BITTER PELELIU

OSPREY
PUBLISHING

THE FORGOTTEN STRUGGLE ON THE PACIFIC WAR'S WORST BATTLEFIELD

BITTER PELELIU

JOSEPH WHEELAN

OSPREY PUBLISHING
Bloomsbury Publishing Plc
Kemp House, Chawley Park, Cumnor Hill, Oxford OX2 9PH, UK
29 Earlsfort Terrace, Dublin 2, Ireland
1385 Broadway, 5th Floor, New York, NY 10018, USA
E-mail: info@ospreypublishing.com
www.ospreypublishing.com

OSPREY is a trademark of Osprey Publishing Ltd

First published in Great Britain in 2022

A catalog record for this book is available from the British Library.

ISBN: HB 978 1 4728 4950 2; PB 978 1 4728 4951 9; eBook 978 1 4728 4947 2;
ePDF 978 1 4728 4949 6; XML 978 1 4728 4948 9

22 23 24 25 26   10 9 8 7 6 5 4 3 2 1

Plate section image credits are given in full in the List of Illustrations (pp. 13–15).
Maps by www.bounford.com
Index by Mark Swift

Typeset by Deanta Global Publishing Services, Chennai, India
Printed and bound in Great Britain by CPI (Group) UK Ltd, Croydon CR0 4YY

Osprey Publishing supports the Woodland Trust, the UK's leading woodland conservation charity.

To find out more about our authors and books visit www.ospreypublishing.com. Here you will find
extracts, author interviews, details of forthcoming events and the option to sign up for our newsletter.

Contents

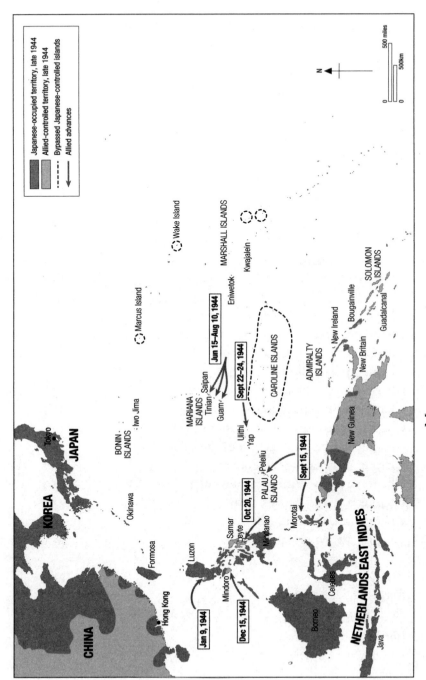

MAP 1: Western Pacific Ocean

Prelude

D-Day on Peleliu, September 15, 1944

We're going to catch some red fire.
Colonel Lewis B. "Chesty" Puller,
responding to the suggestion that
Peleliu would be a walkover.[1]

Sleep had eluded many of the men of the 1st Marine Division, even veterans of the division's two previous Pacific War campaigns. They had never faced heavy enemy fire on the beach during the landings on Guadalcanal and Cape Gloucester but there was always a first time.

It would be today.

They had meticulously oiled and polished their weapons, and their carrying gear was carefully packed, but their racing minds could not be so easily put in good order. It had made for a restless night.

On the crowded transports, reveille sounded at 3 a.m. Depending on the transport they were aboard, the Marines were awakened by either a bugle call over a ship's loudspeaker, or a clanging bell, or with lights suddenly glaring in the stuffy, odoriferous holds, followed by the barked order, "Hit the deck!"

A thin crescent moon gleamed overhead, and choppy silver seas stretched beneath a sky that was "startlingly clear," having been swept clean by a brisk northerly breeze. From the transports' decks the men saw a sight that they would never forget: warships afloat for as far as they could see.[2]

The Marines lined up in their mess for the landing day breakfast. Most of them got grilled steak and eggs, a Kiwi custom adopted as a Marine Corps tradition beginning at Tarawa. On some ships, steak sandwiches were piled on trays in the officers' wardroom. Other messes offered scrambled eggs, bacon, coffee, and fresh fruit, or the option of a lighter meal of coffee, toast, and an apple. The latter alternative was a tacit recognition that anxiety about the impending landing tamped down appetites, and also that a big breakfast tended to worsen stomach wounds. Pfc Russell Davis's company breakfasted on black coffee, dry toast, and one apple or orange per man in a "stand-up meal."[3]

As the eastern sky brightened, preparations quickened aboard the amphibious assault fleet. At 5 a.m., aboard the Landing Ship, Tanks (LSTs) carrying the first-wave assault battalions, Marines began descending ladders to the tank decks and climbed into the tracked amphibian Landing Vehicles, Tracked – LVTs, or "amtracs" – idling in choking clouds of diesel smoke.

On the tank deck of LST 227, the roar of the amtrac engines was "deafening ... blue, swirling exhaust ... began to clog my lungs and make my eyes water," despite the great fans whirling overhead, observed Captain George Hunt, commander of the First Marines' "K" Company.[4]

The sweltering heat caused sweat to bead on the men's faces; their jackets grew damp with perspiration and clung to them. A first sergeant began turning green and appeared ready to vomit, as Hunt's men patiently waited for 227's bow doors to open and release them from the suffocating diesel fumes into the fresh oceanic air.

On other ships, rumbling power winches and creaking davits and pulleys hoisted shallow-draft Higgins Boats over the side preparatory to the landing troops on deck descending into the boats from cargo nets draped down the ships' hulls. The Marines used the idle time before going down the nets to apply "the last oil in the gun, the last whet to the knife." Some men daubed their cheeks with paint and burnt cork, giving them a fierce, primordial warrior appearance.[5]

At 5:30 a.m., 15 minutes before sunrise, Admiral Jesse Oldendorf, the Fire Support Group commander, ordered his flotilla of battleships, cruisers, and destroyers to "commence firing." The Marines watched from the railings of their transports, some of them chanting, "Burn! Burn!", as explosions enveloped the island, 5 miles distant, in dense clouds of dust and smoke.

The bombardment was ear-splittingly loud. To *Life* magazine artist Tom Lea, the firing of the big guns sounded like "the slamming of huge doors." Pfc E.B. Sledge of the Fifth Marines described each discharge as a "thunder clap." The 16-inch shells "tore through the air toward the island, roaring like locomotives"; the Marines had to shout to be heard.[6]

"From all the firepower we were seeing and hearing we were wondering ... how in the world can anything survive?" said Bill Tapscott of the Seventh Marines. "It was beyond your imagination how anything could be alive, so we were beginning to feel pretty good."[7]

The 1st Division's three regiments would come ashore abreast on the five landing beaches: the First on the left, on White Beaches 1 and 2; the Fifth in the middle, on Orange Beaches 1 and 2; and the Seventh on the right, on Orange Beach 3.

The beaches spanned 2,500 yards of Peleliu's southwest coast. If all went according to plan, 5,700 Marines from five battalions would alight from more than 300 amtracs and six-wheeled amphibious trucks called DUKWs during the assault's first 19 minutes with all their weapons except their big guns, which would be landed later. Within an hour, up to 9,000 men would be ashore.

But a major complication in the task of shuttling the assault troops to the beaches was Peleliu's 500-yard-wide coral reef, which lay 700 yards from shore and guarded the shoreline like a stone moat. The treaded amphibians could crawl over the reef and swim the rest of the way to the beaches, but the flat-bottomed Higgins Boats could not. During the Normandy landings on June 6, Higgins Boats alone were used because there was no reef to cross.

There were just enough amtracs to carry the first three waves from their ships, over the reef, and across the lagoon to the beach.

Higgins Boats would have to take the next five waves from the transports to the so-called "transfer control line," about a mile from shore. There, they would wait for the amtracs to return from landing the first three waves. The Marines in the Higgins Boats would then climb into the amtracs, which would turn around and carry them over the reef to the beaches.

In the last five assault waves would be more combat troops, supplies, support troops, and 30 medium Sherman tanks.[8]

Admiral George Fort, who commanded the Marines' transports and their convoy, and General Roy Geiger, who led the III Amphibious Corps, observed the deafening opening act from the command ship *Mount McKinley*. From the bridge of the troop transport *DuPage*, the

1st Division commander and his assistants, Generals William Rupertus and O.P. Smith, tensely watched the bombardment and their Marines emerging from the maws of the LSTs.[9]

The first assault waves pushed off in the roaring, open-topped amtracs, amid billowing blue exhaust fumes. Beside the massive warships, "the pygmy tractors crawled around them like bugs," wrote Captain Hunt.

The landing vehicles circled offshore like schooling fish before forming a ragged formation two and a half miles from shore – the so-called "line of departure."[10]

At a signal at 8 a.m., the amtracs began their 30-minute approach to the beaches, led by more heavily armored amtracs – LVT(A)s and nicknamed "amtanks" – equipped with either a turreted 37mm gun, or a "snub-nosed" 75mm gun and .50-caliber machine guns. Under the aegis of the 3rd Armored Amphibian Tractor Battalion, the fire support amtanks would go in first, clearing a path for the riflemen behind them.

At the very tip of the murderous phalanx – even ahead of the amtanks – 18 landing craft armed with rocket launchers and four others equipped with 4.2-inch mortars barreled toward the beaches. Their job was to sweep the shoreline of any enemy soldiers that might meet the Marines at the water's edge.

The Marines in the first three waves endured jarring rides in the amtracs, which belonged to various vintages. Earlier model LVT-1s and LVT-2s could carry 18 men, while the latest-model LVT-4s had a 30-man capacity and rear exit ramps. The older models had no ramps; passengers exited simply by vaulting over the sides.

The destroyer *Hazelwood*, assisted by five submarine chasers for each landing beach, was responsible for shepherding the landing craft ashore in an orderly fashion. *Hazelwood* used signal flags to identify which wave was to proceed next; each wave was led by Higgins guide boats that peeled off before reaching the reef.[11]

As the amphibious force headed toward the beaches, Admiral Oldendorf's bombardment force carried out a final, vigorous pre-landing mission. All vessels laid down a fierce barrage on the beaches and adjacent areas to pin down or kill the Japanese. Then, 48 dive-bombers and fighters from the eight large and light carriers lurking a dozen miles to the southwest struck the landing beaches with bombs, rockets, and machine guns.

From a half-mile offshore, the rocket-firing and mortar-firing landing craft volleyed hundreds of 4.5-inch rockets and mortars onto the beaches and targets behind them. The furious salvos appeared certain to annihilate everything in their path.[12]

Forty miles to the north at Babelthuap, soldiers from the U.S. Army's 81st Infantry Division made plainly visible choreographed preparations to assault the Palaus' largest island, but then did not launch any landing craft.

However, the feint succeeded in persuading General Sadae Inoue, who commanded the Palaus' primary defense force, the 14th Infantry Division, that the Americans intended to assault both Babelthuap and Koror. Inoue fatefully decided to not send the 25,000 infantrymen stationed on Babelthuap to Peleliu.

After leaving the Babelthuap area, the 81st Division resumed its role as the 1st Marine Division's floating reserve; if unneeded on Peleliu, the soldiers would invade tiny Angaur 6 miles southwest of Peleliu on September 17.[13]

Meanwhile, Pfc Jack Ainsworth's Higgins Boat was "tossing around like a matchstick" in the rolling seas off Peleliu. "Huge columns of black smoke" billowed from places on the island smashed by the last-minute naval bombardment. Peering over the Higgins Boat's gunwale, Ainsworth thought it "impossible that anything could possibly remain alive." It was wishful thinking, and nothing more, as events would demonstrate.[14]

General Rupertus, the 1st Division's commander, had optimistically predicted that Peleliu would be a "rough but quick" campaign, and his men were eager to believe him.

"The Marines were almost gay going in," said Pfc Robert Leckie of the First Marines, "for General Rupertus's prediction of four days had made them cocky."[15]

Aboard an amtrac in the first wave, a Marine with a harmonica began playing "Beer Barrel Polka" to break the tension, and the men sang along loudly. In another amtrac, the men belted out "Give My Regards to Broadway." "Just before we hit the beach we were all singing it at the top of our lungs," said a Sergeant Webber. "It sure made us feel good."[16]

Pfc George Peto was also in the first wave. When his amtrac crashed into the reef, "it felt like we were ramming a brick wall, and we all staggered forward, slamming into each other." Its 250-horsepower aircraft engine whining, the amtrac slowly pulled itself over the rough coral.[17]

Until now, there had been virtually no Japanese counterfire. Marine and naval leaders were hopeful, if not confident, that the three-day preliminary bombardment and air strikes and that morning's barrage had silenced the enemy guns on Peleliu. "We thought the landing would be a piece of cake," said Lieutenant Clifford West, a First Marines forward controller. "Nobody on shore could have survived all that shelling and bombing."[18]

Before leaving the transport *Crescent City*, Colonel Lewis B. "Chesty" Puller, the colorful, much-decorated First Marines commander, thanked Captain Lionel Rowe for his ship's gracious treatment of Puller's men.

Rowe confidently predicted that Puller and his men would have little to do on Peleliu. "Everything's done over there. You'll walk in."

Manifestly skeptical that Peleliu would in fact be a walkover, Puller told Rowe that if he believed what he said, Rowe should join him on the beach at 5 p.m. for supper and to pick up souvenirs.

Rowe replied, "Puller, you won't find anything to stop you over there. Nothing could have lived through that hammering."

"We're going to catch some red fire," Puller shot back.

Rowe said he would see Puller at dinner that night.

"If we get out of this one, you'll be back in Hawaii before we're through with the job," Puller replied.[19]

As if to confirm Puller's deep misgivings and to make a lie out of Rupertus's prediction of a quick, at most four-day battle, enemy artillery fire began to crash down on the reef. Japanese engineers had carefully pre-registered their guns and mortars to hit the reef and the landing beaches. The terrible result could now be seen up and down the reef, where amtracs were exploding and burning furiously.[20]

Pfc Leckie said the gunfire threw ice water on the festive atmosphere aboard the amtracs. "They stopped calling to one another, stopped throwing kisses, stopped waggling four confident fingers."[21]

"The vessel beside us was hit while I watched helplessly," said Corpsman Brooking Gex. "Its occupants never reached the beach." The water, suddenly filled with floating bodies, "surged with explosions … the air was thick with the screams of the wounded and dying – half of our troops were killed on the way to shore."[22]

During the first minutes of the assault, 26 amtracs took direct hits and burned on the reef. Twenty-eight men were killed, 78 were wounded, and four were reported missing. Over the next 90 minutes, another 35 amtracs were damaged or destroyed on the reef or on the beaches.[23]

The rough part predicted by Rupertus had begun. But would Peleliu still be the quick campaign that the general had optimistically predicted?

List of Illustrations

Colonel Herman Hanneken, commander of the Seventh Marine Regiment. (USMC photo)

Amtracs headed toward the Peleliu beaches on D-Day, September 15, 1944. (Photo by Interim Archives/Getty Images)

A D-Day scene on Orange Beach 3. (USMC photo)

Paul Douglas, the oldest Marine recruit at age 50, is shown during an inspection at Parris Island Recruit Depot. (USMC photo)

D-Day on White Beach 2. (USMC photo)

Marines take cover behind an amtank on a Peleliu landing beach. (Everett Collection Inc / Alamy Stock Photo)

Tom Lea of *Life* magazine portrayed this Marine moments after he was wounded on Orange Beach 3 on D-Day. (*The Price, 1944*, Tom Lea, 1944, Copyright Catherine Lea Weeks, Courtesy of the Tom Lea Institute)

An amtank moves inland after coming ashore on Peleliu. (USMC photo)

Seventh Marines set up their command post in a tank trap near Peleliu's beach. (USMC photo)

The Fifth Marines shown in the act of capturing Peleliu's airfield, a harrowing experience for those crossing the flat, exposed airstrip while under enemy fire. (USMC photo)

Marines fight in the rubble of Japanese buildings on Peleliu airfield's northern perimeter. (USMC photo)

A Navy corpsman gives water to a wounded Marine. (Bettmann/Getty Images)

Marines armed with a .30-caliber machine gun and a Browning Automatic Rifle battle entrenched Japanese soldiers. (USMC photo)

A Marine war dog and its handler. (USMC photo)

An amtrac flamethrower in action. (Photo by Interim Archives/Getty Images)

Marines advance into the ridges of the Umurbrogol. (USMC photo)

Marine infantry-tank assault proceeds in rugged terrain on Peleliu. (USMC photo)

The first Corsairs arrive at Peleliu airstrip. (National Archives)

A Corsair bombs Peleliu's ridges. (USMC photo)

Dead Marines prior to burial. (National Archives, #205586277)

List of Maps

Chapter 1

The "Old Breed"

*They ran curiously to type, with drilled shoulders
and a bone-deep sunburn, and a tolerant scorn of nearly
everything on earth... The Marine Corps was home,
and war an occupation, and they transmitted their
temper and character and viewpoint to the high-hearted
volunteer mass.*

Colonel John W. Thomason[1]

Peleliu's place in Marine Corps history can be traced to the early 1920s. Intelligence operative Lieutenant Colonel Earl "Pete" Ellis, a charter member of the Marines' "Old Breed" who won the Navy Cross, the Silver Star, and the French Croix de Guerre in France during World War I, prowled the Palau Islands to find out what the Japanese military was up to. It was believed that the Japanese were fortifying the islands in violation of the League of Nations Mandate of 1920.

Japanese agents shadowed Ellis during the cloak-and-dagger operation, as he gathered material for what would become his prophetic 80-page "Advance Base Operation in Micronesia," written in 1921. In it, Ellis boldly predicted that Japan would start the next war. The Navy's Pacific Fleet and Marine landing forces would have to capture Japanese-occupied islands to win it, he wrote.

Ellis died in Koror in May 1923 after a bout of heavy drinking. A New York newspaper story about Ellis's death appeared under the provocative headline, "Was Marine Murdered by Japs While on U.S.

Spy Mission?" The question was never answered, and it appeared that Ellis's death most likely resulted from his severe alcoholism.[2]

Spanish explorer Ruy López de Villalobos is credited with discovering the Palau Islands in early 1543 while on an expedition from Mexico to the archipelago later known as the Philippines.

The 110-mile-long Palaus – 340 islands that lie on the western edge of the Carolines – comprise one of the largest island chains in the world. The Carolines extend along 33 degrees longitude from their southern terminus at Peleliu and Angaur – small, steamy islands just 7 degrees north of the equator, at the same latitude as central Africa. The Japanese would call the Palaus "the spigot of the oil barrel," the barrel being their fuel-rich East Indies conquests.[3]

Spain originally annexed the Palaus, but the Spanish did nothing to develop the island chain. In 1899, as the Spanish Empire was dissolving, Spain sold the islands to Germany for $4 million. Germany discovered phosphate on Angaur, the southernmost Palau island, and began processing it into fertilizer. The Germans also required the Palauans to plant palm trees for copra, which was pressed into coconut oil.

Twenty years later, the League of Nations awarded Japan all of Germany's former colonies north of the equator – the Palaus, Carolines, and Marianas – as a reward for having supported the Allies during World War I.

The Palauans themselves were of Polynesian, Micronesian, and Malayan descent – the latter influence evident in the place names beginning with the unusual consonant combination "ng." Before the Pacific War, about 1,000 Palauans lived on Angaur and its northern neighbor, Peleliu – the Palaus' southernmost islands. Their inhabitants subsisted, as they had for millennia, on mullet, taro, bananas, mangos, papayas, sweet potatoes, and tapioca. Crabs and coconuts supplemented their diet.[4]

The industrious Japanese built harbors, roads, seaplane ramps, and water and sewer systems. They made Koror their administrative capital, and constructed a harbor at adjacent Malakel. They also took over the Angaur phosphate processing plant.

During the 1930s, Japanese engineers found more phosphate deposits on northern Peleliu. Near the village of Akalokul, they built a phosphate crushing plant and a hand-operated narrow-gauge railroad. But the operation was not as productive as the one on Angaur. By 1944, when the Allies were pushing into the Western Pacific, both processing plants had been abandoned.[5]

Far more significantly, in 1939, the Japanese military began transforming the Palaus into a base for military operations. The Kossol Passage, a 10-mile-wide strait through the northern Palaus, became a protected anchorage. Japanese engineers built an airfield on Babelthuap, the Palaus' largest island, and another airstrip was begun on the only flat piece of ground on Peleliu, south of the hill mass that dominated the central island.

The 3,000-man naval construction detachment sent to Peleliu to build runways arrived in April 1939 with steam shovels, rollers, cranes, trucks, and bulldozers. Two of Peleliu's five villages were emptied and razed to clear a path for the airfield. By the end of the year, construction crews had built two crisscrossing runways – of 6,000 and 3,500 feet – along with revetments and a 2,700-foot taxiway.

Along the runways' northern perimeter, above which loomed hills and ridges up to 300 feet high that extended into the central highlands, builders erected barracks, hangars, a two-story headquarters building, machine shops, and a power plant. They laid a coral-surfaced road from Peleliu's southern tip to Ngesebus, a small island connected to northern Peleliu by a 500-foot causeway near the abandoned phosphate refinery. On Ngesebus, the Japanese commenced work on a fighter airfield.

Peleliu became a way station for Japanese troops sailing to other destinations, and a refueling stop for new aircraft en route from Japan's factories to battlefields in the South Pacific and Southeast Asia.[6]

An event that might have suggested the lobster-claw-shaped, 6-mile-by-2-mile island's importance in the Pacific War occurred on December 7, 1941 – the day of Japan's surprise attack on Pearl Harbor. Japanese Navy dive-bombers took off from Palau airfields and flew 430 miles west to strike Mindanao, the southernmost Philippine island.

The attackers targeted the U.S. seaplane tender *William Preston* and two PBY wing-over-fuselage patrol bombers in Davao Harbor. *William Preston* evaded the dive-bombers, but both PBYs were sunk. Aboard one of them was the first American serviceman to be killed in action in the Philippines – Navy Ensign Robert Tills.[7]

Two and a half years later, as American forces pushed into the Central and Western Pacific, U.S. Navy carrier planes struck the Palaus. On

March 3–4, 1944, they bombed and strafed the Japanese airfield on Peleliu, inflicting heavy damage on its parked planes and support facilities.

The Japanese Combined Fleet had recently withdrawn to the Palaus from Truk in the eastern Carolines. Known as the "Gibraltar of the Pacific" because of its large naval and air bases, Truk had been lashed by Admiral Marc Mitscher's Task Force 58 for two days in February. American warplanes sank two cruisers, four destroyers, two submarines, and 200,000 tons of shipping, and destroyed 250 planes.

Truk had been an important crossroads for arms and aircraft shipped from Japan to Southeast Asia. But after the dust settled from Mitscher's Operation *Hailstone*, the Combined Fleet abandoned Truk and sailed to the Palaus' capital, Koror.

Following the March 3–4 Palau raid, the fleet moved again, this time to the southern Philippines.[8]

Mitscher's task force of 11 fast carriers hit the Palaus again at the end of March during Operation *Desecrate* to support General Douglas MacArthur's New Guinea campaign. Helldivers, Dauntless dive-bombers, and Grumman TBF Avenger torpedo bombers swarmed the Palau airfields and destroyed shipping in the island group's harbors and lagoons. "We were terrified," wrote Dilchuuch Ermang, a Peleliu native. People fled to the hills and hid in caves. "We saw many Japanese planes destroyed."[9]

Indeed, after-action reports claimed that 110 Zeros and "Betty" medium bombers had been shot down, and 214 others were blasted on the ground. In June and July, during the invasion of the Marianas, carrier planes returned to the Palaus to crush potential opposition. None of Peleliu's Japanese aircraft survived the raids, and no replacements were sent, as planes were being hoarded for MacArthur's anticipated invasion of the Philippines.[10]

Air Force bombers from the Admiralty Islands struck the Palaus periodically throughout August, and in September the air strikes resumed, but with the object of softening up Peleliu's and Angaur's defenses for the amphibious assaults on those islands scheduled in mid-September.

Admiral Chester Nimitz, commander in chief of the Pacific Ocean Area Command, had issued a "warning order" on May 29 to seize the Palau Islands on September 8.

The impending campaign, Operation *Stalemate*, would come to seem an apt description of the campaign during the frustrating weeks of intensive combat that lay ahead. *Stalemate* initially targeted Peleliu and Angaur in the southern Palaus, and Babelthuap in the northern islands. Its original purpose was to seize Japanese airfields in the Palaus that could interfere with General MacArthur's planned Philippines invasion that fall.

But the carrier air raids in March had wrecked the airfields; they no longer posed a threat to any Allied thrust into the Philippines.

Partly for that reason, *Stalemate*'s objectives were scaled back on July 7. The change was also due to a shortage of available shipping tonnage because of the unexpectedly prolonged Marianas campaign.

Saipan, the initial Mariana target in June, proved to be a tougher objective than expected. Its defenders had fiercely resisted the assaults of the 2nd and 3rd Marine Divisions and the Army's 27th Infantry Division. Saipan's obduracy had delayed by one month the scheduled assaults on neighboring Guam and Tinian. Consequently, vessels and supplies remained tied up in the Marianas for those campaigns while preparations for *Stalemate* were being made.[11]

Changes made to *Stalemate* on July 7 included dropping Babelthuap from the invasion's objectives. Babelthuap was the largest Palauan island, and it had one airfield. However, planners concluded that the rugged terrain surrounding the airfield made its expansion nearly impossible, while Peleliu's airfield, built on flat terrain, was better suited for enlargement.

Moreover, Babelthuap's large size and its 25,000 defenders portended a long campaign. The Army's 7th and 96th Divisions, which were to have assaulted the island, were instead sent to MacArthur for the Philippines operation, leaving *Stalemate* with just two divisions.[12]

The Yap island group and Ulithi atoll were added to *Stalemate* on July 7 – the latter because its excellent anchorages would support future U.S. Western Pacific military operations. The updated operation became known as *Stalemate II*.

The elements for the invasion of the southern Palaus fell into place. The 1st Marine Division and the Army's 81st Infantry Division were to assault Peleliu and Angaur in mid-September: Peleliu on September 15, and Angaur a day or two later.

Before *Stalemate* ended, every major command in the Pacific would participate in it: 800 vessels, 1,600 aircraft, and an estimated 250,000 Navy, Marine, and Army personnel.[13]

While *Stalemate* unfolded, the Army's 31st Infantry Division would invade lightly defended Morotai in the Netherland East Indies, 480 miles to the southwest; it would become another Allied air base that could support MacArthur's Philippines campaign. Yap and Ulithi were penciled in for invasion on October 8.[14]

From a Navy Catalina flying at an altitude of several hundred feet, General Roy Geiger chose the island of Pavavu as the place where the 1st Marine Division would recover from its Cape Gloucester campaign, which ended in April 1944. To Geiger's eyes at that distance, Pavavu appeared idyllic, offering a banquet of inviting beaches, blue seas, and palm trees.

It lay 50 miles northwest of Guadalcanal, the place that Geiger wished the 1st Division to avoid. After the pitched battles of 1942 and 1943, new airfields and port and logistics facilities had blossomed on Guadalcanal and its neighbor, Tulagi. The islands became a major staging area for future amphibious campaigns.

The 3rd Marine Division, which Geiger had led on Bougainville as part of the I Amphibious Corps, had had the misfortune of arriving for R&R on Guadalcanal during one of its busiest periods – and when its senior logistics officers were conscripting every available man for work parties. Thus, rather than resting and refitting on Guadalcanal, the 3rd Division was required to supply 1,000 men a day to toil at the ports and airfields. There was little time to rest, or to train replacements. Geiger was determined that the 1st Division would not suffer the same fate.[15]

The stocky, white-haired 59 year old was an energetic hands-on leader, a fast learner, and one of the better-educated generals in the Marine Corps. After graduating college, he became a school principal at the age of 20 and began attending law school. By the time he was 22, Geiger was a fully fledged lawyer. But he was restless and craved adventure. Toward that end, he applied to the Marine Corps Officer Candidate School – and was rejected: heart murmur, eye strain, low body weight for his height. So Geiger enlisted as a mere private in the Marines in November 1907. Rapidly promoted to corporal, he was commissioned as a second lieutenant a little more than a year later. Assigned to the Atlantic Fleet, Geiger gained recognition for his swimming prowess.[16]

In 1916, Geiger volunteered for flight training at the Navy's two-year-old aviation school in Pensacola, Florida. When he graduated in 1917, Geiger became the fifth aviator in Marine Corps history, and the 49th naval aviator.

During World War I, he led a Marine bomber squadron of two-seat de Havilland DH-4B biplanes – known as "flaming coffins" – with the Royal Flying Corps out of Dunkirk. The squadron went on to fly 14 missions as the 1st Marine Aviation Force. Major Geiger earned a reputation as a fearless flyer and an inspiring squadron leader. He received his first Navy Cross for his World War I service.[17]

Between wars, he was a squadron leader in Haiti during the U.S. campaign against the insurgent Cacos, personally leading close-air support and reconnaissance missions.

Acknowledging Geiger's potential, his superiors sent him to the Command and General Staff College at Leavenworth, Kansas; the Army War College; and the Naval War College.

In 1942, Geiger led the Cactus Air Force during its perilous early weeks on Guadalcanal in the Solomon Islands. From Guadalcanal's Henderson Field, often under enemy fire and operating from runways pitted by shell holes, the Cactus Air Force supported the 1st Marine Division in its desperate struggle to keep the airstrip out of Japanese hands.

Geiger, himself a superb pilot, sometimes took off in one of his warplanes to drop a bomb or to reconnoiter the waters around Guadalcanal. In bad weather one night, he insisted on going up and spotted enemy warships approaching the island. The Cactus Air Force sank two of the enemy destroyers with aerial bombs.

Shelled at night by Japanese battleships and sleep-deprived, the Cactus pilots subsisted on two skimpy meals a day and often operated without sufficient fuel or ammunition. Yet Geiger and his pilots defied the odds, and the Marines held. For his leadership on Guadalcanal, Geiger was awarded his second Navy Cross and a Distinguished Flying Cross. Admiral William Halsey was so impressed by Geiger that he selected him to lead the I Amphibious Corps at Bougainville when General Charles Burnett died in an accidental fall. *Time* magazine described Geiger as "thick-set, poker-faced, chilly eyed … another Marine's Marine."[18]

Before landing in July with his III Amphibious Corps at Guam – Operation *Stevedore* – Geiger risked his life to swim alongside Navy frogmen on several of their pre-landing missions. He even reconnoitered the island in a boat in broad daylight.

The United States had seized Guam from Spain during the Spanish–American War of 1898 and occupied it until December 10, 1941. On that date, the Japanese invaded the island, and its governor surrendered it and its 150-man U.S. Marine garrison. In the ensuing years, the recapture of Guam was a field problem at the Marine Corps School in Quantico, Virginia, and a festering wound to Marine pride. The Marines meant to retake Guam in good time.

However, because of the protracted Saipan campaign, Guam's invasion was delayed from June 18 to July 21. The 19,000 Guam defenders, fully expecting to be attacked, took advantage of the additional time to fortify their defenses around the island's crown jewel, Apra Harbor. The Americans used the interregnum to shell Guam for two solid weeks.

Geiger passed up the standard Marine Corps School solution to Guam – landing on the island's more lightly defended eastern coast – and instead assaulted the strongly defended western beaches, where the Japanese expected the blow to land. His 40,000 troops included the 3rd Marine Division, the 1st Provisional Marine Brigade, and the Army's 77th Division, which was the corps reserve. Geiger intended to double-envelop Apra Harbor and capture Orote Airfield before driving inland.[19]

The three-week campaign officially ended when Guam was declared secure on August 11, but combat continued. Thousands of enemy soldiers remained alive, although incapable of mounting coordinated counterattacks.

Geiger put Guam behind him and flew to the Russell Islands and the 1st Marine Division to complete the planning for Operation *Stalemate*, due to begin in just one month.

The 1st Division's most recent South Pacific campaign was a dispiriting four-month slog through knee-deep mud in Cape Gloucester's rain-drenched jungles and mangrove and tropical rain forests. The campaign cost the division 310 killed and 1,083 wounded.

The landing at Cape Gloucester on December 26, 1943, was part of Operation *Cartwheel*, a campaign designed to isolate the powerful Japanese base at Rabaul through a dozen offensives begun the previous

June. The joint Marine–Army invasion of Bougainville on November 1 was one part of the overarching strategy.

The plan to isolate Rabaul was later discarded when military strategists instead chose to bypass Rabaul, after destroying its naval and air assets, and to let it wither on the vine. But before *Cartwheel* was scuttled, the 1st Division, commanded by General William Rupertus, landed at Cape Gloucester.

Afterward, Navy historian Samuel Eliot Morison wrote, "The wisdom of hindsight makes [Cape Gloucester] seem superfluous."[20]

The fact that the campaign did little to influence the Pacific War's outcome – aside from eliminating 2,000 Japanese troops – did not diminish the enduring misery of Cape Gloucester, nicknamed the "Green Inferno."

The Marines quickly secured the airstrip, the campaign's primary objective; the flag-raising ceremony was on December 31. The Marines broke the back of Japanese resistance in battles at Hill 660, Suicide Creek, and Aogiri Ridge – renamed "Walt's Ridge" as a tribute to Lieutenant Colonel Lew Walt. His Fifth Marines overcame dense jungle and fierce Japanese resistance to eventually capture the ridge, pushing a 37mm gun uphill and blasting the enemy with canister in a driving rainstorm. From atop the ridge, Walt's men repelled five brutal bayonet attacks.[21]

Thereafter, the campaign became a grueling test of men against mud, rain, nearly impenetrable jungle, and mosquito swarms as the Marines pursued General Iwao Matsuda's tattered 65th Brigade. Enemy snipers hidden in 100-foot-tall trees picked off the Marines, and at night Japanese dive-bombers struck the Marine lines, marked by enemy tracers. Falling trees killed dozens of Marines.

Matsuda's men, ordered to withdraw to Rabaul, were force-marched more than 200 miles over two weeks.[22]

———

General MacArthur summoned General Rupertus to his Brisbane headquarters as the Cape Gloucester campaign was winding down. MacArthur told the Marine general that he wanted to keep the 1st Division in his Sixth Army, under whose auspices the Marines had fought on Cape Gloucester. Rupertus predictably bridled at MacArthur's plan, because the 1st Marine Division was nothing less than the heart and sinews of the Marine Corps during the early years of World War II.

Created in February 1941 from the 1st Marine Brigade, the 1st Division had as its nucleus in 1941 the Fifth Marines, whose exploits in World War I at Belleau Wood and St. Mihiel, and during the Meuse–Argonne offensive, earned the regiment three Croix de Guerre citations and the right to wear the *fourragère* on the left shoulder of their uniforms.

With the formation of the 1st Marine Division, part of the Fifth Marines was carved away to create the Seventh Marine Regiment. The First Marines emerged as a composite of units from the Fifth and the Seventh. These three regiments would lead the assault on Peleliu.[23]

The division was steeped in the tradition of the "Old Breed" of leatherneck regulars. Colonel John W. Thomason, the Marine Corps's celebrated author and artist of the 1930s, wrote that the Marines of the "Old Breed," "ran curiously to type, with drilled shoulders and a bone-deep sunburn, and a tolerant scorn of nearly everything on earth." They regarded the Marine Corps "as home and war an occupation, and they transmitted their temper and character and viewpoint to the high-hearted volunteer mass."[24]

Although Rupertus opposed MacArthur's proposal to retain the division for future operations, he lacked the authority to reject it outright. He sent it up the command chain, where it was coldly received.

Admiral Nimitz objected to MacArthur retaining command of Nimitz's premier infantry division. After Operation *Watchtower* on Guadalcanal, he had reluctantly lent the division to MacArthur for the Cape Gloucester operation, and he now wanted it back. The Marine Corps commandant, General Alexander Vandegrift, who had led the division on Guadalcanal, also denounced MacArthur's plan.

The tug-of-war intensified when MacArthur still refused to relinquish the Marines. Nimitz was forced to appeal to the Joint Chiefs of Staff. The chiefs ordered MacArthur to return the 1st Marine Division to the Pacific Naval Command.[25]

When their campaign on Cape Gloucester ended in April 1944, the 1st Division Marines anticipated once more enjoying R&R in Melbourne, where they had basked in Australian hospitality after being relieved on Guadalcanal in December 1942. The grueling Cape Gloucester campaign had left the men in the combat battalions thin, exhausted, and suffering from malaria and jungle rot. Although they eagerly anticipated returning to Australia, Australia was not under consideration.

By 1944, South Pacific combat units instead were routinely being rotated through Guadalcanal, now a major Allied base. Wanting to keep the division away from the Guadalcanal work details so that the Marines could get a well-deserved rest, Geiger believed that Pavavu would be a better R&R locale. Geiger's motives were certainly well intentioned, but his flyover of the island did not give him a clear picture of what Pavavu had to offer the Marines.

Pavavu proved to be the antithesis of the rest area that the Marines had anticipated during Cape Gloucester's long, wet, steamy, malarial nights. True, the 8-mile-by-4-mile isle, located in the Russell Islands, featured sandy-white beaches and neat rows of coconut trees, which had looked inviting to Geiger from several hundred feet aloft. Before the war, it had been a Lever Brothers coconut plantation, with drying sheds for copra and a plantation house on stilts. But the dilapidated drying sheds, the crumbling plantation house, and the beaches were the extent of Pavavu's amenities; no further signs of civilization were evident, and most of the island was swampland. Abandoned three years earlier, the plantation's legacy was a revolting stew of rotting coconuts and rancid milk that attracted swarms of land crabs and foraging rats up to 2 feet long.

"Great God! Who picked this dump?" shouted an exasperated officer after bursting into the tent of General O.P. Smith, the assistant division commander. "More like a hog lot than a rest camp!"[26]

A naval construction battalion (nicknamed "Seabees") had arrived on Pavavu before the Marines to build roads, docks, and barracks. After beginning work on a steel pontoon pier and a road, the Seabees received an early transfer stateside and left before completing the projects.[27] Consequently, the Marines had to build their own rest area from scratch with picks and shovels in the steam-bath heat. They lived, worked, and slept in mud until they had excavated and hauled enough coral to surface the living area. It meant days of unremitting hard labor. The work parties broke up coral for use as road-paving material. They dug wells, widened the few roads, and built a rifle range, latrines, and a 3-mile track around the island. Because there were no showers at first, the men stripped off their clothing and soaped up whenever it rained, which it did nearly every afternoon, and then tried to hurriedly rinse off before the rain stopped.

Driven to extreme measures by the swarms of rats, the Marines incinerated them with flamethrowers. The blue-black land crabs were about the size of a man's hand. The men shook them out of their boots before dressing each morning. "Periodically we reached the point of rage over these filthy things and chased them out from under boxes, seabags and cots," wrote Pfc E.B. Sledge. "We killed them with sticks, bayonets, and entrenching tools."[28]

A short distance inland from the inviting beaches lay impenetrable swamps and dense jungle. Pavavu's thin ground crust concealed sinkholes and quicksand. Mud and standing water were everywhere. "Conditions weren't good," Lieutenant Clifford West understatedly said. "We initially were sleeping in jungle hammocks and then in tents… We had just a field mess hall… It was jungle living in a coconut grove."[29]

Morale understandably suffered as a result of the primitive living conditions. One night, a Marine bolted from his tent and pounded his fists against a coconut tree, angrily sobbing, "I hate you, goddammit, I hate you!" The only reaction from his comrades came from a nearby tent. "Hit it once for me!" someone shouted.[30]

Navy corpsman Oris Brehmer described Pavavu as "a kind of malaria area"; the Anopheles mosquito, ubiquitous in the Solomon and Russell islands, thrived in Pavavu's jungles and swamps. Brehmer and his fellow corpsmen were responsible for ensuring that the Marines took atabrine every day as a prophylactic against malaria.

It wasn't easy, because the Marines disliked how atabrine turned their skin and eyes yellow. Moreover, it was falsely asserted that atabrine caused impotency. Many of the men simply threw away the pills – until the corpsmen were ordered to issue one to each man at mealtime, and to make sure that it was swallowed. "They'd open their mouths and we'd literally throw it into their mouth," said Brehmer.[31]

Fresh food was scarce on Pavavu, but plentiful on Guadalcanal and nearby Banika, which lay across a narrow channel from Pavavu. Banika's superior terrain and drainage encouraged its quick development as a Navy base depot – with a hospital, an airstrip, and a harbor.

Geiger had believed that Pavavu's proximity to Banika would mean easy access to supplies, but he was wrong. None of Banika's amenities made it across the channel to Pavavu. The Marines slept in tents that were Army rejects: "Our tents were rotten and punctured with holes," wrote Pfc Robert Leckie. "There was no water except what we caught in our helmets at night."[32]

They ate canned food: usually spam, dehydrated potatoes, powdered eggs, and "C" rations heated over Sterno canisters. They drank "ersatz coffee." When canned supplies ran low, they dined on oatmeal and sometimes on the meat of crocodiles killed in the swamps.[33]

The Marines were pleased when they discovered that when the plantation owners had abandoned Pavavu and its nearby islands, they left behind about 600 head of cattle. The Marines rounded up the cattle and built a slaughterhouse. The Australian government, the governing authority over the Russell Islands before the war, objected, and the enterprise was stopped.[34]

Pavavu's cleared area was too small for combat exercises involving up to 15,000 men, so the Marines improvised. Mock attacks were staged on company streets; for artillery practice, gun crews fired rounds into the ocean. Lieutenant Colonel Leonard Chapman Jr., the operations officer for the Eleventh Marines and future Marine Corps commandant, said, "Training was reduced to the pitiful expedient of firing into the water with the observers out in a boat or DUKW."[35]

The Marines built Japanese-style bunkers and assaulted them with mortars, rockets, and flamethrowers. Lieutenant Colonel Ray Davis, who commanded the First Marines' 1st Battalion, believed it was "the best assault team training I ever witnessed and totally realistic," albeit "dangerous."[36]

The Marines' equipment was in poor condition after two campaigns. New portable flamethrowers, bazookas, and demolitions reached the division with little time for the men to receive proper training in their use. And then 4,860 replacements – some of them green, others wounded men returning to duty – arrived to take the places of 260 officers and 4,600 men with 24 months overseas who were being rotated back to the States.[37]

On nearby Banika, life was much better. The Marine pilots and Navy personnel stationed there enjoyed traveling USO shows, fresh food, and unlimited alcohol. The Peleliu Marines' nighttime entertainment consisted of "B" movies reshown so many times that the Marines sometimes recited the lines along with the actors. Alcohol was limited to three cans of beer weekly. And the USO never stopped at Pavavu – until Bob Hope's USO troupe paid an unexpected visit.

Pavavu was not on Hope's itinerary, but the 1st Division's recreation officer happened to be in Banika when Hope and his entertainers arrived to put on a show there. The Marine officer asked Hope if he would be willing to come to Pavavu and entertain the 1st Marine Division. Yes, he would, Hope immediately replied.

Because Pavavu had no airstrip, only a road for emergency landings, the entertainers – Hope, comedian Jerry Colonna, singer-actress Frances Langford, and singer-dancer Patty Thomas – made the short hop from Banika on August 7 in tiny Piper Cubs, one entertainer per plane. Fifteen thousand Marines awaited them in a field, cheering each Cub as it landed. The show was a smash. It "really boosted our spirits. It was the finest entertainment I ever saw overseas," wrote Pfc E.B. Sledge. "For us masses in the Marine line companies [the show] was truly inspiring," wrote Private James Johnson.

Bob Hope later said that his most memorable show was on Pavavu. "It was the most exciting thing that happened on the trip [to the South Pacific in 1944] to see those 15,000 guys all looking up and cheering each little plane as she came in," he later wrote. "When we were doing it, we knew that many of the men we were entertaining would never see the States again."[38]

Stalemate's planners knew that the Marines' toughest initial task would be getting over Peleliu's 500-yard-wide coral reef, beyond which lay a 700-yard lagoon lapping the landing beaches, the so-called "critical pause in amphibious warfare," in the words of one planner. At Guadalcanal and Cape Gloucester, the 1st Marine Division had neither to negotiate a reef nor face enemy gunfire while coming ashore.[39]

Peleliu's reef was of special concern because the debacle at the reef at Tarawa in the Gilbert Islands remained a fresh, tragic memory. In November 1943, the fringing reef had nearly doomed the 2nd Marine Division's Operation *Galvanic*. Because of an unexpectedly low neap tide known as a "dodging tide," even Higgins Boats with their shallow, 4-foot drafts could not clear the reef. Only tracked amphibious landing vehicles – just 125 amtracs of two vintages were available for *Galvanic* – were able to clank over the reef and deliver the first three waves to the furiously contested enemy shore. Marines who boarded the Higgins Boats in waves four and five had to get out at the reef and either climb into rubber boats, or wade 700 yards to shore through chest-deep water churned by enemy machine-gun fire. Many Marines died in the water.[40]

Reefs also guarded Kwajalein and Majura atolls in the Marshall Islands, and Saipan and Guam in the Marianas, posing the same ship-to-shore difficulties. The obvious solution was to increase the number of available amtracs, but with so many operations underway at once, there were never enough "Alligators," as they were nicknamed. Thus, Higgins Boats remained integral to amphibious operations.

An improvised system was developed for *Stalemate* employing both amtracs and Higgins Boats. Amtracs would carry the first waves from the transports all the way to the landing beaches. Because there were not enough amtracs, Higgins Boats would carry subsequent waves of men and supplies as far as the reef. There, they would be transferred to the amtracs after they had landed the early waves.

After taking aboard the Marines and supplies, the Alligators would turn around and carry them the rest of the way to the beach. Wounded men ferried from the beach to the reef on the amtracs would be transferred to the empty Higgins Boats to be transported to hospital ships.

The first amtracs, designed as logistical but not assault vehicles, were lightly armored and lacked exit ramps. Troops had to climb over the sides, dropping 6 feet to the ground; consequently, there were many ankle and knee injuries. The newer Alligators had thicker armor, 37mm guns, and rear exit ramps. The very latest models were armed with a 75mm gun, and operated on land much like tanks. Three of the amtracs that were assigned to *Stalemate* were retrofitted with flamethrowers.

After Tarawa, other Marine divisions had begun using the amtracs to support the infantrymen after they landed them, but Rupertus was initially reluctant to make the change. His inclination was to continue to use the amtracs for logistical support only.[41]

There being no space on Pavavu for maneuvers, much less practice landings, the division rehearsed the Peleliu amphibious assault at Cape

Esperance on Guadalcanal's northwestern coast. The rehearsal site's major drawback was that it lacked a reef.

So the Navy and Marines pretended that there was one – and effected the troop transfer and landing as though a reef in fact existed. Control vessels flagged the imaginary reef. The Marines transferred from Higgins Boats to amtracs with alacrity, as though the boats risked running aground if they continued toward the beach.[42]

Because the new amtracs were late in reaching the amphibious force, their crews studied blueprints until the amtracs arrived and they could begin hands-on learning. The crews were still struggling to master the new machines during the dry run on August 27 and at the dress rehearsal two days later at Cape Esperance.[43]

During the first rehearsal, General Rupertus broke his ankle. He was climbing aboard an amtrac when a handhold gave way and he fell onto the hard coral. When he learned about Rupertus's injury, General Geiger, the III Amphibious Corps commander, questioned Rupertus's ability to lead the 1st Marine Division while on crutches. Rupertus's assistant, General Smith, assured Geiger that Rupertus would recover during the two weeks remaining before the landing, and would be able to perform his duties.[44]

While the Marines were struggling to adapt to the new landing craft, some of them were exchanging their new M1 carbines for the older M1 Garand rifles that the carbines had ostensibly replaced. But the carbine's detractors claimed that it lacked the stopping power of the M1 rifle.

Weighing 9½ pounds and 43 inches long, the M1 Garand rifle, with an eight-round clip of .30-06 ammunition, had a 500-yard effective range, with its rounds traveling at 2,800 feet per second. The M1 carbine was smaller – 3 feet long and 4¼ pounds lighter than the Garand. The carbine was originally designed for "specialized soldiers," such as artillerymen and engineers, to be used in the place of sidearms.

But now the carbine was the Marines' designated standard issue weapon. Equipped with a 15-round magazine, it fired .30-caliber rounds at a lower velocity than the Garand: 1,900 feet per second. Its effective range was 300 yards. For these reasons, many Marines disliked it and reclaimed the older, heavier Garands.[45]

Another new weapon that proved to be unpopular was the 60mm Garrett Model T20 grenade-launcher. It fired a standard high-explosive mortar round – but from the shoulder, so that it could be fired directly into caves and bunkers. Its drawbacks were its tremendous recoil, which quickly exhausted the gunner, and the fact that it was three times heavier than the 13-pound M9 bazooka. The unwieldy shoulder-fired mortar was a flop with the Marines in the Pacific.[46]

The Allies had a lot on their plate in mid-1944. The Combined Joint Chiefs of Staff were juggling multiple Pacific campaigns, foremost among them the capture of the Marianas and MacArthur's New Guinea operation. Admiral Raymond Spruance's Fifth Fleet was seeking out the Japanese Combined Fleet; the Army Air Corps was helping the Chinese repel a major Japanese offensive in southeastern China; submarine warfare against Japanese shipping was reaching an apotheosis. At the same time, the Chiefs were immersed in even larger operations: Operation *Overlord*, the massive invasion of France that had begun on June 6; and the assault on the Philippines scheduled for October.

Stalemate II, involving two divisions and 60,000 troops, was a gnat's whisker compared with Normandy and the impending invasion of the Philippines, and it was overshadowed by the Marianas campaign. For *Overlord*, 39 divisions and a million and a half troops from five nations would be committed to battlefields in France by late July. MacArthur's Sixth Army would use up to a dozen divisions to recapture the Philippines if that operation were green-lighted. Aside from its utility in guarding MacArthur's right flank if he invaded the Philippines, the III Amphibious Corps's two-division assault on Peleliu and Angaur must have seemed like an afterthought.[47]

In late July, MacArthur, Nimitz, and President Franklin D. Roosevelt met in Hawaii to set an operational agenda for the coming months. Nimitz played host. FDR, recently nominated by Democrats to seek an unprecedented fourth term, sailed from California on the cruiser *Baltimore*, and MacArthur flew in from Brisbane, Australia, in his new Douglas C-54 Skymaster. The general paced the bomber's aisle throughout most of the 26-hour trip and at one point grumbled about the "humiliation of forcing me to leave my command to fly to Honolulu for a political picture-taking junket."[48]

Indeed, Roosevelt certainly wanted to be photographed alongside his Pacific War commanders – and MacArthur's voter approval was particularly high among Republicans. With the election just three months away, FDR and his campaign staff hoped that some of the general's popularity would rub off and bring voters to Roosevelt.

A casual observer never would have suspected from their public bonhomie that FDR and MacArthur despised one another. FDR believed that MacArthur aspired to the presidency – the general's political ambitions and his support among Republicans were well known – while MacArthur privately deplored FDR's military leadership.

In a display of one-upmanship, MacArthur, who had landed at Hickam Field an hour before Roosevelt's ship docked, kept the president and the Pacific command waiting while he dropped off his bag and bathed at the residence where he was staying at Fort Shafter. He rolled up to the *Baltimore* in a long open touring car; his grand entrance inspired onlookers' cheers.[49]

The president's Republican opponent, former New York Governor Thomas Dewey, had openly questioned FDR's health and vigor. The Honolulu meeting, FDR's advisers believed, would show that he was still up to the job, while they hoped that the relaxing five-day ocean voyage would recharge him. FDR's physicians had concealed from the public the fact that he was suffering from progressive and ultimately fatal cardiovascular disease; the details would be kept secret for years.

MacArthur, who had not seen Roosevelt in seven years, was shocked by his commander in chief's gaunt, pale appearance. He told his wife Jean, "He's just a shell of the man I knew." To MacArthur's wartime physician, Dr. Roger Egeberg, the general said, "Doc, the mark of death is on him. In six months he'll be in his grave." MacArthur's morbid prediction was only three months off the mark.[50]

With the New Guinea and Marianas campaigns winding down, the three men hoped to agree upon the next major objective of the Allies' march across the Pacific to mainland Japan. During the July 28 meeting, for which no minutes were kept, the invasions of Peleliu and Morotai were briefly touched upon – as islands whose capture would protect MacArthur's flanks as he proceeded northward. However, the more pressing issue facing the leaders was whether the Philippines or Formosa would be the next major invasion target.

Of course, MacArthur was predisposed toward the Philippines to fulfill the "I shall return" pledge that he had made in 1942 when he was evacuated from Corregidor to Australia. Speaking on behalf of Admiral Ernest King, the chief of naval operations, Nimitz advocated bypassing the Philippines and invading Formosa. This would place U.S. forces in a commanding position between Japan and the Philippines, and near China's coast, he said.

MacArthur strongly objected to the Navy proposal. "American honor" required that the Philippines be invaded next, he said, with the recapture of Manila a priority.

Later, during a one-on-one meeting with FDR, MacArthur warned the president that choosing to not invade the Philippines would mean abandoning 7,000 starving prisoners of war and 17 million Filipino Christians. How would American voters react, and during an election year? As MacArthur well knew, by raising such an explosive political issue, he would hit a nerve with FDR.

The principals met again during the morning of July 29. No decision was announced regarding the Philippines and Formosa.

FDR chose his words with great care when asked by correspondents afterward which objective would have primacy. "We are going to get the Philippines back," he said, "and without question General MacArthur will take a part in it. Whether he goes direct or not, I can't say."[51]

The issue was far from settled. The Formosa option, known as *Causeway*, remained very much alive for the Joint Chiefs of Staff, who signed off on all major planning decisions, with Admiral King its chief supporter. Moreover, by 1944 FDR was not as apt to interfere with the JCS as earlier in the war when he had involved himself in military planning, and sometimes had even overridden the Chiefs.

The Chiefs balked at *Causeway*'s enormous manpower and materiel requirements – more than 650,000 troops and the commitment of virtually all of the Pacific Theater's air and naval resources. Not only would it consume all available manpower and resources in the Pacific, but *Causeway* likely would require additional troops from the European Theater as well.

General Henry "Hap" Arnold, commander of the Army Air Forces, said *Causeway* would snatch the rug out from under the AAF's base development plan for the strategic bombing of Japan's Home Islands. Admiral Raymond Spruance said he favored recapturing the

Philippines, followed by Iwo Jima, and Okinawa; these objectives could be accomplished with the resources at hand, he said.

The Joint Chiefs of Staff debated the Philippines–Formosa issue for several weeks after the Hawaii conference. They left open the question of whether to proceed from Mindanao in the southern Philippines to Luzon and Manila, or to move directly to Formosa.

In early September, U.S. intelligence determined that Leyte was far more vulnerable than previously believed and that it would be a better target than Mindanao. Then, at a follow-up in San Francisco to the Hawaii conference at the end of September, Admiral King withdrew his insistence on *Causeway*. He said that he would instead recommend to the Chiefs that American forces proceed to Luzon, to Iwo Jima, and thence to Okinawa, which lay just 350 miles from the Home Islands. Formosa was permanently scratched from the invasion agenda. Formosa, noted Nimitz, would require nine divisions – many of them unavailable until the European war was concluded.[52]

With the Philippines now established as the Allies' next major Pacific objective, the invasion of Peleliu and Angaur would proceed in September.

Following the rehearsals for the now green-lighted Operation *Stalemate*, the Marines returned to Pavavu to prepare to ship out. On Pavavu's beach road, somewhat ominously they passed a carpentry shop where white crosses were being made – grave markers that would be landed with the troops on Peleliu.[53]

Chapter 2

Second Thoughts, A Brash Prediction

Let me assure you this is going to be a short one, a quickie. Rough but fast. We'll be through in three days. It might take only two.

General William Rupertus,
1st Marine Division commander[1]

Everything about Peleliu left a bad taste in your mouth.

Colonel Merwin Silverthorn,
chief of staff of Geiger's III
Amphibious Corps[2]

Two days before D-Day, Admiral William Halsey tried to cancel Operation *Stalemate*.

Early in his career, Halsey, along with nearly every naval officer in the world, believed that the battleship was the ultimate naval weapon, and the bigger the better. But Halsey was the rare battleship admiral who, in the 1920s and 1930s, recognized that naval aviation and aircraft carriers were the future of naval warfare. When chosen to command the carrier *Saratoga* in 1934, he jumped at the chance to educate himself in the new science of carrier warfare. He enrolled in a naval aviator program to better understand the challenges faced by carrier pilots, graduating in 1935 at the advanced age of 52, the oldest person in Navy history to do so. "The naval officer in the next war had better know his aviation, and good," Halsey said.[3]

In late August 1944, Halsey was en route to the Western Pacific from Pearl Harbor to take charge of the Fifth Fleet from Admiral Raymond Spruance, its commander for the past year. Under Halsey, the Fifth Fleet would become the Third Fleet. This was part of the Navy's new plan to rotate the fleet command periodically in order to give the incumbent staff adequate time for planning and rest. In six months, Spruance and his staff would return to take the place of Halsey, and the Third Fleet would once more become the Fifth Fleet. For the sailors and officers who manned the warships, there was no change in their day-to-day duties – and no rest.[4]

The fast carriers of Admiral Marc Mitscher's Task Force 38 – formerly TF-58 – cast off on August 28 from Eniwetok on a mission to degrade Japanese air power in the Western and Central Pacific. Over the next two weeks, its planes bombed Yap, the Palaus, and Mindanao in the southern Philippines, and launched a diversionary strike against the Bonin Islands.

Naval intelligence had estimated that 650 Japanese warplanes were based in the southern Philippines, but during the two-week campaign Halsey's pilots reported a surprising lack of opposition. In 2,400 sorties over two days in the Philippines, naval aviators destroyed 200 planes on the ground, sank many ships, and flattened numerous installations. They had expected to meet more determined opposition than they did.

The weak resistance suggested to Halsey that Japanese air power in the region had been badly crippled in June during the Battle of the Philippine Sea, known by Americans as the "Great Marianas Turkey Shoot." Nearly 600 enemy planes were destroyed during the great carrier battle.

Then, on September 12 Filipino guerrillas received a downed pilot from the *Hornet* – 20-year-old Ensign Thomas Tillar. His Grumman F6F Hellcat had been shot down over Leyte Gulf during a dogfight with three Japanese fighters. Plucked from the water by Filipinos in an outrigger, Tillar was able to make contact with the pro-American guerrillas, who radioed the U.S. fleet. While with the guerrillas, Tillar learned that there were about 15,000 Japanese on the nearby island of Cebu – but no troops or air bases on Leyte. A floatplane picked up Tillar and flew him to Admiral Turner Joy's flagship, the cruiser *Wichita*. There, Tillar shared his information about Japanese troop strength on Cebu and Leyte.

When Admiral Halsey received the report on the battleship *New Jersey*, he speculated that enemy air defenses in the central and southern Philippines might be a "hollow shell." "Enemy's non-aggressive attitude [was] unbelievable and fantastic," Halsey reported to Admiral Chester Nimitz, the Pacific Ocean Area commander. "In my opinion, this was the vulnerable belly of the imperial dragon."[5]

If so, the planned invasion of Yap, the Palaus, and Mindanao – the latter previously believed to harbor 70,000 troops and hundreds of aircraft – might be cancelled, and Mindanao bypassed. MacArthur's Sixth Army could instead target the central and northern Philippines, and bring the Pacific War to a quicker conclusion.

On September 13, Halsey radioed Nimitz and proposed a new strategy. His air strikes had dealt a "crippling blow to the enemy," he said, and the Japanese were "operating on a shoestring in those areas." He recommended that Nimitz cancel the assaults on Peleliu, Angaur, Yap, Ulithi, Morotai, the northern Palau Islands, and Mindanao. He suggested that troops committed to those campaigns be attached to MacArthur's Sixth Army in order to invade undefended Leyte in October instead of December as previously planned. Halsey believed that the Japanese in the Palaus would no longer pose a threat to MacArthur's operations in the Philippines under his proposed new timetable.[6]

In the back of Halsey's mind also lurked the fear that Peleliu could become a bloodbath on the order of Tarawa, where 3,400 men were killed or wounded in 76 hours in November 1943. In May and June, Halsey had questioned the need to invade Peleliu at all – and in July, even Nimitz had suggested that Peleliu might be bypassed in favor of a more direct path to the Japanese Home Islands.[7]

In his response to Halsey's September 13 radio message, Nimitz agreed with his recommendation to scratch the invasions of Yap, Mindanao, and the northern Palaus, and move up Leyte's invasion to October. But he said the Peleliu and Morotai operations were too far advanced to call off – the Navy had already begun shelling Peleliu, and troop transports were en route. Moreover, the campaigns' objective – to secure MacArthur's flanks as his army advanced toward the Philippines – had not changed, said Nimitz. Sailing under radio silence with the Morotai invasion force on the cruiser *Nashville*, MacArthur could not be consulted about a last-minute cancellation of the Peleliu invasion.[8]

Nimitz believed that it was just as important to secure Peleliu's airfield and the Kossol Passage for the Leyte campaign as it had been for the invasion of Mindanao. Ten-mile-wide Kossol Passage lay north of the Palaus' largest island – coral-reef-girdled Babelthuap – and Nimitz thought it could become an important staging area for the Leyte campaign. The Peleliu campaign had scarcely begun when the Navy secured Kossol Passage and anchored 66 Allied vessels there.[9]

For the Leyte campaign's sake, too, Nimitz refused to drop the *Stalemate* plan to invade Ulithi. With a secure anchorage and a deep, capacious lagoon that could accommodate up to 600 warships, Ulithi would serve the Navy as an important forward base.[10]

The Combined Joint Chiefs of Staff, meeting in Quebec with President Franklin Roosevelt and Prime Minister Winston Churchill, approved Nimitz's revised plan, as did MacArthur's chief of staff, General R.K. Sutherland, acting in his commander's absence. Sutherland said MacArthur would be able to invade Leyte on October 20, two months before the original landing date. The Peleliu and Angaur landings would go forward.[11]

Pacific War historian Ian Toll suggested that another factor might have influenced Nimitz's decision to proceed with the Peleliu invasion. Nimitz was known for his ability to quickly adapt to changed circumstances. Toll wrote that it was unusual for him to stick to a plan that was possibly outdated.

Yet, if Nimitz had cancelled *Stalemate*, argued Toll, the 1st Marine Division and all of its amphibious equipment would have been returned to MacArthur's Southwest Pacific Area Command. SWPAC had overseen the division's 1943–44 Cape Gloucester campaign on the island of New Britain and would likely have utilized the Marines during the Philippines invasion. After having just wrested the 1st Division from MacArthur after Cape Gloucester, Nimitz could not permit MacArthur to reappropriate the Marine Corps's premier division.[12]

General Rupertus was in Washington, D.C., when planning for Operation *Stalemate* began on June 2. Rupertus had led the division during its rain-drenched, four-month campaign on Cape Gloucester, New Britain, that had ended in April. Afterward, he was ordered to report to Marine Corps Headquarters in Washington by Commandant Alexander Vandegrift, his superior and friend. Rupertus had served as Vandegrift's assistant division commander during the Guadalcanal campaign.

Vandegrift ostensibly summoned Rupertus to Washington to sit on a board that would recommend candidates for promotion to colonel and lieutenant colonel. Traveling to Washington with his chief of staff, Colonel John Selden, Rupertus planned to lobby Vandegrift and other senior officers at Marine headquarters for replacements and equipment that the division needed after two hard campaigns. It was unusual for a combat division commander on the cusp of a new campaign to embark on a journey of thousands of miles for a promotions board. That duty could easily be performed by ranking officers closer at hand.

However, it might have been Vandegrift's way, under the cover of government business, of granting his old friend compassionate leave so that he could spend time in Washington with his new wife and the infant son that Rupertus had not yet seen.[13] Fifteen years earlier, when Rupertus was stationed in Peking, scarlet fever had claimed the lives of Rupertus's wife Marguerite and their son and daughter. The tragedy changed Rupertus; previously known for his affability, he became moody, uncommunicative, and stingy with compliments and rewards.

Rupertus was a hardened, sun-bronzed lifelong Marine of the "Old Breed" school, having spent 30 of his 55 years in the Corps. During World War I, he commanded a Marine detachment on the battleship *Florida*, which was then attached to the British Grand Fleet. After the war, he campaigned against insurgents in Haiti, performed two tours of duty in China, and graduated from the Army Command and General Staff College at Fort Leavenworth, Kansas. Rupertus appeared to be on a path to succeed Vandegrift as commandant.[14]

Vandegrift's good intentions notwithstanding, the timing of the general's trip to Washington could not have been worse. Rupertus was absent when Peleliu's invasion plan was drafted. That task fell to assistant division commander O.P. Smith and the division staff – luckily, all competent, experienced planners.

When he returned to Pavavu on June 21, Rupertus approved the first draft of the Peleliu campaign. However, more detailed planning had to await the completion of the Marianas campaign, whose prolongation continued to occupy *Stalemate's* Marine and Navy commanders.

Guam's invasion by Geiger's III Amphibious Corps had been pushed back one month to late July because it had taken longer than expected to secure Saipan. By August 8, General Julian Smith, the expeditionary force commander, Geiger, and Admiral George Fort, in charge of the Western and Peleliu attack groups, were finally free to meet and discuss *Stalemate*. The scheduled September 15 landings were now just seven weeks away.[15]

During the first planning conference in August, Fort warned Geiger and his III Amphibious Corps staff to not expect the pre-landing gunfire support on Peleliu that III Corps had received on Guam, which had been a lavish 13-day affair. "I don't have the ships, and we don't have the ammunition," Fort bluntly said. Peleliu's much shorter pre-landing fire support would ultimately create friction between the Navy and the Marines.[16]

The Navy initially proposed seizing Angaur before Peleliu, but Smith vetoed the idea. If Angaur were invaded first, Smith argued, the Japanese could rush reinforcements from Babelthuap to Peleliu before the Marines landed there.[17]

Geiger, Fort, and their staffs studied aerial and submarine reconnaissance photos taken between May and July, and reviewed the analyses of several potential landing beaches. Ultimately, the southwestern beaches were selected because they lay closest to the Peleliu airfield and had the fewest drawbacks. The five landing beaches were designated, north to south, as White 1 and 2, and Orange 1, 2, and 3.

Three other landing sites were considered and rejected: Purple Beach on eastern Peleliu; Scarlet Beach along the southern shore; and Amber Beach on northwest Peleliu. While LSTs could bring men and supplies directly to Purple Beach, where the reef was just 200 yards wide, it also appeared to be heavily defended, and a short distance inland lay a mangrove swamp. Traversed by a single-lane road, the swamp would almost certainly become a bottleneck. Scarlet Beach was rejected because of its many tactical drawbacks and its proximity to the known Japanese defenses on Peleliu's southern promontories.

Amber Beach was overshadowed by part of the ridge system that dominated central Peleliu. If the heights could be quickly captured, the campaign might be shortened; if they could not, Amber Beach would become a death trap for the assault troops, much like Anzio in Italy. "Anything less than 100 percent execution would have been fatal," with the Marines stranded on a narrow beachhead with the enemy "literally looking down their throats," said the Marine Corps account. Another drawback was that Amber's northern flank could be enfiladed from nearby Ngesebus Island.[18]

The submarine *Seawolf* had photographed the potential landing beaches through its periscope from June 23 to 28. From these photos and aerial photos taken from high altitudes, the Army's 64th Engineering Topographical Battalion created the maps that would be used by combat units. Lieutenant Colonel W.F. Coleman, the 1st Division's assistant intelligence officer, later said that the maps proved to be "extremely inaccurate." Although they correctly depicted the island's network of roads and trails, "the hill masses were not portrayed anything like the actual terrain," Coleman said. Indeed, Peleliu's high ground would confound the American invaders.

Until nearly the last minute, no one could confidently say that there would be enough ships to carry out *Stalemate*, or where they would be found. Early in the Pacific War, there had been an acute shipping shortage. Now new ships were coming off the slipways nearly every day, but assembling enough vessels for amphibious operations remained problematic. Multiple campaigns were being planned and prosecuted simultaneously across the Pacific, and long distances between bases and objectives was another hurdle.

In *Stalemate*'s case, the ongoing Guam and Tinian campaigns in the Marianas and the naval-air battle in the Philippine Sea had made it difficult to gather the vessels needed to transport troops and their equipment to Peleliu and Angaur. MacArthur's impending Philippines operation, too, had begun to siphon off materiel.[19]

Stalemate's vessels rendezvoused at ports sprawling across the South and Central Pacific – from Manus, in the Admiralty Islands; to Tulagi in the Solomons; to Eniwetok Atoll, 1,500 miles northeast of Peleliu. Besides transporting troops and weapons, the ships carried rations for 32 days; water for five days at 2 gallons per man per day; 30 days' worth of medical supplies; and a 20-day supply of clothing, fuel, lubricants, and miscellaneous equipment.

Ammunition was rationed in units of fire – a unit of fire comprising what was needed for one day of combat. All weapons were allotted five units of fire for the assault phase. Two additional units were apportioned for 155mm howitzers, and five additional units for 57mm antitank guns. Anticipating that Peleliu's rugged topography would place heavier demands on weapons that were not normally used in combat on flatter terrain, the division allocated ten additional units of flamethrower fillers and ten extra units of explosives.[20]

It soon became apparent that there were not enough ships. Admiral Theodore Wilkinson informed Rupertus that seven transports that were to have carried 6,000 Marines and their gear were unavailable. Because fighting men and equipment could not be left behind, they had to be crammed into transports that were already at capacity.[21]

Tanks proved to be an exception. The 1st Marine Tank Battalion had to cast off with just 30 of its 46 Sherman tanks; only two Landing Ship Docks (LSDs), instead of the three needed, were provided to transport the tanks. The battalion's commander, Lieutenant Colonel Arthur "Jeb" Stuart, described the lapse as "a serious error, indefensible from the tank viewpoint ... as events proved it was extremely unsound in view of the desperate need for tanks throughout the first five days of the operation."[22] The gunners and maintenance crews for the 16 tanks that were left behind boarded the transports to Peleliu to serve as ready replacements. The tanks that did reach Peleliu did excellent service; 16 more would have been welcome.[23]

Accidents beset the *Stalemate* staging sites. The battleships *California* and *Tennessee* collided in Guadalcanal's Iron Bottom Sound, and the Navy was compelled to withdraw *California* from Peleliu's bombardment force because of the damage it sustained. Two fleet oilers rammed one another, as did a transport and its destroyer escort. The transport sank, but without loss of life.[24]

The invasion force was poised to weigh anchor when the 1st Division discovered that it had no naval gunfire officer to coordinate firing missions requested by combat units. In its two South Pacific campaigns on Guadalcanal and Cape Gloucester, the division had had little need for naval gunfire support during its unopposed landings and campaigns in the islands' dense jungles. But the Central Pacific campaigns required supporting naval gunfire. At the last minute, Navy Lieutenant Marvin Morton was flown in from Pearl Harbor to act as the gunfire officer.

At last, in early September, 868 ships set sail with the 17,490-man 1st Marine Division and 4,950 additional Marines in attached units. Sailing with the Marines were the Army's 12,601-man 81st Infantry Division, and 7,334 supporting unit troops. The 81st would invade Angaur if it was not urgently needed to reinforce the 1st Division on Peleliu. Accompanying the armada was a 129-ship "striking force" ready to engage any Japanese warships encountered by the invaders.

During the 2,100-mile journey from Guadalcanal to Peleliu, Admiral George Fort's transports and their escorts traveled in two groups that stretched across 30 miles of ocean. Thirty slower-moving LSTs averaging 7.7 knots (their initials jocularly interpreted by the Marines to mean "Large, Slow Targets") left on September 4 with amtracs, amtanks, Higgins Boats, amphibious trucks or DUKWs, and assault troops aboard. With the LSTs traveled 23 combat vessels that protected the convoy and its accompanying 32 Landing Craft, Infantry (LCIs) vessels that had been converted into rocket- and mortar-firing gunboats.

Lashed to the sides of the LSTs were 24 pontoon barges that would later be assembled into a pontoon causeway over the reef to the beaches. Nine of the barges had been modified so that cranes could be mounted on them; before the pontoon bridge was built, the cranes would transfer supplies across the reef to amtracs that would ferry them to the beaches. Until they were needed for the causeway, the other barges would serve as floating dumps for ammunition and supplies.[25]

An innovation that would be first seen on Peleliu was the amphibious cargo trailer. It had an axle and two pneumatic tires, it could float, and it was waterproof on top. Preloaded with supplies, the cargo trailers would be lowered from the transports and towed to the reef, where amtracs would hook onto them, drag them over the reef, and tow them across the lagoon to the beaches.[26]

The invasion force's LSDs and the 17 troop transports cast off on September 8, four days after the slower-moving LSTs and LCIs. Traveling at a speed of 12 knots, they carried the rest of the division and were accompanied by a slew of auxiliary, escort ships, and aircraft carrier escorts.

At sea, Marine officers lectured their men on the latest intelligence reports about Peleliu, and the naval and air support that they could expect during the amphibious assault. There were debarkation drills, and the Marines began taking their three atabrine tablets a day to pre-emptively combat malaria.[27] They lavished care on their rifles, BARs, carbines, Thompson submachine guns, pistols, and shotguns. The mortar men polished their tubes. Machine-gun crews test-fired their weapons and loaded their ammunition belts. K-Bars were honed to a razor-sharp edge.

Calm seas made the LSTs' 11-day sail to Peleliu uneventful. But because of the shortage of ships, the vessels were crowded. Belowdecks, the air was hot and fetid. For that reason, the Marines remained topside as much as possible and slept under the stars.

When not attending to their weapons, they roamed their ships, threading their way among the jumble of amtracs, DUKWs, and supplies. They played cards, read pocket books, and drank copious amounts of coffee. On some of the LSTs, the naval officers and sailors tried to be good hosts, and made certain that the Marines dined well – on roast beef, fresh green beans, fresh eggs, even ice cream.[28]

Not every ship's crew was so gracious. Upon finishing their journey on one of the transports, the Marines posted a sardonic farewell message on the bulletin board in the officers' wardroom:

A MESSAGE OF THANKS
From: Marines aboard U.S.S. *Repulsive*
To: Officers and Men aboard U.S.S. *Repulsive*

1. It gives us great pleasure at this time to extend our sincere thanks to all members of the crew for their kind and considerate treatment of Marines during this cruise.
2. We non-combatants realize that the brave and stalwart members of the crew are winning the war in the Pacific. You Navy people even go within ten miles of a Japanese island, thereby risking your precious lives. Oh how courageous you are! Oh how our piles bleed for you.
3. Because of your actions during this voyage it is our heartfelt wish that:

    a. The U.S.S. *Repulsive* receives a Jap torpedo immediately after debarkation of all troops.

    b. The crew of the U.S.S. *Repulsive* is stranded on Beach Orange Three where Marine units which sailed aboard the ship may repay in some measure the good fellowship extended by the crew and officers during the trip.

4. In conclusion we Marines wish to say to all of you dear, dear boys of the Navy: "Bugger you, you bloody bastards!"[29]

The Marines enthusiastically welcomed General Rupertus's prediction that Peleliu would be a short campaign. Guadalcanal and Cape Gloucester had been four-month ordeals. The 1st Division Marines hoped that this time, at least, they would catch a break.

In late August, during a critique of the rehearsal landings on Guadalcanal, Rupertus had acknowledged that there would be casualties on Peleliu, but he had added, "Let me assure you this is going to be a short one, a quickie. Rough but fast. We'll be through in three days. It might take only two." The general said that he wanted someone to bring him the Japanese commander's sword.[30]

"We were encouraged," wrote Pfc E.B. Sledge, for whom Peleliu would be his first campaign. "We all dreaded a long, protracted campaign that would drag on beyond endurance like Guadalcanal and Cape Gloucester."[31] Eighteen-year-old Pfc Fred Fox's superiors told the men that 30 days after they captured Peleliu's airfield, MacArthur's army would land in the Philippines. "He wanted that airfield for support," said Fox.[32] Pfc Robert Leckie, a veteran of Guadalcanal and Cape Gloucester, fervently hoped that Rupertus was right about the campaign's duration. It was Leckie's third amphibious assault, and it would likely be his last before he was rotated Stateside. "We rejoiced. That was the best way – short and sweet."[33]

Aboard the assault ships, sealed envelopes were distributed to several ranking Marine officers and to civilian news correspondents – with instructions to not open them until September 14, the day before the landings. Each envelope contained a note from General Rupertus that reiterated his optimistic prediction about *Stalemate*: "a hard-fought 'quickie,' that will last four days, five days at the most, and may result in a considerable number of casualties. You can be sure, however, that the 1st Division will conquer Peleliu."[34]

The unintended consequence was that most of the 36 accredited correspondents, photographers, and artists, convinced that Peleliu would be a minor story, elected to not go ashore at all. They lobbied their bosses for reassignment to what was expected to be the big show – MacArthur's anticipated invasion of the Philippines – or to the next major Central Pacific campaign. Just six correspondents remained to cover *Stalemate*.[35]

Peleliu would become the most underreported major campaign of the entire Pacific War.

Admiral Jesse B. Oldendorf, a member of the U.S. Naval Academy Class of 1909, led the Fire Support Group that would soften up Peleliu with naval gunfire and air strikes and, it was hoped, destroy enemy installations before the Marines hit the five landing beaches. Oldendorf's ships and planes would continue to support the Marines after they had gone ashore.

Before the bombardment began, U.S. planes dropped leaflets over Peleliu that urged islanders to leave while they could. However, none remained on the island. Hundreds of native Palauans had lived in villages on Peleliu and Angaur before the U.S. carrier raids in March. Afterward, the Japanese removed them to the northern Palaus. They now inhabited the Rock Islands, Babelthuap, and Ngaraard.[36]

Oldendorf's Fire Support Group consisted of five battleships, eight heavy and light cruisers, 14 destroyers, and minesweepers. The 32 LCIs would add to the cacophony with their automatic cannon, mortars, and rocket launchers. Three hundred fighters and dive-bombers crowded the decks of the seven escort carriers in Oldendorf's group, ready to carry out pre-landing strafing and bombardment assignments and future ground support missions.[37]

The air strikes began on September 6, when more than 600 planes lifted off from Admiral Marc Mitscher's fast carriers of Task Force 38. During 1,470 sorties over three days, they bombed and strafed ammunition and supply dumps, barracks, and warehouses. They encountered no opposition.

During September 10–12, the onslaught from the air resumed, concentrating on the Peleliu beach defenses and suspected antiaircraft battery sites.[38] At 5:30 a.m. on September 12, Oldendorf's ships began their bombardment of Peleliu. Arrayed along a 2-mile front 4 miles offshore, the five battleships – *Pennsylvania, Maryland, Mississippi, Tennessee,* and *Idaho* – battered their assigned targets on Peleliu with 48 fourteen- and sixteen-inch guns that blazed fiery orange. Three miles from shore, heavy and light cruisers lashed out at their targets. They shelled pre-selected targets for two hours. The warships checked their fire while the escort carrier planes flew missions for the next two hours. This would be the pattern until D-Day.[39]

III Amphibious Corps had requested 11 days of naval preparatory gunfire, but Oldendorf would commit to just two. In June, Saipan was shelled for three days before the landings, and it had not been enough. Adjustments were made for the next two objectives in the Mariana Islands: Guam, bombarded for 13 days; and Tinian, a much smaller objective, shelled for several days by naval vessels and long-range artillery on southern Saipan. Guam was a III Corps operation led by General Geiger, although larger-scale than Peleliu, with the Army's 77th Infantry Division and the Marines' 3rd Division and 1st Provisional Brigade – the latter composed of the Fourth and 22nd Marine Regiments (and months later combined with the 29th Marines to form a new 6th Marine Division).[40]

The extensive bombardment of Guam was one reason that Peleliu was allotted just two days. The Navy was experiencing a temporary ammunition shortage, partly because of the Marianas campaign, and partly due to the Navy stockpiling ammunition for the Philippines invasion in October.

When Geiger pressed Oldendorf for a longer pre-landing bombardment of Peleliu, the admiral reluctantly agreed to add a third day of shelling. In actuality, he added nothing; his bombardment force would use the same amount of ammunition that would have been expended during the two-day bombardment; it would merely be fired at a slower rate to make it last three days. It was no concession at all.

The weight of the metal fired on Peleliu over three days would not even equal the weight fired at Tarawa in three hours."[41]

When he was later criticized for the brevity of the pre-landing bombardment, Oldendorf wrote with obvious exasperation, "No matter how many shells you fire, or their caliber, you cannot destroy enemy gun emplacements on an island the size of Peleliu, unless the enemy will oblige by disclosing the position of his guns."[42]

Admiral George Fort said Oldendorf was "entirely correct" in ending the bombardment after three days. The "idea which some people seem to have of just firing at an island is an inexcusable waste of ammunition," he wrote.[43] Colonel William Harrison, who led the Eleventh Marines artillery regiment, said that he doubted "whether ten times the gunfire would have helped."[44]

Indeed, when they landed on the island, Marine infantrymen would quickly discover that the Navy had in fact not hit every enemy strongpoint; some would necessarily have to be silenced with the weapons at hand, and at considerable human cost.

The Japanese did not contest the barrage with organized counterfire. Peleliu's defenders rode out the bombardment in their caves, bunkers, and pillboxes. An unidentified diarist belonging to the 33rd Independent Machine Cannon Battalion wrote that, at 5:40 a.m. on September 12, "I heard the roar of motors to the south, where the moon was paling... All retired thereupon to the concrete bunkers and didn't fire at all during the whole day." The bombardment was "so fierce that we could not even lift up our heads."[45]

Colonel Tokechi Tada, the 14th Infantry Division's chief of staff at Koror, reported the first day's bombardment killed six Japanese soldiers and wounded four others, and the shelling on September 13 killed 13 defenders. On the 14th, four Japanese soldiers died.

The bombardment transformed Peleliu into "a wasteland," the Machine Cannon Battalion gunner wrote. "Not a sign of the original aspect that greeted us when we first arrived remains."[46]

Besides preparing for landing day with naval gunfire and air sorties, the Navy sent minesweepers to clear the landing beach approaches at

---

'In an after-action report, the Navy with its usual meticulousness would enumerate Peleliu's preparatory bombardment: 17,745 shells – about 2,255 tons of ammunition – including 519 sixteen-inch shells and 1,845 fourteen-inch shells.

Peleliu and Angaur. During the night of August 13, frogmen from Navy Underwater Demolition Teams 6 and 7 reconnoitered Peleliu's assault beaches at low tide. The swimmers, predecessors of the Navy SEALS, were volunteers who were variously nicknamed "mermen" and "half fish, half nuts." They had previously scouted the beaches from the submarine *Burrfish*.

Thirty-six hours before D-Day, while under sporadic rifle and machine-gun fire, frogmen from Team 7 blasted paths through a forest of obstacles off Orange Beaches 1,2, and 3: steel pyramids, wooden posts, and tetrahedrons. Off White Beaches 1, 2, and 3, Team 6, also under enemy fire, used tetrytol explosives to carve channels for amtanks, amtracs, and DUKWs through tetrahedron barriers, coconut logs, and barbed wire. Team 8 performed a similar service at Angaur's three landing beaches, which the Japanese had sown with steel rails to thwart landing craft.[47]

———

The aerial photographs of Peleliu made from carrier planes and long-range Army bombers showed that the central island was dominated by a long ridge swathed in lush jungle, trees, and undergrowth. This extremely misleading portrait had severely skewed the planners' perception of Peleliu's anticipated difficulty as a military objective, and inspired General Rupertus's optimistic prediction of a brief campaign.

The bombardment, however, had begun to strip away the green canopy from the deceptively symmetrical ridge that rose north of the airfield. Gradually revealed were Peleliu's true coral-limestone contours: heart-stopping cliffs, knife-edged ridges, deep gulches, and box canyons.

Looking through his binoculars at the unclad terrain, a gunnery officer on the cruiser *Portland* saw an enemy artillery piece emerge from a previously hidden coral fissure, fire rapidly at the American ships, and then disappear into a cave. The gunnery officer instantly ordered his guns to fire five salvos of 8-inch shells. Afterward, the gun re-emerged and fired again. "You can put all the steel in Pittsburgh onto that thing and still not get it," the frustrated officer said.[48]

The torrent of gunfire had diminished neither the Japanese defenses, nor the defenders' fighting spirit. "Who is afraid of the Americans or the British?" wrote the Machine Cannon Battalion diarist. "We will defend Peleliu."[49]

At the end of the three-day bombardment, Oldendorf announced that he had run out of targets. Indeed, the enemy defenders had made themselves scarce, but Oldendorf had also overlooked credible targets, such as a large blockhouse and a rocky, 30-feet-high promontory that jutted into the ocean at the northern edge of the five landing beaches. The latter would become known as The Point, and its capture would require an effusion of blood that would add to the Marines' displeasure over the bombardment's brevity.[50]

As *Stalemate* careered toward D-Day, it should have been clear that decisions and preparations had been made on the fly by division and Navy staff officers at Pavavu and Pearl Harbor in the absence of General Roy Geiger, preoccupied with the assault on Guam in the Marianas. General Rupertus himself had been thousands of miles away in Washington. The planning was done in the hugely mistaken belief, based on poor intelligence, that Peleliu would be quick and easy.

Those factors alone would have compromised any campaign. But neither the Allies nor the 1st Marine Division were yet aware that a seismic strategic shift had recently occurred in the Japanese Army. No longer hoping to achieve a "decisive victory," Japanese military leaders had embraced a new, "endurance engagement" strategy. They planned to fight a smart defensive battle from carefully prepared fortifications, using "fukkaku" tactics – meaning fighting from "underground, honeycombed defensive positions."

They would wage a so-called "defense in depth" battle from caves, tunnels, blockhouses, and pillboxes that were mutually supporting. Rather than stage large-scale, futile banzai attacks, the defenders would wait for the invaders to attack their cleverly designed defenses. Their purpose was to kill as many Americans as possible before inevitably being annihilated by the invaders' overwhelming firepower. Victory was no longer the object; attrition was.[51]

Stalemate's leaders would be caught flat-footed, initially watching in incomprehension and horror as their casualties soared. Blood-soaked weeks would pass before the Marines adjusted their aggressive offensive tactics to the new paradigm.

The Japanese attritional strategy, first fully implemented on Peleliu, would become the model for the defense of Iwo Jima and Okinawa in 1945. It was a desperate expedient by an adversary that recognized that although the war was no longer winnable, a reasonable peace might yet be salvaged. "Everything about Peleliu left a bad taste in your mouth," concluded Colonel Merwin Silverthorn, chief of staff of Geiger's III Amphibious Corps, after the battle finally ended after 74 days.[52]

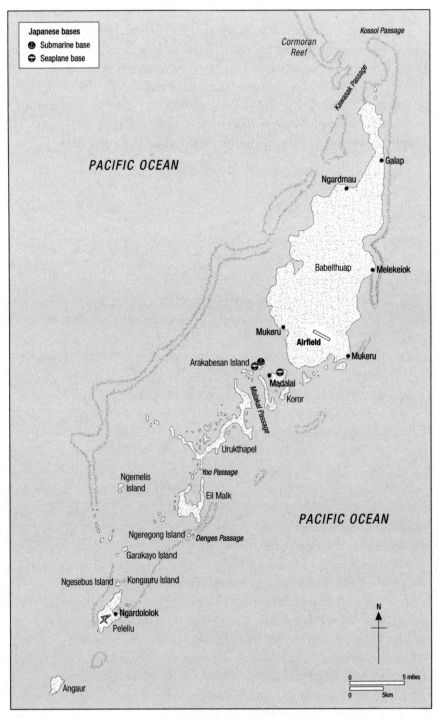

Map 2: The Palau Islands

Chapter 3

The Japanese

On this small island, we must fortify it like a big
warship – a large, unsinkable warship.
Sergeant Major Masao Kurihara, quoting a recent
Cadet School graduate who helped build
Peleliu's defenses[1]

Rouse ourselves for the sake of your country! Officers
and men, you will devote your life to the winning of
this battle, and attaining your long cherished desire of
annihilating the enemy.
Exhortation by General Sadae Inoue,
14th Infantry Division commander[2]

Japanese commanders in the Palaus were alerted on September 3 that an American invasion force was approaching. Within days, they knew where and when it would strike – Peleliu, on September 15, and, at about the same time, Angaur, the Palaus' southernmost island.[3] A week before the anticipated landings, the Japanese Navy withdrew its 150 floatplanes from Peleliu and sent them to the Philippines.[4]

The Japanese had in fact been expecting the Americans for months. All of Peleliu's and Angaur's civilians were evacuated weeks earlier. Since the Allies had shattered the enemy's first defensive line in the Central Pacific – by capturing Tarawa in the Gilbert Islands and Kwajalein in the Marshalls in late 1943 and early 1944 – Japanese leaders had been feverishly strengthening their second-line defenses. Admiral Marc Mitscher's two carrier raids against the Palaus in March – raids that wrecked Peleliu's airfield facilities and planes – persuaded the Japanese that the Palaus would be invaded first.

Imperial Japanese Headquarters had a decision to make. With just 3,000 troops garrisoned on Peleliu and others scattered around the northern Palaus, the question was whether to withdraw them, or to reinforce the Peleliu garrison and fight.[5] Prime Minister Hideki Tojo, who was also Japan's war minister, believed that the Palaus were worth fighting for, if for no other reason than to kill large numbers of Americans. In March, he met in Tokyo with General Sadae Inoue, whose 14th Infantry Division had been fighting in China. He ordered Inoue to transfer his men to the Palaus. The so-called "Shining Division" arrived on April 24.

The 14th Division's combat history can be traced to the 1905 Russo–Japanese War, and the climactic attack on Port Arthur. During the 1930s, the division served with the Kwangtung Area Army in Manchuria and northern China, where it acquired a reputation for its fighting spirit and its fealty to the emperor. The 14th Division proudly adopted the motto "Breakwater of the Pacific" when it received that tribute following a northern China battle in which it had distinguished itself.[6]

After studying the Palaus from a reconnaissance plane, Inoue identified two of the island chain's keystones as Peleliu with its airstrip, and Angaur, 6 miles to Peleliu's southwest. Inoue deployed most of his men to Babelthuap and Yap, but to Peleliu he sent the 2nd Infantry Regiment, reinforced to 6,500 men by two battalions of the 15th Infantry Regiment. With the blessing of Imperial General Headquarters in Tokyo, he assembled building materials, Korean and Okinawan laborers, and engineers on Peleliu in order to construct strong fortifications.[7]

However, senior Japanese military leaders had misread the situation. The Mariana Islands, and not the Palaus, were the Allies' first objective in their drive through the Japanese Central Pacific secondary line toward the Home Islands and Tokyo. Thus, Peleliu received building materials before Saipan, Guam, and Tinian in the Marianas got them. When the Americans invaded the Marianas in June 1944, they encountered partially completed defenses, heavy weapons that had not yet been emplaced, and unused construction materials scattered about; there had been too little time for the Japanese to finish the fortifications.

It is unlikely that new defenses would have appreciably changed the outcome of the Marianas campaign. By August, the defenders on all three islands had succumbed to the overwhelming numbers and humbling firepower of the U.S. V and III Amphibious Corps.[8]

Colonel Kunio Nakagawa, the commander of the Japanese forces on Peleliu, was a heavy-set man in his mid-40s. Known as a brilliant tactician, Nakagawa had been involved in the Marco Polo Bridge incident in 1937 that ignited the Second Sino-Japanese War, and he had led combat units in China during that war.

On Peleliu, he commanded the 2nd Infantry Regiment, one of the oldest, proudest regiments in the Imperial Army. Most of its soldiers were recruited from Japan's Ibaraki Prefecture, northeast of Tokyo. In addition to the 2nd Infantry's three battalions and the two battalions of the 15th Infantry Regiment, Nakagawa commanded a battalion of the 53rd Independent Mixed Brigade; the 45th Navy Guard Force Detachment; 2,200 men from various naval construction battalions; air base personnel; a provisional artillery battalion; two tank companies; a field hospital; and antiaircraft units. The Okinawan and Korean laborers who were conscripted to help build Peleliu's defenses could be shifted to combat roles if needed, giving Nakagawa a total of more than 11,000 men.

Pacific War historian Joseph Alexander subsequently wrote that Peleliu's defenders, man-for-man, "represented the best fighters in the Japanese Empire."[9]

Besides the construction of defensive works on Peleliu, fortification work also proceeded on neighboring Angaur. Unlike Peleliu and its coral-limestone highlands, Angaur was mostly flat and lacked terrain that might provide natural defenses, except for Romauldo Hill in the island's rugged northwest corner.

Two battalions of the 59th Infantry Regiment and Major Ushio Goto's own battalion prepared Angaur's defenses. In early September, the 59th Regiment's battalions were transferred to Peleliu, leaving only Goto's reinforced battalion of 1,400 men on Angaur. Aware that Goto's small force alone could never repulse an invasion, General Inoue requested reinforcements; he did not receive them.[10]

Before work began on Peleliu's fortifications, a row over rank erupted: the Japanese Navy refused to cooperate with Nakagawa because the colonel presumed to issue orders to naval construction units commanded by a rear admiral, Yoshioka Ito, Nakagawa's superior in rank.

Believing the army "was not receiving the cooperation it needed" from Admiral Ito, General Inoue sent 53-year-old Major General Kenijiro Murai, who out-ranked Ito, to assist Nakagawa in July. Nakagawa remained overall commander and supervised construction of the defenses, but Murai, known as an expert on fortifications and beach defenses, played a role in preparing Peleliu for the anticipated American onslaught. He and Nakagawa reportedly got along famously. Nakagawa had studied Peleliu from a navy dive-bomber and from the roads that bordered the highlands looming over the airstrip. From his observations from the air and ground, Nakagawa drew up a brilliant plan for his version of a "fukkaku" defense. When defended by troops of the caliber of Nakagawa's men, such a defensive network would be nearly impregnable. Work began in April and continued from dawn to dusk daily.[11]

Peleliu would mark the debut of Japan's new defensive strategy. In time, it would force Americans to radically change their tactics in order to minimize their losses.

But Peleliu was not the Allies' initial encounter with what would be recognized as the attritional in-depth defense. That had occurred four months earlier, in May 1944, on the island of Biak in the Sehouten Islands during General Douglas MacArthur's New Guinea campaign.

MacArthur had believed that the Army's 41st Infantry Division would capture Biak and its three airfields in just three weeks. Instead the campaign lasted two months.

Biak's airfields were coveted as buttresses for MacArthur's planned invasion of the Philippines in the fall of 1944. The Japanese, however, regarded the airstrips as keystones to the defense of their southern perimeter; they would fight hard to keep them. "Biak Island is the most critical crossroad of the war," Admiral Matome Ugaki wrote in his diary.[12]

On May 20, christened Z-Day, the Americans were confident that the campaign would be an easy one after encountering only sporadic resistance on the landing beaches. They quickly drove inland. However, this was by Japanese design. General Takazo Numata, chief of staff of the 2nd Area Army, happened to be on an inspection visit to Biak when it was invaded. Numata and Colonel Kuzume Naoyuki, who commanded Biak's 10,000-man garrison, spontaneously decided to shelve the conventional strategy of opposing the enemy at the water's edge, believing it led to unnecessary losses from naval gunfire.

Numata and Naoyuki instead deployed the defenders in natural caves; on high ground overlooking the principal airstrip, Mokmer airfield; and in pillboxes and strongholds around the airstrip. As the Americans neared Mokmer, they were stopped in their tracks by a hurricane of gunfire.

Thereafter, the battle for Biak became a grinding jungle campaign – what the Japanese described as an "endurance engagement." During the unexpectedly difficult campaign, the 41st Division commander, General Horace Fuller, was sacked, and the 24th Division's 34th Regimental Combat Team was dispatched to reinforce the 41st Division.[13]

Having resolved to fight to the death, 6,100 Japanese soldiers were killed, and a mere 450 were made prisoners. The 4,000 other defenders were unaccounted for. American casualties totaled 3,000.[14]

Biak foreshadowed Peleliu and the island battles that would follow it, but the valuable details of the novel Japanese defense in depth never reached the 1st Marine Division. As the Marines approached Peleliu, they had no idea that they were about to enter a hornet's nest.[15]

The effectiveness of Biak's resistance did not escape the notice of Imperial Japanese Headquarters, grappling with the demoralizing loss of the Marianas. It was now clear that Japan's colonial empire – the "Greater East Asia Co-Prosperity Sphere" – was slipping away. The Co-Prosperity Sphere was a natural progression of the Shinto concept of "Hakko-Jehi-u," the belief that Japan's destiny was to place "the whole world under one roof." It evidently was not; the roof was collapsing.[16]

In seizing the Marianas, the Allies had not only pierced the Japanese second line of defense but also toppled a Japanese government. Hideki Tojo, the Pacific War's architect as prime minister and army minister, was forced to resign on July 22, and a new cabinet was hastily formed.

The fall of the Marianas shattered the illusory belief that the United States could be defeated. At the same time, there had fallen the hammer blow of the Japanese First Mobile Fleet's crushing naval and air defeat during June's Battle of the Philippine Sea. Americans called it the "Great Marianas Turkey Shoot," destroying 400 planes and many of Japan's remaining top pilots.[17]

Having now seen the mastery of the sea and skies that Japan had enjoyed in 1942 shift to the Americans, the more realistic Japanese military leaders began to acknowledge that Japan had lost the war. The Japanese now strove to compel the United States, by exacting copious amounts of American blood, to drop its demand for "unconditional surrender" and agree to negotiate. A negotiated peace, the thinking went, might preserve the emperor's authority and prerogatives, and some of Japan's conquests, averting a humiliating full-scale defeat.

In Biak's wake, Imperial General Headquarters staff drafted and distributed to its senior officers in August a document titled "Defense Guidance on Islands," a detailed description of the new defensive paradigm. Its primary feature was a radical new prohibition against contesting enemy landings at the water's edge from beachside pillboxes and by launching large-scale banzai attacks. Some of the more thoughtful Japanese generals had already come to the realization, as had General Inoue, that the banzai attack "wasted manpower which could be put to more effective use."[18]

Under the new IGHQ guidelines, when invaders landed on a Japanese-held island, they would be raked by mortar and artillery fire and subjected to delaying actions from prepared positions. Then, as the enemy penetrated deeper into the Japanese defensive systems, he would find himself on ground carefully prepared for the purpose of killing as many invaders as possible. Every island and atoll would become a fortress. Peleliu would be the template for the 1945 battles on Iwo Jima and Okinawa, and ultimately for the defense of the Home Islands.

Colonel Tokuchi Tada, the 14th Infantry Division's chief of staff, would ordinarily have met strength with strength. No more. Saipan had taught the Japanese that with the enemy now controlling the sea and skies, stupendous U.S. naval and air bombardments – "beyond imagination" – would precede future beach landings. "We had no fleet arm to oppose the American fleet; we had no air power to oppose the American air force; we had no tanks capable of defeating the American tanks," Tada later recalled.[19] He went on to say:

[What remained was a situation that] closely resembled a contest between a large man armed with a long spear and a small man armed with a short sword. The man armed with the short sword must crowd in close to the large man so that his spear is useless. We had to attempt to infiltrate into the American lines to render American air attacks, naval bombardments, and tank attacks ineffective.[20]

While losing Guam, the Japanese had nonetheless learned to use shore defenses merely for the purpose of attempting to disrupt the landings. Farther inland, the defenders must prepare "deep resistance zones" and strongpoints from which to launch counterattacks. It went without saying that Japanese soldiers must fight to the death; surrender was unthinkable.

The subject of surrender was avoided in the Japanese Army. "It is better to choose death than the dishonor of surrender," Colonel Tada later remarked, adding disingenuously, "therefore, we would not care to prevent them from achieving their honor."[21] The defenders' best hope, Tada said, was "that the great number of American losses would cause them to think that the price was not commensurate with the value of Palau and therefore withdraw."[22]

It was a revolutionary overarching strategy of "endurance engagement," replacing Japan's years-long quest for a "decisive engagement." Rather than the Japanese acting to immediately crush the invaders, the enemy must be allowed to deplete himself in attempting to surmount the Japanese defenses. The core of the IGHQ's "Defense Guidance" was the "fukkaku" system of underground defensive combat – the very strategy that Nakagawa was employing on Peleliu. The document stressed the importance of utilizing terrain to mount a "defense in depth." On the landing beaches, the goal was to temporarily delay the enemy, with the primary defensive line, if possible, far enough inland to escape naval bombardment. The document also stipulated that sufficient forces must be held in reserve to mount a counterattack at the critical moment.[23]

The new attritional strategy jibed with General Inoue's July 11 order titled "Palau Group Sector Training for Victory." It warned Japanese defenders to steel themselves for a naval and aerial firestorm prior to the enemy's amphibious landing. Afterward, if possible, they were to destroy his beachhead "at one blow" before it could be fully consolidated. If the enemy's landing forces could not be stopped, the Japanese must withdraw to their prepared positions and wage an attritional battle. In anticipation of a prolonged struggle, Peleliu's defenders had been supplied with abundant canned fish, canned meat, and rice.[24]

By employing the same tactics that had been used on Biak, Peleliu's defenders would bloody the invader and erode his fighting spirit, while raising morale in the Home Islands, which had plummeted after Saipan's capture. "If we repay the Americans (who rely solely upon material power) with material power it will shock them beyond imagination," General Inoue wrote. "We are ready to die honorably," said Inoue's order, "[but] even if we die delivering our territories into the hands of the enemy it may contribute to the opening of a new phase of the war ..."[25]

The "endurance engagement" defensive philosophy was a good fit for the Japanese soldier. From childhood, he had been inured to sacrifice and hardship, and then had received a finishing course in the Imperial Army's harsh training, rigid discipline, and adherence to the strict bushido moral code that shaped the medieval samurai warrior. Soldiers in no other army in the world were better suited than the Japanese to fight to the death under such torturous circumstances – nor would they have readily consented to it.

Prior to the war, Japanese children grew up in a culture in which the individual was subordinate to the group, and obedience to one's elders and superiors was reflexive. Absolute conformity was expected. Beginning at age eight, schoolboys received military indoctrination for two to four hours a week from teachers who were themselves former soldiers or reservists. From that young age, they participated in annual maneuvers lasting up to a week, and the tradition continued through primary and middle school, high school, and college. Youths also trained for years to master judo, karate, and other martial arts, and were schooled in the belief that human endurance is limitless. A young man's family was exhorted to hand over his life to the "Divine Emperor" when he entered military service.

Military training was arduous. Soldiers drilled day and night in bayonet-fighting – the 20-inch Japanese bayonet had a wicked 16-inch blade – in the belief that the bayonet alone could force the enemy to yield ground. There were 50-mile marches with full equipment in hot summer weather, and "snow marches" in northern Japan and Korea in the wintertime. In garrison, a soldier's simple diet might include a large bowl of rice, a cup of green tea, smoked fish, fried bean paste, fruits, and vegetables. In the field, he subsisted on milled wheat and rice, which were mixed in a pot and eaten thrice daily.[26]

During maneuvers, Japanese soldiers learned to carry out bold, rapid movements without regard to terrain or casualties. Mentally prepared to fight until killed, the Japanese soldier anticipated joining his warrior ancestors at the Yasukuni Shrine in Tokyo, the resting place of Japan's "guardian spirits."[27]

The Palauans called the hill mass that dominated central Peleliu "Omleblochel"; the Americans corrupted the name to "Umurbrogol." Author and historian Robert Leckie, who fought on Peleliu as a Marine Pfc, described it as "neither ridge nor mountain but an undersea coral reef thrown above the surface by a subterranean volcano… It was a place that might have been designed by a maniacal artist given to painting mathematical abstractions – all slants, jaggeds, straights, steeps, and sheers with no curve to soften or relieve."[28]

After the coral was eroded by the elements, what remained was durable limestone standing up to 300 feet high, riddled with caves – some of them with stalactites and stalagmites – and cliffs and ravines. The terrain was ideal for defense, but "a nightmare's nightmare" for attackers, in the words of one Marine.[29]

Nakagawa asked General Inoue to send mining and tunnel engineers to help him utilize the hundreds of naturally occurring coral-limestone caves – some of them 500 feet deep – that were common on Peleliu, and to use explosives to create new ones. The colonel divided the island into four zones. He reasoned that troops in inactive zones could move swiftly through tunnels and along interior lines to areas under attack. It was a good plan – so long as the invaders did not isolate a zone before it could either be reinforced, or before its defenders could escape.

Nakagawa assigned 550 men from the 346th Independent Infantry Battalion under Major Michero Hiikino to defend northern Peleliu. They would fight alongside up to 1,000 naval construction troops that occupied the area. Five hundred infantrymen, along with an artillery unit, were sent to the tiny island of Ngesebus, formerly joined to northern Peleliu by a 500-yard causeway. The 15th Regiment's 3rd Battalion – 750 men under a Captain Senkasi – was dispatched to Scarlet Beach on Peleliu's southern tip. Defending the western approaches were 600 men from the 14th Infantry's 2nd Battalion under Major Hoji Tomita.

Another 600-man battalion defended Purple Beach on Peleliu's eastern shore. The Purple Beach units had orders to withdraw if the battle developed to the west. The battalion at Scarlet Beach, however, was expected to stand fast and fight to the death. The rest of Nakagawa's men – the majority of Peleliu's defenders – occupied the island's rocky central highlands under Nakagawa's personal command.[30]

Whenever possible, Japanese engineers utilized underground water cavities and streams as tunnels – entered by way of camouflaged ground-level trapdoors, or down vertical shafts accessed by ladders. They also built "balcony caves" around horizontal fissures high on the ridge faces. Tunnels connected these fighting positions to adjacent balcony caves, sometimes on a ridge's opposite side.[31]

Among the Japanese soldiers that built the island defenses was Sergeant Major Masao Kurihara, who belonged to General Murai's headquarters detachment and later became a war prisoner. "We spent many days and nights in constructing the pillboxes," recalled Kurihara, who came to Peleliu in late April, "although the thickness of the cement was not up to expectation due to lack of manpower and machinery."[32]

Engineers carved out firing ports and small, well-concealed entrances to the caves, some shielded by armor-plate doors set in concrete. Their locations were picked for their ability to provide covering fire for one another, so that attacking one Japanese fortification would attract lethal supporting fire from numerous positions nearby. Inside the cave entrances, the passageways were contrived to turn sharply and deflect direct gunfire and flames from the caves' interiors.

"Blast walls" made of reinforced concrete, and oil drums filled with crushed coral shored up the caves' interiors, some of them containing ammunition storage areas and rest areas for gun crews. The largest caves could hold 1,000 men and had multiple exits, laterals, and bays.[33]

A Japanese officer who had recently graduated from the Cadet School observed that because the defenders lacked air and naval support, "On this small island, we must fortify it like a big warship – a large, unsinkable warship." This they strove mightily to accomplish.[34]

Army and naval construction units operated independently of one another. Army engineers built combat caves for ground defense. Naval engineers created shelters in northern Peleliu – initially without regard for protection against tank-infantry assaults. However, many of these were later converted into defensive positions.

The tunnels were dug by a special Naval Tunnel Construction Unit led by a civilian engineer who supervised men who had built tunnels in Japan.[35] After the engineers and laborers completed the fortifications, Peleliu had been transformed into an underground fortress of more than 500 caves – 200 man-made, 300 naturally occurring but improved – some of them seven stories deep and connected by tunnels. Living areas often had wooden floors, tin roofs, and electric lighting.[36]

When the Japanese were burrowing into the coralline-limestone rock, they undoubtedly cursed its obduracy. But the defenders would later be grateful for the protection their caves and tunnels afforded them from artillery and naval gunfire, and aerial bombing, which reduced every above-ground structure to rubble but seldom penetrated the underground fortresses. Moreover, they stayed relatively cool when above-ground temperatures soared over 100 degrees.

Inside the roomier "L"- and "T"-shaped caves were Nakagawa's twenty-four 75mm cannons, 30 dual-purpose antiaircraft guns, and mortars, which were usually positioned on reverse slopes. Engineers carefully registered the guns on Peleliu's beaches and reef so that invaders would pay a price for the privilege of coming ashore.[37]

The smaller caves, inhabited by riflemen and machine gunners, were carved out of cliffs, sometimes one above the other to provide enfilading fire. Often, sharpshooters occupied positions deep inside caves, where they were especially difficult to locate and neutralize.

The "I"-shaped caves were the most numerous – and were essentially suicide caves because they had one entrance and no escape route. The "L"- and "T"-shaped caves had more than one access tunnel, and the largest caves were used for storage, air raid shelters, and hospitals.[38]

Dense tropical under- and over-growth concealed the cleverly contrived defensive complex from snooping American flyovers. From the air, Peleliu's highlands and what became known as Bloody Nose Ridge appeared to be a long, gently sloping ridge generously swathed in dense rainforest foliage – and nothing more. Peleliu's ridges did not begin to reveal their secrets until naval gunfire and air strikes began stripping the highlands of their vegetation, baring the shocking labyrinthine landscape that lay beneath: a broken, non-contiguous jumble of sheer walls honeycombed with cavities, precipitous cliffs, razor-edged crags, and debris-strewn canyons.*[39]

The Japanese soldiers, having been trained in offensive warfare, struggled to adapt to the new defensive strategy. Sergeant Major Kurihara and a Japanese prisoner identified only as "On" stated that their army training did not prepare them to wage a strictly defensive battle on Peleliu. "We were not familiar with defensive warfare, especially defensive island warfare," recalled On. Moreover, the Japanese, proficient in jungle warfare, were not prepared to fight in Peleliu's rocky terrain in terrific heat. But neither were the Americans.[40]

General Inoue was inspecting Peleliu's northern island defenses a few days before D-Day when American carrier planes bombed and strafed the airfield. When he went to assess the damage, Inoue found that "the naval headquarters had suffered a direct hit and all of the Navy staff officers had been wounded (except for the rear admiral [Ito]); the fuel depot had been hit and was burning fiercely, blackening the sky with smoke." The bombardment foreshadowed what was to come.[41]

Accurately apprised that the approaching invasion force was a Marine division led by General Julian Smith, who was in fact the overall expeditionary commander, Inoue issued a spirited address to his officers and men, reminding them of the coming battle's stakes:

> The battle may have a part in the decisive turn of tide in breaking the deadlock of the "Great Asiatic War." The entire Army and people of Japan are expecting us to win this battle... Rouse ourselves for the sake of your country! Officers and men, you will devote your life to the winning of this battle, and attaining your long cherished desire of annihilating the enemy.[42]

---

*Several months after the Battle of Peleliu ended, Navy Lieutenant W.C. Phelan explored every cave on the island and meticulously catalogued their shapes and uses. He wrote that millennia of erosion from rain and wind had abraded the coral rock faces into precipitous cliffs, fissures, and faults, some plunging 50 feet or more. By then, the Marines had already discovered these features the hard way.

By the third year of the Pacific War, American soldiers understood that the Japanese fighting man possessed an unfathomable willingness to withstand profound hardships and to forfeit his life in battle; it exceeded the bounds of normal human endurance. Yet, unbroken victories across the Pacific during two years of hard campaigning against Japanese forces had convinced the Allies that technological prowess, superior numbers, and overwhelming firepower could overcome every obstacle thrown up by the Japanese. Just as Japanese leaders recognized that their wartime dreams were doomed, so did Americans believe that they would ultimately triumph.

From the voluminous Japanese 31st Army records seized when Saipan fell – along with a captured Japanese intelligence officer to interpret them – *Stalemate*'s leaders had learned how many Japanese defended the Palaus. The enemy infantrymen, they were nearly certain, belonged to the 14th Infantry Division, one of the Imperial Army's best combat units – veterans of years of fighting in China and Manchuria.[43]

Of the approximately 27,000 Marines on the transports bound for Peleliu, just 9,000 infantrymen from three regiments would storm Peleliu's defenses, manned by upwards of 10,600 enemy combatants – a number indicated by the captured documents. The relatively small size of the assault force violated the standard rule-of-thumb, which recommended that attackers should possess a 3-to-1 numerical advantage over defenders.[44]

Being Marines, however, the rest of the division – various specialists not trained as infantrymen – could certainly go into combat if necessary. Until they were summoned to the front lines, they served in artillery, medical, transportation, and logistics units; and shore parties and headquarters units. They drove tanks, amtracs, and DUKWs, and they were engineers.

One had to wonder, though, whether the confidence earned during two unbroken years of island conquests had become overconfidence.

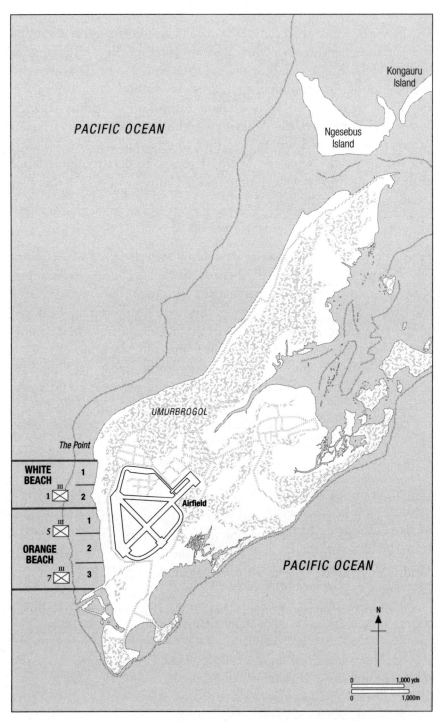

MAP 3: Peleliu Island

Chapter 4

The Bloody Beaches

I couldn't believe what I was seeing. Boats were burning
and I saw one boat ... [and] it took a direct hit...
Marines were spinning around in the air just like in slow
motion, flopping back in the water.
                                          Corporal James Young[1]

Everywhere the air hummed and sang. The zip, zip, zip
became so steady it settled into one drone at high pitch.
I ran into the humming smoke...
                                          Pfc Russell Davis[2]

During the first assault waves' lunge toward Peleliu's beaches, the thunder of naval gunfire was stupefying. The Marines dared to hope that it had silenced the enemy batteries. United Press's Richard Johnston, watching from the bridge of the III Amphibious Corps flagship *Mount McKinley*, said the bombardment "rolled up a 4,000-foot black curtain in the windless tropical air... It seemed impossible that a single Jap was left alive."[3]

Aboard the amtracs and Higgins Boats bumping through the choppy waters toward the reef, some Marine riflemen vomited up the sumptuous breakfasts that they had eaten a few hours earlier. As they squinted through the smoke veiling the beaches, they glimpsed geysers of sand and shattered trees. The water around the landing craft suddenly came alive in spurts and splashes. Bullets pinged off the amtrac hulls. There would be opposition after all.

Nearing Peleliu's landing beaches, the tense Marines struggled to control their fear. "It was like a scar or a limp that I had to learn to live with. I learned always to control what showed in my face, my hands and my voice. And I let it rage on inside," said Pfc Russell Davis of his first amphibious assault. "I never lost my fear, but lost my fear of fear, because it became such a familiar thing."[4]

"A group of Hellcats flew over, cracking the air, sounding like a string of firecrackers popping in their wake," said Pfc Sterling Mace, a BAR man bound for Orange Beach 2 with the Fifth Marines' first wave. One of the Hellcats, hit by Japanese ground fire and trailing smoke over the distant airfield, disappeared from view. "Those of us who had never been in combat had an idea of what it would be like – but we were completely wrong. Mortally wrong," Mace later recalled.[5]

The amtracs in the first assault waves struck the stout coral reef with teeth-rattling jolts that knocked the Marines off their feet, before the vehicles' tank treads took hold and pulled the amphibians over the reef. "Ours stood almost on end," said Corporal James Young. "We thought it was going to topple over. I was hanging on and bam! It went down and off we went."[6]

A mortar round hit the front end of Young's amtrac. One of the two coxswains slumped over, and the other motioned to the men that the amtrac could not continue to the beach. The men splashed into the water and waded ashore. "I couldn't believe what I was seeing," said Young. "Boats were burning and I saw one boat ... [and] it took a direct hit... Marines were spinning around in the air just like in slow motion, flopping back in the water."[7]

Pfc Robert Leckie landed with the First Marines in one of the early assault waves, "yet the beach was already a litter of burning, blackened amphibian tractors, of dead and wounded, a mortal garden of exploding mortar shells. Holes had been scooped in the white sand or had been blasted out by the shells; the beach was pocked with holes – all filled with green-clad helmeted Marines."[8]

Men in subsequent waves could plainly see the cost that the assault was exacting from the 1st Division. Pfc Loren Abdulla of the First Marines and his comrades came ashore on White Beach, where they faced "a big coral wall, and nothing but Marines stacked around it, lying flat dead" – casualties from the previous landing wave.[9]

A mortar smashed into radio operator Kenneth Harrell's amtrac in the second wave, killing one of the gunners. Harrell ended up in the water, crawling over the reef. The coral shredded his hands and knees. Another amtrac picked him up and the crew gave him new trousers, a T-shirt, and a gunner's helmet, and took him to the beach.[10]

The Guadalcanal and Cape Gloucester assaults had been nothing like this. The Marines of the 1st Division had never landed on a contested beach; D-Day on Peleliu was a terrible shock. "The whole beach was fire and smoke," said Pfc Ray Hechler. "You could hear the bullets whizzing."[11]

Colonel Lewis "Chesty" Puller, too, had never encountered a beach landing as hot as Peleliu's. Landed by an amtrac in the first troop wave, Puller "went up and over that side as fast as I could scramble and ran like hell at least twenty-five yards before I hit the beach flat down," he wrote. "That big promontory on my left [soon to be known as The Point] hadn't been touched by the ship's guns and planes, and we got a whirlwind of machine gun and antitank fire." Five reinforced concrete pillboxes on The Point raked the White beaches with enfilading machine-gun and 47mm cannon fire.[12]

Hissing shrapnel and shards of splintered coral filled the air as Puller sprinted across the beach, his leg throbbing with pain from an unhealed shrapnel wound that he had received on Guadalcanal in 1942. When he looked back at the amtrac that had landed him, it suddenly vanished in a plume of smoke, crushed by a flurry of enemy shells. Most of its crewmen died.[13]

The Marines unexpectedly encountered a mongrel dog roving the beach, "wet, shaking from tail to muzzle vibratory. The dog's eyes are insane," said Sterling Mace, the BAR man. "Crossing the beach was like running between raindrops," said Pfc Joe Clapper of the First Marines. "You just got the hell off the beach."[14]

Pfc Hechler dove into a shell hole. An enemy shell exploded beside it, blowing off his helmet, rupturing an artery in his nose, and knocking him out. Evacuated to a hospital ship, Hechler's role in *Stalemate* had ended.[15]

Pfc Giles McCoy, a sniper with the Seventh Marines who later became a medical doctor, found himself in the water beside a Marine whose right arm had been blown off by a machine-gun blast. "He was squirting blood about twenty feet and I knew he was going to faint, so I got him over and got him up on my hip and I tried to calm him down and reached around and got hold of the blood vessel that was blown off and I pinched it ... 'til my fingers cramped." On the beach, McCoy flagged down a corpsman who, after examining the wounded man, said, "Son, he's already gone. Turn him loose."[16]

Ceaseless enemy mortar fire kept the corpsmen scrambling to treat the wounded. "Big mortars just every time," said Corpsman Burnett Napier. "A lot of casualties. Every kind of wound in the world we had to treat. It was a constant yell for corpsmen." Some of the cries came from the Japanese, who tried to lure corpsmen into the open so that they could shoot them.[17]

Hit by mortar fire while crossing the reef were five amtracs carrying the First Marines' communications equipment and headquarters personnel. As a consequence, the regiment would be without radio contact during most of its first day ashore, and was forced to rely on runners to convey messages and orders. A mortar round smashed into the regimental command post after it was set up, compounding the First Marines' woes.[18]

Yet, most of the first-wave landing craft negotiated the fiery gantlet with relatively few men killed or wounded. But then the enemy gunfire intensified, and the casualties mounted in subsequent assault waves. Those who survived the murderous mortar fire alive and unhurt, like the chaplain who passed through the fiery crucible untouched, thought it nothing less than miraculous. "The bursts were everywhere, and our men were being hit, left and right," he later wrote.[19]

By the time the fifth wave arrived, the carnage was widespread. Lieutenant Clifford West, who had expected the landing to be "a picnic," said, "Bodies and stuff were floating in the bay."[20]

In the 700-yard lagoon between the reef and the beach, the amtracs and amtanks faced new hazards. After watching Navy frogmen remove hundreds of landing obstacles the day before, Nakagawa that night had sent "stealth swimmers" to re-sow the waters with 300 single- and double-horned anti-invasion mines. Fortunately for the invaders, the swimmers who planted them neglected to remove the safety pins from most of them and they did not detonate.

But there were hundreds of 110-pound aerial bombs jury-rigged as mines and buried in the beaches. Their detonators protruded from the sand; they were wired to be detonated remotely. However, the preliminary bombardment shredded the wires, and the bombs were crushed by the amtanks and amtracs without exploding.[21]

Pfc Davis was in the first wave with the First Marines' 2nd Battalion when it landed on White Beach 2 at 8:32 a.m., two minutes behind schedule. As he splashed ashore through the shallows, "everywhere the air hummed and sang. The zip, zip, zip became so steady it settled into one drone at high pitch. I ran into the humming smoke …"[22]

The Japanese artillery and mortar fire appeared to be coming from the hill mass northeast of the landing beaches. The mortar would be the Japanese weapon most often remembered by Peleliu veterans. Especially unforgettable was the enemy's massive 150mm mortar, capable of firing a 56-pound projectile – so large that it could be seen in flight – up to 2,000 yards. It was the Marines' first encounter with the weapon. It was most active during *Stalemate*'s early stages, when the beaches and the nearby airfield were within the giant mortars' range.[23]

Machine gunners in well-camouflaged pillboxes a short distance from the beaches lashed the Marines with swarms of bullets. The Nambu machine guns' rapid, high-pitched buzz steadily rose to a full-throated roar. By the time the third wave arrived at the reef, the machine guns and gunfire from Peleliu's heights were cutting bloody swaths through the invaders.[24]

Equally deadly were the 47mm anti-boat guns and machine guns that plastered both ends of the landing beaches with enfilading fire – White Beach 1 and the First Marines' 3rd Battalion on the north; and Orange Beach 3, the Seventh Marines' narrow landing zone on the south. The enemy gun emplacements had been untouched by the three-day naval bombardment.

Daniel Lawler, a Fifth Marines ammunition carrier, looked up and down the beaches as he came ashore, "and all you could hear was screaming, and men were falling and dying." The Fifth Marines, however, landing in the middle on Orange Beaches 1 and 2, were relatively buffered from the anti-boat gunfire chewing up White Beach 1 and Orange Beach 3, and were able to quickly move inland to the airfield's western edge, their objective.

As they moved toward the airfield, Lawler's comrades spotted Japanese troops wheeling a 75mm gun from a blockhouse 200 feet away and preparing to fire it. It resembled "the hood of a Buick halfway out of a garage." A tank summoned from the beach destroyed the 75, as well as a nearby 37mm gun and two mortars. When the firefight ended, about 15 dead Japanese lay scattered around the ruined guns – many of them victims of Marine small-arms fire. "The high coppery tang of dropped blood and the low odor of feces" permeated the air, remembered Pfc Mace.[25]

When 16-year-old Pfc Charles Owen leaped over his amtrac's gunwale onto Peleliu's beach, it was "like falling into hell." Gunfire of many calibers exploded around him, and the shallows were red with the blood of his comrades. "There were bodies and parts of bodies all around," said Owen. "I was terrified." Another teenage Marine, Pfc Harold Clay, was appalled by the casualties. "You could almost walk on the bodies," he said. "I mean, there were that many of them."[26]

Although a veteran of two campaigns, Pfc Charles Loeschorn, too, was shocked by the number of dead Marines in the surf. "You never get used to seeing bodies floating in the water," he said. In the equatorial heat, which by mid-morning approached 100 degrees, "some of them had started to bloat and that wasn't a pretty picture."[27]

Pfc Wayburn Hall, a First Marines mortarman who landed on White Beach 2 with the first wave, had a very brief experience on Peleliu. A Japanese mortar round clipped the corner of Hall's amtrac, and he was blown into the water. His face torn by shrapnel, Hall crawled into a shell hole, where a corpsman put sulfa on and wrapped his wound. Hall hobbled to an outbound amtrac that took him to a hospital ship. He was later evacuated to Pavavu.[28]

Amtracs landed Pfc Jack Ainsworth's "C" Company on the wrong White Beach, and it became mixed in with the First Marines' 2nd Battalion at the base of a cliff. From this vantage point, Ainsworth and his mates witnessed the horrifying sight of Marines "being blown to bits by mortar and artillery fire and our own tractors being blown out of the water and burning the occupants alive." He later remembered how the white beach sands were, in many places, stained red with the blood of his comrades in arms.[29]

Japanese artillery and mortar fire shredded the sixth wave, which consisted largely of unarmored DUKWs; six of the six-wheel amphibious crafts were destroyed. An enemy anti-boat gun firing from a peninsula south of the landing beaches was especially effective.[30]

The southernmost landing beach, Orange 3, was beset by myriad problems. To begin with, the beach was a narrow corridor for an entire regiment – a mere 550 yards wide, permitting just one battalion to be landed at a time.

Before the Seventh Marines reached shore, their amtracs, advancing slowly in a column, had to first negotiate a deadly gantlet of anti-boat barriers, tangles of barbed wire, and anti-boat, antitank, and anti-personnel mines. The lethal underwater obstacles and wooden posts planted in the surf were intended to steer landing craft into kill zones targeted by pre-registered artillery and mortars. Crashing shells transformed some of the landing craft into fiery wrecks and forced the surviving occupants to wade ashore.

When Japanese 75mm artillery rounds plowed into a half-dozen amtracs nearing the beach, "pieces of iron and men seemed to sail slow-motion into the air," wrote *Life* magazine illustrator Tom Lea, who landed with the Seventh. An enemy shell flattened a file of Marines wading toward shore from one of the smoking amtracs, and Lea saw other Marines lashed by sheets of machine-gun fire as they "fell with bloody splashes into the green water."[31]

A mortar round passed so close to Lea that its "red flash stabbed my eyeballs." It landed 15 yards away, crashing into four men from his boat. "One figure seemed to fly to pieces. With terrible clarity I saw the head and one leg sail into the air."[32] A man who had been wounded on the beach staggered past Lea toward amtracs that were shuttling men to the hospital ships. What Lea saw and later made into an iconic illustration captured the dreadfulness of Peleliu's beaches. "His face was a half bloody pulp, and the mangled shreds of what was left of an arm hung down like a stick," wrote Lea. The wounded man fell behind Lea, "in a red puddle on the white sand."[33]

The Seventh Marines were able to gingerly negotiate the beach minefield as gunfire plucked at their green herringbone jackets and cut down some of them, but it was trickier for the tanks that came ashore a short time later. Thirty waterproofed Sherman tanks landed in the fourth wave, in six columns of five tanks. At the head of each column was an amtrac carrying food, ammunition, and maintenance supplies. Fifteen tanks were damaged by artillery and mortar fire during the ten minutes that it took to cross the reef, but they pushed on with the rest. Half of the tanks went to the White beaches and the rest headed to the Orange beaches.[34]

The commander of the lead tank on Orange Beach 3 solved the problem of navigating the minefield by dismounting and proceeding on foot while trailing toilet paper so that other tanks could safely follow his lead.[35]

The Seventh's 3rd Battalion was the first infantry unit to reach Orange 3. It was met by torrents of fire from anti-boat guns, mortars, and machine guns concealed on Peleliu's southern promontories; on Ngarmoked Island; and on a nearby tiny, unnamed islet that had somehow escaped the pre-landing naval and aerial bombardment. The avalanche of metal caused the Seventh Marines' "K" Company to veer to the left to avoid it. "K" Company ended up beside the Fifth Marines' 3rd Battalion, which also had a "K" Company; confusion ensued.

Navy Lieutenant (j.g.) John Carboy, the naval gunfire officer assigned to the Seventh Marines' 1st Battalion, discovered when he tried to direct naval gunfire onto Ngarmoked Island that no gunfire support ship had been assigned to the regiment. Carboy was told that no one had anticipated having to shell the southern promontories. But within an hour, the destroyer *Leutze* began bombarding Ngarmoked, and the enfilading fire slackened.[36]

Admiral Fort, the amphibious assault commander, expressed "surprise and chagrin" when he was informed that naval gunfire had failed to suppress the enemy guns on southern Peleliu. Admiral Oldendorf, who had declared a day earlier that his Fire Support Group had run out of targets, said the gunfire came from the "shore side" of the unnamed islet, which naval gunfire had been unable to reach because of the intervening reefs.[37]

Commanding the Seventh Marines on Orange Beach 3 was Colonel Herman "Hard Head" Hanneken, a leathery, 30-year-veteran "Old Breed" Marine like Puller and the III Amphibious Corps commander, General Roy Geiger. In 1915 in Haiti, where U.S. troops were defending American business interests against peasant revolts, Hanneken tracked down and killed Charlemagne Peralte, a resistance leader, and then assassinated his successor, Osiris Joseph. In Nicaragua in 1929, he captured rebel chief Augusto Sandino's chief of staff. For his exploits in Haiti and Nicaragua, Hanneken was awarded the Congressional Medal of Honor and two Navy Crosses. In 1942, he became commander of the Seventh Marines on Guadalcanal, then led the Seventh on Cape Gloucester, and now, on Peleliu.[38]

The beaches where the Fifth and Seventh Marines had landed were bloody shambles. Wounded and dead Marines lay amid shattered ammunition crates, discarded rifles, helmets, packs, and supplies. In the shallows, half-submerged amtracs burned among corpses bobbing in the surf. Men darted from shell hole to shell hole. Mortars flashed and exploded amid the high-pitched clatter of the Japanese machine guns, creating a terrific din that even shouted orders sometimes failed to penetrate.[39]

On the beach, Pfc Ivan Elms was manning a machine gun in his amtank when a shell ripped through the armor-clad amphibious vehicle. He and a corpsman fled under machine-gun fire. Behind them, an artillery shell smashed a Jeep to smithereens; its two occupants simply disappeared. A piece of Jeep debris struck Elm, carving a lemon-sized hole in his knee, where an artery dangled, pumping blood. "I'm hit!" he shouted to the corpsman, but then saw that the corpsman's left arm had been blown off. "I'm sorry, but I don't think I'll be able to help you," the corpsman said politely before he fell over, dead.[40]

Sergeant "Swede" Hanson leaned over to aid a Marine lying wounded at the water's edge, and the man told Hanson, "No, Mac. Please don't touch me. Leave me be." Hanson, however, could not bear to leave him, but when he tried to lift him up, to his horror he saw the lower half of the man's body was gone. "See what I mean?" the Marine said. "Get some cover for yourself."[41]

Navy Lieutenant Edward Hagan, a doctor attached to the Seventh Marines' 3rd Battalion, hugged the ground after reaching the beach. "I can't imagine how anything could be worse," he said. "In turning your head from side to side lying on the beach, you could see dead Marines on both sides."[42]

Corpsman Brooking Gex said his amtrac passed through a gantlet of roaring gunfire and floating bodies. "The air was thick with the screams of the wounded and dying," he said.[43]

Pfc Owen and his Seventh Marines company lay flat on Orange Beach 3 as enemy mortar shells crashed around them, spraying them with sand and body parts. No one moved. Then, through the gunfire strode Major Arthur Middleton Parker Jr., the executive officer of the 3rd Amphibious Tractor Battalion – the first Marine unit to land on Peleliu. Cradling a Thompson submachine gun, he shouted, "Get the hell off this beach, or I'll shoot your ass!" Parker had left his disabled amtank to light a fire under the stalled assault troops; his was one of 30 amphibious vehicles that were knocked out during the landing, at a cost of 28 killed and 78 wounded.

Convinced "that crazy sonofabitch is going to kill me if I don't get the hell off this beach," Owen and his comrades got going, and it "undoubtedly saved my life," he later acknowledged.[44]

A short distance inland from the beach was a 6-foot-deep tank trap that ran the length of the beach. Not only did it provide welcome shelter for Marines who tumbled into it after their harrowing journey across the beach, but it served a useful tactical purpose. "It proved an excellent artery for moving troops into the proper position for deployment and advance inland, since it crossed the entire width of our zone of action," wrote Major Hunter Hurst, the commander of the Seventh Marines' 3rd Battalion.[45]

———

At almost the exact moment that the 1st Division was landing on Peleliu, the Army's IX Corps under General Charles Hall was coming ashore on the 44-mile-long island of Morotai, the northernmost of the Molucca or Spice Islands of eastern Indonesia.

About 28,000 assault troops spearheaded by the Army's 31st Division waded to Morotai's beach through shoulder-deep water. The invasion was calculated to edge General Douglas MacArthur's forces closer to the Philippines. Accompanying the assault troops was MacArthur himself. As he paced the beach, MacArthur reportedly turned and gazed northward toward the Philippines. He was overheard saying to himself, "They are waiting for me there. It has been a long time."[46]

Outnumbered 50-to-1, Morotai's 500 defenders did not oppose the landings. But during the night of September 15–16, they launched a doomed banzai attack that resulted in the slaughter of most of the enemy soldiers.

The invasion's object was to transform the mountainous, jungle-clad island into an airfield complex that Army bombers could use to strike Mindanao and Leyte. Seven thousand construction troops came ashore with the assault troops and began work immediately. They built two airstrips, a 1,000-bed hospital, and fuel storage facilities.

The Japanese sent hundreds of reinforcements to Morotai to disrupt the airfield construction program, but the counteroffensive failed. Eventually, in January 1945, the 136th Regiment of the Army's 33rd Division, transported to Morotai from New Guinea, mounted an offensive that crushed the last Japanese resistance; 870 Japanese soldiers were reportedly killed or captured.[47]

Sticking to their new attritional strategy, Peleliu's Japanese defenders did not make banzai counterattacks at the beach and attempt to drive the Marines into the sea. But a short distance inland, enemy troops in trenches, dugouts, and pillboxes resisted fiercely with mortars, machine guns, grenades, and small arms.

Their firing ports were at ground level, and the positions were camouflaged with live shrubs and vines, protected by coconut logs, and covered by layers of sand, rock, or cemented coral 3 feet thick. Difficult to detect, they were also difficult to knock out. Nearby, snipers infested the scrub and perched high in the trees, picking off Marines.[48]

Driven to the ground by a machine gun in a pillbox 300 yards ahead of him, Pfc Warner Pyne attempted to flank it, with the intention of throwing a hand grenade into the pillbox. But when Pyne got into position, he realized, to his horror, that he had neglected to bring hand grenades with him. He felt even more foolish when he saw that he did not have a weapon of any kind.

Two comrades joined him, and one of them tossed him a grenade, which Pyne threw into the pillbox. The Japanese survived the blast and continued to fight back even after a tank stuck its 37mm gun barrel into the pillbox and fired two rounds. A grenade defiantly sailed out of the pillbox, wounding Pyne, who was evacuated.[49]

Although the Japanese soldiers that were dug in behind the beach bitterly resisted until they were killed, they were "groggy, disorganized, and devoid of communication" as a result of the pre-landing bombardment, said Colonel Hunter Hurst of the Seventh Marines.

"At no time did we feel him capable of organizing a successful counterattack."[50]

Within an hour, Hurst's battalion seized the Orange 3 beachhead at a cost of 40 casualties and pushed inland 500 yards.[51]

The Seventh Marines saw evidence among the scattered bodies of the defenders that the pre-landing naval and air attacks had not been in vain. Succumbing to curiosity, Captain Don Wyckoff of "B" Company searched a dead Japanese soldier's "horsehide, pinto pony pack with hair on the outside." Inside were neatly packed provisions for a three- or four-day battle: a small straw box of rice; a box of canned condiments; pickled plums; and crab meat.[52]

Mortarman E.B. Sledge came ashore on Orange 2 with the Fifth Marines. Pfc Sledge's baptism by fire was "a nightmare of flashes, explosions, and snapping bullets... My mind was benumbed by the shock of it." The Japanese shells fell so fast that individual explosions could not be discerned; it was "just continuous, crashing rumbles with an occasional ripping sound of shrapnel tearing low through the air overhead amid the roar."

"The beach was a sheet of flame backed by a huge wall of black smoke, as though the island was on fire," Sledge said. "Every Marine in that amtrac was sickly white with terror... Heavy Jap artillery and mortars were pounding the beach, and Marines were getting hit constantly. We piled out of our amtrac amid blue-white Japanese machine-gun tracers and raced inland." A DUKW rolled up on the sand near Sledge and took a direct hit from a mortar. It was instantly engulfed in "thick, dirty black smoke." No one emerged from the wreckage. Smoke rose in pillars from the beach and the reef where DUKWs and amtracs burned furiously.[53]

Sledge's description notwithstanding, compared with the Seventh Marines' problems with flanking fire, mines, and obstacles on their way to Orange 3, the Fifth Marines' landing went relatively smoothly. Orange Beaches 1 and 2 were largely beyond the range of the murderous fire coming from the high ground to the north that mainly targeted the White beaches and from the promontories to the south whose guns targeted Orange 3.

Instead, the Fifth Marines encountered enemy opposition in the coconut groves a short distance inland. Sergeant Jim McEnery of the 3rd Battalion spotted eight to ten Japanese soldiers trying to wrestle a 75mm gun into a firing position behind a rock pile 30 yards from the beach, intending to fire on Marines that were still coming ashore. McEnery attempted to radio for artillery support, but the radio did not work. An amtank appeared at that very moment. Its commander asked McEnery if he was with the Seventh Marines. He was not, but McEnery said that he had a pressing job for him and pointed at the Japanese 75mm gun. "Consider it done, sergeant," the amtank commander said.

Ten seconds later, an amtank round flashed into the enemy field piece, knocking it onto its side. A second round instantly followed, and the gun disappeared in "a cloud of dust, chunks of coral, and several enemy bodies," said McEnery. The survivors tried to run but were killed by Marine riflemen.[54]

Less than an hour after coming ashore on Orange Beach 2, 20-year-old Corporal Lewis K. Bausell of the Fifth Marines earned the first Medal of Honor of the campaign while fighting in the scrub near the landing beach. After his squad used a flamethrower to flush Japanese soldiers from a pillbox, one of them blew himself to pieces with a grenade while rushing the Marines, wounding four of them. A second enemy soldier was immediately shot dead. A third hurled a hissing grenade into the middle of Bausell's squad. There being no place for the men to find cover, Bausell threw himself on the grenade. The explosion mortally wounded him; Bausell died on the hospital ship *Bountiful* three days later.[55]

When a mortar round smashed into the Fifth Marines' command post, located in a captured Japanese trench near the airfield, three staff officers and the naval gunfire liaison were wounded. The regiment's commander, Colonel Harold "Bucky" Harris, was buried in smashed coral and debris with a badly wrenched knee. Although his mobility was now limited, Harris remained in command, assisted by his able executive officer, Lieutenant Colonel Lew Walt.

One of the wounded officers was Major Walter McIlhenny, the regimental operations officer and a Louisiana tabasco scion. With blood streaming from his ears as the result of an apparent concussion, McIlhenny babbled incoherently in Cajun French as he was evacuated.[56]

Because Harris's staff was now severely undermanned, Walt requested that division headquarters send down "that white-haired old s.o.b." If he still wanted to see front-line action, "tell him this is his chance," Walt said.[57]

During the two years since he enlisted as a 50-year-old private, Captain Paul Douglas had been single-mindedly trying to reach the front lines, even though he was a Quaker. Douglas believed that only force could stop aggression, and he wanted to do his part. Before he enlisted in the Marine Corps in 1942, Professor Douglas was a celebrated University of Chicago economist who was internationally recognized for his work on production analysis. He served on the National Recovery Administration's advisory council on consumer finance. Douglas became a political activist and was elected as a Chicago alderman in 1939. Three years later, he ran for the U.S. Senate and lost. Days later, he joined the Marines.

For a 50-year-old man to merely enter the Marine Corps as an enlisted man, the Navy Secretary would have to waive rules that would have barred Douglas because of his age, poor eyesight, and bad teeth. Fortunately for Douglas, Navy Secretary Frank Knox was an old friend. Previously, as *Chicago Daily News* publisher, Knox had been Douglas's ally in fighting corruption in Chicago.

When Douglas arrived at boot camp on Parris Island, South Carolina, a corporal shouted at him, "Pop, aren't your papers wrong? You are listed for active duty." Douglas replied that there had been no mistake and "that I was going to do my best to make the grade." The oldest recruit in Marine Corps history to go through recruit training at Parris Island, Douglas graduated at the top of his class of men 30 years his junior. Douglas earned their respect through his humility and raw determination. Excelling in bayonet fighting and a crack shot with a pistol, Douglas was selected by his boot camp comrades for the honor of carrying the platoon guide-on at graduation.

After passing the examination to become a private first class, he said he was "far prouder than I had been in winning my Ph.D. or being promoted to a full professorship." He was soon promoted to corporal, and then sergeant. He was assigned to write training manuals and give inspirational speeches, but Douglas disliked the desk jobs and repeatedly asked to go overseas; he had enlisted to fight, not write manuals. Each request was denied. Told that he was too old to ship out as an enlisted man, Douglas again pulled strings.

With the aid of his commanding officer at Parris Island, and of Secretary Knox and Knox's assistant, future presidential candidate Adlai Stevenson, Douglas obtained a captain's commission and was sent to the

South Pacific. Douglas joined General William Rupertus's 1st Marine Division staff during the Cape Gloucester campaign, occasionally serving alongside Marine combat troops.[58]

Now summoned to the front lines by Lieutenant Colonel Walt, Douglas became the Fifth Marines' troubleshooter. His job was to ensure that the regiment received enough food, water, ammunition, and weapons; that the wounded were collected, treated, and evacuated; and that reports were prepared nightly on casualties and unit strength. Douglas also spent an hour each day on the battle line and "developed a comradeship that was precious to me."[59]

One of the most singular Marines on Peleliu, Douglas became a familiar figure during resupply runs to the front, where he was often seen lugging 5-gallon cans of drinking water in 110-degree heat. His labors earned him the sobriquet "Gunga Din" among the division's fighting men.[60]

Pfc Sledge and four other men were unloading an amtrac that had brought water, ammunition, and rations to their company when Japanese mortar fire began zeroing in. Shrapnel was flying, and the Marines were working as fast as possible when a middle-aged man in dungarees and wearing glasses asked them if they needed help.

They gladly accepted the offer and asked him which unit he was in. He said he was Captain Paul Douglas, the Fifth Marines' R-1 (personnel officer). "I always want to know how you boys up here are making out and want to help if I can." He told them that he was a friend of their popular "K" Company commander, Captain Andrew "Ack" Haldane, a fellow Bowdoin College alumnus. Douglas knew no better company commander, he said.

They finished unloading the amtrac, and it drove away. Douglas helped the Marines stack some of the ammunition, advised them to disperse, and departed. One of the Marines asked, "What's that crazy old gray-haired guy doing up here if he could be back at regiment?" Their NCO snapped, "Shut up! Knock it off, you eight ball! He's trying to help knuckleheads like you, and he's a damned good man."[61]

Douglas was later wounded by shrapnel on Peleliu while bringing up flamethrower ammunition. He recovered and returned to the division as a major for the Okinawa campaign in April 1945. On Okinawa, he stripped off his oak leaf insignia and served in the line as a rifleman until he was shot in the left arm. The bullet cut an artery and nerves, and he spent over a year at Bethesda Naval Hospital, where he underwent four operations. He never regained the use of his left hand, which he said was "only a good paperweight."

Returning to Illinois and the University of Chicago after the war, Douglas ran for and was elected in 1948 to the first of the three terms that he would serve in the U.S. Senate. A liberal Democrat, Douglas became known for his strong principles and for his support of a minimum wage, public housing, civil and voting rights, and consumer protection. After his death in 1976 at the age of 84, the Marine Corps named its visitors' center at Parris Island for Douglas.[62]

A mortar fire concentration struck the Fifth's 3rd Battalion Command Post (CP) at about 5 p.m. on D-Day, wounding the battalion commander, Lieutenant Colonel Austin Shofner, and killing his communications officer, Captain Raymond Kehoe Jr. Shofner was evacuated, and Harris sent his executive officer, Lew Walt, to assume temporary command.

Walt discovered that the battalion's three companies, "I," "K," and "L," were neither in contact with the CP nor with one another or with the Seventh Marines on their right. The companies had evidently become disoriented after they entered the dense woods east of the airfield while pushing toward Peleliu's eastern shore.

Accompanied by a runner, Walt set out to track down the wayward companies. He first located "L" Company, which had pushed all the way across Peleliu to the eastern beaches – the only Marine unit to reach the opposite shore on D-Day. Walt was still searching for "I" and "K" after nightfall. It was extremely dangerous to be moving around in the dark in an area alive with Japanese soldiers as well as jumpy Marines, but Walt and his runner pressed on.

After an hours-long hunt, Walt located the companies and the left flank of the Seventh Marines' 3rd Battalion, which had strayed into the Fifth's zone. By 11 p.m., Walt had organized them in a line facing southward.[63]

Before Operation *Stalemate*'s convoy left Pavavu, General William Rupertus had summoned his commanders and division chief of staff to a meeting. On crutches because of his broken ankle, Rupertus told the officers that he would remain aboard his flagship *DuPage* throughout D-Day and possibly even D-plus-1.

He then proceeded to display the inflexibility that would become his hallmark in the weeks to come. "I want you to understand now that there will be no changes in orders regardless," he said, and then continued with words that astonished his commanders, "even if General Smith attempts to change my plans or orders, you regimental commanders will refuse to obey."[64]

Rupertus had made no secret of his disdain for his assistant commander, General O.P. Smith, even though Smith had drafted Peleliu's invasion plan in Rupertus's absence. While on Pavavu, Rupertus had banished Smith from his mess, ordering him to dine elsewhere.

Smith, a quiet Marine veteran of the Banana Wars and New Britain with 27 years' service, later diplomatically described his relationship with Rupertus as "at best aloof" and sometimes "confused and strained." During the Korean War six years later, Smith would command the 1st Marine Division during the amphibious assault at Inchon and throughout the epic breakout from Chinese encirclement at the Chosin Reservoir.[65]

On D-Day morning, Rupertus ordered Smith to go ashore alone to set up a message center, as General Lemuel Shepherd had done on Cape Gloucester. Smith strongly objected. "I told the general frankly to send me ashore in advance of himself with no authority to control the situation ashore [Rupertus had already stripped him of that] put me in a very anomalous situation; I could not escape responsibility for what transpired ashore." Rupertus grudgingly permitted Smith to bring a skeleton staff with him. They set up the division command post in a beachside tank trap.[66]

Throughout D-Day, Rupertus repeatedly insisted on leaving his folding chair on the deck of the *DuPage* and coming ashore on crutches. The burning amtracs off White Beaches 1 and 2 disturbed him deeply. Smith discouraged him, as did Rupertus's chief of staff, Colonel John Selden. "It was all I could do to keep him from going in immediately," Selden later said.

The general then decided to send his staff ashore without him; he would follow on D-plus-1. Selden argued that it was too risky under the dangerous conditions on the beachhead. A Japanese mortar or artillery round might wipe out the entire division staff. It was far better to wait. Rupertus reluctantly desisted. In actuality, General Smith had the situation well in hand, and was very likely doing a better job than Rupertus would have done.[67]

Smith established radio contact with the Fifth and Seventh Regiments, but was unable to reach Colonel Puller's First Marines; mortar fire had destroyed the First's radio equipment, the short-range SR-536 walkie-talkies nicknamed "spam cans."

Puller's liaison officer reached the division CP about 1 p.m., and Smith sent him back with a communications team that laid telephone land line to Puller's CP. After the phone link was established, Smith asked Puller if he needed help. Puller said that things were "all right" and estimated that the First Regiment had suffered just 40 casualties. Puller was making the situation look much better than it really was; by the end of D-Day, his regiment would lose 500 men.[68]

Landing with the division were dozens of Native American "code talkers" – specially recruited and trained Navajos who sent and received messages by radio and telephone. The Navajo tongue was an oral language, without an alphabet or symbols, and it was incomprehensible to anyone without extensive training, as the Japanese soon discovered.

Philip Johnson, son of a missionary to the Navajos and fluent in the language, had originally proposed using Navajos as communicators to the Marine Corps in 1942. At that time, fewer than 30 non-Navajos worldwide knew the Navajo language. The Marine Corps quickly grasped the value of using a language that the Japanese had never encountered to transmit coded radio messages on the battlefield.

In 1942, Marine recruiters visited Chester Nez's high school on the Navajo reservation in Tuba City, Arizona. Nez and his roommate decided to become Marines. They and 28 other Navajos comprised the first code talker class at Camp Elliott, California. That class developed a Navajo dictionary of common military terms that had to be memorized during training. Recruits were tested by having to transmit and decode into English a three-line message in 20 seconds.

When Corporal Nez landed on Peleliu – his third campaign following Guadalcanal and Bougainville – he carried a TBX radio. He sent coded reports and requests to Navajo radiomen on the gunfire support ships and to the command posts on the island. By the end of 1944, more than 300 Navajo code talkers served in the Marine Corps. The Japanese were never able to crack their code.[69]

Alarmed by the sight of the burning amtracs and DUKWs, General Geiger hailed a passing amtrac from his command ship, *Mount McKinley*, and ordered the coxswain to take him to the beach. He wanted to see things firsthand.

Striding across the beach of his fourth enemy-held island of the Pacific War, Geiger had to thread his way through a jumble of supplies, ammunition crates, and wounded men. He passed Graves Registration men who were busy collecting dog tags and information from the bodies of the dead, which lay in rows among trees shattered by gunfire. It was the first of what would be Geiger's nearly daily visits from his flagship to the Peleliu battlefield.

Geiger arrived at O.P. Smith's tank trap headquarters at about 1 p.m. Surprised to see the corps commander ashore, Smith said, "Look here, general, according to the book, you're not supposed to be here at this time." Geiger told Smith that he wanted to see the airfield, *Stalemate*'s primary objective. Smith said it was on the other side of the embankment. When Geiger climbed it to get a look, a shell whizzed by, nearly decapitating him. Shaken, he asked Smith where Rupertus was. Informed that he was aboard the *DuPage* with his broken ankle, Geiger replied, "If I'd known that, I'd have relieved him [before the landing]."

Yet Geiger had known of Rupertus's injury during the division's rehearsals at Guadalcanal, when Smith reassured him that Rupertus's ankle sprain would heal before *Stalemate* began. It had not. It is likely that Geiger's remark reflected his disappointment that Rupertus had not recovered enough to land on D-Day with his division.[70]

When Geiger informed Smith that he planned to visit the First Marines CP, Smith told him that it was a bad idea – it was simply too dangerous. Enemy troops were believed to be in the 800-yard gap between the beach positions of the Fifth and the First Regiments. The corps commander headed in the other direction.

Meanwhile aboard the *DuPage*, Rupertus obsessed over rapid movement and momentum – both essential to the 1st Division completing the campaign within the three or four days that he had predicted. Monitoring his radios, he listened to the reports of a Japanese gun on one of Peleliu's southern promontories enfilading Orange Beach 3, knocking out amtracs and DUKWS, and inflicting heavy casualties. The scribbles of black smoke from burning amtracs blotting the sky increased his anxiety. Without consulting his commanders ashore, Rupertus impulsively sent the division Reconnaissance Company to Orange 3.

General O.P. Smith acidly commented, "This company was thrown in on the right with the 1st Battalion [Seventh Marines] and suffered heavy casualties. This was an improper use of the Reconnaissance Company, as there later developed several opportunities for employment of this company in the matter for which it was trained."[71]

Then, that afternoon, with D-Day just seven hours old, Rupertus committed the last division reserve – the Seventh Marines' 2nd Battalion – in the hope of speeding up the Seventh Marines' advance on Orange 3. "All right, Johnny, go ahead," he said to division chief of staff John Selden. "But I've shot my bolt when they go in." Anxiously, he added, "This won't stop us … We'll still take the island on schedule … a week at the most."[72]

Lieutenant Colonel Spencer Berger was ordered to take his 2nd Battalion to the transfer line near the reef and to wait there for amtracs to take them across the reef to Orange 3. Just before 4 p.m., Spencer's men began debarking from their transport, the USS *Leedstown*, into Higgins Boats that had been procured from other ships. Because the battalion had not been expected to land on D-Day, the *Leedstown's* boats had been assigned to other units.

But this was only the first hurdle. When the battalion's lead company reported to the Orange 3 beachmaster's control vessel, the beachmaster said that he neither had orders to land the battalion nor amtracs available to do so. Many landing craft had been destroyed or were badly damaged, and the rest were either ashore supporting the infantry, or shuttling men and supplies between the beach and reef, he said. When the Orange 2 beachmaster was asked to land the Marines, he, too, said that he did not have the orders or amtracs to meet Berger's request.[73]

As his battalion bobbed in the waves in its borrowed Higgins Boats, Berger sought guidance from the division command. Try the Orange 3 beachmaster again, he was told. But the beachmaster told Berger that there were still no amtracs available; he said that if he did somehow obtain enough amtracs, he would land the battalion.

In desperation after no spare amtracs had surfaced by 5 p.m., the 2nd Battalion tried to reach shore in the Higgins Boats before it got dark. The boats, shallow draft though they were, could not clear the reef. Berger's landing force was forced to withdraw when enemy mortar rounds began splashing around it.

At 8:15 p.m., the division CP directed Berger to return with his battalion to the *Leedstown* and to land the next morning. At sea in the inky darkness, the Higgins Boats became scattered. Many of the boats lacked compasses and the boat pilots were unable to find their way back to the *Leedstown*. Complicating matters, *Leedstown* and the other transports had changed positions since that afternoon, making them harder to find.

Berger finally located the *Leedstown* around midnight, but the transport's by-the-book captain refused to allow the Marines to come aboard; his orders were to land the troops, not to reboard them. However, the captain allowed Berger to use the ship's radio, and Berger contacted the 1st Division. *Leedstown* was given new orders to take the Marines aboard and land them at first light. Even so, more than half of Berger's battalion spent the night in small boats scattered at sea because they were unable to find the ship, and efforts to locate them were unsuccessful.

With daylight on September 16, prospects for Berger's men greatly improved, and the 2nd Battalion landed on Orange 3 around 8 a.m. Later, when the First Marines' precarious situation became known, Berger's men were transported to White Beach 2, where they were temporarily attached to Puller's regiment.[74]

White Beaches 1 and 2 were by far the most dangerous beaches on Peleliu. They were where two First Marines battalions had landed – and had been instantly pinned down by intensive artillery, mortar, and machine-gun fire. Clouds of smoke billowed from amtracs and DUKWs burning on the White beaches and the reef offshore. "The ammo which had been aboard them was exploding, and occasionally one of the tractors would blow up, scattering burning debris over the beach," said the 1st Battalion report.

The First Marines' 1st Battalion, led by Lieutenant Colonel Ray Davis, and later reinforced by Berger's regimental reserve battalion, landed in front of a 100-yard-long coral shelf that was the boundary between the White and Orange beaches. Davis, wounded in the lower leg by a shell fragment during the landing, received first aid and remained in command.

The coral shelf was a hive of tunnels, machine-gun positions, and two Japanese 47mm guns that were knocking out amtracs to the north and south. Davis's men killed the defenders with grenades, flamethrowers, and satchel charges – explosives in a satchel or messenger bag with shoulder straps, detonated with a pull ignitor. Enemy soldiers were driven from rifle pits and shot down.

On the chaotic beach, and in the weeks to come, "only one cry was more disheartening than the cry for stretcher-bearers, and that was, 'Never mind the corpsman,'" said Davis's battalion report.[75]

The First Marines' amtracs had drawn unexpectedly fierce fire even as they approached the reef. It came from three sources: the coral shelf under attack by the 1st Battalion; the rising hills inland known as the Umurbrogol; and a 30-foot-high coral ridge that jutted to the water line. The coral ridge formed the northern boundary of White 1, and no one would ever forget it.

It was called The Point.[76]

Chapter 5

The Point, The Airfield

Should we fail to capture and hold The Point, the entire regimental beach would be exposed to heavy fire from the flank.

Captain George P. Hunt,
"K" Company, First Marines[1]

To be shelled by massed artillery and mortars is absolutely terrifying, but to be shelled in the open is terror compounded beyond the belief of anyone who hasn't experienced it.

Pfc E.B. Sledge, describing the Marine
assault across Peleliu's airfield[2]

The Point bristled with pillboxes, small caves, spider holes, and a camouflaged bunker harboring a 47mm anti-boat gun. About 500 Japanese soldiers manned the unanticipated stronghold. The big gun, along with mortars, cannons, machine guns, and riflemen, lashed the beaches with enfilading fire. Riddled by the fusillade of steel, dying and wounded Marines sprawled on the bloodstained beach, and wrecked amtracs blazed like torches.

Inexplicably, Admiral Fort's naval bombardment had left The Point untouched – aerial reconnaissance evidently had not identified it as a target. It was now imperative that the First Marines destroy The Point's defenders and their guns. The job fell to Captain George P. Hunt's

"K" Company of the 3rd Battalion. A magazine writer before the war, Hunt had already been awarded the Silver Star for gallantry at Cape Gloucester.

When Hunt and his men came ashore, White Beach 1 was already a slaughterhouse. "I saw a ghastly mixture of bandages, bloody and mutilated skin; men gritting their teeth, resigned to their wounds; men groaning and writhing in their agonies; men outstretched or twisted or grotesquely transfixed in the attitude of death; men with their entrails exposed or whole chunks of their body ripped out of them," Hunt later wrote.[3]

Amid snapping bullets and jarring explosions, Navy corpsmen darted among the wounded, stanching bleeding, dispensing plasma, and applying sulfa powder to arrest bacterial infections and morphine to relieve pain. About 1,800 medical personnel came ashore on D-Day and were assigned to the three infantry regiments, the Eleventh Marines artillery regiment, and attached units. Up to four Navy corpsmen accompanied each rifle platoon, in addition to stretcher-bearers.

It would be several days before hospital facilities were up and running on Peleliu. Until then, casualties were trundled to the beach. There, they were loaded onto amtracs and taken across the reef to small boats that ferried them to the nearest hospital ship seen flying a signal flag indicating that it had empty beds.[4] The dead remained on the beach – and were covered with a shirt, a poncho, or a blanket and placed in rows to await burial.[5]

During the first month of the fighting on Peleliu, 59 Navy corpsmen attached to the 1st Marine Division were either killed in action or died of their wounds.[6]

The Japanese called The Point the "Ishimatsu position." Thirty feet high, the jagged coral promontory rising from the water's edge was a concatenation of sharp pinnacles, deep crevasses, and enormous boulders. It was no less than a mini-fortress, guarded by five south-facing pillboxes, each manned by six to 12 defenders. Reinforced with steel and concrete, they frowned down on the landing beaches and reef. Four pillboxes contained 20mm cannons, each capable of firing 500 rounds per minute. The fifth held a 47mm anti-boat gun whose range was 4 miles, greater than the length of the landing beaches. Surrounding each pillbox were nests of light machine guns, and spider holes and depressions full of concealed riflemen.

"It surpassed by far anything we had conceived of when we studied the aerial photographs," observed Captain Hunt. Moreover, none of the enemy positions had been damaged by naval gunfire or air strikes.[7]

Hunt's "K" Company acted at once to seize The Point. The enemy-held position posed an existential threat to the 1st Division's left flank. "Should we fail to capture and hold The Point, the entire regimental beach would be exposed to heavy fire from the flank," Hunt said.[8]

"K" Company attacked with 102 men from two of its three platoons – the 1st and the 3rd; the 2nd Platoon was pinned down in the tank trap behind the beach and could not be utilized. Believing that attacking The Point frontally would result in unacceptably high casualties, Hunt's Marines moved inland, turned, and struck The Point from the rear. The sharp coral cut their knees and elbows as they crawled forward under heavy fire in the intense heat. Soon they and their sweat-soaked clothing were coated in gray coral dust. During the first 40 minutes of their attack, half of the Marine attackers became casualties.[9]

One of them was Sergeant Rudolph Culjak, a mustachioed company scout who had fought on Guadalcanal and Cape Gloucester. He was one of the Marines hemmed in by the tank trap but was determined to join the attack on The Point. Bursting from the tank trap, Culjak killed an enemy soldier and jumped into a shell hole as bullets ricocheted off the coral around him. Finding himself a yard away from two Japanese who were setting up a machine gun, Culjak killed them with a concussion grenade, and in so doing was shot in the arm. The wound bled so profusely that Hunt sent him to an evacuation station.[10]

Although isolated from the rest of the 3rd Battalion and from its 2nd Platoon, "K" Company nonetheless systematically neutralized the spider holes surrounding the pillboxes. During the chaotic fighting, Pfc Lindsey Jones was bandaging a wounded Marine when he spotted an enemy soldier creeping toward him. "Git away from heah, you Jap!" he shouted, waving him off. "Can't you see I'm fixin' a man?" The startled Japanese hid behind a tree. Jones then picked up his BAR and fired a bullet through the tree that struck the enemy soldier in the head.

The 47mm gun was tackled by Lieutenant William Willis, who crept down onto the pillbox from above and dropped a smoke grenade in front of it to mask a frontal approach. Another Marine fired a rifle grenade into the pillbox's firing aperture. The grenade struck the anti-boat gun's barrel, disabling the gun, and ignited an explosion and a roaring fire. Shrieking gun crewmen bolted from the pillbox, as the ammunition in their belts cooked off. Marines waiting outside the pillbox's rear exit shot them all down.

Inside the gutted pillbox, Hunt found dead Japanese soldiers that were "fried black, and the whites of their eyes shone in the dark like phosphorus." The gun was "twisted and yanked cockeyed from its mount."[11]

By 10:30 a.m., 9,500 Marines were ashore on Peleliu, and The Point belonged to "K" Company, although just 33 of the 102 men from Hunt's two attacking platoons were still able to fight. The bodies of more than 100 enemy soldiers were sprawled around The Point's base, in its niches and holes, and on its rocky summit. The Japanese dead were "big, healthy men, and had new equipment," Hunt observed. Hunt's Marines crouched behind boulders, forming an all-around defense.[12]

While "K" Company struggled to hold The Point, several hundred Japanese soldiers emerged from the jungle behind the beaches and occupied the gap between The Point and a coral ridge behind White Beach 1 – Chevatel Ridge. The ancient strongpoint had been used by Palauan warriors for centuries to repel invaders. The new Japanese salient further isolated Hunt's men.[13]

Ordered to eliminate the threat, the First Marines' "A" Company became mired in the same tank trap that had paralyzed Hunt's 2nd Platoon. Working with Hunt's men and supported by tanks, the Marines stormed out of the tank trap and into the salient. A torrent of gunfire stopped the assault and disabled the tanks. Then, a Japanese counterattack eviscerated Hunt's 2nd Platoon, making casualties of two lieutenants, a sergeant, and many riflemen.

On The Point, the situation was now dire. Hunt's 33-man remnant, which remained isolated from "A" Company and the 2nd Platoon, would alone have to hold the promontory against the anticipated nighttime counterattacks and infiltrations. Low on ammunition, food, water, and medical supplies, the Marines commandeered a Japanese machine gun to help defend their position.

Weirdly, with the batteries nearly dead in Corporal Joe LaCoy's hand-held "spam can" radio – "K" Company's link to three 60mm mortars on the beach – LaCoy was able to hear only a broadcast of Japanese military marches.[14]

The First Marines feared that a coordinated nighttime counterattack from the salient would roll up White Beach 1 and then sweep down the other landing beaches. To counteract this, Colonel Lewis Puller organized a "defense in depth" line south of The Point with a patchwork of men from the Seventh Marines' 2nd Battalion, headquarters personnel from the First Marines, and 100 men from the 1st Engineers Battalion.[15]

Surprisingly, during the night of September 15, the Japanese did not attempt to exploit their overwhelming numerical advantage at The Point with a major attack. Instead, they harassed Hunt's men with mortar fire and small-scale infiltrations through the adjacent woods.

Pfc George Peto of "K" Company's mortar platoon discovered that some of the infiltrators toted sacks of grenades, and others were armed with 8-foot bamboo poles tipped with bayonets. "That way, they could stab you from a distance with a lunge, or toss a grenade, a new danger to worry about," Peto wrote.[16]

Captain Theodore Harbaugh, a 30-year-old Dartmouth graduate, spent that night crouched in a foxhole with a flashlight, translating captured documents for the 1st Division command and hoping that enemy troops would not overrun him. The Marines had sent Harbaugh to school for 14 months until he became fluent in the Japanese language. When he finished translating the documents, he was able to identify every Japanese commander and unit. Later, Harbaugh tried without success to persuade enemy soldiers in the woods to surrender. "They answered with bullets, shooting over my head, didn't kill me because I was using their language."[17]

With the new day, Lieutenant James Haggerty's mortar men were ready to defend Hunt's beleaguered position against the Japanese counterattack they were certain was coming. Haggerty had spent most of D-Day reassembling his scattered 3rd Battalion mortar platoon after landing with just two mortars and no ammunition; three other mortars and 17 men had gone missing. By dark, however, he had reconstituted his platoon, which laid down harassing fire all night long.[18]

At first light on September 16, the sporadic enemy mortar fire swelled to a steady roar. Japanese snipers that had crept into the trees and bushes during the night engaged Hunt's men in "a vicious melee of countless explosions, whining bullets, shrapnel whirring overhead or clinking off the rocks," punctuated by "hoarse shouts [and] shrill-screaming Japanese." Hunt's Marines held, but when the battle finally subsided, just 18 effectives remained.[19]

Reinforcements filtered into Hunt's positions until 50 men defended The Point. Ten came from "K" Company's 2nd Platoon, drained from its original strength by a day of fending off counterattacks in the tank trap. Then, an amtrac finally brought Hunt more men, supplies, and ammunition.[20]

The First Marines' "B" Company tackled the Japanese salient that had isolated "K." At great cost, it fought its way through a maze of antitank ditches, log barriers, and hidden enemy pillboxes connected by trenches.

With the support of tanks, "B" Company by 3:30 p.m. succeeded in crushing the Japanese salient. It then linked up with "K" Company – ending 30 hours of isolation for Hunt's men. "K" Company was able to restore communications with both "B" and "K" Companies' mortar platoons.[21]

———

The Japanese might have overpowered Hunt's tiny band during the night of September 15, but they did not attempt to do so. Twenty-four hours later, on September 16, the situation favored the Marines. Evidently following an outdated plan, the Japanese launched their major counterattack on The Point at 10 o'clock that night.

Amid a heavy mortar and grenade barrage, about 500 enemy soldiers poured out of the jungle. "They're comin' in on us," someone shouted. The attackers charged into the Marine lines, screaming, "Banzai! Banzai!"

The Marines were ready. A hurricane of Marine rifle and machine-gun fire from prepared positions, along with pre-registered artillery and mortar fire, smashed into the charging Japanese as Hunt bellowed, "Give 'em hell! Kill every one of the bastards!"[22]

Pfc Peto said his mortar platoon, under Hunt's close supervision, laid down its fire dangerously close to the Marines' lines. "The ground shook with the detonations. We could hear shrapnel angrily buzzing just above us," Peto wrote. "We were satisfied to hear some Japs screaming in the night."[23]

Japanese soldiers wading along the shoreline launched a secondary attack. It, too, failed. The survivors hid in crevices at the cliff base.[24]

Pfc Fred Fox had participated in "K" Company's assault on The Point, as well as the first night's circle-the-wagons defense with 17 comrades. Many in the tiny band were wounded but "most of 'em just bandaged up and kept fighting. Those what were dead were dead."[25]

During the second night's battle, Fox left his clifftop position near the water to report to Hunt's command post below. Hearing footsteps behind him, Fox whirled around, knocking away a bayonet that a Japanese soldier behind him was poised to plunge into Fox. Fox struck him in the face with his pistol, causing the soldier to drop his rifle. Fox bayoneted him with it. "I pulled it out and started yelling, "Nips! Nips!" There was an explosion beside Fox, and he rolled down the cliff. Another Japanese soldier stabbed him in the back; Fox blacked out.[26]

After repelling the main enemy counterattack, the Marines threw thermite grenades to flush the Japanese hiding at the cliff base. With loud shrieks and flames licking their bodies, they ran to the water as the ammunition in their belts exploded like "strings of fireworks." They rolled over and over in the water in a futile attempt to extinguish the flames. Their bodies burned in the shallows, "crackling human bonfires that lit up the night." Hunt said that their "shrill screams resounded so piercingly that I realized that the noise of the battle had suddenly ceased."[27]

Around dawn, a Marine spotted Fox, who was lying unconscious in the shallow water at the base of the cliff. Braving heavy sniper fire, he carried Fox to shore. Fox survived; his rescuer, Corporal Andrew Byrnes, was subsequently awarded a Silver Star.[28]

The bodies of more than 500 Japanese soldiers lay in the rocks, in the woods, and on the beach around The Point. In places, the enemy dead were grotesquely heaped four deep. "Many of them were huddled with their arms around each other as though they had futilely tried to protect themselves from our fire," Hunt wrote.

Along the shoreline, enemy corpses washed in with the tide and bled on the white sand. "They were horribly mutilated, riddled by bullets and torn by shrapnel ... legs and arms and heads and torsos littered the rocks and in some places were lodged grotesquely in the treetops. A sickening, putrid stench was emanating from the ones we had killed yesterday."[29]

Found among the battle's detritus was a crate containing a new 47mm anti-boat gun. The counterattacking Japanese had evidently planned to reoccupy the bunker where the first anti-boat gun had been destroyed, and to resume their enfilading fire down the beach.[30]

On the morning of *Stalemate*'s third day, September 17, "I" Company relieved "K" Company, which was sent into reserve for a rest. Of the 235 "K" Company Marines that had landed on the 15th, just 78 had escaped being killed or wounded.

A journalist at heart, Hunt, who after the war would become managing editor of *Life* magazine, interviewed some of his own men immediately after the battle. From these interviews and his own observations, he wrote *Coral Comes High*, his electrifying account of the fierce battle for The Point.

A replica of The Point was built after World War II on the Marine Corps base at Quantico, Virginia. For a decade, new second lieutenants were required to draft a battle plan for successfully assaulting its defenses.[31]

———————

Each Marine came ashore with two canteens of water and three chocolate energy bars. "We were supposed to conserve and drink as little as possible," said Lieutenant Clifford West. But in the oppressive heat – 105 degrees, and above 80 percent humidity – the water was gone by early afternoon. Some of the severely dehydrated Marines became violently ill.[32]

Major Waite Worden, the executive officer of the Seventh Marines' 3rd Battalion, later said that dehydration felled scores of his men. They became "unfit to fight, unable to continue. Some were carried out with dry heaves," he said. "Others had tongues so swollen as to make it impossible for them to talk or swallow… Others were unable to close eyelids over their dried, swollen eyeballs."[33]

Lieutenant Prate Stack Jr., a tank platoon commander, said that inside the tanks it was "torrid as hell," even with blowers going full blast. "I don't think the Marines ever fought on any other island where the heat was worse than on Peleliu," he said.[34]

Fifty-five-gallon drums of water were sent ashore from the transports, but most of them were contaminated. The drums had contained diesel fuel and gasoline and had not been properly steam-cleaned. The tainted water caused cramps, diarrhea, and vomiting. Hundreds of Marines became incapacitated after drinking the water. The worst cases were evacuated to hospital ships.[35]

Determined to find out whether underground reservoirs of non-saline water existed, engineers drilled down into Peleliu's coral and limestone. To their delight, they found potable water, although fouled by rotting coconuts and decomposing vegetation. Moreover, the Marines discovered that even shallow holes dug in the sand yielded water that became drinkable with the addition of halazone water purification tablets and lemonade from their K-rations.

The engineers set up water distillation equipment to purify groundwater on a larger scale, and water in clean containers began to arrive from Pavavu. By the campaign's fifth day, 50,000 gallons of potable water was being distilled each day from the newly dug wells.[36]

As sweat from the tropical heat and humidity dripped from the Marines, their dungarees became salt-streaked and stiff. They gobbled salt tablets to replenish the salt that they sweated out. Six tablets were allotted daily, instead of the usual two, for every canteen of water consumed. Many Marines, however, swallowed 12 to 14 tablets per day. When a salt tablet shortage developed, naval commanders were asked to send all available salt tablets from their ships to the island. "Those who take from six to ten tablets a day are able to keep going, but the others, their utility clothes completely soaked with sweat, suffer badly," observed Lieutenant Colonel Davis of the First Marines' 1st Battalion.[37]

The equatorial heat drilled through the men's helmets and clothing, and scorched the ground under their feet. "It was like walking barefoot on top of a stove," said one Marine. Phosphorus grenades left in the sun sometimes spontaneously exploded. To protect themselves from the relentless sun and the sting of the rock dust floating in the air, some men removed their helmet covers and draped them across the backs of their necks, like kepis. "The riflemen looked like desert soldiers," wrote Pfc Russell Davis. He said some Marines discarded their helmets altogether and donned the "old, soft, floppy fatigue cap of the Army. The round hat was a favorite in the First Division."[38]

Pfc Davis described a comrade who cracked up because of the heat. "One big, redheaded man, horribly burned and cracked around the face and lips, suddenly reared out of his hole like a wild horse," said Davis. "'I can't go the heat!' he bellowed. 'I can take the war but not the heat!'" The man shook his fist at the sun, and he brushed off two Marines who tried to force him to the ground. He was finally able to get control of himself, and undoubtedly received a tongue-lashing from his NCO.[39]

In 1939, Japanese engineers completed an airfield on Peleliu that had runways of 3,500 and 6,000 feet to accommodate fighters and bombers. The airstrips were surfaced with hard-packed, finely crushed coral, and were adjacent to auxiliary taxiways, turning circles, and servicing facilities. Along the airfield's northern perimeter, at the foot of the rugged ridges and hills collectively known as the Umurbrogol, were barracks, hangars, machine shops, a power plant, a two-story administration building, and a radio transmission station.[40]

The Fifth Marines' D-Day objective was the airfield. It was a few hundred yards inland, and the regiment reached it quickly. The 1st Battalion dug in along its southwestern edge before noon, while the 2nd Battalion continued to advance eastward – almost to Peleliu's far shore. The 2nd then occupied positions beside the airstrips.

Pfc Sterling Mace's fire team was sent to the airfield to find the Hellcat that had been shot down during the amphibious assault. They found it, its nose embedded in the ground, and the pilot inside, dead. As the Marines neared the wreckage, one of them happened to spot a thin wire; it led to a string of grenades. The cockpit was booby-trapped. Nonetheless, an enterprising Marine managed to carefully prize the pilot's .38-caliber revolver from its holster and take possession of it.[41]

The Fifth's commanders were aware that the Japanese had tanks. As a precaution, they had landed the two assault battalions with heavy machine guns and 37mm guns, and placed them in forward positions. Bazooka teams and three Sherman tanks set up nearby. This was indeed fortuitous, because the Japanese had planned to disrupt the landings by counterattacking with tanks. Had the attack been launched that morning, while the Marines were struggling to come ashore, it might have been devastating.

But the Japanese waited too long. By 4:50 p.m., when the counterattack finally began, thousands of Marines and their supporting arms were ready for them.[42]

Thunderous enemy artillery and mortar fire suddenly erupting in the ridges signaled the overture to the attack. Clouds of boiling dust suddenly rose from the airfield's northern perimeter. Then, hundreds of dispersed infantrymen – a battalion of Colonel Nakagawa's 2nd Infantry Regiment that had received special training for conducting tank-infantry assaults – began advancing toward the Marines, using shell holes and natural terrain for cover. The rest of Nakagawa's men watched from the hills overlooking the airfield.

Hundreds of yards away, ranged along the western and southern edges of the airstrip, waited the much larger American force – nearly three Marine battalions, supported by Sherman tanks and heavy weapons. When they were 500 yards away, the Japanese soldiers began firing. Then, with a piercing roar, more than a dozen enemy tanks – reports ranged from 13 to 18 – poured out of hiding places along the airfield's northern perimeter in two columns. They raced toward the Marines; camouflaged snipers clung to the tanks' rear decks and flanks.

They were Type 95 Ha-Go light tanks – the Marines called them "tankettes" because of their relatively diminutive size. Their armor was just 14mm thick, a fraction of the Shermans' 76mm armor, and each tankette was lightly armed with two machine guns and a 37mm gun. Captain Joe Gayle said they "looked like Model T's on tracks."

At 5:15 p.m., someone cried, "Here they come!"[43]

Pfc Robert Leckie of the First Marines said the tanks "swooped suddenly upon us. They came tearing across that airfield, a dozen or so of them. It was startling."[44] Attacking in echelon formation, the tanks and infantrymen aimed for where the Fifth Marines adjoined the First in a wooded area southwest of the airfield.[45]

The tanks overtook the Japanese foot soldiers about 400 yards from the Marine lines. Then the drivers floored it, pushing the tankettes' shrieking engines to their top speed of 28 mph in a bizarre simulacrum of a 19th-century cavalry charge. The little armored vehicles stormed across the runway, firing canister shot. The infantrymen were left in their dust.

The tank commanders' impatience to close with the Americans fractured what began as a coordinated tank-infantry attack into its two components, with neither supporting the other.[46] The tanks "were running around wildly, apparently without coordination, within our lines, firing those 37mm guns, with the riders on those tanks carrying external passengers yelling and firing rifles," said Lieutenant Colonel Robert Boyd, who led the Fifth Marines' 1st Battalion.[47]

The Marines blistered the attackers with heavy machine guns, grenade launchers, and bazookas; amtanks firing 75mm guns; 37mm guns; and mortars, artillery, and pack howitzers positioned behind the Fifth Marines' lines. From 5 miles away, the cruiser *Honolulu* plastered the airfield with 6-inch shells. Then a Navy dive-bomber that happened to be flying overhead spotted the developing battle and dropped a 500-pound bomb amid the tanks.[48]

Corporal Billie Driver, a bazooka gunner, knocked out three tanks and dodged a grenade thrown by an enemy soldier lashed to the rear of one of them. Another bazooka gunner scored hits on four other tanks before a fifth tank blew off his left arm. When that tank, too, was disabled, a Japanese soldier emerged. Marshalling his remaining strength, the Marine somehow fired his bazooka one-handed, hitting the enemy soldier in the chest, recalled Sergeant F. Killeen, who witnessed the exchange. The bazooka man was evacuated – and survived.[49]

As the hurricane of gunfire tore apart the phalanx of tanks, no mercy was shown to the survivors; a soldier who slipped out of a burning tank's escape hatch was instantly killed, and one that raised a bloody white rag in surrender had his hand shot off – followed by a shower of grenades tossed into his tank.[50]

In a diary entry a Japanese soldier with the 33rd Independent Machine Gun Company wrote that the dense gunsmoke created by the torrent of Marine fire obliterated the sun. After crawling into a shelter, he dared not lift his head because of the furious explosions and streaking tracer bullets.[51]

A platoon of American Sherman tanks entered the fray. "The Japanese tanks were no match for our tanks," said Major Gordon Gayle, who commanded the Fifth Marines' 2nd Battalion. The Shermans destroyed every enemy tank that they encountered.[52] An American tank commander said the tankettes' armor was so thin that his armor-piercing shells passed through the tankettes without detonating, so he switched to high-explosive shells, which also had little effect. Finally, he changed the shell fuses to "instantaneous," which blew the enemy tanks to pieces.

The Marines killed two Japanese crewmen who emerged from a disabled tank with a machine gun, bipod, and boxes of ammunition. A third man, an officer, came out firing a rifle haphazardly in all directions. There was a lull as he lay on the ground, attaching a bayonet. When he stood and glared round defiantly, the Marines realized that he was out of ammunition. A Marine rose and challenged the officer to a bayonet duel. They sparred, thrusting and parrying. When the Japanese closed and struck his opponent in the shoulder with his rifle butt, the Marine stepped back four paces and shot the officer dead.[53]

Some of the enemy tanks broke through the Marine lines and raced all the way to the beach. There, five Shermans engaged the tankettes in a gun battle fought over the heads of crouching Marine infantrymen. The Japanese tanks were destroyed. It was the only tank-versus-tank battle fought by the Marines during the Pacific War, although Marine tanks served as supporting arms in nearly every campaign.[54]

Other Japanese tanks veered into the lines of the First Marines' 2nd Battalion, bowling over and scattering men. Pfc Russell Davis said that a tank "cut a swath through the line, rolling men and weapons before it." Two Marines were crushed to death. The tank landed nose-down in a swamp, and no one emerged from it. While dodging another tank, Pfc Dan Toledo dove into a shallow hole that he had dug "and scrunched my body into a tight little ball. The tank tread rolled directly over me" without injuring him. Then, the tank wheeled around with its barrel pointed at Toledo. "Just at that moment when I should have died, for some unexplained reason the hatch opened and one of the tank crew popped his head out to have a look around." A Marine leaped onto the tank and dropped a grenade down the hatch, killing the crew. Another tank hurtled off the edge of the airstrip and over the prone Lieutenant Colonel Russell Honsowetz, the First Marines' 2nd Battalion commander. It splashed into a bog, where Pfc Harold Miller tucked a grenade into its open turret. The crewmen scrambled out and were all killed.[55]

Pfc Leckie approached one of the burning tanks. Inside were dead Japanese, and on the tank's exterior "the snipers hung in their nets like dolls stuffed in a Christmas stocking."[56]

Just two enemy tanks escaped destruction. Most of the infantrymen melted away without closing with the Marines after the tanks left them behind. Japanese Superior Private Takeo Sugimura said that neither the other members of his platoon nor the tank company that they accompanied returned from the attack. Scores of Japanese soldiers died in what would be the campaign's only enemy tank assault.[57]

The Japanese report on the attack was typically hyperbolical: "Our tank unit attacked the enemy with such a cat-like spring at dusk, that they were able to inflict heavy damages on the enemy."[58]

After the fighting ended, the Fifth Marines' 2nd Battalion dug in for the night near the middle of the airfield.[59]

Late on D-Day, the Japanese began probing the Marine lines for weaknesses, using "fire and maneuver" tactics.

All along the line of the Seventh Marines' 3rd Battalion, enemy infiltration teams lashed the Marines with Nambu and 6.5mm machine guns. "Streams of glowing bullets crossed in the night," noted one Marine. The Japanese fired blue-and-white tracers, easily distinguishable from the Marines' red tracers, enabling the combatants to track one another's movements.

At 2 a.m., Japanese infiltrators emerged from a swamp and attacked "C" Company of the Seventh. Repulsed after a two-hour battle, the Japanese launched a second counterattack at 4 a.m. that lasted an hour and a half and also failed. Fifty enemy bodies were counted at daybreak.[60]

The infiltrators had donned "tabis" – canvas split-toed shoes made for silent movement – and armed themselves with bayonets, swords, and knives. Some of the Japanese wore the helmets of dead Marines and slipped into foxholes behind the Seventh Marine lines, where they cut throats and were, in turn, slashed or shot by the Marines in frenzied life-or-death struggles.[61]

Two infiltrators got into the same foxhole and, in the dark, each mistook the other for a Marine. They fought savagely at close quarters until one of them bayoneted the other to death. The victor then wounded a Marine before being shot dead.[62]

The nighttime enemy counterattacks were stronger and more concentrated in the First and Fifth Marines' sectors, where rifle and machine-gun fire crackled continuously along the entire front, and was frequently punctuated by artillery and mortar blasts. The fighting lasted for hours but the Marines' lines held.

At the airfield, two Japanese tanks – possibly the survivors of the earlier counterattack – struck the seam between the First and Fifth Marines. The Marines destroyed them both before they could break through. Later that night, the Fifth Marines repulsed two mortar and grenade counterattacks.[63]

Pfc E.B. Sledge later stated that 15 Japanese that had been cut down by a machine gun had mines tied to their bodies. The enemy soldier who fell the closest to the Marine position clutched an unexploded grenade in his right hand, and he also had a mine tied onto his back above his shoulders and a mine on each hip.[64]

D-Day on Peleliu cost the 1st Marine Division 1,148 casualties, including 210 men who had been killed, died of their wounds, or were reported missing. Before the landing, the losses had been projected to be less than half of the actual total. Heat-related illnesses incapacitated uncounted other Marines. The First Marines reported the most casualties – more than 500, one-sixth of the regiment's strength.

The landing's human cost was apparent in a tank crewman's description of the Peleliu beach on D-Day evening. When the tide went out, he said, a man could have walked hundreds of yards on the bodies of dead Marines without touching the ground.

Along Peleliu's southwest coast, the Marines occupied a 2,800-yard-long beachhead. Their first-day objective was to advance to the so-called O-1 Line, which was about 400 yards inland and, if possible, to push across the airfield to the O-2 objective. While the Fifth Marines accomplished both of these goals and the Seventh Marines nearly did, the First Marines, landing nearest Peleliu's heavily fortified ridges, fell short by 200 yards. Five hundred yards was the 1st Division's average penetration on D-Day, with the maximum being 1,500 yards.[65]

The Japanese account of D-Day was a compendium of exaggerations and inventions. Based on reports evidently concocted by the 14th Infantry Division in Koror, Radio Tokyo reported, "Our glorious forces have again slaughtered thousands of bloodthirsty Marines in a stupid invasion attempt, this time in the Palau Islands." The defenders, said Radio Tokyo, shattered the first attempted landing, "putting the screaming enemy hordes to flight." During a second attempt, "the fiendish Yankees were put to rout once more, with the sea red with their blood."[66]

Admiral Chester Nimitz's communique at the close of D-Day was colorless and understated compared with Radio Tokyo's florid account. Nimitz minimized both enemy resistance and Marine casualties: "Our casualties during the first day of the assault were light, although the landing beaches have been under sporadic mortar and artillery fire."[67]

The blandness of Nimitz's communique belied the great anxiety that he felt while awaiting news about the Peleliu landings. Subordinates said that Nimitz spent hours on the small pistol range that he had set up beside his Pearl Harbor headquarters, firing thousands of rounds from his target pistol. Under the strain of his responsibilities in 1942, Nimitz had developed a tremor, and his doctor had suggested target-shooting to calm his nerves. Sometimes he placed a half-dollar on the pistol's barrel and fired it without allowing it to fall off. When he was feeling upbeat, Nimitz pitched horseshoes. But on this day, he fired the target pistol to alleviate his anxiety.[68]

On *Stalemate*'s second day, the temperature stood at 80 degrees an hour before dawn, and a low mist hung over the airfield before the sun appeared and burned it off. By afternoon, it would be 105 in the shade.

At 8 a.m. on September 16, four Marine battalions – about 4,500 men – launched a harrowing assault across the barren, billiard-table-flat Peleliu airfield to secure the campaign's primary objective. Naval gunfire and air strikes pounded the ridges north of the airfield before the attack began. One thousand yards of level, treeless terrain crisscrossed by the paved runways lay between the attackers and their objective – the airstrip's northern perimeter.

"We were filled with dread as we lay on the scorching hot coral and looked north across the open toward Bloody Nose Ridge," Pfc E.B. Sledge later wrote. Advancing to the north and east, the perspiring Marines' faces were quickly caked with gray coral dust. "As we moved forward, I clenched my teeth, prayed and squeezed my rifle stock," wrote Sledge.[69]

The Marines began the attack in a wave, then spread out so that 10- to 20-yard intervals separated them. One Marine described the attack as "an inspiring and never to be forgotten sight." "Dirty little mushrooms of dirt and smoke started blossoming around us almost instantly," said Sergeant Jim McEnery of the Fifth Marines. All three Fifth battalions made the attack.[70]

A hot wind was "blowing down from the scalded hills," said Pfc Russell Davis, and heat waves shimmered over the airstrip. They began the assault at a walking pace. "We just stood up and started walking across," said Corporal Billie Driver, the bazooka man from the Fifth Marines' "A" Company, adding that it was "just an amazing display of discipline. I didn't even see anybody hesitate."[71]

Soon, they were jogging, bent over at the waist as though unconsciously bracing themselves against the gale of rifle, machine-gun, mortar, and artillery fire singing around them discordantly. Deafening Japanese shellfire produced "a wall of spurting earth and flaming explosions and vicious, whirring shrapnel," said Pfc Davis. "I felt that the artillery was trying to shake us loose from the earth itself."[72]

Around Corporal R.V. Burgin and his comrades there erupted "the hiss and zing of shrapnel and bullets ... We were as exposed as bugs on a breakfast table."[73] "Men were walking across the open runway one minute, then dropping like flies the next as Japanese picked them off from their hillside caves," said Pfc Dan Toledo.[74] Men overcome by heat prostration began to fall to the ground, too, "shivering and exhausted, with mottled gray and red visages," wrote one Marine.[75]

Sledge said that it was his worst experience of the war. "To be shelled by massed artillery and mortars is absolutely terrifying, but to be shelled in the open is terror compounded beyond the belief of anyone who hasn't experienced it." "We were exposed, running ... through a veritable shower of deadly metal," Sledge wrote. "Tracers went by me on both sides at waist height ... steel fragments spattered down on the hard rock like hail on a city street."[76]

It would be Pfc Robert Leckie's final battle. As Marines fell around him like "clay ducks in a shooting gallery," Leckie dove into a large shell crater, where an officer ordered him to report the fraught situation to his company command post.[77]

As Leckie set out for the CP, Japanese gunners began walking artillery fire toward him; the target was not Leckie, but an ammunition dump to his rear. Suddenly, the dump exploded with a terrific roar. It felt like "a giant lemon squeezer had crushed me dry." Leckie stumbled and sank to his knees, shell-shocked and unable to walk or speak. He was evacuated to a hospital ship where he finally regained his faculties after three days. But Leckie's war was over after three campaigns.[78]

Corpsman Brooking Gex set up an aid station at the northern end of one of the runways and quickly had his hands full of casualties. Stretcher-bearers brought Gex Marines hit by bullets and shrapnel, and he applied sulpha and battle dressings to their wounds. "Shells exploded all around us and screams echoed from victims as they lay in pools of blood, dismembered, entangled in their gear," Gex said of the chaotic, dreadful scene. "Men fell faster than we could reach them." He saw four men gunned down, one after the other, while trying to reach a wounded Marine. Unable to just watch, Gex sprinted to the fallen man, who was bleeding heavily from a stomach wound, and assisted him.[79]

The assault troops reached the relative shelter of a mangrove copse. It was clogged with dead Japanese soldiers, "black-crusted, blimped, belching and farting noxious gases, their swollen tongues plugging their mouths, almost taunting," wrote Pfc Mace. Corporal Robert Shedd, a veteran of Guadalcanal and Cape Gloucester, was stunned by the losses suffered by the Fifth's "A" Company: of the 225 men who had landed 24 hours earlier, just 90 effectives remained.[80]

Shortly after 10 a.m., the commander of the Fifth's 1st Battalion sent an urgent request for help to regimental headquarters. "B" and "C" Company's casualties were as severe as "A" Company's and the battalion needed reinforcements, he said. Ninety minutes later, "I" Company arrived to reinforce the depleted battalion.[81]

While the Fifth Marines stormed across the airfield, the First Marines' 2nd Battalion advanced eastward along the airfield's northern periphery, through the rubble of the smashed support facilities. Danger menaced them from along the debris-choked streets – and even from unexpected quarters. "F" Company became locked in a fierce firefight with what it described as "a really organized force," before it determined that it had drifted across its southern boundary and was battling a Fifth Marines unit.

From pillboxes, cellars, and concrete shelters, the Japanese fought back furiously with machine guns, mortars, and antiaircraft and antitank guns. Enemy artillerymen in the ridges north of the airfield indiscriminately shelled friend and foe alike as they fought in the ruins of the smashed airfield buildings.[82]

Corporal Laurence Norris, who landed on Peleliu with a flamethrower on his back, lost a friend when "E" Company plunged into the jungle at the edge of the airfield. Like Norris, "Porky" Gazette was on his third campaign. He was killed while attacking a pillbox. Norris said Gazette had recently received a letter from his father that prophesied his fate with morbid accuracy, "Well, I guess, son, they're going to keep you over there 'til they kill you."

During the fighting north of the airfield, Norris held the hand of a dying comrade whose belly had been split open by shrapnel. "He said … 'I'm not going to make it.' He squeezed real tight and every once in a while he said, 'Am I getting weaker?' And I said, 'Nah, you're all right.' And he lived about 15 minutes."[83]

By afternoon, the First Marines' 2nd Battalion had blasted through the building rubble and a 300-yard strip of enemy rifle pits. At the base of the hill mass, the Marines reached a road that linked the island's two main north-south roads, one on each coastline. The battalion reported 144 casualties for the day.[84]

———

General William Rupertus came ashore in an amtrac just before 10 a.m. on September 16. Using a walking stick to help propel him and his plastered foot across one of the central landing beaches, he reached the tank trap that General O.P. Smith was using as the division command post.

Rupertus wasted no time in commandeering the tank trap and making it his personal headquarters. From here, he intended to manage the campaign virtually alone. He banished the division CP – along with Smith, whom he openly detested – to a nearby shallow depression, deliberately keeping the quiet, brainy Smith at arm's length, just as he had on Pavavu. Smith was never invited to the division planning meetings, despite the fact that he was Rupertus's assistant commander.[85]

Rupertus was convinced that resistance would collapse in a few days if the 1st Division could just push the Japanese beyond their breaking point. He had no inkling that he had woefully misread Peleliu's defenses and underestimated its defenders.

To achieve the campaign-ending breakthrough that Rupertus envisioned, the division must maintain momentum, never relenting in its attacks. From the outset, the general was convinced that the naval bombardment and air strikes would destroy most of the Japanese defenses and defenders. The remaining Japanese would then have no recourse but to launch futile banzai attacks, during which they could be dispatched en masse, as they had been on Tarawa and Saipan.[86]

He appeared satisfied with the progress made by the Fifth and Seventh Marines, but was displeased with the small gains of Colonel Lewis B. "Chesty" Puller's First Marines on the northern landing beaches.

The fact that the regiment had lost 500 men in one day while capturing The Point, Chevatel Ridge behind it, and the fortified coral shelf behind White Beach 2 appeared to make no impression on the irascible Rupertus. "Can't you move faster?" he barked at Puller. "Goddammit, Lewie, you've gotta kick ass to get results. You know that, goddammit!"[87]

Rupertus had resolved that the 1st Division would complete Peleliu's conquest without the involvement of *Stalemate*'s reserve, the Army's 81st Infantry Division. He had no intention of bringing Army units to Peleliu, and he told General Geiger that the 81st was unneeded. Not questioning Rupertus's decision, Geiger released General Paul Mueller's division to assault Angaur. He would later have good reason to revisit this decision.[88]

In a news statement that night, Admiral Nimitz's headquarters claimed that 1,400 Japanese were killed during the airfield assault but provided no U.S. casualty figures. Later, it was determined that the attack cost the Fifth Marines alone 38 men killed in action, 259 wounded, and three missing.[89]

Among those who died while storming the airfield was Damien Parer, killed by machine-gun fire while filming the fighting for Paramount News. The 27-year-old Australian cameraman had stalked battlefields since 1940, in both North Africa and the South Pacific. He was as revered in Australia as the newspaper correspondent Ernie Pyle was in the United States. In 1943, Parer won an Academy Award for Best Documentary for his film of the fighting on New Guinea – the only time a newsreel cameraman was so honored.[90]

During the early fighting, the Marines captured a Japanese ration document showing that, a week before the landings, there were up to 11,000 Japanese soldiers, naval personnel, and construction troops on Peleliu and Ngesebus.[91] That meant many more enemy awaited the Marines in the jumbled ridges north of the airfield.

The large number of Marine dead in such a short time overwhelmed the burial details. Peleliu's intensive heat accelerated the bodies' decomposition. Senior officers became concerned that this would create a serious health threat unless something was done.

As a temporary solution, a bulldozer began digging a mass grave along the beach. For those who watched the bulldozer fill the hole with their comrades' bodies, "that was the lowest point" of the campaign, said one Marine. The dead were later reburied in marked graves in a proper cemetery at Orange Beach 2.[92]

A Catholic chaplain who landed with the assault troops would have liked to conduct services, but the situation was still so chaotic that there was no possibility that he could celebrate Mass, much less administer Last Rites. He had plenty to do, though. "I stopped to pull some bodies out of the water so they wouldn't be run over by landing craft coming in after our wave," and then quickly got off the beach because of the enemy mortar and artillery fire. The chaplain attended to the wounded, "comforting the jittery and digging the usual foxholes."[93]

As darkness fell after the day-long fighting around the airfield, a lone figure could be seen sitting amid the airfield's carnage and debris. When the Marines investigated, they found that it was Corpsman James Lee, nicknamed "Admiral Lee" after the Navy task force commander. Corpsman Lee had been bandaging a wounded Marine with his medical kit in his lap when a Japanese machine gunner killed him and his patient. The medical kit had kept Lee's body upright.[94] "Our intense hatred of the enemy grew as they shot our helpless wounded and the dedicated corpsmen who were struggling to give what aid and comfort they could on that battlefield," Pfc Sledge later wrote.[95]

That night, Lieutenant Domenic DiLuglio, "F" Company's executive officer, and his radioman were in a foxhole on the north side of the airfield when a Japanese soldier armed with a bayonet jumped into the foxhole with them. The three men struggled furiously in the confined space. DiLuglio snatched up a piece of corrugated tin, pressed it down on the enemy soldier, and sat on it.

"He thrashed around and, Christ, I must have fired a clip from a forty-five through the tin every time he moved," said DiLuglio. When morning came, the Japanese soldier was still alive.

"He was a tough bastard, and big," said DiLuglio. "These guys were big and well-fed. Fat. And dirty, unshaven."[96]

New to combat, the replacements who had joined the division on Pavavu had had to learn fast, or else become casualties. Among other things, they learned to distinguish in the darkness the sounds made by friendly fire from those made by enemy weapons. Pfc Russell Davis compared it to identifying by ear the instruments of a symphony orchestra. "It was easy to tell their weapons from ours," he wrote. "Their rifles had a lighter sound and a higher crack. Their machine guns fired faster than ours. Their artillery was more wobbly in flight than ours."[97]

Their new ability to discern weapons' sounds might have somewhat mitigated their nighttime jitters, but a long symphony of terrors yet awaited them after the effusive bloodletting on D-Day and during the battle for the airfield.

At the end of September 16, the 1st Marine Division reported a total of 1,454 casualties during its two days in action on Peleliu: 117 killed, 1,262 wounded, and 75 missing. Especially hard-hit were the First Marines, whose losses over 48 hours exceeded 1,000 men. The number of enemy soldiers killed during the two-day period was estimated to be 2,445.[98]

Chapter 6

Into the Ridges

The hills opened up and fire poured down on our heads.
Private Russell Davis[1]

If I had my choice of a defensive position anywhere in the world, this is the kind of spot I would pick.
A Marine officer describing the Umurbrogol[2]

"I" Company of the Seventh Marines pushed eastward across southern Peleliu early on September 16, intending to drive all the way to the eastern shore. The advance was the 1st Division's first test of the enemy's new defensive scheme.

After repelling Japanese counterattacks and battling infiltration teams through the nighttime, the Seventh Marines were bedraggled-looking after one day and one night on Peleliu. "The whiskery, red-eyed, dirty Marines had spent the night fighting in foxholes filled with stinking swamp water; they were slimy, wet and mean now," wrote combat artist Tom Lea, who was attached to the regiment.[3]

"I" Company got off to a good start the next morning. Its progress was unimpeded until the Marines came upon a huge blockhouse 200 yards from the eastern beaches. The blockhouse suddenly blazed with machine-gun and cannon fire that scythed through the advancing column, stopping it cold.

Based upon a German design, the fortification was one of the stoutest ever built by the Japanese. Circular and 40 feet in diameter, it had

4-foot-thick walls made of reinforced concrete; its roof was 2½ feet thick. Inch-thick steel doors guarded the below-ground-level entryways. Supported by three nearby dual-gun positions, the massive structure harbored heavy machine guns and 20mm rapid-fire cannons protected behind gun ports by sliding steel cover plates that were three-eighths of an inch thick. The blockhouse resisted all infantry weapons, including flamethrowers. Naval gunfire failed to neutralize it. A tank fired its 75mm gun point-blank at the blockhouse; the shells bounced off.

Demolition engineers were summoned. Laden with large quantities of Compound C, they crept close to one of the entry doors under a smokescreen and prepared a tremendous charge. The huge explosion killed or stunned all of the Japanese inside the blockhouse. The Marines shot and killed those who lived through it.[4]

"I" Company resumed its advance and reached the eastern shore at 9:25 a.m. The drive disrupted Nakagawa's four-zone defensive scheme by severing the defenders in the southern sector from units in the other three areas, denying them the use of interior lines to receive reinforcements. Conceding the loss of his southern zone troops, Nakagawa concentrated his remaining men in the ridges north of the airfield.[5]

Planners were aware before the campaign began that the First Marines, given the task of attacking Peleliu's central highlands, would have *Stalemate*'s toughest assignment. But they had not expected the regiment to do it alone. The Seventh Marines were to have come to the First's aid after capturing southern Peleliu, an offensive optimistically expected to be completed in one day. Despite "I" Company's success in quickly reaching Peleliu's eastern shore, it would take four days rather than one for the Seventh to conquer the southern island in its entirety.

More Japanese than anticipated defended the area, and they happened to belong to one of the Imperial Army's elite units – the reinforced 3rd Battalion of the 15th Infantry Regiment. They occupied concrete blockhouses, pillboxes, bunkers, rifle pits, and trenches blasted from the coral on a southeastern promontory, on Ngarmoked Island, and on another island appearing on the Marines' maps as "Unnamed Island." The islands lay across heavily mined sand spits that could be crossed on foot, but only at low tide and at great peril.[6]

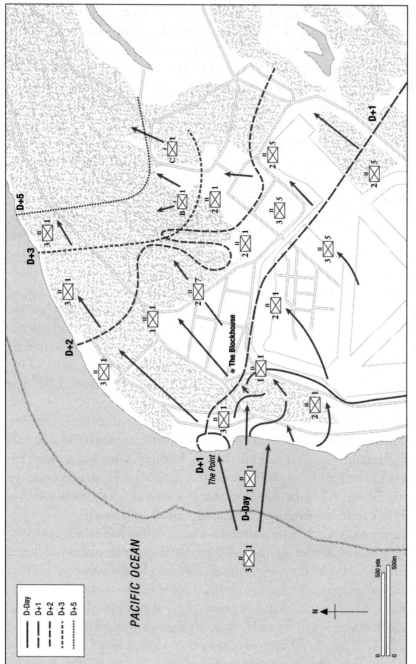

MAP 4: Peleliu's Central Ridges

The Seventh's first attempts on September 16 to penetrate the heavily defended area encountered fierce opposition. Preparatory fire from the cruisers *Indianapolis* and *Honolulu*, air strikes, 105mm artillery fire, and 4.5-inch rockets fired by an LCI(G) targeted the bunkers and pillboxes.

But the strongpoints withstood the onslaught. Two companies that advanced on a massive pillbox that had been a primary target found it intact after the bombardment; the pillbox's gunners knocked out a Sherman tank and an amtrac. Another amtrac hit a mine and was destroyed.[7]

The regiment halted, set up defensive lines for the night, and brought in more supporting weapons, including four 37mm guns and a half-track. The drawn-out battle for the southern island would delay the Seventh Marines' anticipated support of the First Regiment in the Umurbrogol.

The First Marines began to discover the terrible reality of the Umurbrogol on *Stalemate*'s third day, September 17, as the Seventh was poised to resume its attack on southern Peleliu's promontories.

The First Marines were probing the edge of the enemy's coralline-limestone fortress for the first time. At its center was a horseshoe-shaped canyon that ran roughly south to north, known thereafter as the Horseshoe. East of the Horseshoe rose Hill 100, Hill 200, and a series of connected ridges. To the west was a line of sharp peaks separated by steep-sided gullies: the Five Sisters. On the Sisters' west side, running parallel to the Horseshoe, was another canyon – christened Wildcat Bowl, abutting China Wall to its west.

The 1st Division held the airfield and the southeastern beaches, but the central ridges remained firmly under the control of Colonel Nakagawa's men. It fell to Puller's First Marines, who had landed the closest to the Umurbrogol, to wrest the jumbled hills that dominated central Peleliu from the Japanese. Little honor or glory would attend the First's furious assaults – only blood, horror, and death.

Naval and artillery bombardments and air strikes had steadily stripped the 300-foot highlands of their deceptively lush green mantle. Beneath lay terrain that was "the worst ever encountered by the regiment in three Pacific campaigns," according to the First Marines' official narrative. "Ravines, which on the map and photographs appeared to be steep-sided, actually had sheer cliffs for sides, some of them 50 to 100 feet high," wrote General O.P. Smith. "There were dozens of caves and pillboxes worked into the noses of the ridges and up the ravines. It was very difficult to find blind spots, as the caves and pillboxes were mutually supporting."[8]

The First Marines' regimental narrative described the Umurbrogol as "a contorted mass of decayed coral, strewn with rubble, crags, ridges and gulches thrown together in a confusing maze." It was roadless, trails were few, and the footing was poor. Marine officers described the terrain as "the most difficult of any in the world." Said one officer, "If I had my choice of a defensive position anywhere in the world, this is the kind of spot I would pick."[9]

The infantrymen quickly grasped the grim reality that their chances of survival in the ridges decreased by the day. They struggled to accept their fate. Pfc Dan Toledo worked out what appeared to him to be a rational strategy for staying alive: "I stayed near Japanese pillboxes which had been neutralized because, I reasoned, Japanese weapons from the surrounding hills were probably not zeroed in on them."[10]

It was nearly impossible to break into the tough coral with entrenching tools. "You couldn't dig a foxhole," said Lieutenant Clifford West, a forward air, artillery, and naval gunfire controller. "You could get a little crevice, but nothing that was any protection."[11]

"It was like sitting in the middle of a concrete parking lot," said Sergeant Robert Arkey. The men piled coral and debris around their positions, and even laid their packs – or those left behind by Marines who had become casualties – in front of their positions, hoping for the best. When enemy mortar rounds struck the coral, it became nothing less than granular shrapnel. "There'd be rock and shrapnel and everything else flying all over the place," said Sergeant Arkey. "It almost tripled the effect of a mortar shell."[12]

The Marines scrambled and crawled uphill, trying to avoid becoming casualties. The jagged coral tore at their elbows, knees, shoes and clothing. Often, "we gained the summit, but we still didn't own the hill," because the Japanese, secure in their tunnels, were "popping out and firing, then popping back in before we could get a bead on them," said Pfc Toledo.[13]

Armed with machine guns, mortars, and artillery in cleverly concealed caves, ravines, and spider holes, the Japanese positions provided maximum support for one another. Each time the Marines attacked a ridge or fortified position, they drew fire from places they had never anticipated.

Lieutenant Colonel Russell Honsowetz's 2nd Battalion stormed across the road that skirted the base of the hill mass, and followed it to where it joined the East Road, the north-south thoroughfare east of the Umurbrogol. Proceeding north on the East Road, the lead companies came under intensive fire from a hill to their west; its prosaic name was simply Hill 200, denoting its elevation. The Japanese called it Nakayama. Caves honeycombed it. From inside them, enemy observation teams were able to direct artillery fire from the Umurbrogol onto the airfield.

Honsowetz's Marines wheeled left and began assaulting Hill 200. Enemy artillery fire smashed two amtracs and sprayed the 2nd Battalion command post with shrapnel. Puller badly wanted Hill 200 and pressured his battalion commander to capture it. "Look, Honsowetz, I want that sonuvabitchin' ridge before sundown. I mean, gawdammit, I WANT it!"[14]

The Marines were climbing toward the summit in 105-degree heat when "the hills opened and fire poured down on our heads," said Pfc Russell Davis. "Two riflemen and I were plastered down into a hole and there we lay while the world heaved up all around us. We could do nothing but huddle together in terror… We were witless and helpless, with nothing to do but take it."[15]

A preview of the day's events had occurred at 5:30 that morning when 60 Japanese soldiers assaulted Honsowetz's "G" Company. The attack was a debacle. The First Marines' 2nd Battalion after-action report said, "The 50-caliber machine guns which were set up in the line proved invaluable. Only two of the enemy got as far as the lines and they were killed in hand-to-hand combat." The counterattack began a very long day of bitter fighting and severe losses for Honsowetz's battalion in the deadly, scorching-hot ridges. By noon, "G" Company reported 87 casualties.[16]

The rapid loss of 2nd Battalion officers over a brief period was especially egregious. Honsowetz's "E" Company was the first unit to attack into the ridges. The captain who led the assault was struck in the neck by shrapnel and evacuated to a hospital ship. Two minutes earlier, at 9:40 a.m., "F" Company's commander, Captain Tiscornia, had been wounded.

At 10:10 a.m., Lieutenant Russo, acting in the stead of the wounded Captain Tiscornia, was also wounded. A battalion runner reached "F" Company's command post about that time and was unable to find any other officers except the wounded Russo. The runner told the battalion CP that "F"'s Marines were "badly scattered and not under control." At 10:14 a.m., a battalion officer instructed Russo to gather all of the men that he could find and, if he were not too badly wounded, to "stand by with them for orders."

Over the next few minutes, the 2nd Battalion directed the quartermaster on the beach to send an amtrac loaded with small-arms ammunition to the battalion front line. The CP also told the air liaison officer, "We are getting observed fire from some OP. Hits are being registered on tanks and in the CP area. Get planes for observation."

At 10:25 a.m., two amtracs were knocked out by Japanese artillery fire, showering the battalion CP area with shrapnel. The CP requested artillery fire on target 134 LMN. Twenty-five minutes later, a battalion staff officer, a Lieutenant Didler, was wounded at the CP and evacuated.[17]

As the day proceeded in the shadeless coral-limestone hills and the temperature rose to 112 degrees, the Marines fought hand-to-hand with enemy soldiers bursting out of caves. A Japanese officer dashed from a cave swinging a sword and charged a Marine 50 feet away as the Marine fired his rifle at him. Lieutenant R. Bruce Watkins saw the bullets striking the officer, but he kept coming. The enemy officer made a final lunge and fell dead, his saber reaching the Marine's boot tip as the clip ejected from his rifle, "signaling the last of eight rounds."[18]

Despite sustaining heavy casualties from machine-gun and small-arms fire and from dual-purpose and 37mm mountain guns, the Marines managed to reach Hill 200's crest. They tenaciously clung to their prize.

Hill 200's crest was just 20 yards wide, however. Japanese troops atop slightly higher ridges to the north and west – Hills 205 and 210 – lashed the hilltop with gunfire. A deep ravine teeming with enemy soldiers separated Hills 200 and 210, and prevented the Marines from attempting to capture 210 as well. At day's end, Honsowetz had lost half of his 400-man assault force. Yet, the Marines still held the narrow summit of Hill 200.

They strung wire and hung empty ration cans on it to alert them to approaching enemy. During the night, the cans began rattling and the Marines hurled grenades at the noise. "At daylight we went to see how many Japs we had killed," said rifleman John Brewer. "We had gotten a wild sow and her piglets ... We had pork and shrapnel for breakfast."[19]

After Watkins's platoon had spent the night fending off repeated counterattacks on Hill 200's crest, it was mistakenly shelled by a Navy ship at dawn on the 18th. The friendly fire wounded many of

Watkins's men and accomplished what the Japanese could not: it drove them off the ridge. Shrapnel severed Watkins's helmet strap. "My knees turned to water," he wrote.[20]

Watkins requested smoke to conceal his platoon's withdrawal. "As men and stretcher-bearers stumbled down the steep slope, I saw a red-haired private take a direct hit," wrote Watkins. "He was vaporized! One minute he was there and the next gone without a trace."[21]

Japanese gunners in the hills around Hill 200 poured "murderous fire" on 2nd Battalion Marines that still held the hill's forward side. Japanese counterattacks briefly drove the Marines from the hillside, but Honsowetz's men got it back.

Pfc Frank Pomroy, shot in the leg three times the previous day during an ambush that killed his companions, had spent the night alone in a nearby dry gulch. He was awakened by the loud rattle of a Japanese officer and an enlisted man pulling a machine-gun cart loaded with supplies. Although weak from loss of blood, Pomroy shot them both. A short time later, an amtrac appeared. Seeing Pomroy's bloodstained trousers, the amtrac crewmen drove him to the beach, from where he was taken to a hospital ship.[22]

The 2nd Battalion's ordeal on Hill 200 was the First Marines' disturbing introduction to the enemy's new attritional strategy. Nearly invisible inside rock formations, caves, and tunnels, the Japanese occupied ideal firing positions protected by nearby concealed pillboxes and strongpoints.

Honsowetz requested reinforcements, and Puller dispatched Company "B" from his regimental reserve. It attacked nearby Hill 205 in the hope of gaining access to Hill 200. To the Marines' disgust, Hills 205 and 200 were not connected as they were shown to be on the regiment's map. The tactic failed in its goal of helping to recapture Hill 200. Hill 205 became an observation post.

"B" pushed on, though, until a hurricane of gunfire coming from the nearby Five Sisters emphatically repulsed it. The row of upended peaks was the area's most daunting topological feature. Oriented east-to-west, the Five Sisters' southern faces appeared as a single, sheer-sided wall impeding any northward advance. Plunging ravines made it nearly impossible to move from one peak to its neighbor.

Marine historian Frank Hough subsequently wrote that this was Peleliu's original Bloody Nose Ridge, so christened by the earliest troops – Puller's First Marines – that battered themselves against it. Other units would promiscuously confer the sobering nickname on other cliffs and ridges where the enemy furiously resisted, blurring its true location.[23]

The 2nd Battalion's feat in seizing Hill 200 might have seemed like a pyrrhic victory, yet its capture denied the Japanese their last direct sight line to the landing beaches. Moreover, Colonel Nakagawa was forced to abandon his command post near Hill 200 with the Marines now dangerously close by.

It must have been with a pang of regret that the colonel walked away from his CP and its many attractive features: electric lighting, decks and stairways, a refrigerated storeroom, and radio and telephone communications – Nakagawa maintained continual telephone contact with Koror via "suboceanic cable." The CP was also furnished with wooden desks, wall maps, filing cabinets, built-in bunks, and a well-supplied galley. Nakagawa's new CP lacked nearly all of these amenities, except for the communications links. It was located in a cave at the bottom of a deep hole a mile to the north.[24]

A Marine concisely expressed his frustration with an enemy that fought from inside hills and ridges: "When we hit them on top, they popped out of the bottom; when we hit them in the middle, they popped out of both ends."[25] Another Marine said, "Once you got on top of a hill ... it was like getting on top of an ant nest... at night they'd crawl out and try to crawl in the hole with you." The Marines who huddled atop Hill 200 during the night of September 17–18 were highly incensed when they smelled rice cooking in the Japanese-held caves beneath them.[26]

Late in the day on September 17, Puller reached Honsowetz by telephone and asked him how things were going. Honsowetz replied that things were not going very well; he had lost a lot of men, about 200. Asked by Puller how many Japanese they had killed, Honsowetz said about 50. Puller exploded. "Jesus Christ, Honsowetz, what the hell are the American people gonna think? Losing 200 fine young Marines and killing only fifty Japs! I'm gonna put you down for 500."[27]

A battalion commander wrote of the difficult terrain in which the First Marines now found themselves, "There was no such thing as a continuous attacking line. Elements of the same company, even platoon, were attacking in every direction of the compass, with large gaps in between." "The country was so difficult, cut up, and poorly mapped that it was difficult at best to locate oneself," added Lieutenant Colonel Spencer Berger, commander of the Seventh Marines' 2nd Battalion, the division reserve unit fighting alongside the First Marines.[28]

One of Berger's infantrymen, Pfc Charles Roan, became trapped in a rocky depression with four companions during a fierce grenade duel with the Japanese. Wounded by one grenade, Roan threw himself on a second one that landed amid him and his comrades. For his selfless action, Roan was posthumously awarded the Congressional Medal of Honor.[29]

Pipe habitually clenched in his teeth, the usually shirtless "Chesty" Puller cajoled, exhorted, and prodded his commanders from his shabby little command post. His CP consisted of a poncho and a piece of scrap tin that shaded him from the broiling sun while he studied his maps. Puller's CP was just yards from the battle line, closer to the action than any of his regiment's battalion command posts. When enemy shells occasionally exploded nearby, Puller did not flinch.[30]

Here Puller lived his philosophy of leading from the front. On Guadalcanal he had berated his officers, then new to combat, for taking cover when he said they should have been on their feet and leading. He expected his officers to expose themselves to danger. "I want to see my officers leading... Officers should be forward with their men at the point of impact. That is where their character stands out and they can do the most good," Puller believed.[31]

Puller regularly inspected his lines, limping from the shrapnel that he still carried from Guadalcanal in his left leg. His bodyguard, Sergeant Jan "Bo" Bodey, armed with a Thompson submachine gun, shadowed Puller wherever he went.[32] When he observed low casualty figures among lieutenants in his regiment, Puller interpreted it as evidence that they were not leading vigorously enough.[33]

Lieutenant Prate Stack Jr., the tank platoon commander, witnessed firsthand Puller's demand that his platoon leaders take risks to inspire their men. Stack was reporting to Colonel Harold "Bucky" Harris, the Fifth Regiment commander, when Puller appeared. Although Puller and Harris now each commanded a regiment and were essentially equals, Puller had been Harris's commander on Cape Gloucester and was accustomed to acting as his superior.

Puller bluntly asked Harris, "How many second lieutenants have you had killed so far?" Harris replied with a number that Puller found unsatisfactory. "What the hell are you doing, having a Sunday school picnic?" Puller bellowed.[34]

Unsurprisingly, turnover was high among Puller's company commanders, but seeing him walking around "being as fearless as he was helped an awful lot. He was a good leader," said Lieutenant West, the forward air and gunfire controller.[35]

Several weeks earlier, Puller's younger brother, Lieutenant Colonel Sam Puller, the Fourth Marines' executive officer, had been killed on Guam. Over the summer, the brothers had spent three days together on Guadalcanal before shipping out for their respective campaigns. They had reminisced about their rural Virginia boyhood and the war. It was their last reunion.[36]

Sam's death, some Puller acquaintances maintained, made Puller, already aggressive by nature, even more so and, at times, even "quite irrational," said West. "Puller was a changed man after that. He was anxious. He wanted to kill Japs. He did not want them captured and that was made very clear."[37]

Indeed, during a regimental assembly on Pavavu, Puller had reminded his men that Japanese soldiers on Guadalcanal had bayoneted Australian priests and raped and bayoneted nuns. "We will not take prisoners," he said, although adding that captured Korean laborers might be spared.[38]

Yet it was not his brother's death or his own aggressive nature that compelled Puller to order the costly frontal attacks that would ultimately destroy his regiment. General Rupertus, obsessed with securing Peleliu inside of a week, continually prodded Puller, who never would admit that he could not complete a job, no matter how impossible.[39]

Before attacking the Umurbrogol's ridges, Lieutenant Colonel Ray Davis's 1st Battalion had to first knock out a reinforced blockhouse on the airfield's northern perimeter. Its walls were 4 feet thick, and 12 pillboxes, connected by tunnels, surrounded it. Although clearly marked on aerial maps and on the maps issued to ground units, it had not been so much as touched by the pre-landing naval bombardment.

After losing 25 men during a first attempt to capture the blockhouse, the 1st Battalion pulled back. Its naval gunfire forward observer,

Lieutenant N.R.K. Stanford, called on the battleship *Mississippi*, the battalion's direct gunfire support that day, to deal with the blockhouse with its 14-inch guns. The second round scored a direct hit that destroyed the target.

"Everything in it was smashed, twisted, blasted," wrote Tom Lea of *Life* magazine. "In two of the pillboxes I saw some of the bodies were nothing more than red raw meat and blood mixed with the gravelly dust of concrete and splintered logs." About 20 enemy soldiers lay dead, some without a mark on them – killed by concussion.[40]

Now poised to storm Hill 160, one of the so-called "outpost hills" rising in front of them, Davis's Marines endured 45 minutes of fire from a Japanese 6-inch naval gun and a 70mm mountain gun fired at point-blank range from a concrete-hardened cave. Bazookas took out the naval gun. Two tanks were summoned to deal with the mountain gun, which was fired when it emerged from the cave on a railroad trestle, and retracted before counterfire could be trained on it.

After the mountain gun disabled one of the tanks, the other Sherman took up a position 100 yards away. Lieutenant Stack's tank crew was ready to fire when the gun reappeared. "It was like a shootout in one of the Western movies," said Stack. His gunner "lets go with our 75 and blows the hell out of the Jap gun" and its ten-man crew, said Stack. "Thank God our gunner was a crack shot."[41]

With the mountain gun destroyed, Davis's 1st Battalion now tackled Hill 160. Scrambling over coral pinnacles, down the sheer sides of gullies, and among boulders dotting the hill's slope, the Marines neutralized 24 caves.

By the early afternoon, Davis's "A" Company reached the top of Hill 160. Its losses had been shocking. The company commander told Davis, "We're up here, but we're knee-deep in Purple Hearts." Davis understatedly conceded that it "was the most difficult assignment I have ever seen."[42]

Forced to withdraw under heavy fire, "A" Company claimed to have killed more than 300 Japanese, and to have knocked out 37 pillboxes and four large guns.

"C" Company penetrated the farthest – 800 yards – during the 1st Battalion's initial attack into the Umurbrogol. To cement the gain, Davis threw in the remnants of Companies "A" and "B" – those not killed or wounded while attacking adjacent ridges with less success – along with engineer and pioneer units. By nightfall, "C" held the forward slope of the first range of hills.[43]

During "C" Company's initial assault on the ridges, Sergeant Jack Ainsworth said Japanese machine gunners inflicted many casualties from a pillbox that the Marines were unable to see until they were practically on top of it. "There were many dead Marines throughout our entire layout but we have no time to bury them," he wrote. Their comrades covered them with ponchos or shelter halves until burial parties could reach them.[44]

That night, the Japanese attempted to exploit a gap between the 1st and 2nd Battalions, hoping to isolate and destroy the 1st Battalion salient. Two companies of the division reserve, the Seventh Marines' 2nd Battalion, were rushed from the beach to plug the hole in the lines, stopping the attack.[45]

While staging in a shell-torn coconut grove for "C" Company's initial attack into the ridges, Ainsworth observed that the area was littered with the bodies of both Marines and Japanese – some sprawled over one another – who had died in a tank and artillery duel. Ainsworth said the gruesome sight was hard for him to comprehend even when he saw it with his own eyes. "Mortar and artillery fire leaves its victims in horrible grotesque positions, partially decapitated, minus limbs, and sometimes fully draped in their own intestines."[46]

The enemy's zealous determination to fight to the death was manifest. Colonel Puller reported that his men found dead Japanese soldiers shackled to their weapons inside caves and pillboxes, evidently to prevent them from withdrawing during aerial and naval bombardments. Pfc Bernard Martin, a rifleman, later said that he had seen Japanese machine gunners chained in their pillboxes with their right arms left free to fire their guns.[47]

The First Marines' CP warned the battalions as they began to push into the ridges: "Practically all [dead] enemy officers are booby trapped. Use caution" – as though contending with live enemy soldiers wasn't stressful enough.[48]

Indeed, the campaign's intensity and manifold horrors began to wear down the Marines psychologically. Some became calloused to the incredible violence, but others exhibited signs of severe distress. A common symptom was the unfocused "thousand-yard stare." Others broke down altogether. Second Lieutenant Jesse Hollingsworth, whose rifle company lost more than 100 men, said he had fought on Guadalcanal and Cape Gloucester, but those experiences were "never anything like this."[49]

A Marine who found his company commander sitting on the ground weeping said, "He just cracked up. I remember thinking, 'What the hell is going on here?' … his eyes were pouring." After being evacuated to an aid station, some combat fatigue casualties were eventually able to rejoin their units, but many did not.[50]

Late on September 16, *Life* magazine artist Tom Lea arrived at the beach in an amtrac prior to returning to his transport ship. On the beach he saw a shell-shocked Marine standing quietly beside a corpsman in a makeshift sick bay in a shell hole. That Marine became the subject of Lea's most famous World War II portrait, *The Two Thousand Yard Stare*. The man was "staring stiffly at nothing," Lea wrote. "His mind had crumbled in battle, his jaw hung, and his eyes were like two black empty holes in his head."[51]

James Jones, the author of *From Here to Eternity* and *The Thin Red Line*, observed that before Lea went to Peleliu, his work was "excellently done but high-grade propaganda. There was very little American blood, very little tension, very little horror." "But something apparently happened to Lea after going into Peleliu," Jones wrote. "There is the tension of terror in the bodies here, the distorted facial expression of the men under fire show it, too."[52]

After just three days, the First Marine Regiment's losses were shockingly high: 1,236 killed or wounded – about 40 percent of the regiment's landing force. "Frontline units were decimated," a report said. One hundred fifteen pioneers were sent to the regiment as replacements. In the 3rd Battalion, just 473 effectives remained, and 200 of them were headquarters personnel serving as combat troops.[53]

Corpsman Burnett Napier was an unhappy witness to the destruction of "B" Company of the First Marines. By the fifth morning, just 38 of the company's original 225 men answered roll call, including one lieutenant and Napier, the last of the nine corpsmen. Later in the day, Napier was wounded during a Japanese mortar barrage and evacuated.[54]

Assigned to the 1st Sniper and Recon Company, Corpsman Oris Brehmer was evacuated on the second day after being wounded by

The pre-landing bombardment, September 15, 1944. (Getty Images)

General William Rupertus, commander of the 1st Marine Division. (USMC)

General Roy Geiger, commander of the III Amphibious Corps. (USMC)

General Paul Mueller, commander of the 81st Infantry Division. (U.S. Army)

Admiral William Halsey, commander of the Third Fleet. (U.S. Navy, NARA)

General Oliver P. Smith, assistant commander of the 1st Marine Division. (USMC)

Colonel Lewis B. "Chesty" Puller, commander of the First Marine Regiment. (USMC)

Puller at his command post. (USMC, NARA)

Colonel Harold "Bucky" Harris, Fifth
Marines commander (center) with Geiger
(left) and Rupertus (right). (USMC)

Lieutenant Colonel Ray Davis's
1st Battalion of the First Marines suffered
71 percent casualties on Peleliu. He is
shown here after the Korean War. (NARA)

Colonel Herman Hanneken, commander of the Seventh Marine Regiment. (USMC)

Amtracs headed toward the Peleliu beaches on D-Day, September 15, 1944. (Getty Images)

A D-Day scene on Orange Beach 3. (USMC)

Paul Douglas, the oldest Marine recruit at age 50. (USMC)

D-Day on White Beach 2. (USMC)

Marines take cover behind an amtank on a Peleliu landing beach. (Alamy)

Tom Lea of *Life* magazine portrayed this Marine moments after he was wounded on Orange Beach 3 on D-Day. (*The Price, 1944*, Tom Lea, 1944, Copyright Catherine Lea Weeks, Courtesy of the Tom Lea Institute)

An amtank moves inland after coming ashore on Peleliu. (USMC)

Seventh Marines set up their command post in a tank trap near Peleliu's beach. (USMC)

The Fifth Marines shown in the act of capturing Peleliu's airfield. (USMC)

Marines fight in the rubble of Japanese buildings on Peleliu airfield's northern perimeter. (USMC)

A Navy corpsman gives water to a wounded Marine. (Getty Images)

Marines battle entrenched Japanese soldiers. (USMC)

A Marine war dog and its handler. (USMC)

An amtrac flamethrower in action. (Getty Images)

Marines advance into the ridges of the Umurbrogol. (USMC)

Marine infantry-tank assault proceeds in rugged terrain on Peleliu. (USMC)

The first Corsairs arrive at Peleliu airstrip. (NARA)

A Corsair bombs Peleliu's ridges. (USMC)

Dead Marines prior to burial. (NARA)

Black 16th Depot Company Marines served as stretcher-bearers on Peleliu. (NARA)

A wounded Marine being evacuated to a hospital ship. (USMC)

A weary Marine. (Getty Images)

A Marine displays stress of combat. (Getty Images)

Marines prepare for action. (USMC)

Life magazine illustrator Tom Lea's depiction of the "2,000-yard stare" resulting from battle fatigue. (*That 2,000-Yard Stare, 1944*, Tom Lea, 1944, Copyright Catherine Lea Weeks, Courtesy of the Tom Lea Institute)

Marines advance in the Horseshoe, skirting Grinlinton Pond. (USMC)

Captain Everett Pope was awarded
the Medal of Honor for his leadership
on Hill 100. (USMC)

Tank "Lady Luck" crushing an
enemy gun. (USMC)

Three Native American code talker Marines who fought on Peleliu, pictured here on their way to Okinawa in late March 1945. (USMC)

Arthur Jackson of the Seventh Marines, a Medal of Honor recipient. (USMC)

Marines taking a smoke break. (Getty Images)

mortar shrapnel. Released from a hospital ship a few days later, Brehmer returned to his unit, but "there was practically nothing left. Lots of the people [were] gone."[55]

Admiral William Halsey arrived aboard his flagship *New Jersey* in the waters off Peleliu during the late morning of the 17th with Task Group 38. After briefly observing Operation *Stalemate* from afar, Halsey met for an hour and a half with Admirals Wilkinson, Fort, and Cochrane, and with General Julian Smith, the expeditionary force commander, and General Roy Geiger, the III Amphibious Corps commander. Halsey departed without going ashore, and resumed making preparations for the imminent Philippines campaign.[56]

General Rupertus's prediction that *Stalemate* would be rough but quick had let the air out of the campaign as a news story. After D-Day, Peleliu disappeared from American newspapers' front pages. As naval vessels peeled away from the *Stalemate* amphibious force to join the armada transporting the Sixth Army to Leyte in the Philippines, along with them went most of the correspondents credentialed for Peleliu. They elected to follow the bigger story – General Douglas MacArthur's triumphal return to the Philippines.

Days after Peleliu's D-Day, major developments in Europe dominated newspaper headlines: General Bernard Montgomery's bold, but ultimately unsuccessful Operation *Market Garden* through the Netherlands, whose object was to breach the Siegfried Line and cross the Rhine River.

Nine days after the Peleliu landings, MacArthur invaded Leyte.

Thereafter, correspondents' stories about the Battle of Peleliu were trimmed and relegated to the inside and back pages of U.S. newspapers, where they attracted fewer readers. As Peleliu's bloodletting and horrors were intensifying by the day, the battle's place in the annals of the Pacific War was waning and would nearly disappear.[57]

"A blazing sun, reflected off the white sand and coral, turned the entire arena into a scorching furnace," said a First Marines report. Some front-line Marines collapsed from heat exhaustion while scrambling up the ridges' steep slopes, laden with weapons and ammunition. In addition, "countless numbers suffered minor discomfort from blistered faces and cracked, bleeding lips," the report said. As temperatures exceeded 110 degrees, heat prostration casualties rivaled those from combat wounds.[58]

Corporal James Young said his First Marines mortar crew was exhausted after four days of getting by on catnaps. But even catnaps were problematic. "We would just lay our head back on our helmets and try to doze a little bit," but then "the sweat would run down over your eyelids and coagulate and you couldn't get them open. You had to get cups of water and soak your eyelids to open your eyes."[59]

Yet neither his men's travails nor his division's heavy casualties for meager gains had disabused Rupertus of his conviction that the campaign would soon end in a climactic battle and the enemy's defeat; his Marines must only continue to apply intensive pressure and maintain momentum. He continually strove to "put more fire in the bellies" of his field commanders.

Rupertus's headquarters invariably issued the same orders daily, no matter how severe the losses had been the previous day: "All infantry units will resume the attack with maximum effort in all sectors at 0830 hours."[60]

But Colonel Puller now understood that his First Marines, which were leading the headlong attacks against the heavily fortified Japanese defenses, were being rapidly depleted by heavy casualties. In just three days, he had lost half of his men. When Lieutenant Colonel Lew Walt saw Puller at a meeting on September 17, Puller "was absolutely sick over the loss of his men." Walt said Puller thought "we were getting them killed for nothing."[61]

Usually reluctant to acknowledge that he needed help, Puller now did. That evening, he asked Rupertus's chief of staff, Colonel Selden, for replacements. Selden told him that no replacements were available. Puller pointed out that the division was using just one-third of its manpower on the battle line because of "all these damned specialists" – up to 17,000 1st Division Marines that were performing noncombat duties. They were not infantry-trained, said Selden. If he got them, Puller replied, within a day they would be trained infantrymen. Selden abruptly ended the conversation.[62] However, Selden later relented and released part of the division reserve to Puller, adding Sherman tanks and 100 shore party men to serve as combat troops.[63]

On the campaign's fourth day, September 18, Puller's regiment faced Peleliu's most formidable terrain features – the Five Sisters, on the regiment's left; and Hills 300, 200, and 100 on its right. Jutting skyward north of the airfield, they barred the way to Peleliu's other highlands to the north. Amid this jumble of dirty-white coral ridges the real battle for Peleliu would be fought.[64]

Ray Davis's 1st Battalion reported that until this point the Japanese dead were "all clean, well fed and equipped and rather large in stature – most were 6 feet in height." The report added, "The Japs we fought were not the wild, attacking hordes of the early stages of the war. These Japs were from a Manchurian division, well equipped, well fed, well trained and well disciplined."[65]

The Marines' first prisoner was a former fisherman from Koror who was inducted into the Japanese Army in July and belonged to a special counter-landing force. The prisoner had little to offer in the way of information, but when asked about the defenders' morale, he immediately replied, "Though they die, they will defend."[66]

About this time, a Japanese message center chief captured by a First Marines patrol told his captors that the 2nd Infantry Regiment was the principal Japanese unit on Peleliu. The prisoner claimed to be the sole survivor of the 6th Company, which had been overrun. His comrades who were badly wounded had killed themselves with grenades, he said. The prisoner drew a map that identified major enemy strongpoints.[67]

But he was very much the exception. The few Japanese regulars that were taken prisoner were not only uncooperative, but aggressively defiant. "They'd spit at you with the muzzle [of a weapon shoved] in their mouth," said a Marine. "Haughty types of people. They'd just give you the old evil eye like they were going to get you somewhere down the line."[68]

This was the result of the Imperial Japanese Army's Code of Battlefield Conduct – "Senjinkun" – issued in January 1941 by Prime Minister Hideki Tojo. The code made it impermissible for Japanese soldiers to be taken prisoner under any circumstances. "Never live to experience shame as a prisoner," it said. "By dying you will avoid leaving behind the crime of a stain on your honor." Surrender or capture, the code stated, would also bring disgrace to family members and prevent a soldier's remains from being accepted at the Yasukuni Shinto shrine for war dead in Tokyo's Kudan district.

Calculatedly designed to end the rash of Japanese surrenders that had occurred during the fighting in China in 1937–41, the code invoked samurai values from the shogun era, a time when war prisoners could expect to be tortured and possibly beheaded. Hara-kiri – ritual suicide – was encouraged as a way to evade capture and execution.[69]

In a poem penned during the Pacific War, a captured Japanese soldier lamented:

My comrades are crossing the seas
To the shrine of Kudan.
But I, like a caged bird,
Cannot join them.[70]

The Marines were justifiably suspicious of surrendering Japanese soldiers, who sometimes only feigned submission in order to get close enough to the Marines to kill them. In one instance, Marines held their fire when an enemy soldier emerged from a pillbox with his hands in the air. Then, one of the Marines abruptly shouldered his M1 rifle and emptied a clip into the surrendering soldier, momentarily shocking his comrades. The Japanese soldier literally blew up when struck by the bullets, and the acrid smell of explosives hung in the air. The Marine who shot him had glimpsed the explosives strapped to the man's back.[71]

The morning of September 18 began another tense, bloody day for the First Marines. At 6 a.m., Honsowetz's 2nd Battalion said that it had received intermittent fire all night long near Hill 210. "G" Company reported 23 casualties; "E" reported ten. At 6:10 a.m., "E" said that it was receiving heavy rocket, mortar, and artillery fire. Two minutes later, U.S. artillery and naval gunfire responded.

"G" Company urgently requested stretcher-bearers at 6:20 a.m., and 15 minutes later, "E" Company's radio was knocked out and the operator was wounded when shells and shrapnel tore through the company area. At 7 a.m., the 2nd Battalion resumed its attack into the ridges. "F" Company reported an hour later, "We have been hit heavily by mortar and machine gun fire. Send all available stretcher-bearers." "E" Company requested stretcher-bearers and corpsmen at 10:05 a.m.

"The request is urgent." Five minutes later, "E" asked for reinforcements. "Very badly cut up. Needs all types of medical supplies."[72]

About 11 a.m., Honsowetz asked Puller for reinforcements for the assault on Hill 210. He said the attack could not be made without more men. Puller irritably replied, "You sound all right, you're there. Goddammit, you get those troops in there, and you take the goddamn hill!"[73]

After 30 minutes of preparatory naval and artillery fire and air strikes, Honsowetz personally led the 2nd Battalion's attack on Hill 210. When the supporting fire ceased, Japanese soldiers emerged from caves and gullies, and rolled grenades down onto the Marines climbing the hill.

"Clawing and crawling up the cliff went platoons that were no more than squads, and companies that were no more than large platoons," said Private Russell Davis. One platoon, he said, that normally numbered about 40 men now consisted of just 18. The assault troops clubbed and stabbed their way to the hilltop, slowly driving out the enemy defenders with the help of the Seventh Marines' 2nd Battalion.[74]

They were unable to hold. Honsowetz wept when he and his battered battalion returned from the futile attack. Pfc Gabriel Caggiano said just 30 men remained in his "G" Company from the original complement of about 230, and all of its officers were gone.[75]

The 3rd Battalion attacked the ridges from the west side until a torrent of enemy gunfire drove it back to its starting point. "We got the crap beat out of us and took many casualties," stated Pfc George Peto.[76]

At the close of the campaign's fourth day, September 18, the First Marines had not come closer to achieving a breakthrough in the Umurbrogol. They instead clung to tenuous positions among the sharp-edged coral outcroppings while the Japanese flayed them around the clock from many directions with blizzards of large and small steel projectiles. Honsowetz's 2nd Battalion reported 81 men killed, 331 wounded, and 79 men missing since D-Day – a casualty rate approaching 50 percent.[77]

The Marines defended their minimal gains with teams of riflemen and scouts spaced 5 feet apart to minimize the possibility of mass casualties. They were armed with Thompson submachine guns, .50-caliber machine guns, and M1 Garand rifles. On the valley floor below, armored half-tracks with 75mm and 37mm field guns, more machine-gun units, and rifle teams stood ready to provide support. After dark, the Marines fired at everything that moved.

Even so, a Japanese soldier somehow managed to infiltrate the lines, enter a foxhole, and cut a Marine's throat before being stabbed to death. Like many of the infiltrators, he was clad in black clothing that at night made him nearly invisible, and he wore rubber-soled shoes that muted his footfall. Three other infiltrators crept down into the valley and set up a machine gun in front of the American lines, killing a Marine before a half-track gunner wiped out all of them.[78]

The Umurbrogol's jumbled terrain fragmented the Marine assaults into an often incohesive series of individual battles waged by rifle companies. Nakagawa's care in fortifying every ridge, cliff, and gully was doing exactly as he had intended: exacting a high price in blood from the First Marines.

Squad leader Rudolph Fanska led his men over a natural bridge that spanned a 12-foot-deep crevice. "I ran up to the point where I could see the bottom of the crevasse and it was just filled with [dead] Marines … So other people had assaulted that hill and I knew immediately that that was extreme danger by crossing that bridge," he said. When he ordered his squad to stop, Fanska was shot in the left shoulder. "I went down to my knees and I said, 'Uh-oh. Dead duck.'" But he was able to get to his feet and walk out. He was evacuated to a hospital ship.[79]

The corrosive effects of days spent clambering about the punishing terrain in the oppressive heat, sustained by snatches of sleep and hastily eaten rations, were stamped on the Marines' smudged faces and ragged clothing. Their voices cracked when they spoke. Their dungarees, torn by the jagged coral and stained by bodily functions and comrades' blood, were coated in gray coral dust. Some men had cut them off below the knees to obtain relief from the heat. For the same reason, many had dispensed with underwear, T-shirts, and leggings.[80]

"We have paid dearly in lives and blood for the meager holdings already conquered," said Sergeant Jack Ainsworth. "It has been a desperate fight for every inch of ground taken."[81]

Corporal Albert Bouley's machine-gun section attacked enemy positions in the ridges, following in the train of an infantry platoon. Cresting a ridge, the Marines were suddenly struck by a cyclone of gunfire. Bouley and his men took cover behind a large coral boulder. "All you could hear … was guys yelling for corpsmen, plasma, and stretcher-bearers," Bouley said. "The riflemen were getting hit really hard."

He overheard his company commander telling Colonel Puller on the walkie-talkie, "Well, God damn it colonel, why don't you get up here and find out what is going on." Puller appeared a short time later. "Well, captain, here I am," he said. "Now what the hell is going on? Why aren't you moving out?"

The captain told Puller to listen to the cries for corpsmen from his shot-up company. Minutes later, Puller ordered the captain to withdraw his company to its previous night's position.[82]

While the First Regiment was hemorrhaging men in the Umurbrogol on September 18, the Seventh Marines continued their slog through swampy southern Peleliu.[83]

Fortunately for the Marines, the carefully prepared Japanese defenses, which bristled with interlocking fields of fire, faced seaward – and not landward, in the direction from which the Marines were attacking.

Nakagawa had mistakenly believed the Americans would attempt amphibious landings along Peleliu's southern coastline. His assumption might have made the Marines' job marginally easier, but the Japanese rapidly adapted to the situation and fought with the desperate fury of doomed men. Nakagawa had in fact ordered the defenders to stand their ground and fight to the death.[84]

Early on September 17, the 3rd Battalion attacked the "Unnamed Island" as it was labeled on maps, but the heavily mined sandspit and its environs stalled the assault. It took two hours for engineers to remove or detonate 32 mines.

At 10 a.m., "L" Company led a new attack on the island and captured it after encountering just moderate resistance. The Marines shot fleeing Japanese in the water as they tried to swim to neighboring Ngarmoked Island. The 3rd Battalion reported that it killed 116 Japanese soldiers.[85] Arrowhead-shaped Ngarmoked covered 70 acres. Its defenders, more numerous than on the Unnamed Island, had transformed its more rugged terrain into fortified positions.[86]

The first attack, led by "B" Company at 8 a.m., failed when the Marines ran into a 100-yard-long chain of bunkers, pillboxes, and rifle pits that had survived the pre-attack bombardment.

Tall, lanky Captain Leonard Migliori, who had played football at Columbia, was at the head of "B" Company when his executive officer, Lieutenant Philip Bayer, was killed on the sand spit. Bayer had also been a Columbia football player, and Migliori paused long enough to remove Bayer's class ring from his finger before forging ahead.

The Japanese plastered the Marines with mortar fire, and casualties soared. Migliori twice asked Colonel Herman Hanneken, the Seventh's crusty "Old Breed" commander, for permission to withdraw "B" Company. Both requests were denied. The Seventh's executive officer, however, managed to persuade Hanneken to allow "B" to pull back, and to send more tanks.

The Marines wrestled artillery onto the just-captured Unnamed Island to support a second attack on Ngarmoked. Tanks, half-tracks, amtanks, and 37mm guns were also brought up. At 2:30 p.m., under a broiling sun and after an air strike targeted a blockhouse and pillboxes, "A" Company, supported by three tanks, spearheaded the assault as artillery and mortars pounded the Japanese positions. This attack gained 100 yards in 20 minutes, with the infantrymen crouching behind the tanks as they fired on the enemy's mutually supporting coral bunkers, concrete blockhouses, reinforced foxholes, trenches, and caves.

"A" Company pressed the attack for an hour, pushing ahead 300 yards before running into a dense pocket of resistance that the air strikes, artillery, and naval gunfire had failed to suppress. "C" Company was thrown into the battle, along with "B" Company. Roaring enemy gunfire stopped the Marines at the edge of a swamp, and they dug in for the night.[87]

Giles McCoy, a Seventh Marines sniper, said that he usually targeted Japanese officers, "because they were the ones that committed the atrocities on our young men." The enemy officers wore high boots, and for that reason the Marine sniper acquired the nickname "High Boots McCoy."

On September 17, however, McCoy became embroiled in a bloody duel with an enemy sniper 200 yards away. The Japanese drew first blood, shooting McCoy twice in the left side. The Marine sniper stuffed his wounds with rags and bandages to stanch the bleeding. Then, he gathered himself and sighted in on the enemy position.

"I finally nailed him and dropped him, so he didn't shoot me again," said McCoy. "He made a mistake; he moved to get another shot at me and … that was the wrong thing for him to do." Afterward, McCoy examined his dead rival and his gear. "He had good equipment. He had good weapons," was McCoy's succinct summation.[88]

The next day, September 18, the 1st Battalion resumed its attack on Ngarmoked, bypassing cave openings and pillboxes in order to maintain momentum. After the Marines had gone ahead, the enemy, practicing "passive infiltration," swarmed from their underground positions and attacked the advancing Marines from behind. "I" Company and the division Reconnaissance Company were summoned to bring the rear area under control.

In "C" Company's wake, 80 Japanese stormed out of an undisturbed coral mound that was a hive of bunkers and pillboxes connected by tunnels. With machine guns and rifles, the Japanese pinned down Pfc Arthur Jackson's platoon. Machine-gun fire killed the platoon's commander and the senior sergeant, and threatened to annihilate the other men hugging the ground.

Jackson's first assignment in the Marines had been an unusual one: to physically condition Marines recovering in Australia from the rigors of the Guadalcanal campaign. It is unlikely that Jackson endeared himself to combat veterans that probably resented being forced to keep up with a strong, fit, 210-pound 19 year old. After his assignment in Australia, Jackson ended up in the infantry; during the Cape Gloucester campaign, he lugged around a Browning Automatic Rifle.

While on mess duty before landing on Peleliu, a cook gave Jackson a 14-pound ham to take ashore with him. Jackson gained a measure of oddball fame for carrying the ham everywhere in his pack. It became a nuisance. "Every time I hit the deck that damned ham would rap me in the head," he said.*[89]

Pinned down with his platoon in the area of southern Peleliu known as the "fishhook," Jackson looked up to see his company commander and the battalion weapons officer kneeling beside him.

Because of Jackson's physical condition, they thought he might be able to successfully assault a chain of bunkers in a shallow depression

---

*Later during the campaign, Jackson shared his ham with his mates. Initially delighted by the rare treat, they later regretted having eaten it because it made them terribly thirsty.

ahead of them. His platoon would cover him. They asked him whether he would be willing to try. Jackson readily agreed. He took off his helmet and pack (with the ham inside it) to lighten his load, and took off running with his BAR.

He didn't zig-zag. "I went straight to where this trench was," he said. Enemy automatic weapons fire kicked up dirt around him as he ran. He reached a large bunker made of coral, coconut logs, and earth. The firing aperture faced seaward. "I could hear them jabbering in there" when he threw a white phosphorus grenade into the bunker. Smoke poured out, and he could hear men coughing inside.

Jackson moved around outside the bunker, firing his BAR. He killed two guards that tried to surrender. "Some ran out, and I blew them back into the hole." He jammed the muzzle of his BAR into the aperture and emptied a 20-round magazine. The suddenness and violence of Jackson's assault froze the Japanese in the bunker, giving his squad leader time to bring him a pack containing up to 40 pounds of plastic explosives, along with blasting caps, time fuse, and primer cord.

Jackson, who was trained in demolitions, armed the bomb with a 30-second fuse and stuffed it through the aperture, along with phosphorus grenades that his comrades had also brought to him. The stupendous explosion hurled logs and stones into the air. When the dust settled, nothing remained of the bunker, and the 35 men that had been inside were all dead, "laid down like cord wood and bleeding from the ears and mouth."

Jackson's platoon, now free to maneuver, provided backup firepower as Jackson stormed nearby enemy positions, knocking out about a dozen of them. No one came out to fight. When he was finished, Jackson was credited with 50 kills.[90] For his bold, selfless actions Jackson was awarded the Congressional Medal of Honor. Unusual for a Medal of Honor recipient on Peleliu, Jackson had not suffered so much as a scratch.

A few days later, four Japanese soldiers made the mistake of attacking Jackson in his foxhole. He killed three of them with his BAR and clubbed the fourth to death.[91]

"B" Company pushed into Ngarmoked's eastern barb, which was dense with defensive works. During a three-hour battle, the company swept down the island's eastern side with armored vehicles equipped with 75mm cannon, and infantrymen armed with bazookas, satchel charges, flamethrowers, and thermite grenades.

The Japanese had difficulty reorienting themselves to defend against an onslaught from the rear, and "B," although outnumbered, drove the last 40 Japanese into a 50-square-yard pocket. Some of the diehards killed themselves with grenades and pistols, while others dove head-first from rocks into the shallows. "B" Company reported having killed 425 enemy soldiers, at a cost of just 22 casualties.[92]

Meanwhile, "A" and "C" companies skirted the swamp and pushed south until they reached the sea. The conquest of Ngarmoked, completed at 3:30 p.m., marked the extinction of the 3rd Battalion of the enemy's vaunted 15th Infantry Regiment.[93]

During four days of fighting on southern Peleliu, the Seventh Marines killed 2,609 Japanese soldiers. They took no prisoners. The Seventh's losses included 27 killed in action, 414 wounded, and 36 missing.[94]

The 1st and 3rd Battalions – the 2nd, which was the division reserve under Lieutenant Colonel Spencer Berger, was fighting alongside the First Marines in the Umurbrogol – spent September 19 resting and rummaging through the Japanese supply dumps in southern Peleliu.

During the interregnum, a Seventh Marines officer catalogued the personal effects of his men who had been killed – everything that they possessed at the time:

Cory: books, a handkerchief, ten cents, and a cat's eye.
Tyson: a razor, a pen, and a wallet.
Ives: a prayer book, wallet, one peso, ten shillings, a key, a razor.
Fisher: letters, a comb, a towel, a sewing kit. Poor son of a bitch.
Silberson: a dictionary, letters, pictures.
Marone: none.[95]

Late on September 19, a communique issued by CINCPAC from Pearl Harbor reported that Marines had killed 5,195 Japanese on Peleliu. Five days later, the total of enemy killed reached 7,020.[96]

The Seventh was ordered on September 20 to move north and take over the First Marines' right flank. On the heels of that order came a new one: Hanneken's regiment was to relieve the remnants of the First Regiment's 1st and 2nd Battalions.[97]

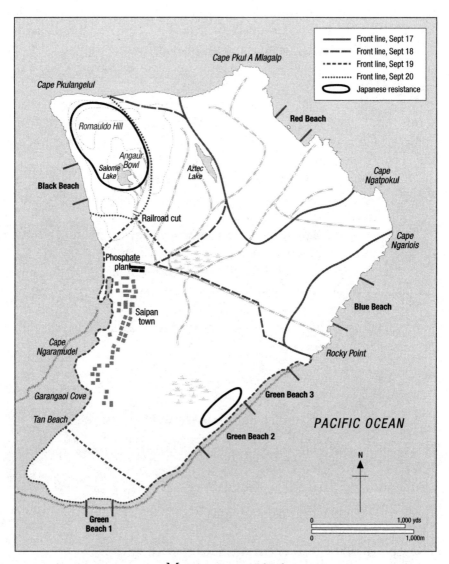

MAP 5: Angaur Island

Chapter 7

Combat on Angaur and Peleliu

*I fully believe that combat with the Japanese at close range in
bad weather is the closest thing to hell on earth that there is.*
Sergeant Brooks Nicklas,
322nd Infantry on Angaur[1]

*Their artillery shells whined and shrieked, accompanied by
the deadly whispering of the mortar shells. We were getting
the first bitter taste of Bloody Nose Ridge.*
Pfc E.B. Sledge, Fifth Marines[2]

The Army's 81st Infantry Division, which was the other division in
Operation *Stalemate*, had not been idle while the Marines were fighting
on Peleliu. On D-Day, elements of the 81st had feigned a landing
on Babelthuap 40 miles north of Peleliu to divert the attention of
the Japanese. The feint was a success: it prevented Japanese troops at
Babelthuap from being sent to reinforce Peleliu.

Afterward, the 81st, nicknamed the Wildcat Division, remained afloat
off Peleliu on September 15 and 16, prepared to land there if the Marines
asked for its assistance. No such request was made; General Rupertus
declared the situation well in hand. Furthermore, he was determined
that his division would capture Peleliu without the Army's help.

The 81st Division was released to carry out its other mission: invading
the island of Angaur 6 miles southwest of Peleliu, in order to build an
airfield for American bombers.

The division had not seen combat since its activation in June 1942. In World War I, the 81st had fought in the Meuse–Argonne campaign. It became the first Army division to wear a shoulder patch – a black wildcat on an olive background – before being deactivated in 1919. The division acquired its nickname from Wildcat Creek at Fort Jackson, South Carolina, where the 81st had trained.

Reactivated at Fort Rucker, Alabama, in 1942, the division underwent desert training in Arizona and then, accompanied by its live mascot, "Tuffy" the wildcat, it underwent amphibious training at Camp San Luis Obispo, California. There, Marine General Holland Smith, who later commanded V Corps during the invasion of Saipan, schooled the soldiers in amphibious warfare doctrine. Jungle warfare training followed in Hawaii. The division was quintessentially American; its soldiers came from every state and U.S. possession. Under General Paul Mueller, the 81st sailed in August 1944 from Hawaii to the Solomon Islands, where it conducted three practice landings at Cape Esperance, Guadalcanal.[3]

Intelligence officers initially estimated that Angaur was defended by 2,500 to 3,000 Japanese soldiers, but the estimate was too high; about 1,400 enemy troops occupied Angaur. Commanded by Major Ushio Goto, they were part of the veteran 15th Infantry Regiment of General Inoue Sadae's 14th Infantry Division – the same 15th Regiment that tenaciously defended southern Peleliu.[4]

Angaur was small – 2½ miles long and about a mile wide – mostly flat, and it was shaped like a pork chop with the bony tip pointing south. It had no coral reef, greatly simplifying amphibious landing operations.

Angaur broiled in the same equatorial heat as Peleliu and, like Peleliu, received 140 inches of rainfall annually. Consequently, riotous undergrowth, tropical rainforest, and swamps covered the island, with the exception of its handful of small towns and Angaur's phosphate mining area. The latter was pitted with depressions and two small lakes – Aztec and Salome. A narrow-gauge railroad linked the mining area to an abandoned phosphate processing plant on Angaur's west coast.

In 1935, Angaur was inhabited by 420 native Palauans, 406 Japanese civilians, and six people labeled as "foreigners" – most of them living in Saipan Town on the western coast. In July and August 1944, about half of the native Micronesians were evacuated to the northern Palau Islands by the Japanese. Left behind to prepare the island for the anticipated American invasion were Goto's battalion, the remaining Angaur natives, and some imported laborers.[5]

Goto's workmen built fortifications all over the island, but they especially concentrated on the southeastern coastline, where Goto believed an amphibious assault was likeliest. Designated Green Beaches 1 and 2 by General Mueller's intelligence officers, they were protected by offshore anti-boat barricades and mines, and numerous pillboxes near the beaches.

After studying the data showing the fortified southeastern coastline, Mueller elected to land his division on Angaur's lightly defended northeastern beaches.

While afloat on September 15 and 16, the 81st awaited orders to either land on Peleliu to support the 1st Division, or to hit Angaur. "As we waited offshore, looking out we could see bodies floating – bodies of dead Marines," said Pfc Ed Frazer of the 317th Artillery Battalion. Expecting to land at any moment, the soldiers did not attempt to retrieve them, Frazer said.[6]

Capturing Angaur, planners believed, would deny the Japanese a stepping stone from which to reinforce Peleliu, while providing the Allies an ideal location for a bomber airfield. B-24 Liberators based on Angaur would be within striking distance of the Philippines and could support General MacArthur's invasion in October.[7]

Major Goto was prepared to employ the new attritional defensive strategy developed in Tokyo in July to defend Angaur. He was determined to make the Allies pay for every hill and gully, every foot of ground. His men would mount well-planned local counterattacks, preferably at night. They would fight from fortified positions farther inland and hide during bombardments.[8]

Goto's men would defend Angaur much like Colonel Nakagawa's troops were defending Peleliu by fighting for every strongpoint before withdrawing to higher ground. However, there was a major difference: Angaur was almost entirely flat, marshy, and clotted with undergrowth and dense jungle. With the exception of Romauldo Hill in the northwestern corner of the island, there were none of Peleliu's ubiquitous jumbled coral-and-limestone hills riddled with caves and laced with sheer-sided cliffs and ravines that might be easily transformed into defensive strongholds.

It would make the 81st Division's task of capturing Angaur easier.

"Fox Day," the code name for D-Day on Angaur, was scheduled for Sunday, September 17. Before dawn, Admiral Jesse Oldendorf's Fire Support battleships, cruisers, and destroyers began bombarding Angaur, followed at 8 a.m. by air strikes on the island's interior by carrier planes.

The assault troops of the 321st, 322nd, and 323rd Regimental Combat Teams (RCTs) breakfasted on pork chops, steak, mashed potatoes, and peas. They then descended into the exhaust-choked cargo areas of their LSTs to board amphibious craft that roared into the open water at 5:30 a.m. They circled for two hours before assembling at the line of departure, 2,500 yards from shore.

Led by seven gunboats firing 20mm and 40mm guns and rockets, landing craft carried the 321st RCT to Blue Beach on eastern Angaur. There being no coral reef to cross, the first of the six waves made landfall at 8:30 a.m. in an array of amphibious vehicles. Six minutes later, the 322nd RCT's first wave, spearheaded by six mortar-firing gunboats, went ashore on Red Beach on the island's northeastern shoulder. Within an hour, 8,000 Wildcats were ashore on Angaur.[9]

The Japanese had expected the blow to fall 2 miles to the south on the Green beaches. As a result, they were able only to meet the invaders with sporadic rifle fire from the thin defenses near the beaches, and with mortar fire from Romauldo Hill.

Casualties were light during the landing. Enemy machine gunners in scattered pillboxes 100 yards from the beach killed a few soldiers before amtanks destroyed the pillboxes.

The reserve regiment, the 323rd RCT, feinted toward the code-named Black beaches on Angaur's west coast, but did not land. Barring a disaster on Angaur, the 323rd would soon be given another assignment elsewhere in the Caroline Islands.[10]

Armored bulldozers cut trails through the dense rainforest, enabling the 321st to advance slowly through sniper fire. With spikes and ropes, camouflaged snipers had climbed high into the towering trees. Other snipers fired on the Americans from the roots beneath the huge trees, while machine gunners in bunkers concealed by foliage raked the Wildcats.

The 322nd made better progress pushing westward across northern Angaur; there were fewer defenders but more rugged terrain than in the 321st's sector.

After moving inland, the 321st turned south – toward the strongly defended southeastern Green beaches where Goto had expected the invaders to land.[11] The 321st was ably led by Colonel Robert Dark, who had been commissioned from the enlisted ranks during World War I. During the Great War, he led an infantry company before commanding a battalion of the 4th Division through four major campaigns. Cited for bravery in action, Dark remained in the Army after the war, steadily rising through the ranks until he was assigned to command the 321st Regiment.[12]

As it advanced southward toward the Green beaches, the 321st ran into Goto's in-depth defensive system of caves, bunkers, and pillboxes, each one supporting fortifications nearby. The Americans attacked with BARs, demolitions, bazookas, and flamethrowers. They struggled through heavy sniper fire to capture Rocky Point near the northernmost enemy-held beach before stopping and digging in.

That night, enemy soldiers attempted to infiltrate a 1,000-yard gap between the 321st and 322nd RCTs, but they did not break through.

It was the 81st's first night on a hostile shore, and the inexperienced infantrymen not only had to cope with infiltrators, but with some of the local fauna. Noisily scuttling in the darkness were huge land crabs "about the size of a pretty good dinner plate," said Sergeant John Climie. Frequently mistaken for infiltrators, the crabs drew a large part of the nervous soldiers' gunfire.[13]

At 5 a.m., a Japanese mortar barrage smashed into the command post of the 321st's 1st Battalion near Rocky Point, wounding the battalion commander, Lieutenant Colonel Lester Evans, and four staff officers. Then, 200 Japanese soldiers shouting, "Get up, Joe!" and supported by light machine guns and knee mortars, which were in fact grenade launchers, launched a counterattack against Evans's battalion. Hardest hit was "B" Company, the 321st reserve. It repelled two attacks as it pulled back 75 yards. At dawn, Navy planes bombed and strafed the Japanese. "B" repulsed a third attack at 9:35 a.m.[14]

Initially thought to be an attempt to roll up the Blue landing beach, the attack in fact was a diversion. The 321st discovered this later in the morning, when bulldozer tanks carved an approach to the Green beaches and found only vacant defensive positions. During the night, Major Goto's men had slipped out of southern Angaur and marched through the jungle to Romauldo Hill in the island's northwestern corner. They got out just in time, before the Americans could block their avenue of retreat.

On Romauldo Hill, Goto intended to make his last stand.[15]

Advancing with his company along the now undefended southeastern beaches, Pfc Keith Axelson saw his first dead Japanese soldier. He had been blown in half, "legs to the right of me, torso and head on the left. His body appeared to be standing in a foxhole. I was lying on his viscera, still connected to both body parts." The Wildcats seized enemy documents in the empty defensive works revealing that Japanese leaders had known for weeks about Angaur's impending invasion.[16]

After discovering that the Japanese had abandoned southern Angaur, the 321st and 322nd turned north in pursuit. About 2 p.m. on the 18th, the 322nd was marching to the phosphate plant northeast of Saipan Town when U.S. carrier planes bombed and strafed its 3rd Battalion. The friendly fire killed seven soldiers and wounded 46 others.[17]

Friendly fire deaths were not so rare that they were automatically cause for official inquiries, and they were commoner than might be supposed, especially in units new to combat that were prone to mistakes and miscommunication. In fact, the previous night, the 321st's 2nd Battalion reported 19 friendly fire casualties from short rounds fired by the 316th Field Artillery Battery. Four of the wounded men later died. By day's end on September 18, the 81st Division reported losses of 22 killed and 177 wounded – about one-third of them felled by friendly fire.[18]

At 7:30 a.m. on September 19, the 321st and 322nd began a drive to capture the entire northern half of Angaur, including Saipan Town, Middle Village, and Romauldo Hill. The 322nd seized Shrine and Polomas Hills as part of a plan to envelop Romauldo Hill. Polomas Hill became an observation post.

Above a 50-yard-long railroad cut, the 322nd's 3rd Battalion ascended a ridge that overlooked shallow Salome Lake, nestled in a bowl that covered a 400-by-450-yard area. On every side of the bowl steep coral cliffs cloaked in dense jungle growth rose 100 feet or more. This was Angaur Bowl, the site of the former phosphate strip mine – and defended by hundreds of Goto's remaining men.[19]

The 81st sent three M8 75mm self-propelled guns through the railroad cut on the western side of the bowl. An enemy mine and 75mm gunfire disabled the first two M8s. Japanese mortars and machine guns raked the 322nd's 2nd Battalion as it entered the bowl. Nonetheless, a reconnaissance platoon managed to launch rubber boats on Salome Lake, circle to its northern shore, and knock out the 75mm gun. Intensive enemy gunfire forced the battalion to withdraw before nightfall to its previous position near the phosphate plant.[20]

The next morning, preparatory to an infantry attack into the bowl, the artillery pounded the area for an hour, followed by air strikes by carrier planes that strafed and dropped napalm, and then by another, 30-minute artillery barrage.

When the 2nd Battalion attacked at 8 a.m., it discovered that Goto's men had occupied the railroad cut overnight. The Japanese had barricaded the entrance into Angaur Bowl with the two disabled M8s and set them on fire. The Wildcats towed away the M8s, and three Sherman tanks rolled into Angaur Bowl, where they were pelted by sheets of enemy gunfire from every side of the bowl. At nightfall, the tanks and infantry once more withdrew through the cut to their previous night's positions.[21]

Despite strong resistance at Angaur Bowl and Romauldo Hill firmly in enemy hands, late on September 20 General Paul Mueller pronounced Angaur Island to be secured. Goto's diehards, however, remained committed to fighting to the death.

Yet, Mueller's declaration resulted in Angaur's naval gunfire support warships departing to join the Third Fleet for the Philippines invasion. Moreover, engineers could now begin building the bomber airfield on southern Angaur.

The 322nd RCT was given the assignment of destroying Goto's last holdouts. The regiment would soon be the only 81st Division unit remaining on Angaur. The 321st would be sent to Peleliu to reinforce the Marines, while the 323rd RCT, which had been held in reserve, was given an altogether different mission: on September 20, Admiral William Halsey ordered the 323rd to invade Ulithi Atoll.[22]

Ulithi was a chain of 30 islets ringed by coral reefs in the western Carolines. It lay 380 miles northeast of Peleliu and midway between Guam and Peleliu. At the center of the serpentine atoll was a deep, 209-square-mile lagoon – large enough to accommodate the entire Third Fleet. The Navy coveted it as a prospective forward naval base for operations against the Philippines.

General Julian Smith, *Stalemate's* expeditionary commander, believed that it was risky to send away *Stalemate's* reserve regiment with the campaign just a week old. His objection was brushed aside, and the Ulithi operation proceeded.[23]

The 323rd invaded Ulithi on September 23, "Jig Day." No shots were fired; the invaders met no opposition, only friendly Micronesians. The Japanese garrison had decamped to Yap after American carrier strikes struck the island chain in March and April. "We were pleasantly surprised to find that the Japanese had pulled out," said Pfc John Hirsch, who went ashore on Falalop Island, one of the five atolls where landings were made.[24]

By October 1, two carrier groups had dropped anchor at Ulithi. Soon afterward, Seabees expanded and improved the existing airstrip on Falalop Island and began work on an advanced fleet base capable of accommodating more than 700 vessels. The base eventually encompassed a recreation center, a 100-bed hospital, and other amenities.[25]

The 323rd remained on Ulithi until October 10, when some of its units left for Peleliu. By that time, the 321st RCT was involved in the fierce battle for the Umurbrogol.[26]

Angaur had been pronounced secured, but this did not mitigate the fighting on Romauldo Hill in the island's northwestern corner, where Goto's men defended rugged coral ridges that resembled Peleliu's.

On September 22, companies "E," "G," and "C" of Colonel Benjamin Venable's 322nd Regiment made a third attempt to enter Angaur Bowl through the western railroad cut, now nicknamed "Bloody Gulch." Tanks from the 710th Tank Battalion and mortars from the 88th Chemical Weapons Battalion supported the creeping attack, knocking out one Japanese position after another. Enemy gunfire killed two men and wounded 35, and a ricocheting antitank round injured Colonel Venable and killed his radio operator. Late in the day, the 322nd again withdrew through the cut for the night.

Rugged terrain had discouraged consideration of any attempt to enter the bowl from the east, so two companies were sent northward along Black Beach, where the 323rd had feigned a landing on Fox Day, to reconnoiter the island's western side.[27]

On the 24th, during another attack into Angaur Bowl, the 322nd pushed northward past Salome Lake, but withdrew again that night after losing 18 killed and 75 wounded. Five frontal attacks on Angaur Bowl had failed to dislodge the several hundred remaining defenders from their entrenched positions. Goto's small defending force was ably preventing a superior force from overwhelming it.

The frustrated Americans now attempted to advance from the east and northeast while broadcasting a surrender appeal. Two Japanese came forward and surrendered. The captives helpfully pointed out the Japanese strongpoints and described the types of weapons used to defend them. They told the Americans that about 300 Japanese troops remained alive and combat-capable.[28]

The 322nd's engineers bulldozed a new road from the northeast, and on September 26, the 3rd Battalion advanced to the eastern rim of Angaur Bowl without a single casualty. The 1st and 2nd Battalions closed in on the bowl from the south and northeast. Upon entering the bowl itself, with flamethrowers and satchel charges the Wildcats knocked out enemy positions in the tall cliffs. For the first time since reaching Angaur Bowl, the Wildcats did not withdraw to their previous night's positions; they dug in and repulsed a counterattack as heavy rain began to fall.

Three days later, on September 29, rain was still pouring down. But after suffering more than 100 additional casualties, the 322nd had tightened its grip on Angaur Bowl, and extended its lines to block the escape routes from Ronauldo Hill.

American soldiers continued to die in the downpours.

On Black Beach, "C" Company waged a vicious firefight against a Japanese stronghold. "Mortars were being shot practically straight up, that's how close we were to them," recalled Herman Soblick. "We were able to get our wounded out with the mortars and smoke grenades. The BAR man, his assistant, our squad leader, and the assistant squad leader were all killed."[29]

On another patrol to Black Beach, Soblick and his comrades targeted Japanese holed up in cliffside caves. Holding onto a tree,

Soblick climbed a cliff to gain access to one of the caves. He was startled when an enemy soldier crawled from a cave into the same tree. When Soblick shot the Japanese in the leg, the man blew himself up with a grenade.[30]

Snipers targeted "G" Company's command post, killing the commanding officer and six other men, cutting the CP phone line, and shooting repair crews. "G" lost nine men to sniper fire. "I fully believe that combat with the Japanese at close range in bad weather is the closest thing to hell on earth that there is," said Sergeant Brooks Nicklas of "G" Company.[31]

Goto's remnants made their last stand on Romauldo Hill, a rugged, oval-shaped hill covering an area 500 yards by 150 yards. Enemy snipers hid in the rocks and picked off soldiers. Every movement was filled with extreme peril. Sergeant Nicklas said snipers had a spot covered that his men had to cross to connect with "F" Company. "Anybody that tried to go to the other side was shot," Nicklas said. The snipers killed a BAR man, took his weapon, and rifled his pockets. A staff sergeant was wounded in the arm, and a medic was shot in the head when he went to the sergeant's aid. The sergeant was shot again and later died.[32]

The soldiers found that showing leniency toward the enemy could backfire. James Fitzgerald of "E" Company spotted a Japanese soldier cowering in a hole and was about to shoot him when his lieutenant stopped him. "That night he [the prisoner] broke out and killed three of our men before committing suicide," Fitzgerald said.[33]

On September 30, two battalions from the 322nd attacked and captured an approach ridge to Romauldo. The next morning, all three of the 322nd's battalions resumed the attack. The ensuing chaotic battle was fought in a maze of ridges, defiles, and sheer cliffs, with snipers everywhere. The Japanese fought back with machine guns. They dropped grenades on the Americans from cliffs and caves.

The terrain isolated units from one another. "You had no idea what the next squad was doing, or the next platoon, or the company commander, or what, you had no idea," said Kenneth Anderson.[34]

All the while, the regiment tightened its noose around the Romauldo Hill defenders; there was no place for the Japanese to go.

Concluding that further infantry attacks would be futile, regimental leaders shifted from assault to siege tactics. Heavy weapons were moved close to the battle line to pound the enemy caves and fortifications, sometimes at point-blank range. Fire teams then moved in to finish the job with satchel charges, flamethrowers, and rifle fire.

The trapped Japanese deliberately wounded Americans to lure others to their aid – and then killed the medics and litter-bearers. So many medics were shot that those still alive removed their red cross insignia. The badges of their noncombatant status had become bullseyes for Japanese snipers. Japan had never signed the Geneva Conventions, and Japanese infantrymen, sailors, and pilots routinely ignored their provisions.

"A report came that so many of our medics had been hit or killed when crawling up into the hills to drag back fellows who had been wounded or killed that they needed men from our outfit who would replace the medics," said Sergeant Ray Melheim of the 316th Field Artillery. After dark, night patrols went into the ridges to retrieve dead comrades who could not be reached during the daytime because of enemy gunfire.[35]

On October 6, the 322nd zeroed in on Major Goto's headquarters with infantry attacks, and shelled it with 155mm guns and 105mm and 81mm mortars, often firing directly into caves. Two days later, 87 starving Micronesians – Goto's laborers – emerged from caves in the ridges and surrendered, and the next day 89 more came out.

"Every woman that was old enough was pregnant," said Elzie Brown of the 2nd Battalion's Headquarters Company. The Navy cared for the women in a big tent. "Babies were born one right after the other," said Brown. "Those Japanese got every one of them pregnant, all those that were old enough."[36]

The siege squeezed the pocket to the size of a football field by October 19. On that day, 37 Japanese soldiers were killed, while the 322nd lost four killed and ten wounded from enemy counterattacks that became progressively feebler.

The Wildcats spent the days sniping in the ridges. "We would go up in the rocks early in the morning and stay there all day, searching with telescopes and field glasses all through the rocks for any Japs that might move," said Sergeant Nicklas of "G" Company. "It was much like being in a deer stand all day, only searching for a different target."[37]

About this time, B-24 Liberators began successfully flying missions from Angaur's new bomber airstrip during the daytime. The key objective had been achieved.

A Japanese prisoner subsequently told his American captors that Goto had ordered his surviving band to slip through the American lines to the seashore, build a raft, and escape. However, no raft was built, and there was no escape.

The battle for Angaur ended on October 23. The 81st reported having killed 1,338 enemy troops, including Major Goto, who died in one of the last counterattacks. A mere 59 enemy soldiers were captured. The 81st Division had lost 264 killed and 1,354 wounded. An additional 940 men were treated for non-battle injuries, illness, and combat fatigue.

With American battle and non-battle casualties amounting to nearly twice the number of enemy losses, the Japanese attritional defensive strategy appeared to have been successful on Angaur. Marine General O.P. Smith, the 1st Division's assistant commander, said of the Army's losses on Angaur, "This methodical business doesn't always pay off."[38]

While the 81st Division's campaign on Angaur was winding down, there was no letup in the savage fighting still being waged on Peleliu.

After seizing Peleliu's airfield, the 1st Marine Division's Fifth Regiment led by Colonel Harold "Bucky" Harris turned east to carry out its mission of securing the eastern half of Peleliu. Skirting the base of the Umurbrogol, the Fifth's 3rd Battalion advanced toward the north-south thoroughfare known as the East Road.

From the highlands, the Japanese commanded a panoramic view of the Marines and their movements, and they took advantage of it. "Their artillery shells whined and shrieked, accompanied by the deadly whispering of the mortar shells," wrote Pfc E.B. Sledge of the Fifth's 3rd Battalion. "We were getting the first bitter taste of Bloody Nose Ridge." The Japanese appeared to fire only when they expected to inflict multiple casualties, and stopped firing when the opportunity passed, noted Sledge, who was impressed by their fire discipline.*[39]

That night, Japanese loudspeakers blared, "Marine, you die tonight."[40]

Meanwhile, on September 17, Major Gordon Gayle's 2nd Battalion pushed across the low ground east of the Umurbrogol, hacking through

*Marine Corps regulations forbade Marines to keep diaries, but Eugene Sledge jotted notes in the pocket New Testament issued by the military during World War II; "Death Ridges" video.

dense underbrush in a skirmish line toward the Ngardololok peninsula, one of Peleliu's lobster claws. The punishing heat was "our worst enemy," a Marine wrote. Heat prostration cases soared, and frequent rest breaks had to be taken. "Thousands of branches pull at our equipment, beg for our weapons, and grope at our clothing," wrote Pfc Sterling Mace of the tedious, nerve-wracking passage through the jungle, swamps, and towering mangrove stands bathed in dim crepuscular light.[41] The undergrowth was so thick that the Marines killed three Japanese snipers who were unable to raise their rifles to defend themselves because of the dense vegetation.[42]

A road over a 300-yard causeway led to Ngardololok village, a Japanese radio direction finder station, and Purple Beach. Although he believed that Peleliu's western beaches would be the likeliest place for the Americans to come ashore, Colonel Nakagawa had hedged his bets and assigned a battalion to defend Purple Beach in the event that it, too, was targeted.

Purple Beach's formidable defenses, which faced seaward and featured mines and tank traps, were never tested. After D-Day, the Japanese troops defending Purple Beach were withdrawn into the Umurbrogol.

Gayle's battalion began crossing the undefended causeway to the Ngardololok peninsula during the morning of September 18. Although it appeared that the village had been abandoned, Gayle called in an air strike on its ruined buildings as a precaution.

Instead of hitting the village, the Navy planes strafed Gayle's "F" Company as it was crossing the causeway. Then, "E" Company was hit by a "friendly" artillery concentration on the causeway approaches, and was bombarded by friendly mortar fire on the causeway itself. The battalion reported 34 casualties for the day, nearly all of them inflicted by friendly fire.[43]

Pfc James Isabelle was livid with rage after seeing friendly fire kill four of his comrades and wound several others. "I wanted to go shoot those artillery guys... It really shook me up... It was an accident, it wasn't deliberate, but I had that anger."[44]

Two 3rd Battalion companies also went over the causeway and set up a command post before dark. They organized a 40-man combat patrol to push to the east coast along Peleliu's smaller lobster claw. A war dog and its handler ranged ahead to alert the Marines to potential ambushes.[45]

Gunnery Sergeant Elmo Haney volunteered to accompany the patrol. Remarkably, the 46-year-old Arkansan's service dated to World War I, and he had also fought in the Banana Wars of the 1920s and 1930s. He landed with the 1st Marine Division at Guadalcanal, and he was awarded the Silver Star on Cape Gloucester. Haney belonged to the Fifth Marines' "K" Company, but like some experienced, long-serving Marine noncommissioned officers – for instance, Gunnery Sergeant Lou Diamond, the unconventional Guadalcanal mortarman – Haney was a "floater" with no assigned place in the company hierarchy.

Haney was small-boned, lean, hard, muscular – and eccentric in the extreme. He was an object of endless curiosity to the young Marines nearly 30 years his junior with whom he served. They enjoyed observing his thrice daily routine of meticulously cleaning his M1 rifle on the ship's fantail while talking quietly to himself and then performing bayonet drills – thrusting, parrying, and butt-stroking the air. He fit Captain John W. Thomason's description of the archetypical "Old Breed" Marine: someone "with drilled shoulders and a bone-deep sunburn, and a tolerant scorn of nearly everything on earth."[46]

Several sailors asked Pfc E.B. Sledge, a "K" Company comrade of Haney's, if Haney had gone "Asiatic," implying that he might be deranged. When Sledge mischievously replied that Haney was typical of the men in his outfit, "they would stare at me as they had at Haney."[47]

Haney and the patrol slogged through dense undergrowth and swamps where huge man-o-war birds glowered at them from their nests high in the mangroves. The Marines dug in near an abandoned enemy bunker, ate their rations, checked their weapons, and received the password for the night.

All of the Marine passwords contained the letter "L," which the Japanese had difficulty pronouncing; they often pronounced "Ls" as "Rs," and could be tripped up by tricky passwords. During a two-week period on Peleliu, the division passwords were Belleau Wood, Bull Run, Waterloo, Guadalcanal, Tulagi, Vella Lavella, Valley Forge, Stalingrad, Lexington, El Alamein, Bougainville, Pearl Harbor, Manila, and Sicily.[48]

During the night, Haney several times crept from position to position in the inky darkness, demanding to be told the password. His nerves evidently were frayed by the heavy silence that was broken only by the sounds made by jungle animals.[49]

Then a cry shattered the quiet. "Help! Help! Oh God, help me!"

It was the war dog handler.

Fearful that the handler's cries would alert the Japanese to their location, the Marines attempted to silence him. They first tried to reassure him. When that didn't work, they pinned him to the ground.

He screamed louder. "Help me, dog! The Japs have got me! The Japs have got me and they're gonna throw me in the ocean!"

Someone punched him in the jaw, but the blow had no effect. A corpsman gave him several doses of morphine, hoping that it would calm him. But he continued to bellow in terror. He had lost his mind.

"Hit him with the flat of that entrenching tool!" boomed a voice from the command post.

There was a loud clang, and the shouting stopped. But the man was dead.[50]

In the morning, the platoon leader contacted battalion headquarters and said the patrol needed to come out; the men's nerves were shot. A relief patrol and a tank arrived a short time later. The dead dog handler was loaded onto the tank. Accompanied by the first patrol, the tank retraced its route through the jungle and swamp.

"None of us was proud of it," wrote Corporal R.V. Burgin, but "we'd done what we had to do." The Marines never discussed the incident among themselves, and their superior officers did not question them about it. "The strange thing is that the Doberman was silent during the whole deal," wrote Burgin.[51]

It was not long afterward that Haney withdrew himself from the front lines, conceding that he could no longer stand the heat or the rigors of combat.[52]

————

Purple Beach became an American strongpoint. Ironically, it had been built by the Japanese to repel American landings, but it now was a bulwark against Japanese counter-landings. It also served as a rest area for exhausted assault units.

The Fifth Marines made the former Japanese headquarters on Ngardololok its regimental headquarters. The Japanese had adorned the area with ornamental gates, rock gardens, and goldfish ponds. All of these decorative flourishes were dispensed with during the Marines' occupation.[53]

The Fifth Marines went on to methodically seize the small islands off northeast Peleliu's coast – "Island A" and Ngabad Island were the first ones captured – without meeting any opposition.[54]

After completing their initial assignment of landing and supporting Marines on the beachhead, amtracs and amtanks became essential resupply and infantry support vehicles. Rupertus and *Stalemate*'s planners had not intended to use them in this manner on Peleliu, although other Marine divisions had already begun to utilize armored landing craft in these ways.

However, company and battalion commanders on Peleliu swiftly integrated the armored, steel tread-equipped amphibians into their tactical operations, and they became indispensable. Some of the amtracs were equipped with the Navy Mark-1 version of the Canadian Ronson flamethrower and could scorch enemy targets 75 to 150 yards away. Those firing a gasoline-oil mixture could spew flames for 55 seconds, while those using napalm could burn for 80 seconds. Both were effective in destroying the vegetation that concealed firing ports, and then incinerating the enemy soldiers inside.[55]

Resupplying the Fifth and Seventh Marines in eastern Peleliu from the southwestern beaches meant crossing the airfield. Before Marine infantrymen neutralized Japanese firing positions in the southern Umurbrogol, the amtracs zigzagged across the airstrips at top speed to avoid enemy fire. The crewmen nicknamed the airfield "Mortar Valley" and their resupply mission "The Purple Heart Run."[56]

Radio operator Kenneth Harrell's fraught service on Peleliu ended on September 19. On D-Day, his amtrac had been hit by artillery fire, and he had bailed into the water and crawled over the coral reef, which shredded his clothing and bloodied his knees and legs. Assigned to another amtrac, Harrell helped support the Fifth Marines – until an enemy infiltrator stabbed him in the belly; the bayonet was not attached to a rifle, but to a long stick. Harrell was evacuated to a hospital ship. His relatively brief service on Peleliu was not unusual for Marines who were sent into combat areas each day.[57]

Four hundred Naval Construction Battalion troops – better-known as Seabees – had landed on D-Day with the object of making the airfield operational, but their construction equipment remained offshore on LSTs for days. Until their gear could be landed, the Seabees volunteered as stretcher-carriers. Twenty-four Seabees became casualties while evacuating wounded men from the battlefield.

When the 33rd and 73rd Seabees eventually began clearing the airfield of mines under sporadic sniper fire, they counted 130 derelict Japanese planes; they had been destroyed or heavily damaged during the U.S. air attacks in March. Amid the wreckage, the Seabees found a new model of the "Betty" medium bomber and a previously unknown medium bomber that became known as the "Frances."[58]

Lieutenant Charles McCandless, dispatched to Peleliu in early October to help the late-arriving 71st Seabees extend a runway across a swamp, was struck by the island's tatterdemalion appearance. "The whole vista was like a scene from the *Inferno*," he wrote, framed by "topless, shattered, burned out palm trees." On the ridges rising from the airstrip's northern side, he saw cave entrances ringed by the black soot residue left by flamethrowers. Over the ridges rose a wall of gray-black smoke from northern Peleliu, where battles continued to rage.

That night, McCandless was kept awake by the concussive blast of nearby howitzers shelling the other side of the island. "Once in a while enemy guns returned the gunfire, knocking down trees, starting fires, and creating more craters on the airstrip." Above the ridges, "I could see the red-orange glare of fire and hear the rumble of war-like continuous thunder."

The next day, while surveying the projected path of the runway extension across the swamp, McCandless and his party were suddenly set upon by about 50 shrieking Japanese soldiers. The Seabees and their escort of more than a dozen Marines armed with Thompson submachine guns wiped them out to the last man. McCandless himself killed two attackers with his .45-caliber pistol.[59]

Weeks earlier, two artillery spotter planes had landed at the airfield. They were the first arrivals of Captain Wallace Slappey's seven "Bird Dog" observation planes of VMO-3. Soon after taxiing to a stop on September 18, the "Piperschmidts" and "Messercubs" began identifying targets for the Eleventh Marines' artillery regiment and the III Amphibious Corps's 155mm howitzer battalion.

That same day, September 18, a Navy carrier plane made an emergency landing on the potholed airstrip when its engine lost power during a strafing mission over the Umurbrogol. On the 20th, the Seabees' construction equipment arrived, and airstrip improvements proceeded rapidly. The Seabees completed rudimentary runway repairs with bulldozers and road rollers despite being sporadically harassed by Japanese mortar and artillery fire.

Eight night-fighters arrived on September 24, and more warplanes began landing every day. By the end of September, the 24 "white-nosed" Corsairs of VMF-114, known as "The Death Dealers," were operating from the airfield under the command of Major Robert Stout – nicknamed "Cowboy" because he had grown up on a ranch near Fort Laramie, Wyoming.

The Death Dealers' insignia was a hand severed at the wrist that featured the legendary Wild Bill Hickock's "Death Hand" – the cards he had been dealt when he was killed in Deadwood, South Dakota: two aces, a four, and two eights. The two aces and the four spelled out the Death Dealers' squadron number.

While flying with the Cactus Air Force on Guadalcanal, Stout became an ace and won the Navy Cross.[*] From Peleliu, he led his high-spirited pilots on numerous missions against Babelthuap Island 30 miles north of Peleliu, looking for landing barges to destroy. The pilots were sometimes attired in Japanese flying helmets lined with rabbit fur, and "zoot suits" captured by Marine infantrymen from Japanese caves and then sold to the pilots.

The gull-wing Vought F4U Corsair, the first U.S. warplane to exceed 400 mph by virtue of its large Pratt & Whitney engine, debuted in 1943 in the Solomons, where it quickly gained air supremacy over the vaunted Japanese Zero. Originally designed as a carrier-based fighter-bomber, the Corsair had been eclipsed by the slower but more carrier-friendly Grumman F6F Hellcat.

The Corsair instead replaced the F4F Wildcat as the mainstay of Marine Corps land-based operations – famously in the Solomons in 1943 as the fighter plane of Major Gregory "Pappy" Boyington's "Black Sheep Squadron."[60]

When VMF-114 arrived on Peleliu on September 26, howitzers were firing on the ridges, and "Peleliu looked to us like it was on a

_____

[*]Stout would not survive the war, perishing in early 1945 when his plane was struck by antiaircraft fire over Koror.

planet in another universe," wrote Lieutenant Glenn Daniel. "Almost all of the trees had been blown to shreds or splintered into pieces. The surface, nothing but coral rock, was also blown apart... In the distance, stretcher-bearers were trying to bring dead and wounded Marines down the coral precipices."[61]

During the squadron's first bombing run over the Umurbrogol on September 29, Stout's pilots dropped 1,000-pound bombs. A week later, the munitions were 265-gallon tanks of napalm.

The airfield's proximity to the Umurbrogol made for short bomb runs: from takeoff to target took just 15 seconds. "We hold the record for the shortest bombing hop in history," said Lieutenant Bill Cantrell. "It was eleven hundred yards from takeoff to target and our ground crew could stand out like cheerleaders at a football game and yell for us." The Corsairs often didn't even bother to raise their landing gear. Delayed fuses gave the pilots enough time to escape from their bomb blasts.[62]

For the first time since the Solomon Islands campaigns, Marine fighters were used to conduct multiple strafing and steep-angle precision bombing missions against cave positions. Infantrymen marked the cave openings with circles of smoke, with the center denoting the entrance, and the outer circle signifying the Marines' positions. "Out of necessity we became very precise," said Lieutenant Daniel.[63]

Air operations steadily expanded. In October, more Marine fighter squadrons from the Second Marine Air Wing joined VMF-114 on Peleliu: VMF-121, and VMF-122; a squadron of 15 night-fighting F6F Grummans, VMF(N)-541; and a squadron of Navy Avenger torpedo bombers for anti-submarine patrols.

The day after the arrival of VMO-3 on September 18, Colonel Harold "Bucky" Harris went up in a Piperschmidt with Captain Slappey. Harris wanted to look over the Umurbrogol, which his Fifth Marines would soon take their turn in assaulting.

At 41, Harris was the youngest of Rupertus's three regimental commanders. He grew up outside Laramie, Wyoming, and graduated with the Naval Academy Class of 1925. During the 1920s, he was wounded while fighting the Sandinistas in Nicaragua, and he was later posted to Tientsin, China.

Regarded by his superiors as "something of an intellectual," Harris was selected to attend the prestigious École Supérieure de Guerre in

Paris in 1938–39. At Cape Gloucester, he was executive officer of Colonel Puller's First Regiment. Then, just before Operation *Stalemate*, Harris became commander of the Fifth Marines when Colonel William Fellers was incapacitated by malaria.[64]

Of his flight with Captain Slappey over Peleliu's highlands, now shorn of vegetation by American artillery and naval gunfire, Harris said, "I was appalled by the sight of those ridges from the air." It was a desolate landscape, he wrote: "sheer coral walls, with caves everywhere, box canyons, crevices, rock-strewn cliffs, and all defended by well-hidden Japs." It was obvious that there could be no sudden breakthrough from the south against such a formidable defense in depth, Harris concluded.[65]

Harris met with Rupertus and Puller to brief them on what he had seen. He told them that attacking the Umurbrogol from the north could be more productive and result in fewer casualties. Go up with Slappey to see for yourselves, Harris urged them. But Rupertus and Puller smiled and said, "they had their maps," shrugging off Harris's recommendations. They continued to order attacks on the highlands from the south.[66]

Harris's reconnaissance flight had convinced him that he would be wasting his men's lives by continuing to attack such seemingly unassailable positions frontally. He resolved to be "lavish with ordnance and stingy with men's lives" – by first softening up his regiment's objectives with artillery, air strikes using napalm, and naval gunfire.

His newfound prudence would place him at odds with the aggressive, impatient Rupertus, who believed that only by sustaining forward momentum would the Marines conquer Peleliu.[67]

Chapter 8

The Destruction of the First Marines

*As the first tremendous rain of bullets hit us, you could feel
more than see as people dropped around you.*
Lieutenant Bruce Watkins,
First Marines[1]

*What once had been companies in the First Marines looked
like platoons; platoons looked like squads. I saw few officers.*
Pfc E.B. Sledge's description of the regiment
as it descended from the ridges[2]

Northeast of Bloody Nose Ridge, Hill 100 loomed over the East Road
and two nearby swamps. "C" Company of the First Marines was
assigned to capture it on September 19 to give the Marines a foothold
in Peleliu's eastern Umurbrogol. Other units planned to simultaneously
try to crack Hill 300 west of Hill 100, and the Five Sisters.

The First Marines' companies had been whittled down to shadows
of their landing-day strength. At 9:02 a.m., "F" Company reported,
"I have approximately 60 men left and four officers, including myself.
Lieutenant Russo has three pieces of shrapnel in his back. Maples has
been wounded in the shoulder." Despite "F"'s severe losses from a
landing force of 235 men, the company commander ended his report
with a defiant coda: "We are still in the fight."[3]

After the fighting moved into the ridges, the Battle of Peleliu had
become a succession of localized engagements waged by small infantry

units. Company-size attacks targeted cave and pillbox strongholds. Each presented a unique problem requiring a degree of improvisation. The Marines' toolbox included combat engineers and their dynamite and plastic explosives; flamethrowers; satchel charges; bazookas and mortars; and field guns. But the essential weapon was always the Marine rifleman.[4]

On *Stalemate*'s fifth day, scorching-hot, evil-smelling, 12-square-mile Peleliu teemed with 45,000 combatants: Marines, naval personnel, and enemy defenders.

The First Marines' objective on September 19 – the Five Sisters and Hill 300 – presented a thick east-west barrier to movement into the Umurbrogol. The ridges rose from the north side of the airstrip like a rampart, the rock face "flat as if it had been cleft by a giant axe," wrote one Marine. The five peaks barred the way north through Peleliu's highlands.

Here lay some of the Umurbrogol's most daunting defenses: cave complexes with overlapping fields of fire from artillery, mortar, and machine-gun emplacements. Steeply plunging ravines separated each sheer-sided "Sister" from its neighbor, vastly complicating the task of capturing the heights. Moreover, their ascent at times required alpine climbing equipment.[5]

From their fortified caves inside the Sisters, Japanese snipers and machine-gun crews were able to reach the summits through interior shafts fitted with ladders, and over prepared paths. Artillery and mortar fire and air strikes did not discernibly reduce the enemy resistance.

It was no easy matter guiding air strikes to their targets in such a small area. Lieutenant Clifford West, the First Regiment's air controller, said, "If you had planes coming in, you never knew whether they were your planes or not," because other controllers were calling in strikes at the same time. During his two weeks with the First Marines, West operated in an area of less than a square mile. "You could never identify your strike coming in," and he had no way to directly contact the pilots from the ground; air controllers at the Peleliu airstrip assigned the missions.[6]

Hill 300, the assigned objective of Lieutenant Colonel Spencer Berger's 2nd Battalion of the Seventh Marines, lay between Hill 100 and the

Five Sisters and guarded the entrance to the U-shaped valley known as the Horseshoe. Another series of ridges, nicknamed the Five Brothers, rose north of the entryway to the Horseshoe.

The attack on September 19 proceeded slowly and tortuously over the rough terrain, which impeded the visibility of the attackers while affording the defenders optimal views of the advancing Marines. Shells and bullets rained down from the hill mass with an unbroken rumble and crackle.

In Berger's opinion, the 300 yards that his battalion gained on this day "was a miracle," although on division maps the achievement appeared miniscule. Berger's battalion reported 87 casualties, including 16 men killed.[7]

By 11 a.m., Lieutenant Colonel Russell Honsowetz's 2nd Battalion of the First Marines was moving toward the center of the Five Sisters' forbidding wall of peaks, which were honeycombed with caves and fortified firing positions. Thundering mortar fire stopped the advance in its tracks.

In short order, "E" Company reported that it had just one effective squad left on the battlefield due to exhaustion and heat prostration. "We need more men to continue the advance," the battalion CP radioed regimental headquarters, and the First Marines' depleted 1st Battalion, held in reserve during the 2nd Battalion's initial attack, was sent forward.

Japanese gunfire coming from caves in the Sisters' interior faces pinned down the assault companies. Relays of enemy snipers and machine gunners moved through tunnels from one firing position to another. They also climbed from the caves to the peaks' summits. From atop the Sisters they were able to fire on every approach. The Japanese, in effect, held a master class on how a few defenders could thwart a superior force.

Throughout the assault, U.S. artillery and mortar fire and air strikes pounded the peaks, but the avalanche of metal appeared to have no effect. "It was just like throwing a handful of BBs against the wall for all the good it was doing," said one discouraged observer.[8]

Even concentrated artillery fire aimed at a single Japanese gun emplacement too often was unable to knock it out. At midday on the 19th, Colonel Puller's regimental headquarters reported that 900 rounds of 105mm and 155mm ammunition had been fired at a position identified on maps as 141U. Yet the Japanese gun in the position continued to fire back. A Marine officer said thousands of rounds of 75mm shells were fired at a single cave 200 yards in front of the First Marines "without disturbing anything appreciably below the foliage and topsoil."

Despite accumulating evidence to the contrary, Rupertus and Puller obstinately believed that a breakthrough was imminent. They insisted that the attack continue.[9]

A survivor of the futile assault told a friend in the Fifth Marines that the Marines made "frontal attacks with fixed bayonets on that damn ridge and they can't even see the Nips that are shootin' at 'em. One poor kid was really depressed; don't see no way he can come out alive."[10]

Tanks accompanied some units of Honsowetz's battalion when entering the Horseshoe for the first time. The result was a bloody repulse. Afterward, a tank platoon leader who had seen enemy mortars plaster a Marine squad, reducing it to just two men, told Honsowetz with tears streaming down his cheeks, "Colonel, we couldn't do enough for them. We couldn't reach the mortars that killed them like flies all around us."[11]

At 12:45 p.m., Honsowetz's "F" Company requested 15 stretchers and all of the bearers that could be rounded up. Five minutes later, the company reported that enemy machine-gun fire had stalled its advance, and tanks were needed to clear a path.

At 1 p.m., "F"'s sister, "G" Company, sought permission to withdraw. "The men are dropping from exhaustion and our casualties are great from heavy machine-gun fire and knee mortars. The position is untenable." Smoke shells were laid on the hill so that the company could pull back to the reverse slope, away from the deadly enemy machine-gun fire.[12]

"A" Company's 56 men passed through Lieutenant Colonel Honsowetz's 2nd Battalion to tackle gunfire-swept Hill 160 and relieve pressure on Honsowetz's men. When the skeletal company reached the ridge about 1 p.m., the 2nd Battalion CP asked, "Can you go forward at all?" The response, "No."

Honsowetz replied, "You will advance at once across the ridge."

"We cannot move out as there is heavy machine-gun fire raking the entire ridge," responded "A."

Honsowetz refused to accept "no" for an answer.

"It is necessary that you move out at all costs," he said. "I am giving you a direct order. You will move out at once. If you move in small rushes your casualties will not be great."

"All contact lost with 'A' Company," noted the battalion entry minutes later.[13]

Yet "A" Company did move out. Under heavy fire, with wounded men falling to the ground every few seconds, the company managed to cross Hill 160 on the left side of the attack zone as ordered. However, the Marines' maps were wrong. What appeared on paper to be an unbroken ridgeline in fact ended in a 150-foot cliff. The Japanese defenders riddled "A" Company until it withdrew with just seven unwounded men.[14]

Pressured by Puller, Honsowetz continued to push every available man into the inferno. When "G" and "F" companies became stalled with large numbers of casualties, "E" Company was sent forward. Every man that could be spared from the battalion CP was sent to the lines; five of them were wounded by mortar fire before they got there. Reinforcements were then dispatched from the Pioneer Battalion.

"E" and "G" companies had to be withdrawn when the roaring Japanese gunfire did not abate. "G" Company's commander, a Lieutenant Fournier, was riddled by machine-gun bullets.[15] Colonel Berger's "E" Company of the Seventh Marines dug in for the night on a nearby coral ridge. At 9 p.m., the Japanese began to counterattack.

An enemy patrol suddenly materialized behind the Marines' lines and sprinted toward "E"'s command post, shouting the password for the night while hurling hand grenades. Four officers and several enlisted men were killed, and Captain Warrick Hoopes, the "E" commander, was wounded. An enemy soldier who barged into the battalion aid station was shot dead by the assistant battalion surgeon.

Sergeant Francis Roberts climbed a hill overlooking the command post with a .30-caliber machine gun. Cradling it in his blistered hands, he fired at the Japanese who were screaming in the dark until his weapon jammed. Just as he cleared it, a Japanese soldier loomed before him with a grenade in one hand and a bayonet in the other. From 4 feet away, Roberts fired his now-operable machine gun, cutting the intruder in half.

Thirty Japanese bodies were later counted. When the wounded Hoopes set up a new command post on the front line, just four survivors from the previous CP accompanied him.[16]

———

While its sister "A" Company was fighting alongside Honsowetz's battalion before the Five Sisters, "C" Company, led by 25-year-old Captain Everett Pope, attacked Hill 100 to the east. Pope's company now consisted of just 94 men who were still able to fight. Four days earlier, 242 men had come ashore with "C" Company.[17]

In the late afternoon of September 19, two tanks led "C" to a causeway across a lagoon at the base of Hill 100. While attempting to negotiate the narrow, slippery path, the tanks slid off either side of the causeway, blocking egress to all motorized traffic. Now without supporting arms, Pope's men – two dozen participated in the assault – kept moving forward. They passed over the causeway in "squad rushes" and scrambled up Hill 100.

Pfc Jack Ainsworth, a "C" Company runner, watched his company swarm the face of the ridge "like so many Moros running amok. They were shouting and hollerin' as they [went] up the steep slope." The Japanese atop Hill 100 recoiled from the wild attack.[18]

But when they reached the summit, Pope's men were dismayed to learn, as "A" Company had found out, that the maps were wrong. Hill 100, shown on the map to be standing tall and alone above the surrounding terrain, in fact was the nose of a long ridge. Moreover, 50 yards away, an even loftier knoll overshadowed it, enabling the enemy to fire down on Pope's men. "We were quite startled that we were not on top of the hill, but on a plateau with high ground dominating it to the south," noted Pope.

Sheets of gunfire from the knoll and a parallel ridge to the west pelted "C" Company. Pope asked the 2nd Battalion for reinforcements. Honsowetz, who was also directing "C" Company's attack, replied that reinforcements were unavailable. Expecting counterattacks at any moment, Pope set up a tight perimeter about the size of a tennis court atop the hill.[19]

"The line is flimsy as hell, and it is getting dark," reported "C" Company's war diary. "We have no wires and need grenades badly."

The anticipated counterattacks from the high ground began at nightfall, with groups of 20 to 25 Japanese infantrymen charging the tiny Marine perimeter. The attacks continued through the night.

"Squads of the enemy broke through our line in several places," Pope later wrote, "and the fight was literally hand to hand," often waged with rocks and fists because Pope's men were running out of ammunition that could not be replenished. The attackers were "good troops, well led, well trained, and determined to die."[20]

The Marines clung to the hillcrest through the night, fending off the enemy attacks. At one point, two Japanese soldiers assaulted Lieutenant Francis Burke. When one of them bayoneted him in the leg, Burke beat him senseless with his fists. Sergeant James McAlarnis bludgeoned the second attacker to death, and both bodies were hurled over a precipice.[21]

"The edge of the fight moved back and forth like a wave," amid the continual thunder of mortar fire, wrote Pope.[22]

A Marine mortarman estimated that 3,000 rounds, most of them high explosive shells, were fired by the mortar detail from Hill 100's base. "We fired all night long, from sundown to sunup," said Pfc Barnett Bell. Some of the mortar tubes became overheated and swelled to the point that they would not fire until cooled by immersion in water.[23]

Just before dawn, Pope's men ran out of machine-gun ammunition. Concentrated Japanese artillery, mortar, and small-arms fire crashed down on the tiny Marine position, knocking out several BARs. Enemy troops then launched "a vicious counterattack." A desperate hand-to-hand fight ensued, which Pope described as "a mixed-up melee. We had a few grenades and some bayonets and some brave Marines."[24]

"It was so bad at times that empty grenade boxes, canteens full of water, rocks, and other malfunctioning weapons were hurled at the advancing Nips," wrote Pfc Ainsworth.[25]

"Throw three rocks," Pope instructed his men, "and then one of your remaining grenades and slow them down a bit."[26]

With the extinction of his command imminent, Pope requested and received permission to withdraw. Under a smokescreen and a curtain of artillery fire, nine of the 24 men who ascended the hill on September 19 descended it early on September 20, twelve hours later. They slid and tumbled to the bottom, with Pope limping from a shrapnel wound to his leg. The dead were left behind.

The Japanese quickly reclaimed the hill and drove Pope's men back over the causeway with a torrent of machine-gun, rifle, and mortar fire. Enemy artillery fire inflicted 30 casualties on the division Reconnaissance Company, which was supporting Pope's men.

Counting the eight survivors of its mortar platoon, "C" Company was now able to muster just 17 combat-capable men.

Pope hobbled to the battalion aid station, borrowed some pliers, and pulled the shrapnel from his leg. He then returned to his company.[27]

To the west, "F" Company requested stretchers and corpsmen. It had just ten men remaining who were combat-capable. A canvass that morning of the First Marines' 1st and 2nd Battalions and supporting units, which began the campaign with nearly 2,000 men, showed that they now had just 150 effectives.[28]

In the afternoon of September 20, Honsowetz, at Puller's direction, ordered Captain Pope's "C" Company to attack up a deep ravine between Hill 100 and the ridge to its west. "C" now amounted to little more than a squad, and half of Pope's men lacked weapons and ammunition.

Certain that they would soon die, Pope's Marines yet prepared to attack. As they waited for the arrival of a corpsman, Pope radioed his 1st Battalion commander, Lieutenant Colonel Ray Davis, and told him that he had just 15 men and two officers. He asked Davis to intervene.

Davis got the attack order rescinded. "Why Puller wanted us all dead on the top of that hill has never been clear to me," said Pope, who was awarded the Medal of Honor for his actions the previous night. Four other "C" Company Marines received Navy Crosses.[29]

At 7 a.m. on the 20th, the First Marines' 2nd and 3rd Battalions and the division reserve, the Seventh Marines' 2nd Battalion led by Lieutenant Colonel Berger, once more attempted to capture the Five Sisters, as well as Hills 100 and 300.

Just three hours after Captain Pope's men were ejected from Hill 100, a fresh attack was launched to retake it – "an all-out effort," wrote General Smith, the assistant division commander. Every grimy, sleep-deprived, but able-bodied man from the depleted battalions assembled for what might be called a "forlorn hope" – carried out by a slender remnant.

The 150 men constituted little more than an understrength company, and about 7 percent of the 2nd and 3rd Battalions' original strength. To increase the battalions' manpower, other units were drafted for the assault: part of Berger's battalion, as well as men from the division Reconnaissance Company and War Dog Platoon, and Marine engineers.

Lieutenant James Stanfield created a scratch machine-gun battery with a dozen salvaged guns. They were manned by non-essential regimental and battalion headquarters staff. Also drafted for the all-out attack were cooks, and communications and quartermaster personnel – and additional tanks, amtracs, half-tracks, 37mm guns, and mortars.[30]

Before the Marines attacked the hill, a squad leader said to Honsowetz, "Colonel, we can go up there. We've been up there before. And we'll go on up again until there's no one left. But we can't hold that ridge, Colonel. We can't hold it unless there's more of us, sir." Honsowetz did not respond to the squad leader's words.[31]

When the signal was given to begin the attack, Pfc Russell Davis saw a bandy-legged, red-bearded sergeant of about 30 years of age stand and wave his men forward. Some of them stumbled out of their holes, but others did not. Leaning on their weapons, they "looked sick with dread." The sergeant turned away as tears streamed down his bearded cheeks. "Let's get killed on that high ground there," he told his men. "It ain't no good to get it down here." The Marines left their holes and shuffled toward their sergeant. "There's the good lads," he said.[32]

As he had done earlier, Honsowetz, shouting and waving his .45-caliber sidearm, personally led the charge up the hill.

Pfc Davis noted that during an attack, there were always a few men who kept going when their comrades stopped advancing. They were "the bone structure of a fighting unit... There aren't more than a few dozen in every thousand men, even in the Marines," Davis wrote. "They clawed and clubbed and stabbed their way up. The rest of us watched."[33]

The Eleventh Marines' artillery battalion fired every five minutes at pre-selected targets, and observers called in 27 naval gunfire missions and 18 air strikes, besides summoning additional artillery fire numerous times. Mortar teams fired until "the mortars glowed red," a Marine report said, "and the machine guns blew up, but those that could returned fire."[34]

It made no difference. Soon after the attack began, the Marines climbing the hill were shredded by gusts of enemy artillery, mortar, and machine-gun fire. "As the first tremendous rain of bullets hit us, you could feel more than see as people dropped around you," said Lieutenant Bruce Watkins.[35] "Things started bad and got worse and, finally, hopeless," said Pfc Davis who, as a runner, tried to aid Honsowetz in retaining control of the 2nd Battalion's scattered units.[36]

The attack faltered, and then stalled. A fiery gun battle lasting four hours preceded the inevitable Marine withdrawal. In despair, Pfc Davis picked up a dead Marine's rifle and stopped acting as a runner. "I didn't worry about death anymore. I had resigned from the human race. I only wanted to be as far forward as any man when my turn came," he wrote. "We were no longer even human beings. I fired at anything that moved in front of me ... I had no friends. I just wanted to kill."[37]

Sergeant Shelby Albright's company, which went into the assault with just 50 men, emerged with fewer than 25 effectives. They crept down the hill, carrying their wounded and dead as Marine Corsairs pinned down the enemy defenders with strafing runs.[38]

The Japanese report of the battle said, "Since dawn the enemy has been concentrating their forces, vainly trying to approach Higashiyama (Hill 100) and Kansokuyama (Hill 300) with 14 tanks and the one infantry battalion under powerful aid of air and artillery fire. However, they were again put to rout, receiving heavy losses."[39]

The Marines' official report said, "Cruel terrain and devilishly prepared positions" thwarted the assault. The survivors of the attack that were still able to fell back. They took up positions covering the mouth of the Horseshoe, beyond which lay a valley and shallow lake hemmed by ridges bristling with armed Japanese.[40]

The official report did not state the obvious – that the First Marine Regiment was finished as a functional combat unit.

At 8 a.m. the next day, September 21, it was the turn of the Seventh Marines' 1st Battalion to try its luck in assaulting Hill 100 from the East Road. It had campaigned until now in southern Peleliu and was relatively intact. This was the 1st Division's third attempt to capture and hold the keystone to the eastern Umurbrogol. Capturing Hill 100 would give the Marines a solid foothold on the eastern flank of Hill 300 and the Five Sisters.

Smoke from 81mm mortars helped screen the advancing infantrymen of the Seventh's "C" Company, closely supported by "A" Company and by fire from tanks on the East Road.

Halfway to the summit of Hill 100, the Marines were met by a volcanic eruption of mortar and small-arms fire from nearby caves and concealed pillboxes, and showers of grenades. The violent reaction was too much for the assault troops, who were driven back to the road, where the regimental Weapons Company relieved them.[41]

The bodies of Captain Pope's Marines who were killed atop Hill 100 on September 19–20 would not be recovered until the hill's capture on October 3.[42]

———

Puller's First Marines had suffered a devastating 1,749 casualties in six days. Of the 3,252 men who had landed on D-Day, 311 had been killed and 1,438 were wounded, a 56 percent casualty rate. The regimental losses surpassed any recorded by the Marine Corps until that time.[*]

This was one result of Puller's and General Rupertus's daily mantra to "keep pushing," no matter what. The other result was the 3,942 Japanese killed in the First Marines' sector – two Japanese fatalities for every Marine killed or wounded.

The cold figures and the banality of the daily progress reports masked the daily horrors and bloodletting witnessed by the combat troops. In its report for September 21, III Amphibious Corps said the 1st Marine Division had lost 505 killed, 2,975 wounded, and 340 missing – losses totaling 3,820 men – while 8,792 enemy troops had been killed on Peleliu. The September 21 report understatedly said:

> The First Marine Division made minor gains in a northerly direction along the western ridge of Peleliu Island facing stiff opposition from the enemy troops well entrenched in precipitous terrain. Our attack was preceded by gunfire from cruisers and destroyers and by bombing.

---

[*] Higher regimental casualties would be reported on Iwo Jima and Okinawa in 1945, by the 26th and 4th Marines, respectively.

Meantime, our forces occupied the entire east coast of Peleliu, including the island of Ngabad.

The daily report catalogued the enemy equipment that had been captured, including six trench mortars and 31 machine guns.

"A captured map indicates entire W[est] coast ridge line to be honeycombed with caves and pillboxes," the report continued.[43]

That same day, Colonel Nakagawa reported to General Inoue at Koror that just 1,800 combat-capable troops remained under his command. He advised Inoue to not attempt to "pour more military into Peleliu." The colonel said it would be a waste of manpower.[44]

Of Puller's three battalions, his 1st Battalion reported the highest number of casualties – terrible losses equaling 71 percent of Lieutenant Colonel Ray Davis's three companies. The 2nd Battalion reported 56 percent casualties, and the 3rd Battalion, 55 percent.

The disparity was due to Puller having doled out the 1st Battalion's companies piecemeal since D-Day, mainly to the 2nd Battalion; they fought as a battalion on only one day. At the end of September 20, just 74 combat-capable men remained in the 1st Battalion.[45]

Despite its severe losses, Ray Davis's battalion went back into action. During its single rest day, "B" Company was disbanded, and its 22 survivors were apportioned to the two remaining rifle companies. When the reorganization was completed, and the men had cleaned their weapons, the battalion mustered 239 men – but up to half of them were clerks, cooks, scouts, jeep drivers, mail orderlies, and communications personnel sent to Davis as replacements. On September 22, Davis's men reinforced the 3rd Battalion. After a bitter fight, the 1st Battalion was relieved.[46]

Davis said the Marines were surprised by the discipline displayed by Peleliu's defenders, and their calculated ferocity. On Cape Gloucester, the Japanese troops had perished in futile banzai attacks, and the starving remnants had retreated through the rain forest, with men dropping hourly along the way. After their experiences on Cape Gloucester, the Marines "were unaccustomed to the ferocious and wily foe in front of us who had never before tasted defeat," said Davis.

On Peleliu, the defenders were "too cautious and tactical to waste their efforts in a few banzai charges." They retrieved their dead and wounded whenever they could. "It was not possible to make an estimate of enemy casualties when the only ones to be found were the few snipers that infiltrated our lines," Davis wrote.[47]

———

From the very beginning of *Stalemate*, General Rupertus had adamantly opposed using 81st Infantry Division units to reinforce the 1st Marine Division. The simple reason was that it was Army; Rupertus wanted *Stalemate* to be an all-Marine operation. His refusal violated the Marines' amphibious doctrine, which stipulated that amphibious assault forces should own a 3-to-1 manpower advantage over the defending force.[48]

On paper, the 1st Division had originally numbered 27,000 men, and Colonel Nakagawa's Peleliu defenders had totaled up to 11,000. But little more than 9,000 of Rupertus's men were combat Marines; the rest were support personnel. Thus, on the battlefield, the Marines and Nakagawa's men were nearly equal numerically, although Rupertus could always send his auxiliaries into combat as replacements. Nakagawa, without a ready pool of reinforcements, could not.

In June, General Julian Smith, the expeditionary force commander, had recommended drawing on the 81st Division's regiments for Marine reinforcements. But Rupertus even then had insisted that the Marines alone would conquer Peleliu. Afterward, the Army could mop up and occupy the island.

"I assure you there is little chance of the division needing it," Rupertus had said of the Army's support. He believed that Peleliu would fall so quickly that there would not even be a need to use the Marines' division reserve – the Seventh Marines' 2nd Battalion – which Rupertus in fact sent into action on the campaign's first day.

General Julian Smith did not dispute Rupertus's pre-assault assessment. Unaware of what awaited them on Peleliu, both men would be proved terribly wrong.[49]

By D-Day plus one, September 16, Rupertus had already committed the division reserve as well as the division's Reconnaissance Company, and the well was dry. That day, General Roy Geiger, the III Amphibious Force commander, came ashore, as he would be inclined to do nearly every day, to see the situation for himself.

Geiger recommended to Rupertus that the First Marines, which had sustained 500 casualties on D-Day, either be reinforced or be relieved by Army units. Rupertus rejected Geiger's proposal out of hand, and said he was confident the 1st Division would prevail without the 81st Division's assistance.[50]

But when the Marines began to assault the ridges of the Umurbrogol on the 17th, casualties rose alarmingly day by day. "Keep pushing" became Rupertus's mantra. Yet the sudden breakthrough that Rupertus anticipated did not occur. Days into the campaign, the general and his staff still did not grasp the enemy's shift to an attritional strategy, or its ingenious use of Peleliu's terrain to inflict maximum casualties.[51]

Hoping to instill in his men his own certainty of victory, Rupertus went so far as to distribute an "inspiring message" to them in late September. Its subject was the Army's assistance being unneeded to finish the job on Peleliu. Along the battle lines, Rupertus's message was "met with curses and profound expressions of hope from the troops that unprintable things should be in the general's future," wrote Pfc E.B. Sledge.[52]

Soon, even Rupertus's optimism curdled in the face of the shocking casualty reports that showed that the First Marines had lost half of its men in five days.[53] Colonel Harold Harris, the Fifth Marines' commander, was summoned to the division command post as the fighting raged in the Umurbrogol. Harris found Rupertus alone and in tears.

"Harris, I'm at the end of my rope," Rupertus said. "Two of my fine regiments are in ruins. You usually seem to know what to do, and get it done. I'm going to turn over to you everything we have left. This is strictly between us."

However, Rupertus had no authority to delegate command of his division, and nothing changed. Rupertus and Harris never discussed their conversation. But Rupertus's admission to Harris was an acknowledgement of the division's bleak situation.

About the same time, the 1st Division's personnel officer, Lieutenant Colonel Harold Deakins, found Rupertus sitting on his bunk with his head in his hands. "This thing has just about got me beat," Rupertus groaned. Deakins put his arm around Rupertus's shoulders and tried to reassure him that things would work out.

The man who might have given Rupertus strong moral and intellectual support, Rupertus's assistant division commander, General O.P. Smith, was never asked for it.[54]

While Rupertus's broken ankle tethered him to his command post, Geiger freely roamed the front lines. Throughout the *Stalemate* campaign, Geiger would appear unexpectedly at the 1st Division command post and the various regimental headquarters to ask questions. He visited the battle lines to talk to the infantrymen. In the evenings, Geiger returned to his command ship.

"I think that … it acted as an incentive to the division and regimental commanders to be on their toes," said Geiger's chief of staff, Colonel Merwin Silverthorn. "They never knew when the corps commander was going to come around and ask some real searching questions."[55]

The III Amphibious Corps artillery officer, Lieutenant Colonel Frederick Henderson, said Geiger, as had been his practice on Guadalcanal and Guam, wanted to have "a personal knowledge of the terrain, the action, and the condition and morale of his men. He'd go out and go climbing up the mountains, up on the hills, right up at the front, and talk to the guys… We worried ourselves to death about him."[56]

One day, he walked up to Marines who were lying flat on a ridge, firing at Japanese soldiers 200 yards away. An enlisted man barked at him, "Get down, you old fool! D'ya want to get us all killed?" Rudely reminded that on the battle line he was sometimes more burden than asset, Geiger smiled, apologized, and walked away. At that moment, he might have agreed with the remark of a Fifth Marines company commander about the savage combat in the Umurbrogol ridges. "It was a young man's war," said Captain John McLaughlin. "Only a young man could fight all night, then attack all day."[57]

Sergeant Guy Farrar said as much. "We were fighting all the time" – around the clock, with one Marine on watch while his comrade napped. In spite of the filthy conditions, the contaminated water, and the rotting enemy corpses all around, "we kept our equipment clean," said Farrar. "We cleaned it all the time. We kept it in good shape."[58]

On September 21, the day following the First Marines' failed all-out attack on Hill 100, Geiger went ashore with his corps artillery officer, Henderson, and the corps intelligence officer, Colonel William Coleman. Two sergeants toting Thompson submachine guns served as bodyguards for the senior officers.[59]

The men first visited Colonel Puller's command post at the foot of a small cliff. Stripped to the waist and with a pipe jutting from his clenched teeth, Puller was on his field telephone shouting and cursing at his 2nd Battalion commander, Lieutenant Colonel Honsowetz, while demanding that his battalion keep pushing despite its heavy losses. Geiger took the First Marines commander aside for a private talk.

Puller appeared haggard and exhausted. Moreover, he was in great pain and had difficulty walking. The unhealed shrapnel wound to his left leg acquired two years earlier on Guadalcanal had become inflamed. Doctors who had treated him back in 1942 had failed to remove all of the shrapnel, and now his leg was swollen to nearly twice its normal size. At times the pain was so excruciating that Puller had to be carried on a stretcher to inspect his lines.[60]

Geiger and Puller's conversation was short and, by all accounts, heated. No record of it was kept. However, Colonel Coleman wrote, "It became rapidly apparent that the regimental commander [Puller] was very tired, he was unable to give a very clear picture of what his situation was and when asked by the Corps Commander what he needed in the way of help he stated that he was doing all right with what he had."[61]

Historian Harry Gailey reported that when Geiger left Puller's command post 15 minutes later, he remarked that Puller appeared to be out of touch with reality in his refusal to acknowledge that his regiment was at an impasse.[62]

Geiger's next stop was 1st Division headquarters in the tank trap next to the landing beaches. Arriving during a division staff meeting, Geiger asked to see the First Marines' casualty figures. When he saw that Puller's regiment had lost 1,749 men since D-Day, Geiger said, "The First Marines are finished." The regiment must be relieved, he said, and almost certainly by an Army regimental combat team.[63]

"Greatly alarmed," Rupertus strenuously objected for several minutes, saying no "damn Army unit," especially one virtually untested in combat like the 81st Division, was going to replace his men. In just another day or two, Rupertus said, his division could secure the island without the Army's assistance.[64]

At this point, Geiger's options for dealing with Rupertus were two-fold: bluntly order Rupertus to relieve Puller's regiment or, if he refused, relieve him of command and see to the First Marines' relief himself. No Marine general had ever been relieved of command on the battlefield; it would certainly mean the end of Rupertus's once-promising career.[65]

Geiger asked Rupertus's operations officer, Lieutenant Colonel Lewis Fields, for his opinion. Although clearly uncomfortable at being called out before Rupertus, Fields replied that the First Marines should be replaced.

Geiger turned back to Rupertus and said that he felt the same way as Fields. When Rupertus again began to object, Geiger cut him off and ordered him to take the First Marines off the line. The regiment, he said, was "totally spent." The survivors, along with Puller, must be evacuated to Pavavu, said Geiger.[66]

At 4:25 p.m., Geiger sent a message to the 81st Division commander, General Paul Mueller, on Angaur. "Urgently request RCT 321 immediate transfer from Angaur, and assignment to commanding general 1st Marine Division Peleliu hq."[67]

Rupertus informed Puller of Geiger's decision. Puller notified his 1st and 2nd Battalion commanders, and Berger of the Seventh Marines that their battalions would be relieved that afternoon. The First's 3rd Battalion would remain in place for the present, as would Puller's command post.[68]

Although General O.P. Smith, the assistant division commander, was never consulted by Geiger about relieving the First Marines, he later said that he agreed with the decision – to a point. "What we needed was another regiment to finish the job, but what we needed was a fresh *Marine* regiment."[69]

No allusion to the drama in the Marines' Peleliu command appeared in that day's bland communique distributed by Admiral Nimitz's Pearl Harbor headquarters:

On 21 September 1st MarDiv resumed the attack on Peleliu. 1st and 7th Regts attacked abreast along western arm of the island, while 5th Regt continued the attack up eastern arm and nearby islands (NGABAD Island and the island just south thereof). The attempted advance on the west was halted by heavy enemy resistance located on precipitous cliffs and in deep ravines that prohibited maneuver of our forces. 5th Regt was successful in occupying remainder of east coast including NGABAD Island.[70]

Three of Honsowetz's nine original company commanders in the 2nd Battalion continued to lead; the others were casualties. When they learned that their battalion was being relieved, one of the surviving company COs, Lieutenant Bruce Watkins, said that he and the other two commanders "looked at each other in numbed silence." Watkins then led his remnant company of nine men to the rear.[71]

When the First Marines came out of the line, they passed by the Fifth Marines. Pfc E.B. Sledge, a mortarman with the Fifth, wrote, "I saw some familiar faces as the three decimated battalions trudged past us, but I was shocked at the absence of so many others whom I know in that regiment... It was appalling."[72] "Eyes glazed and distant, they looked like hell, with battered dungarees salted white with sweat, unshaven and filthy from powder burns, bloodstained and near-emaciated," wrote Pfc Sterling Mace.[73]

Sergeant Jim McEnery said the men coming out of the ridges "looked so pitiful that I couldn't help stopping for a minute to watch them. Their uniforms were torn, filthy, and bloodstained in many cases, and their faces were blank and hollow-eyed. They shambled along like walking dead men."[74]

Lieutenant Clifford West, the First Marines' air controller, said, "We dragged ourselves... Walking back down I had no feeling at all."[75]

"What once had been companies in the First Marines looked like platoons; platoons looked like squads. I saw few officers," wrote Sledge. Sledge and his comrades now knew that it soon would be their turn to fight in the Umurbrogol. "We were resigned to the dismal conclusion that our battalion wasn't going to leave the island until all the Japanese were killed, or we had all been hit... It seemed that the only escape was to be killed or wounded."[76]

Sledge asked a friend from the First how many men remained in his company. He replied, "Twenty is all that's left in the whole company, Sledgehammer. They nearly wiped us out."[77]

Colonel Puller approached a small group as it was leaving the ridges and asked the men which platoon they were from. One of them replied, "Platoon, hell, colonel, this is Charlie Company."[78]

A newsman asked one of the exhausted infantrymen, "You the First Marines?" One of them replied, "Ain't no more First Marines."[79]

Although physically and mentally spent, the First Marines had continued to function on reflexes and training. "We survivors were tired from having been pushed into action almost constantly," said Pfc George Peto, "by day and by night, often isolated, sometimes low on ammunition and under heavy fire. We had been subjected to terrible heat and humidity, contaminated water, and unreliable communications."[80]

Some of the Marines bitterly reproached Colonel Honsowetz, the 2nd Battalion commander, as they passed him on their way out of the Umurbrogol. The exhausted, filthy men were "cussing him to a fare thee well," said one Marine. "Well, we hope you're satisfied, you sonofabitch," one of them said to the colonel.

A wounded officer, Lieutenant Francis Rineer, confronted Honsowetz that afternoon at his command post and called him a "butcher." Rineer, awarded the Navy Cross for helping lead one of the attacks on Hill 100, later said that Honsowetz's reaction "was ... very kind. He could understand." Honsowetz was only following orders from Puller, who, in turn, was driven by Rupertus's insistence that his regiments capture high ground, no matter the cost.[81]

At the end of the day on September 22, gunfire still crackled in the ridges, and teams of stretcher-bearers continued to arrive at the aid stations with the wounded. However, Americans now held the airfield, the heights immediately north of it, and all of southern Peleliu. The beaches were open to receive shipping, and all of the division's artillery was now ashore.

It had taken eight days of combat and 3,946 casualties to reach this milestone. Weeks of fighting lay ahead. The Japanese soldiers still fiercely resisting from the Umurbrogol's caves, tunnels, and ravines were certainly not ready to accept defeat.[82]

With Peleliu's beaches secured, gravediggers were able to bury the dead in a former palm grove near Orange Beach 2. They did it by the numbers: 50 bodies to a row, 3 feet between rows. The wooden crosses whose manufacture on Pavavu had filled some Marines with foreboding now proved their utility. Each bore a stenciled name, rank, serial number, and unit. A master chart showed the location of each man.[83]

From Peleliu's airstrip, the pilots of Major "Cowboy" Stout's VMF-114 watched with admiration as Marine infantrymen repeatedly stormed the heavily defended ridges of the Umurbrogol. "There was not one of us [pilots] who would have traded places" with them, said Lieutenant Bill Cantrell. "There isn't any question about it; it could not have been done without these kids that carry a rifle for the Marine Corps."[84]

The pilots aided the infantrymen by flying increasingly daring close-air support missions, which included the generous use of napalm. Napalm-filled belly tanks equipped with instantaneous fuses ignited infernos among the Japanese-held ridges.

Later in October, when the enemy was cornered in a narrow pocket and precision strikes became difficult, the procedure changed. The napalm was dropped without fuses, and the pilots dipped their wings to signal artillerymen to fire phosphorus shells to ignite the napalm.[85] Of this American tactic, Colonel Nakagawa wrote, "The enemy plan seems to be to burn down the central hills post to ashes by dropping gasoline from airplanes."[86]

Robert "Pepper" Martin of *Time* magazine was one of the handful of correspondents that had not abandoned *Stalemate* after Rupertus's prediction that it would be a short but rough campaign. While the other reporters transferred to General MacArthur's Philippines invasion force, Martin went ashore on Peleliu with the 1st Marine Division.

He was appalled by the environmental conditions that he encountered ashore – stifling heat and high humidity. "The muggy rain … brings no relief, only greater misery," Martin wrote. The fighting, he said, was "incomparably worse than Guam in its bloodiness, terror, climate, and the incomprehensible tenacity of the Japs. For sheer brutality and fatigue, I think it surpasses anything yet seen in the Pacific …"[87]

Fighting day and night in the suffocating heat and catnapping whenever possible, the Marines suffered from severe sleep deficit. They became so tired that they could sleep anywhere – even under the muzzle of a barking 155mm howitzer, which one Marine described as "commensurate to having a subway tunnel running between your ears."[88]

The blazing tropical sun blackened the bodies of the slain Japanese soldiers, and they bloated and burst, emitting a terrible stench. The remains became food for huge blowflies that then landed on the Marines' C-rations and had to be picked from the food as the men ate. "The business of eating out of a C-ration can was a constant swirling motion of the hands, because the flies were collecting on the C-ration before you could get it into your mouth," said one Marine.

At night, the biting gnats were so pernicious that the men slept with their cuffs buttoned tightly. To control them, as well as the flies and the clouds of mosquitoes – fortunately the non-malarial variety, but nonetheless spreaders of dengue fever – large quantities of DDT were used for the first time in the Pacific War.

The Marines' misery was compounded by dysentery, which had become widespread, and by diarrhea, which was commonplace.[89]

On September 24, the 1st Division command post was moved from the tank trap at the beach into a two-story former Japanese administrative building on the airfield's northern perimeter. The airfield was no longer a target for enemy gunfire and air operations were now routine.

The Marines christened the new headquarters at a ceremony in which Generals Geiger, Rupertus, and Smith, and Colonels Puller, Harold Harris, and Herman Hanneken saluted the American flag as it was raised.[90]

The Seventh Marines moved into the southern Umurbrogol on September 22, and continued to press the assaults that the First Marines had begun. General Rupertus was sticking to his south-to-north attack scheme, despite his division's huge losses. He still believed the bludgeoning attacks would yield a climactic breakthrough.[91]

The Seventh's 1st Battalion wasted no time before launching a headlong assault against the southern face of the Five Sisters. Following preparatory artillery and tank fire, a smokescreen cloaked "B" Company as it spearheaded the advance. The Seventh's Weapons Company attempted to distract the enemy by feinting toward Walt Ridge.

The ridge, the former Hill 100, was renamed for Lieutenant Colonel Lew Walt, the Fifth Marines' executive officer, because a mapping team happened to encounter Walt near the hill. The former Aogiri Ridge on Cape Gloucester also bore Walt's name; for his leadership during the intensive battle to capture it, Walt was awarded the Navy Cross. A better name for Hill 100 would have been Pope Ridge, honoring Captain Everett Pope and his company's desperate all-night struggle to hold that hill.

At first, the diversion appeared to work. Light sniper fire peppered "B" Company as it advanced 250 yards over rocky ground into what later became known as Death Valley. Then, the Japanese smothered the Marines with machine-gun fire from the front, from the right, and from caves inside Hill 200 to the left. Men fell like dominoes with bullet wounds. Tanks fired point-blank into the cave openings, and the infantrymen pushed ahead – and into a steep-sided draw blocked by a coral formation. There the assault stalled. The Marines withdrew under a smokescreen.[92]

Enemy troops attempted to infiltrate the Seventh Marines' lines that night. An infiltrator killed 10 feet from a half-track and found the next morning had a Molotov cocktail tied to one leg, pockets full of grenades, and explosives strapped to his back.[93]

By this time, it was apparent to everyone that the Battle of Peleliu was different from anything the Marines had yet experienced during the Pacific War. "The campaign had now become a battle of attrition – a slow, slugging yard-by-yard struggle to blast the enemy from the last remaining stronghold in the high ground to the north of the airfield," the 1st Marine Division war diary noted in early October.[94]

More than 3,000 men from Colonel Robert Dark's 321st Regiment reached Peleliu in four LSTs at 2 p.m. on September 23. At the reef, they disembarked and hiked over the new pontoon pier to Orange Beach.

Before the Army's arrival, the Marines hastened to bury their dead. During the campaign's first hectic week, there had been neither time nor opportunity to bury many of those killed in action, and they lay on the open ground.

"Everywhere there were tarps, with people underneath," said Corporal Barnett Bell of the First Marines' "C" Company. "You could see arms and feet sticking out, and maggots coming out of the bottoms of their feet." The coming of the 321st inspired a flurry of burials. "They were making it look pretty for the Army," said Bell.[95]

When Colonel Dark met Colonel Puller, he mistook Puller's regimental command post for an observation post because it was so near the front lines. Puller's CP consisted of a poncho and a piece of tin for shade so that he could study his maps. On the day of Puller's departure, Dark moved the CP 1,000 yards to the rear.[96]

On September 23, the 321st relieved the First Marines' 3rd Battalion on the front line and its 1st Battalion on the West Road, which skirted Peleliu's central ridges along the island's western side. "They were in sad shape," sitting by the roadside, Pfc Ray Deihl of the 321st's "B" Company said of the Marines.

"Oh, they were cocky as hell" after Angaur, Marine Corporal Bell said of the 321st. "'Anything going on over here?' they'd ask. 'Anybody getting shot?' And we said, 'You'll find out.'"

"They were kind of soft looking," Bell said, but "we were tickled to death to see them."[97]

After descending from the ridges, the First Marines boarded trucks that took them to the relative peace of eastern Peleliu's Purple Beach, secured earlier by the Fifth Marines. Purple Beach was a stark contrast to the Umurbrogol's carnage.

Pfc George Peto, the mortarman with the 3rd Battalion, was able to begin eating normally again. He had subsisted on crackers and K-rations since coming ashore because his stomach had been tied in knots the entire time.[98]

For reasons that he alone knew, Puller saw fit to announce that the First Marines would return to action after a three-day rest. The news upset his exhausted men. But the division had no intention of sending the severely depleted regiment back into combat.[99]

Pfc Dan Toledo's "E" Company was relieved by a platoon of cooks, motor transport, and other support Marines and soon found itself at Purple Beach. Toledo had not had anything to eat during the previous five days, other than an occasional apple, orange, or fruit drink. He and a friend spotted a ship in the distance anchored beyond the reef, and they swam to it. "The sailors let down a net and welcomed us aboard," wrote Toledo. "We had a wonderful hot breakfast."[100]

From Purple Beach, the First Marines would ship out for Pavavu "We're not a regiment," said one Marine. "We're the survivors of a regiment."[101]

On October 2, the First Marines were taken by DUKWs to the hospital transport ships *Pinckney* and *Tryon*. Heavy seas swamped three DUKWs, and the Marines in them had to be rescued – a final indignity dealt to the depleted regiment.

Reaching the transport ships, the men laboriously climbed the cargo nets, sometimes helped by sailors who stood at the rails to lend a hand when needed, or to offer encouragement. "You gave it to 'em real good, boys," some of them said.[102]

A young naval officer accosted one Marine, wanting to know if he had souvenirs to trade. The Marine gruffly replied, "I brought my ass outta there, swabbie. That's my souvenir of Peleliu."[103]

Feverish, in great pain, and unable to walk without assistance because of his swollen leg, Puller was taken straight to surgery on the *Pinckney*. Doctors removed a 2-inch-long piece of shrapnel from his leg that had festered for nearly two years.

Fifteen Marines died aboard the *Pinckney* before it cast off for Pavavu. Their remains were wrapped in canvas, weighted by shell casings, and committed to the deep as a bugler played "Taps."[104]

Departing with the First Marines were the 1st Tank Battalion, two pack howitzer units of the Eleventh Marines' 2nd Battalion, and a division headquarters detachment.

Rupertus said that the Marine tanks were worn down by Peleliu's harsh terrain, although there were never fewer than 18 tanks available for operations. The Marine general believed that in the future there would be little use anyway for tanks or pack howitzers in the Umurbrogol's rugged ridges. He was wrong.[105]

The day after the departure of the Marine tanks and pack howitzers, "A" Company of the Army's 710th Tank Battalion was detached from the 321st Regiment and assigned to the Seventh Marines. The Army tanks would be called upon often in the coming weeks and months.[106]

On the night before his transport ship departed for Pavavu, a Marine corporal gazed at Peleliu from the ship's railing and wrote,

"It was red, with the flares going up. God knows it looked like Dante's *Inferno*."[107]

The division's 4th and 5th War Dog Platoons also took a beating on Peleliu. Each platoon began the campaign with 36 dogs and 60 handlers.

The dogs served as scouts and sentinels, and delivered messages. Prior to Peleliu, they were used during the Bougainville and Guam campaigns.

On September 20, Boy, a Doberman patrolling ahead of a Marine company, detected an ambush laid by 20 Japanese armed with two machine guns and other automatic weapons. The ambush was foiled. On the same day, a dog detected and killed a sniper.

A war dog named Rollo was leading a patrol when he suddenly stopped and barked to warn of enemy troops ahead. The Marines flattened out. When nothing happened, Rollo and his handler, Pfc Russell T. Frederick, moved ahead to investigate. Japanese guns suddenly blazed from a hidden pillbox, and Frederick fell to the ground with severe wounds. Rollo, who was unhurt, lay beside his handler and steadfastly ignored the efforts of other Marines to call him as the enemy guns roared. Frederick and Rollo were later found side by side, both dead.[108]

As might be expected, the dogs – Dobermans and German Shepherds for the most part – were vulnerable to the same hazards and nervous strains as the Marines: dehydration, exhaustion, shell shock, and enemy fire. Moreover, the sharp coral cut up their feet.

"Dogs becoming very nervous under heavy mortar fire," said a 4th War Dog Platoon report written a day after a dog was lost to shell shock. Shell-shocked dogs sometimes became uncontrollable and had to be destroyed.

On September 19, two dogs were killed by mortar fire. A week later, nine dogs were evacuated to the rear because of wounds, concussion, or deafness.[109]

War dogs have continued to serve with Marine combat units down through the years.

After Colonel Dark's men relieved the First Marines, General O.P. Smith, the 1st Division's assistant commander, examined the forbidding terrain that Colonel Puller's men had captured. "I didn't see how a human being had captured it, but [Puller] did," Smith said. He continued:

> He believed in momentum; he believed in coming ashore and hitting and just keep on hitting and trying to keep up the momentum until he'd overrun the whole thing ... no finesse. When he destroyed 140 defended caves, that's quite an operation, plus a blockhouse or two. No, there was no finesse about it, but there was gallantry and there was determination.[110]

Chapter 9

Isolating the Pocket

*It was a ghastly place. The feel of this thing was so alien,
and … you couldn't get away from it anywhere…
There was no way to take cover. There was no way to bury
the dead.*
Captain Don Wyckoff, Seventh Marines,
describing the Umurbrogol Pocket[1]

*The Germans in a similar situation would long since have
turned themselves in.*
General O.P. Smith remarking
on the enemy's tenacity[2]

On September 23, Colonel Robert Dark's 321st Regiment reached
Orange Beach after hiking over the pontoon pier from the reef. Dark
sent patrols northward on the West Road. After it was fired on from
the Umurbrogol's heights, the patrol withdrew and Dark's men dug
in for their first night on Peleliu – a relatively peaceful one, by Peleliu
standards.[3]

On the 24th, the 321st resumed its march northward on the West
Road. Its mission was to skirt the Umurbrogol's west side, and to find
a pathway to the East Road. If it succeeded, the 321st would complete
the Umurbrogol's envelopment by sealing its open northern perimeter.

An Army battalion scaled the ridge that lay to the immediate right of
the West Road in order to secure the regiment's flank. Below, its sister

battalions advanced along the 75-foot-wide coastal flat, shielded by a low ridge that paralleled the road.

The Seventh Marines' 3rd Battalion followed the Army battalion onto the ridge – until Dark's flankers encountered their first enemy resistance and summarily abandoned the high ground. The battalion hastily rejoined the rest of the 321st on the road below. The 321st's right flank was now completely exposed.

"They moved forward along the ridge a few yards until they encountered the first enemy position, then gave it all up as a bad idea, and bore sharply to their left front to the coastal road below," said Major E. Hunter Hurst, the Marine 3rd Battalion commander, with barely concealed disgust.[4]

In exasperation, Hurst sent a message to Seventh Marines headquarters and to the commander of the Army battalion that had abandoned the ridge. "3 Bn. 321 has withdrawn from the hills leaving a gap on the left flank of 3/7 undefended," Hurst wrote. "The Japs reoccupied the hills and 3/7 is fighting to retake them." When General Rupertus learned of this, he reportedly crowed, "Now I can tell Geiger, 'I told you so.' That's why I didn't want the Army involved in this in the first place."[5]

The snafu illustrated the sharp differences in the tactical philosophies of the Army and Marines: the Army's deliberate, casualty-minimizing approach employing overwhelming firepower, versus the Marines' aggressive use of manpower to quickly seize objectives. Three months earlier on Saipan, this became a flashpoint when the 27th Infantry Division, fighting alongside the 2nd and 4th Marine Divisions, advanced too slowly to satisfy Marine General Holland Smith, who was the V Amphibious Corps commander.

But the animosity went back to November 1943, when Holland Smith and Army General Ralph Smith differed over the conduct of operations at Tarawa Atoll. While the 2nd Marine Division was suffering grievously heavy casualties during its 76-hour battle on Betio Island, defended by 4,800 enemy troops, Ralph Smith's 27th Division was stalled before 800 defenders on nearby Makin Island.

Holland Smith, who was Ralph Smith's superior, went to Makin to investigate the delay. Informed that there was heavy opposition on northern Makin, the Marine general got in a Jeep and went to see for himself.

The area, Smith sarcastically said upon returning from his scouting mission, was "as quiet as Wall Street on a Sunday." "Howlin' Mad" Smith then lived up to his nickname by administering a blistering tongue-lashing to Ralph Smith for his division's dilatory movement.[6]

On Saipan, Holland Smith took the rare, extremely controversial step of relieving Ralph Smith of his command of the 27th Division. Bitterness over the firing curdled Army–Marine Corps relations for the rest of the Pacific War.

———

Seventh Marines headquarters ordered Major Hurst to extend his left flank and assist the Army battalion. The Army battalion commander promised to send his men back up the ridge, but they did not return.

As the Marines fought to reoccupy the ridge, the 321st raced northward on the coastal flat. The Marines lost 27 men in the ensuing ridgetop battle, including three men killed. One was the commander of the Seventh's "I" Company, whose men blamed the Army for their leader's death. "L" Company was sent to relieve "I."

Within hours, the Army captain whose company had begun the abandonment of the ridge was relieved and assigned to Graves Registration recording the particulars of the dead. Also relieved of his duties was the company executive officer.

Graves Registration was a new unit formed during the recent Marianas campaign under the aegis of the Fleet Marine Force. It retrieved the bodies of Marines, sailors, and soldiers, often at great personal risk. After removing one of the deceased's two identification tags and placing it in a bag with his personal effects, the Graves men transported the remains to the beach for positive identification, record-keeping, and burial.

Corporal Norman Keller said that being a stretcher-bearer for a burial detail meant contact with decomposing corpses. "You might grab hold of one of them under their arms and the arm would come off," he said. "Stink, my god. You don't form too much affection for others."[7]

Meanwhile, south of the abandoned village of Garekoru, situated amid coconut groves in a broad coastal plain between the ridgeline and the shore, the 321st discovered a narrow trail that appeared to meander eastward. Hopeful that the trail might be the passage to the East Road that it was seeking, the Army regiment sent its "E" Company to explore it.[8]

The rest of the 321st remained on the West Road, where a strong patrol backed by tanks and flamethrower-equipped amtanks pushed past Garekoru to an abandoned Japanese radio transmitting station.

The trail being scouted by "E" Company was a lucky find. Not shown on the maps, it climbed into the hills that comprised the northern perimeter of the Umurbrogol before terminating at the East Road.

As it approached the East Road, "E" captured Hill 100 (not to be confused with the hill by that name where Captain Pope's company waged its costly fight) and held the promontory through the night against enemy infiltrators. They came from nearby Hill B, which dominated the saddle over which the trail passed. Strongly held by the Japanese, Hill B also overlooked the East Road and Peleliu's swampy eastern shore.[9]

The next morning, an "E" Company patrol set out for the East Road. Although Japanese soldiers concealed in caves and tunnels inside Hill 100 lashed the Americans with heavy fire, the patrol reached its destination. The shrinking Japanese pocket in the Umurbrogol was now nearly surrounded and isolated.

Proud of the success of its first foray on Peleliu, the 321st christened the pathway the "321st Infantry Trail."[10] The trail was narrow and primitive and crossed swampy ground before climbing into the low coral ridges. Bulldozers immediately began widening it so that it could accommodate American supporting arms: amtrac flamethrowers, self-propelled guns, and tanks.[11]

However, Hill B, on the north side of the trail opposite Hill 100, remained in Japanese hands. It was defended by the 2nd Battalion's 4th Company – which included reinforcements led by Major Yoshio Iida that had landed from barges in northern Peleliu during the previous two nights. Hill B had to be neutralized before American vehicles could safely traverse the 321st Infantry Trail to the East Road without being interdicted by enemy gunfire.[12]

Japanese ground fire hit an artillery observation plane that was attempting to identify enemy positions near the trail, and the plane crash-landed behind Japanese lines. Lieutenant Gordon Costello of the 321st's "F" Company led a patrol to the crash site, reaching it before the Japanese did. The patrol saved the two injured crewmen from an agonizing fate in enemy hands.[13]

The next day, September 26, the 321st's 3rd Battalion was given the mission of capturing Hill B, supported by the 2nd Battalion, which occupied positions around Hill 100.

When the 3rd Battalion, under an umbrella of tank and naval gunfire, attacked at 7 a.m., the Wildcats were met by a storm of grenades and knee-mortar and machine-gun fire from Hill B and adjacent ridges to its west. The intensive enemy fire stopped the advance short of its objective. A second attempt 90 minutes later also failed. "The Japanese would run us off, and then we would go back up there," said rifleman Bert Neill.[14]

"I" Company lost its commander and executive officer to battle wounds. A reconnaissance patrol sent into the ridges never returned; two weeks later, 12 decomposing bodies were found in a ravine.[15] The Japanese on Hill B also mourned their slain comrades, who included two popular second lieutenants. "All personnel turned crimson with rage," said the Japanese 4th Company's combat report.[16]

The 321st made a new attack plan. It called for the 2nd Battalion and an armored column to attack Hill B from three sides: Companies "E" and "F" from the south and west, respectively, while Companies "I" and "L" from the 3rd Battalion provided supporting gunfire from ridges to the west.

The armored column was named Task Force Neal for its commander, Captain George Neal, the 2nd Battalion's operations officer. It would attack from the north after traveling on the West Road north to Junction 15, then turning to the east and south down the East Road. The Neal force consisted of 45 infantrymen, seven medium Sherman tanks from the 710th Tank Battalion, six amtanks, an amtrac flamethrower, and a demolition squad.[17]

At 3 p.m., "E" and "F" companies descended Hill 100 and occupied their assault positions south and west of Hill B. The armored column fought off a Japanese attack 200 yards from Hill B, killing 15 enemy troops, and approached the hill.

The attack began at 4 p.m. when mortars fired white phosphorus shells that enveloped Hill B in smoke. Overcoming strong resistance, "E" and "F" Companies stormed the hilltop. During the 45-minute assault, all of the Japanese defenders were killed; 20 Korean laborers surrendered.

It was the 81st Division's first successful mission on Peleliu. Moreover, it was a significant achievement. Seizing Hills B and 100 and securing the 321st Infantry Trail divided the remaining Japanese forces on Peleliu, trapping most of them in what became known as the Umurbrogol Pocket to the south.[18]

In an after-action report, the Japanese 4th Company discussed the American soldiers' reliance on firepower when they were on the offensive. "The speed of penetration is very slow, and if it ends in failure after displaying firepower, the men retreat out of the danger zone and the attack is repeated later," the report said, adding, "The enemy who heavily relies on firepower is bound to be afraid of firepower." Although that statement might sometimes be true, the report left unsaid how defenders whose firepower was being steadily depleted might profit from it.[19]

From Babelthuap, General Inoue had attempted on September 23–24 to reinforce Colonel Nakagawa's Peleliu forces 20 miles to the south with hundreds of troops from the 15th Infantry Regiment's 2nd Battalion. While being interrogated after Japan's surrender, Inoue said that he made the effort "for the sake of the garrison at Peleliu and to bolster the morale of the troops there."[20] Twenty-two barges, large and small, described as being "in the last stages of deterioration," were assembled for the operation.

The destroyer *H.L. Edwards* spotted the first group of reinforcements in seven barges. *Edwards* sank one barge; however, the other six reached a northern Peleliu beach just after midnight. Air strikes, naval gunfire, and machine-gun fire destroyed the barges, but the reinforcements, 174 men led by Major Yoshio Iida, marched all night and reached the northern Umurbrogol and Hill B just before dawn on the 24th.

The rest of the 2nd Battalion left Babelthuap in 15 barges during the night of the 23rd. A mile from Peleliu's shore, the little flotilla came under fire from American destroyers. Nine barges landed safely around daybreak on the 24th, but the other six ran aground near shore. Amtanks destroyed them, along with some of the soldiers that were aboard. The survivors waded to shore, but without arms, ammunition, or food. They made contact with Nakagawa's main force two days later.[21]

While attempting to search the wrecks on the reef, ten Marines in an amtrac were fired on. They killed six enemy soldiers and captured one. The prisoner said most of his comrades had disappeared into the northern hills.

U.S. intelligence reports estimated that 300 to 600 Japanese soldiers from the 15th Infantry's 2nd Battalion managed to reach prepared positions in northern Peleliu.[22] It was the last major Japanese reinforcement effort. General Inoue had planned to send three battalions from Babelthuap to Peleliu in October, but American warplanes destroyed so many barges that the plan had to be abandoned. "It was impossible to even attempt reinforcing Peleliu because of the lack of shipping," Inoue later said.

Nakagawa urged Inoue to not waste manpower in further reinforcement attempts. He would continue to fight with the troops that he had.[23]

Generals Geiger and Rupertus were now fully awake to the danger that they courted by failing to completely secure northern Peleliu. The 1st Marine Division and the 81st Division were tightening a noose around the Umurbrogol, and fresh Japanese troops from Babelthuap must not be permitted to reinforce Nakagawa's besieged men.

Geiger ordered the Navy to dispatch more picket ships to patrol off Akarakora Point, and he increased aerial reconnaissance flights over Babelthuap. Amtanks began to patrol the northern reefs, which were too shallow for naval vessels.

Geiger and Rupertus sent the Fifth Marines from eastern Peleliu up the West Road to secure Peleliu's northern tip. They planned to also capture the tiny island of Ngesebus, which lay across 500 yards of shallow water from Peleliu; at low tide, the water was just 4 feet deep. A wooden causeway, now broken, had once joined the two islands.

The 321st Infantry would become responsible for the area of northern Peleliu east of the Fifth Marines' sector while the First Marines, awaiting evacuation to Pavavu, took over the Fifth's passive security duties around Purple Beach.[24]

On the 25th, the Fifth Marines and nine tanks moved to the West Road and advanced northward, coming abreast of the 321st near Garekoru. The Fifth passed quickly through the Army regiment and proceeded to northern Peleliu, bypassing Road Junction 15, where the East and West roads met.

Forming a "regimental beachhead," the Fifth dug in near the abandoned Japanese radio station, unsure of enemy strength in the area.

The Japanese announced their presence to the 2nd Battalion with a sudden mortar barrage on its headquarters in the radio station. Men fell, mortally wounded, around Major Gordon Gayle, the battalion

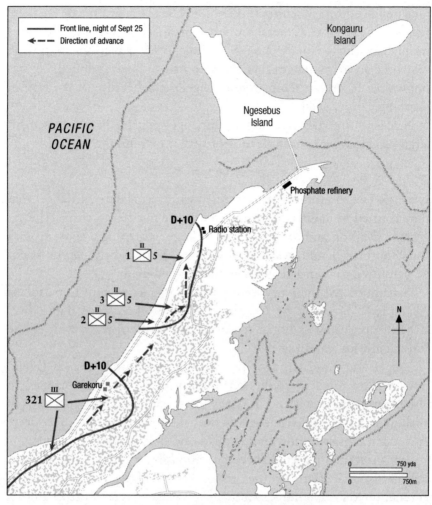

MAP 6: Northern Peleliu and Ngesebus

commander, "but he was lucky and never got a scratch, just sand blown in his eyes, and the helmet blown full of holes. Lucky he didn't have the helmet on," the battalion operations report said.[25]

The 1st Battalion bivouacked 300 yards from a hill that it learned was held by the Japanese. The enemy position was in fact defended by two 70mm guns, as well as mortars and 37mm guns on Ngesebus Island. During the night, the 1st Battalion repelled three Japanese counterattacks.[26]

On the morning of the 26th, the Fifth Marines scouted the four nearby east-west hills that lay athwart the area's most prominent terrain feature, Amiangal Mountain. Hills 1,2, 3, and Radar Hill, on which stood a Japanese radar station, together comprised what became known as "Hill Row." Radar Hill, taller than the others, was steep and sheer-sided.

Artillery, mortars, automatic weapons, and infantrymen – up to 1,500 enemy troops in all – defended the four hills. Each hill stood alone, without pre-registered supporting fire from the others. Most of the defenders belonged to the 346th Independent Infantry Battalion, a mash-up of former service and transportation troops, along with some naval personnel and soldiers from miscellaneous units.

Amiangal Mountain, however, was the apotheosis of Peleliu's underground defensive network. The 214th Naval Construction Battalion, a unit of former miners and mining engineers, had painstakingly excavated it. Multi-level, it featured numerous entrances and exits.

The Fifth Marines quickly recognized that the defenders, although well-armed and fighting from inside cave-and-tunnel complexes that rivaled or surpassed those of the Umurbrogol, were not as tenacious as the Japanese infantrymen that held Peleliu's central ridges. Most of the Amiangal's defenders were the very naval construction troops that had created the elaborate underground network. Although they were superior excavators, most of them lacked infantry training.[27]

As the Marine regiment took positions to begin assaulting Peleliu's northern hills, a Marine found a note pinned to the uniform of a dead Japanese soldier that undoubtedly inspired levity. The note read:

> American brave soldiers, we think you much pitied since landing on this isle despite your pitiful battle. We are sorry that we can give you only fire, not even good water… You have done brave by your duty, now, abandon your guns and come in Japanese military with white flag (or handkerchief), so we will be glad to see you and welcome you as comfortable as we can.

The Marines did not oblige.[28]

Colonel Harold Harris's aerial reconnaissance of northern Peleliu had convinced him of the prudence of using "deliberate tactics" to destroy the Japanese defenders. He did not plan to launch the headlong attacks that had resulted in the First Marines' destruction as a combat unit. Harris instead intended to utilize all available heavy firepower and supporting arms before sending his infantrymen into action.[29]

As it approached Hill Row, the 1st Battalion was pounded by intensive mortar, artillery, and automatic weapons fire from Hill 1 and from a nearby abandoned phosphate mine and processing plant. The Fifth's 2nd Battalion pushed around the stymied 1st's left flank. The battalion bypassed Hill 1 and advanced over flat terrain to the northeast while being fired on by the Japanese troops on Hill 1 and Ngesebus – "far from a happy state," its report ruefully acknowledged. Four tanks were badly damaged.

Before nightfall, however, the 2nd Battalion had managed to capture the southern flank and crest of Amiangal Mountain. At the same time, "B" Company seized Hill 2 after a six-hour gun battle. "It was bad because they were trying to catch us in the valleys," said Sergeant Walter Afflito. "We'd go up one hill and down another, and they'd hit us with grenades and machine gun fire [on the low ground]. You see, once you got down there, it was very tough getting out."[30]

During the night of September 26–27, Major Gordon Gayle, the 2nd Battalion commander, requested that a 155mm gun be brought up from Major George Hanna's 8th 155mm Gun Battalion for the next day's assault on Amiangal Mountain's western caves. In spite of torrential rains that fell overnight, the big gun was wrestled into position for use the next morning. If the gun were able to neutralize the Amiangal's western caves, a bulldozer could fill in a deep antitank ditch that barred tanks from supporting an infantry attack. The infantry-tank assault could then proceed.[31]

Just as the infantry units had been forced to adapt to Peleliu's inhospitable conditions, so had the 155mm howitzer battalion bent its protocols to meet the battlefield's needs after landing at midday on September 16. Since coming ashore, the battalion's three batteries had carried out their missions from a 200-square-yard area near the beachhead, with two batteries firing "trail to trail" in opposite directions and the third one "in march order" nearby for use as needed. Now, a battalion howitzer would go into action at the very tip of the spear.[32]

The 155mm gun went to work on the Amiangal's western caves right after daybreak on September 27. With a 10-mile range, the big gun was massive overkill for reducing a target mere hundreds of yards away – which was precisely why Major Gayle had requested it.

Indeed, at such close range, the gunners were forced to take cover from the debris produced by their own shells. After the gun battered the Japanese guns in the caves into silence, a tank bulldozer crept forward and filled in the antitank ditch. Then, tank-infantry teams pushed around Amiangal to its northern nose. There, the steep terrain crowded the road skirting the island's northern end so closely that there remained only room for the passage of a single tank.

A massive cave mouth dominated Amiangal's northern nose. From inside it the Japanese poured fire onto the attackers. The cave was the island's largest and best-supplied; inside were barracks, mess facilities, a hospital, and large storage areas. It was so capacious that 1,000 enemy troops might eat and sleep there at one time.[33]

The variegated assault on Amiangal utilized the Eleventh Marines' big guns, which bombarded Ngesebus Island in order to suppress the gunfire that had thwarted free movement on northern Peleliu. Navy destroyers shelled Kongauru Island, which lay adjacent to Ngesebus.

Nine tanks lobbed smoke shells onto Ngesebus's beaches to cloak the movement of five amtanks armed with 75mm howitzers. They clambered onto the reef 300 yards north of Amiangal Mountain and blasted the massive cave mouth, which enabled tanks and an amtrac flamethrower to plaster the cave at closer range with 75mm shellfire and napalm. The Marines scrambled to the mountain crest.[34] In the process of reducing Amiangal's defenses, Colonel Harris fulfilled his vow to use deliberate tactics and every available support weapon.

Although the Marines might claim Amiangal's exterior, hundreds of enemy soldiers and sailors remained inside the hill. The aroma of cooking fish and rice that occasionally wafted from its recesses was an irritating reminder to the Marines of their precarious situation. At irregular intervals, the Japanese blasted open the caves that the Marines had sealed and attacked impetuously. The Marines welcomed the opportunity to shoot them down in the open.

In a letter to his wife Esther, General O.P. Smith, the assistant division commander, expressed grudging respect for the enemy's tenacity. "The

Germans in a similar situation would long since have turned themselves in," he wrote.[35]

Amiangal's giant cavern, evidently once part of a phosphate mine, was the terminus of a complex cave-and-tunnel system with nine entrances that reached deep inside the mountain.[36] Nearby lay the ruins of a phosphate processing plant. The Japanese had converted it into a blockhouse, carving gun ports from its reinforced concrete foundation and digging an antitank ditch around it. It was supported by machine gunners in caves 50 yards away.

There being just the one tank bulldozer available, the 2nd Battalion waited until it had filled in the antitank ditch on the west side of Amiangal. The bulldozer then lumbered over to the phosphate plant and filled in the antitank ditch as a hailstorm of machine-gun fire bounced off its blade and the tank's armor.

Major Gayle's battalion, now supported by tanks and a flamethrower-equipped amtrac, attacked the blockhouse and the nearby caves. The amtrac incinerated the blockhouse; 60 enemy bodies were found inside.[37]

The 1st Battalion resumed its assault on heavily defended Hill 1. The attack by "B" and "C" Companies began at 9:30 a.m. and lasted all day. The enemy naval construction troops resisted to the bitter end and had to be wiped out one position at a time, often after frenzied close combat. The Marines destroyed four 37mm guns and four 75mm guns, plus a large number of automatic weapons. While "C" Company secured the hilltop, engineer demolitionists sealed every cave opening.[38]

Gayle's men pushed northward toward a ridge honeycombed with caves that bristled with machine guns. To neutralize the caves, the Marines hit them with every available weapon: grenades, Composition C wrapped around mortar shells, 5-gallon gasoline cans, flamethrowers, artillery, tanks, phosphorus mortar shells, and the 155mm gun. The roaring gunfire and flames drove the Japanese deep into the caves. Then, the Marines brought up the amtrac flamethrower to finish them off. But the amtrac broke down. Determined to utilize it anyway, Gayle's men used tanks and cable lines to drag the amtrac from position to position so that it could pour burning napalm and gasoline into the caves' deepest recesses.[39]

The Fifth Marines now controlled the northern tip of Peleliu. The stage was set for a shore-to-shore assault on Ngesebus and the island adjacent to it, Kongauru.[40]

Five hundred entrenched Japanese soldiers occupied tiny Ngesebus. Its two large naval guns, several 75mm field pieces, and dozens of mortars also supported Japanese positions in Hill Row and on Amiangal Mountain. Reports suggested that Ngesebus had a fighter airstrip that *Stalemate*'s commanders hoped to utilize.

The square mile of Ngesebus was flat, except for a cluster of 20-foot-high hills and ridges in the island's northwestern corner. Japanese soldiers in pillboxes and blockhouses defended the highlands but, like northern Peleliu's fortifications, Ngesebus's had not been integrated into a mutually supporting network.[41]

The Fifth Marines' 3rd Battalion was designated as the Ngesebus landing force. It had been winnowed by heat and enemy steel from 1,000 men on D-Day to about 700. Yet, by the standards of the battered 1st Division, the 3rd Battalion, led by Major John Gustafson, was a relatively intact unit. It would spearhead the infantry attack, with "E" Company and the Seventh Marines' 2nd Battalion acting as its reserve.[42]

The assault scripted by Fifth Marines senior officers Colonel Harold Harris and Lieutenant Colonel Lew Walt was going to be a land, sea, and air operation, and a constellation of VIPs had gathered to observe it from the Fifth Marines' command post on Peleliu's northernmost beach. They included Admiral George Fort; Marine generals Roy Geiger, William Rupertus, Julian Smith, and O.P. Smith; and Army generals Paul Mueller and Marcus Bell of the 81st Division.[43]

At 8 a.m. on September 28, the invasion began with the throaty roar of Marine artillery fire, and naval gunfire from the battleship *Mississippi* and the cruisers *Columbus* and *Denver*. Then white-nosed Marine Corsairs from VMF-114 – Major Robert "Cowboy" Stout's squadron, which had arrived at Peleliu's airfield two days earlier – strafed and bombed the beaches. Ten minutes before H-Hour, Stout's Corsairs returned to strafe the landing beach from an altitude of just 50 feet.[44]

At 9 a.m., the invasion force of 35 amtracs carrying the Marine assault troops, and 13 Sherman amphibious tanks set out for Ngesebus's shore. Then, to the Marines' consternation, the Navy prematurely lifted its bombardment. Instantly grasping the situation, Stout's pilots resumed their air strikes as the Marines on the amtracs cheered and pumped their fists in the air, until the first waves had drawn within 30 yards of the shore.

A Japanese prisoner later said the last-minute air attack was "the most terrifying and effective of any of the preparation fires on the beach." The air strikes pinned enemy troops in their pillboxes and a bunker near the beach until the "swimming" Shermans led the Marines ashore. An impressed General Rupertus later wrote Major Stout: "I hand out very few compliments and when I do they mean something. That was a very 'gutty' show you put on."[45]

The first wave, consisting of the Shermans and amtanks, landed at 9:11 a.m. and overwhelmed the beach defenders before they could mount an effective resistance. Amtracs then put ashore the Marine assault troops in waves two through four at five-minute intervals. The Marines killed or captured 50 Japanese soldiers without suffering a single casualty.[46]

As mortar squad leader R.V. Burgin's team began setting up near a bunker, the Marines discovered that the bunker was still occupied. They sprayed it with machine-gun fire and dropped grenades down the vent pipe. Nearly as quickly as the grenades landed inside, the Japanese pitched them back outside.

Burgin flagged down an amtrac, which blew a hole in the bunker. A flamethrower doused the shrieking defenders through the hole with fire and napalm. Three burning survivors staggered outside, where Marine riflemen cut them down. Seventeen dead enemy soldiers were counted in and around the bunker.[47]

The battalion pushed inland, and "L" Company turned eastward toward Kongauru. "L" landed a platoon and three amtanks there at 1 p.m., and within three hours had completely swept the islet, scooping up Korean and Okinawan laborers as prisoners.[48]

On Ngesebus, Pfc E.B. Sledge and "K" Company had advanced nearly to the airstrip when an enemy light machine gun pinned down Sledge and a comrade. The Nambu's bullets snapped viciously overhead. Hugging the ground behind a rock, Sledge heard a sound like a stick snapping, and his companion shouted, "Oh, God, I'm hit!" and clutched his left elbow.

Sledge dragged the man to a less-exposed place and summoned a corpsman. When they realized that a sniper, and not the machine gun, had wounded the Marine, two men went hunting for the sniper. A few minutes later, one of them waved and called out, "We got the bastard; he ain't gonna shoot nobody else."[49]

While advancing along Ngesebus's shoreline, Pfc Joe Moskalczak was surprised to see two Japanese soldiers walking toward him. He shot and killed the one nearest him, and wounded the other man, who ran toward a small coral island. "As I approached, I heard a Jap grenade go off; he had held the grenade to the left side of his chest," said Moskalczak.[50]

Pfc James Isabelle and his comrades were checking caves near the beach and shouting a Japanese phrase demanding that the occupants surrender when two Japanese emerged from a cave. While they were being escorted down the beach, one of the two prisoners made a break for the water and was cut down by a BAR man. The second prisoner, evidently expecting to also be shot, flung himself on the ground and, grasping a photo of his family, groveled at Isabelle's feet while pleading for his life. Isabelle handed the man a cigarette and led him down the beach.[51]

The Marines overran most of the Japanese positions on Ngesebus by 5 p.m. Holdouts continued to resist from a 300-by-500-yard area on the island's northern extremity, but most of them were wiped out by the middle of the next day, September 29.

While completing the island's conquest, the Marines came upon a strange sight: a Japanese machine-gun squad whose members had died frozen in the act of defending their post. With the top of his head gone, the gunner was seated next to the weapon. By his side lay the assistant gunner. Strung out behind the gun were ammunition carriers, each with a box of ammunition on his back – all struck down by a hurricane of American gunfire.[52]

Ngesebus was pronounced secured on September 29, and the 3rd Battalion, relieved by the 321st's 2nd Battalion, boarded Higgins Boats and sailed to Purple Beach on eastern Peleliu for a hot meal beyond the range of enemy snipers.

Major Gustafson's 3rd Battalion reported that it had killed 440 Japanese troops and had captured 23 others, in addition to the laborers taken prisoner on Kongauru. The operation cost the Marines 15 killed and 25 wounded. Five of the Marine dead were killed when a round fired by the last operable Japanese gun landed in their hole; three of their comrades were wounded.

The capture of Ngesebus and Kongauru might have looked easy to the gallery of watching VIPs, but in fact it was a rare textbook example of a successful combined arms operation. It showed what could be accomplished with Colonel Harris's tactical approach and its emphasis on concentrated firepower. "Infantry and armor performed with a ruthless efficiency unequaled in any previous Pacific operation," the 1st Marine Division battle diary said of the Ngesebus assault.

Ngesebus's fighter airstrip was a disappointment, however; it was built on soft sand that could not support fighter planes.[53]

At the end of September 28, Navy headquarters at Pearl Harbor reported that U.S. troops controlled all of Peleliu, except for "two small Japanese pockets which were still under attack." Those pockets of resistance – in the Umurbrogol and on the island's northeastern tip – would continue to defy U.S. forces for several weeks. The naval communique also stated that the Japanese dead on Peleliu and Angaur numbered 8,537, while U.S. casualties totaled 5,500, including 788 men killed in action.[54]

As Gustafson's 3rd Battalion sailed from Ngesebus to Purple Beach for a rest, its sister 2nd Battalion pressed its attack on Amiangal's nine cave mouths with tanks, machine guns, and flamethrowers. From ingeniously contrived positions, the stronghold's defenders resisted as stubbornly as did Colonel Nakagawa's men in the Umurbrogol Pocket.

On the 29th, the Marines saturated Amiangal's northern entrance with bullets, shellfire, and flames. Fifty Japanese suddenly bolted through the smoking entryway; all but one was killed. Yet scores of enemy troops remained alive inside the mountain as the Marines methodically sealed all of the entrances with explosives – only to have them blasted open from the inside by the Japanese.[55]

On September 30, Marine artillerists again placed a 155mm howitzer outside the Amiangal's largest western cave, while machine-gun crews positioned themselves in defilade on the hill's eastern side. At 10 a.m., Marines fired the "Long Tom" into the cave mouth at such short range that the gun crewmen, as before, were forced to take cover from the shell fragments and debris.

The round ignited a munitions cache inside the mountain that exploded with three sharp thunderclaps. Enemy soldiers poured out of the openings in the hill's eastern side – to be mowed down by the waiting Marine machine gunners. "My God, it was like shooting fish in a barrel," a Marine lieutenant said. "We could see our machine guns turning those poor guys into mincemeat."[56]

A Japanese prisoner told his captors that 50 abled-bodied men remained alive inside Amiangal, plus many wounded men that had been moved into three tunnels. During subsequent Marine assaults on Amiangal's cave entrances prior to their sealing them, flamethrowers incinerated all of the wounded men in the tunnels. Yet more than two dozen Japanese somehow continued to survive inside the hill for months – until early 1945, when an explosion killed 19 enemy soldiers. Afterward, eight others were captured after being wounded, or having been dug out of the debris.[57]

The Fifth Marines' 1st Battalion methodically neutralized nearby Hills 1, 2, and 3 by using every weapon at hand. Of the numbered hills, the most stubbornly defended was Hill 3, captured on September 29 after a day-long siege with bazookas and explosives to clean out its fortified caves. Forty Japanese were killed in the fighting.

On the 30th, the 1st Battalion tackled Radar Hill, dome-shaped and 200 feet high. The Marines attacked it from two sides, reaching the summit late in the afternoon. Demolition teams sealed Radar Hill's largest cave mouth by detonating explosives above it to trigger a landslide that buried the cave entrance.[58]

After Major Gayle's 2nd Battalion secured Amiangal Mountain, it pushed south along Hill Row and flushed Japanese naval construction troops hiding in a swamp, killing or capturing 70 of them. The 2nd also battled 200 enemy soldiers fighting from the rubble of the phosphate refinery.[59]

A wounded Japanese seaman who was taken prisoner told his captors that he, 40 other patients, and medical personnel had managed to survive in a hospital cave on seepage and rainwater. Japanese officers then ordered them to return to their units. Each was issued a stick of dynamite and told to take his own life rather than be captured. Most of the men threw away the dynamite, only to be killed by American tanks before they could surrender, the prisoner said.

Colonel Nakagawa conceded the loss of northern Peleliu in a report to General Inoue's headquarters on September 30. "Our surviving forces are attempting to dash southward, cutting through the enemy in order to join the main force."[60]

The Marines attempted to coax holdouts from their hiding places inside the caves and tunnels, but without success – until a Japanese prisoner, formerly a naval antiaircraft gunner, volunteered to assist them. As the Marines watched, the POW approached two caves. Outside the first cave, he was met by a thrown grenade and automatic weapons fire. After also being driven away from the second cave, he entered a third cave and emerged with nine prisoners.

Colonel Joseph Hankins, the 1st Division's provost marshal and the commander of the Headquarters Battalion, was so impressed by the prisoner's courage that he began taking the diminutive man with him wherever he went. He might have regarded him as a good luck talisman; if Hankins did, he did not recognize its limits.[61]

On October 1, Colonel Harris withdrew the Fifth Marines' 1st and 2nd Battalions to the regiment's rest area near Purple Beach, where they joined the 3rd Battalion. The Army's 321st Infantry Regiment took responsibility for northern Peleliu. Harris left it to the artillery to complete the reduction of Hill 3 and Radar Hill.[62]

While campaigning in northern Peleliu and on Ngesebus, the Fifth Marines reported killing 1,572 enemy soldiers, taking 72 prisoners, and capturing more than 300 fortified positions. The Fifth lost 87 men killed in action, and 217 wounded.

The capture of northern Peleliu's hills completed the isolation of the Umurbrogol Pocket, which on September 27 ranged in length, north to south, from 1,200 to 1,900 yards, and east to west, 550 yards.[63]

On September 27, as artillery fire crashed in the northern hills, Peleliu was declared secured. Marines battling hundreds of Japanese troops entrenched deep inside caves and tunnels in northern Peleliu would have disagreed. That day, too, a ceremony was held at Peleliu's airfield to mark the transfer of overall command of Palau operations from Admiral Theodore Wilkinson to Admiral George Fort.[64]

The Seventh Marines began relieving the 321st Infantry after the Army regiment secured Hill B, and on October 2 the Seventh moved to the northern edge of the Umurbrogol Pocket. That day also saw the conversion of the Marines' 155mm howitzer battalion into an infantry battalion. Because the Pocket each day was being compressed into a smaller area, the artillery was now just as apt to inflict friendly fire casualties as it was to kill Japanese defenders.

"Take off your dungarees and don the infantry uniform. You are to go to the front lines, acting as infantry to hold a defensive sector," the artillery battalion's new orders said. Four hundred eighty-five artillerymen were assigned to defensive positions. Within a few hours of receiving their orders, the artillerymen were issued carbines, grenades, and Thompson submachine guns, and were sent to the Pocket's western and northern perimeters. They adopted a new nickname, "infantillery."[65]

The Japanese wasted no time in testing them. During the infantillery's first night on the battle lines, enemy infiltrators attacked three times but failed to break through. The former artillerymen reported losses of one killed and 14 wounded. Over the next two weeks, until they were relieved, the gunners would sustain 84 casualties; seven of them were killed in action.

The use of specialists as infantrymen became more common as casualties mounted. Among the newly anointed infantrymen could also be found amtrac crewmen; pioneers; stevedores from the 16th Field Depot; and clerks, cooks, truck drivers and communications men. A messman won a Silver Star, and a Marine combat correspondent was wounded while supervising a machine-gun section.[66]

Feeling guilty about their fellow Marines fighting in the ridges while they carried out their duties in the relative safety of secured areas, some men volunteered as stretcher-bearers or ammunition carriers, or to serve on the "containment lines." Among them were the Black Marines of the 16th Depot Company, stevedores who acquired the reputation of being the "volunteeringest" in the Marine Corps.[67]

The Marine Corps began accepting African American recruits in 1942. Recruit training began in September 1942 at Montford Point, North Carolina, where the first class graduated in November. Black Marine stevedores and ammunition carriers came under fire for the first time on Saipan and later on Guam. On Peleliu, the Black Marines initially transferred supplies from transports to vessels bound for the beaches. Upon going ashore, they worked in the supply dumps, they transported supplies and ammunition to the front lines, and they helped evacuate the wounded, which often resulted in casualties.

Private Dyrel Shuler of the 7th Ammunition Company became the first Black Marine casualty on September 20. Two days later, Private Predell Hamblin was hit by enemy fire, and on September 23–24, eight depot Marines were wounded. The 22 Black Marines wounded on Peleliu – one died of his wounds – was the highest casualty rate of any Black Marine unit during World War II.[68]

Unlike the Black Marines and the other volunteers, some men ventured into the ridges not to serve, but to profit – by looting caves and enemy bodies for souvenirs – trophies such as Rising Sun flags, swords, and weapons to trade for food or to sell. Sometimes the souvenir hunters were wounded, and front-line Marines had to risk their lives to rescue the profiteering sailors, Seabees, airfield ground personnel, and other noncombatants.

When caught pocketing souvenirs, the front-line visitors were sometimes handed a weapon, put in the battle line, and kept there by force if necessary. Until company officers permitted them to leave or notified their superiors of their whereabouts, the souvenir-hunters were listed on their unit rosters as absent without leave. It isn't known whether these unhappy outcomes served as a deterrent.[69]

The day after relieving the 321st, the Seventh began squeezing the Umurbrogol Pocket from the north and the west. The 1st and 3rd Battalions pushed southward into the northern parts of the Pocket on October 3, with the goal of seizing Boyd Ridge and Boyd's southern extension, Walt Ridge.

To the south, the 2nd Battalion advanced into the line of ridges above Death Valley, and the Pioneer Battalion occupied static defensive positions near the West Road. The Weapons Company dug in at the mouth of the Horseshoe, with its left flank extended to the base of Hill 300 and the Five Sisters.[70]

Three days after its strafing attacks on Ngesebus's beach, Major Stout's VMF-114 was given a precision bombing mission: its Corsairs were to drop twenty 1,000-pound bombs on a 100-square-yard area inside the Pocket. It might have seemed like overkill, but artillery had failed to knock out the fortified observation point atop the target ridge, which was honeycombed with underground blockhouses on multiple levels.

Beforehand, the pilots were given a detailed briefing that included the precise locations of nearby friendly forces. Squadron and infantry commanders then conducted a joint aerial reconnaissance of the target. At the mission's outset, colored smoke grenades were detonated to mark the Seventh Marine lines.

The planning and precautions paid off: the bombing mission went off as planned, and the thunderous explosions drowned out all other sounds in the Pocket.[71]

Later on September 30, the Seventh Regiment broadcast surrender appeals as aircraft dropped leaflets over the Pocket. Sergeant William Crawmer shoved the leaflets out of a torpedo bomber's tail gunner position as fast as he could. "They looked like snow coming down," said Crawmer. "It looked like snow on top of those coconut palms."[72]

The leaflets said: "As you can see if you look at the planes, the material and the ships, your best efforts are not impeding our work. You still have this choice – raise a white flag and come out unarmed. We will give you water, food, shelter and medicine for your wounded."

No one surrendered.[73]

———

A patrol from the Seventh's 3rd Battalion groped its way through rain and fog west of the East Road until encountering a rocky height that rose like a "wart" from the northern nose of a long, narrow ridge. The Marines named it Baldy Hill. Its defenders spotted the Marine patrol, and the hill suddenly came alive with enemy troops lobbing mortar shells. The patrol withdrew.

At 7:30 a.m. on October 1, the 3rd Battalion attacked Baldy. The frontal attack bogged down amid a blizzard of rifle and machine-gun fire from Baldy and adjacent Hill 120.[74]

Baldy defied capture on October 1. At 4:15 p.m. that day, an entry made in the 3rd Battalion journal read, "The Battalion Surgeon reported to Medical Surgeon that the Third Battalion, Seventh Marines is medically unfit to push." The battalion's combat efficiency was below 50 percent, in large part due to an outbreak of diarrhea.

Torrential rains had begun falling on September 28 as a typhoon approached the Palaus. Under cover of the rains, Colonel Nakagawa sent specially trained raiding parties from the Umurbrogol Pocket to probe the American front lines. They also struck the Seventh Marines' sick bay, its quartermaster command post, and the operations center before withdrawing into the waterlogged ridges.[75]

When the storm's full force began pummeling Peleliu, it made a shambles of the pontoon causeway on Orange Beach 3. Crashing 30-foot waves drove ashore three LSTs at Orange Beach and two LSTs moored at Purple Beach. Resupply operations were suspended for three days. Transports and LSTs had to put to sea.[76] The typhoon's heavy rains dropped the temperature from 110 to a comfortable 80 degrees, turned the coral dust to mud, and clogged weapons.

Because rough seas prevented supplies from being landed by boat, 16 transport planes conducted an emergency airlift of supplies from Saipan to Peleliu. It was the largest emergency mission of its kind of the Pacific War.[77]

The Umurbrogol Pocket's irredeemable harshness sobered the Seventh Marines when they first entered it to fight.

"It was a ghastly place," said Captain Don Wyckoff, the Seventh's "B" Company commander. "The feel of this thing was so alien, and ... you couldn't get away from it anywhere... There was no way to take cover. There was no way to bury the dead."[78] Bodies blackened and decomposed within hours. Maggots quickly infested their eyes and mouths. Some Marines used the bloated Japanese corpses for target practice. "And there were thousands of bodies," said Captain Wyckoff. "They would swell in hours. They would burst. You'd be out there at night and you could hear them pop ... and you'd get this noisome smell of the gases ... It was just a horror."[79]

The widespread decay and ruin inspired a Marine air unit to nickname Peleliu "Nothing Atoll."[80]

Rupertus laid plans for the Seventh Regiment to launch a major offensive against the Pocket. The main effort would target the East Road and the ridges overlooking it, while a diversionary attack would be made against the Five Sisters.

Before the operation began, Lieutenant Colonel Spencer Berger, the Seventh's 2nd Battalion commander, and all nine of his company commanders reconnoitered Walt Ridge from the air. The Japanese closely watched the preparations for the attack against the Pocket. Colonel Nakagawa reported to headquarters in Koror, "It seems that the enemy acted as if preparing for an attack on our surrounding garrison units in the central hills." On October 3, the Seventh Marines' 2nd and 3rd Battalions assaulted Walt Ridge from the south and Boyd Ridge from the north amid typhoon-force winds that had grounded all flights.[81]

West of Walt and Boyd ridges, "K" and "L" companies of the Fifth Marines' 3rd Battalion carried out the diversionary attack into the Horseshoe and against the Five Sisters on the canyon's western side. The Fifth entered the battle zone during a downpour. The advance began with a "Ronson" flamethrower tank scorching a pillbox, and Japanese soldiers then bolting from its single exit, their clothes on fire and their faces blackened. The intense heat caused the ammunition in their cartridge belts to cook off. Fifteen enemy soldiers fell dead in a smoking heap 8 feet from the pillbox exit.[82]

The Marines then pushed into a deep crevice between two of the towering Sisters. It was like passing along a narrow street lined with six-story buildings – buildings brimming with heavily armed enemy troops, said Lieutenant Tom "Stumpy" Stanley, "K" Company's executive officer. It was eerie. "You could feel the eyes on you," said Pfc William Finnegan. "You couldn't see them, but you could feel them."[83]

Inside the rock corridor, the Marines encountered the remains of some of Puller's First Marines who had been ambushed two weeks earlier. "I'm looking left and right and all I see is dead Marines in these [shell] holes," said a shocked Pfc James Isabelle. Some of the dead lay on stretchers. Beside them were the bodies of comrades who had attempted to carry them to safety, "all of them skeletons in saggy, discolored dungarees ... Their bald faces in perpetual skeletal grins."[84]

The high-walled passageway also produced anomalous surprises, such as a large pile of shoes, possibly dumped from a truck. Pfc Joe

Moskalczak had just donned a good-fitting pair to replace his worn-out boondockers when a sniper opened fire. After he took cover behind a hay bale, a tank came up, and Moskalczak and his comrades crouched behind it. The sniper, perched on a 100-foot-high cliff to the right, killed a lieutenant before an amtrac flamethrower incinerated the enemy gunman.[85]

When a machine gun suddenly opened fire, Pfc William Finnegan dove behind a 2-foot berm. The slugs clipped Finnegan's shoes. "The guy next to me got hit and a corpsman ran up and I told him to get down, but he didn't and a couple of seconds later his helmet and a part of his head blew off."[86]

"K" and "L" ascended Sisters 1, 3, 4, and 5. From their summits, the Marines briefly savored an unobstructed view of China Wall and a previously unseen valley to its east that would become known as the Wildcat Bowl. Enemy rifle fire from many quarters drove the Marine companies from the Sisters with heavy casualties.

That night, groups of Japanese repeatedly counterattacked, "jabbering or babbling incoherent sounds, sometimes throwing a grenade, but always swinging a saber, bayonet, or knife." At one point during the confused fighting, two enemy soldiers emerged from a shallow ditch, "arms waving wildly, yelling," and one of them jumped into a foxhole. A Marine jumped out of the hole and a comrade, thinking he was a Japanese soldier, shot him. The Marine's foxhole companion then killed the intruder. The second infiltrator jumped into another foxhole, and there was a fracas and screaming. The Marine, who had lost his weapon, jammed one of his fingers through the eye of his adversary until the man died.

The next morning, the bodies of 27 Japanese were strewn around the area, most of them inside the Marines' lines. The 3rd Battalion reported that seven Marines were killed and 30 others were wounded during the day-and-night fighting.[87]

Typhoon-spawned heavy rains lashed the Seventh Marines in the ridges east of the Horseshoe when its 2nd Battalion attacked at 7 a.m. on October 3 after a heavy artillery and mortar barrage. The battalion followed a path to Walt Ridge – the former Hill 100. Captain Everett Pope's company had seized it on September 19, but had held it for just hours. A night of relentless Japanese counterattacks had driven Pope's men off the ridge.

Supported by cannon fire from half-tracks and Army tanks in the Horseshoe, the 2nd Battalion's "G" Company reached Walt Ridge's crest in just 30 minutes against light opposition. Atop the ridge, the Marines found the decayed bodies of Pope's men who had been killed in the fighting two weeks earlier.

The attackers were suddenly raked by intensive gunfire from Japanese-held caves across the Horseshoe in the eastern face of the Five Brothers, and from the high ground to the north. Enemy fire knocked out an amtrac flamethrower on the East Road below.

While attempting to cross a saddle on Walt Ridge's north side, two of every four men were killed or wounded by Japanese gunfire. The Marines attempted to bypass the deadly choke point via a covered approach on the ridge's 90-foot-high east face. Battalion engineers were dispatched. They widened the approach with explosives, and provided ropes and ladders to aid the Marines in negotiating the tricky route.

When "E" Company had succeeded in traversing the improvised route, it sent up a plume of purple smoke. The smoke was a signal to the 3rd Battalion to begin its advance from the north to nearby Boyd Ridge, 100 feet high and 200 yards long.[88]

Encountering heavy gunfire in a draw, the battalion detoured through a swamp east of the East Road. Just before 3:30 p.m., "K" Company stormed the north side of Boyd Hill and reached its summit. The 2nd and 3rd Battalions made contact at 4 p.m.

That rainy night, the Seventh secured its positions atop Walt and Boyd ridges. Most of the East Road was now in American hands, although traveling along parts of it remained dangerous, especially south of Walt Ridge and opposite the causeway over the swamp. There, enemy gunfire wounded nine members of a 12-man stretcher team, and eight of 12 men in another team.

The storm further depressed the Marines' spirits. It had "a glooming effect. The lightless sky turned the whole island gray. Dust-coated dungarees turned stiff, hard and unpliable when they dried out, and when they were wet, they were very heavy."[89]

In an extremely misleading report to Japanese Army headquarters in Koror recounting the day's fighting, Colonel Nakagawa claimed that his men repelled attacks from the north and south by two infantry battalions. "In this district about 100 enemy infiltrated our front lines secretly but were exterminated during the evening," he said. Five battalions in all participated in the attacks, wrote Nakagawa, adding that they were "believed to be Marines, with one part of the Australian Army."[90]

From atop the eastern rim of the Umurbrogol, the Seventh Marines had a splendid view of the Pocket's interior, now Peleliu's most densely fortified area and easily the strangest battlefield of the Pacific War. It was a weird landscape of razorback hills, pinnacles, knobs, and deep crevices – all shorn of vegetation by weeks of artillery and naval gunfire.

The rubble-strewn open causeway across the swamp to the Horseshoe was one of the two principal approaches to the Pocket. The pathway continued as a narrow road that led into the box canyon. The second approach was from the north. It passed through a chain of steep ridges and cliffs; stubbornly defended Baldy Ridge was its hub.

East and west of the Pocket loomed cliffs that made entry exceedingly difficult. On the east side were Walt and Boyd ridges – now held by the Seventh Marines. Together, they formed what was sometimes called the East Wall. On the west side was China Wall – 200 feet high and 200 yards long – bordered by the imposing Five Sisters and Five Brothers.[91]

The surrealistic landscape bristled with concrete pillboxes guarded by heavy machine guns. Many caves harbored artillery and heavy mortars, and were shielded by steel doors that could be quickly opened and closed. Only point-blank fire from tanks and from flamethrowers mounted on amtracs could neutralize them. The caves appeared to be impervious to naval gunfire.

"They would take them [the heavy weapons] out on these tracks and they'd fired their concentrations before we could even get counter fire on them, [then] they'd roll 'em back again," said Lieutenant Louis Schott, a Fifth Marines infantry platoon leader. "So we had to do it the hard way and just go and get 'em." Schott later reflected that "the most dangerous weapon we had was a 17-year-old kid with a rifle."[92]

Most of the enemy positions were so ingeniously concealed that a man might fight for days in the Umurbrogol without seeing a live Japanese soldier. At times, he might become aware of a strange, unnatural silence, and sense that numerous hostile eyes were watching him – and waiting. Any movement toward an enemy position invited a blaze of gunfire from multiple angles.[93]

Even after the Seventh Marines occupied Boyd and Walt ridges, intensive enemy gunfire often stopped traffic on the East Road, causing drivers and passengers to bolt from their vehicles and seek cover. The Japanese fired through three gaps in the ridges bordering the East Road: one of them originated in the Horseshoe; another was a draw between Boyd Ridge and its neighbors to the north; and the third gap lay between Boyd and Walt ridges.

On October 4, the Seventh tackled the job of stopping gunfire from coming through two of those gaps. The Fifth Marines entered the Horseshoe to stanch the third source. Major Hunter Hurst, the commander of the Seventh's 3rd Battalion, now at just 50 percent strength, sent "I" Company, aided by "F" Company of the 2nd Battalion, into the Boyd–Walt draw. "L" Company set out to suppress the fire coming from the draw on Boyd Ridge's north side. "L" also was ordered to capture three 90-foot-high dome-shaped hills to the west whose defenders provided supporting fire for the Japanese that occupied the draw.[94]

"I" Company's foray into the gap was a bloody affair without a conclusive result, aside from unsustainable casualties; the company emerged with just one officer – two others were killed – and 31 effectives. However, "L" Company seized the three knobs with surprising ease, and Hurst decided that it must push on to Hill 120, a butte that adjoined Baldy Ridge on the Pocket's north side.

Lieutenant James Dunn's 48-man platoon crawled over jagged rocks and crevices, clinging to roots and vines during its ascent of the steep slope. About 4 p.m., Dunn's men reached the summit of Hill 120, which was a 100-yard-long razorback. The platoon began moving southward down its crest. Baldy lay to the west and Boyd Ridge to the east.

Unbeknownst to them, the Marines were walking into an ambush. When automatic weapons opened up on them from a cave in Baldy Ridge, the Marines scrambled over Hill 120's sharp crest to its east side, away from Baldy – only to come under fire from Japanese troops inside caves in the western face of Boyd Ridge.

"Maintaining their excellent fire discipline, the Japanese had refrained from showing their hand until the maximum of U.S. troops had been irrevocably committed," the after-action report glumly noted. "Now, for the men caught in this savage crossfire, that coverless ridge crest became a death trap."[95]

The torrent of enemy gunfire from machine guns, machine cannons, mortars, and rifles swept through the Marines like a powerful wind gust. Point-blank fire flared from other hills near Hill 120's northern nose, making it impossible for the Marines to return to the hillcrest.

There appeared to be no way out.

While desperately seeking an escape route down the ridge's eastern side amid ricocheting bullets and deafening heavy arms fire, Lieutenant Dunn was shot. He plunged from a cliff to his death on the jagged rocks below. "The wounded crawled behind rocks or just lay motionless, bullets hitting them again and again," wrote Marine combat correspondent Jeremiah Leary. "Others cried pitifully for help and begged their comrades not to leave them there."[96] A corpsman was shot and killed when he stood to urge the men to bandage one another and escape a few at a time.

Captain James "Jamo" Shanley, "L" Company's commander, watched in horror from the valley beside Hill 120 as his men were cut to pieces. He ordered "K" Company on adjacent Boyd Hill to throw smoke grenades onto Hill 120 to mask the withdrawal of Shanley's men.[97]

The survivors dropped their weapons, freeing both hands so that they could inch down the rock cliff. Japanese soldiers inside Boyd Ridge picked off some of them; others slid down the rock face on their bellies, arriving at the bottom bloodied but alive. Fourteen men were stranded on a 10-foot-high ledge. In short order, four were killed, and six were shot and wounded. Just four remained unhurt.

One of the wounded men exhorted the four uninjured Marines to get out and leave the others behind "before it's too late." But the four able-bodied Marines vowed to stay "until hell froze over or help came."[98]

The Japanese zeroed in on the ledge. Pinned down, the unhurt men rolled their four most badly wounded comrades off the ledge into the gully; the other two wounded men jumped. They sprinted and hobbled toward a tank parked 50 yards away as the Japanese raked the area with machine-gun fire. The last two men were hit and fell before they could reach the shelter provided by the tank.

Captain Shanley, who was anxiously watching his men's ordeal, went to their aid. After lugging one of the two men lying in the open to the tank, Shanley went back for the second man, but a mortar round exploded behind him, riddling him with shrapnel. Shanley's executive officer, Lieutenant Harold Collins, was killed while attempting to rescue Shanley. Shanley was carried to safety but died that night of his wounds.

Eleven men from Dunn's 48-man platoon returned from Hill 120; just five of them were unhurt. "I" and "L" Companies now mustered 80 men between them, one-sixth of their normal complement of 470 when at full strength.

Later, Lieutenant Gilbert Lindloff, a platoon commander with the 714th Tank Battalion, was speaking with Major Hunter Hurst when Hurst received an order for his 3rd Battalion to renew its attack. Lindloff later wrote that Hurst told his superior that intensive enemy machine-gun fire made another attack impossible.

No machine-gun fire was evident, wrote Lindloff. Hurst turned to Lindloff and said, "I came here with a thousand men in my battalion, and now I have less than 100 left. I'm not going to lose one more man in those ridges."[99]

Hurst's battalion established positions in a ravine below Hill 120. During the night, up to 100 Japanese soldiers infiltrated the Marine lines in small groups, and a melee broke out that lasted until morning. The Marines beat back the attacks, killing 52 enemy soldiers, while 12 of their own died. Two were Marines who flung themselves on live grenades to shield their comrades from the blasts: Pfcs Wesley Phelps and Richard Krauss, both posthumously awarded Congressional Medals of Honor.[100]

The Seventh Marines' losses now nearly equaled the number of casualties that had destroyed the First Marines as a viable fighting unit.

———

Japanese snipers in the ridges along the West Road harassed the American trucks hauling supplies to units in northern Peleliu. On a curve along a chokepoint in the road, the snipers frequently fired at the trucks, stopping traffic as drivers and passengers dived for cover outside their vehicles. The stretch of road became known as "Dead Man's Curve."[101]

Sergeant Jim McEnery and his Fifth Marines platoon from "K" Company were sent to eliminate the Japanese sharpshooters that had turned the road bend into a deadly gantlet. Pfc Seymour Levy, who had earlier received a "million-dollar wound" but had insisted on rejoining his platoon, was on edge. McEnery tried to calm him, and he repeatedly told him to keep his head down. And then Levy suddenly screamed, "I'm sick and tired of this shit! I can't take it anymore!" He leaped into the air and was killed instantly by a sniper's bullet that spattered Levy's blood on McEnery's face.[102]

As provost marshal and commander of the 1st Division's Headquarters Battalion, Colonel Joseph Hankins was responsible for the West Road's security. But his Military Police Company had been unable to suppress the sniping. On rainy October 3, Hankins had had enough. He decided that the sniping had to stop, and he believed that he had the wherewithal to end it. Indeed, Hankins was an experienced combat officer and a crack shot. He had commanded a First Marines' battalion on Cape Gloucester, and earlier in his career he had been a member of several trophy-winning Marine Corps rifle teams.

On this day, however, Hankins acted foolhardily and paid for it with his life.

Arming himself with an M1 and carrying a pair of field glasses, Hankins arrived at Dead Man's Curve intent on doing some countersniping. He found traffic halted by heavy sniper fire coming from a nearby cliff. The enemy gunfire had immobilized an amtrac, forcing several trucks to stop in the middle of the road; their crews were huddled on the shoulder opposite the cliff. Military police were trying to unsnarl the traffic jam. Hankins strode down the middle of the West Road, shouting at the truck crews to return to their vehicles. An eyewitness, remarking on the white pith helmet that Hankins wore, said, "He stood out like the sun on a dark day. He got it right straight between the eyes."[103]

Beside Hankins on the afternoon that he was killed was the Japanese prisoner whom Hankins had made a constant companion after the POW had persuaded nine Japanese soldiers in a cave to surrender. The prisoner wept over Hankins's body and insisted on digging his grave.

Shortly after Hankins was killed, a tank arrived and fired at the enemy positions. The sniping stopped. Traffic began moving again. Hankins was the highest-ranking officer killed on Peleliu.[104]

General Rupertus sent the Fifth Marines' "E" Company to eliminate the threat at Dead Man's Curve. The cliff and the nearby area, it so happened, guarded one of the approaches to Colonel Nakagawa's command post. "E" Company attacked the trouble spot, destroying fortifications, sealing caves, and killing a dozen enemy soldiers. The

Marines cleared an area 75 yards inland and 150 yards northward. Dead Man's Curve was free of sniper fire thereafter.[105]

After fighting for two weeks in Peleliu's ridges, the depleted Seventh Marines were relieved on October 6 by the Fifth Marines. The unit was the second of the 1st Division's three regiments to be withdrawn after sustaining heavy losses in the Umurbrogol.

Of the 3,217 Seventh Marines who landed on D-Day, 1,486 had been killed or wounded – 46 percent of the Seventh's original force. Some of the emaciated survivors were observed trembling involuntarily. Others, filthy and stinking of feces, were doubled over by dysentery. They boarded trucks that took them to Purple Beach, a way station on their journey back to Pavavu.[106]

"Purely and simply, there were no longer enough men left in the unit to continue the fight," wrote General O.P. Smith.[107]

The task of crushing the Pocket now fell to the Fifth Marines.

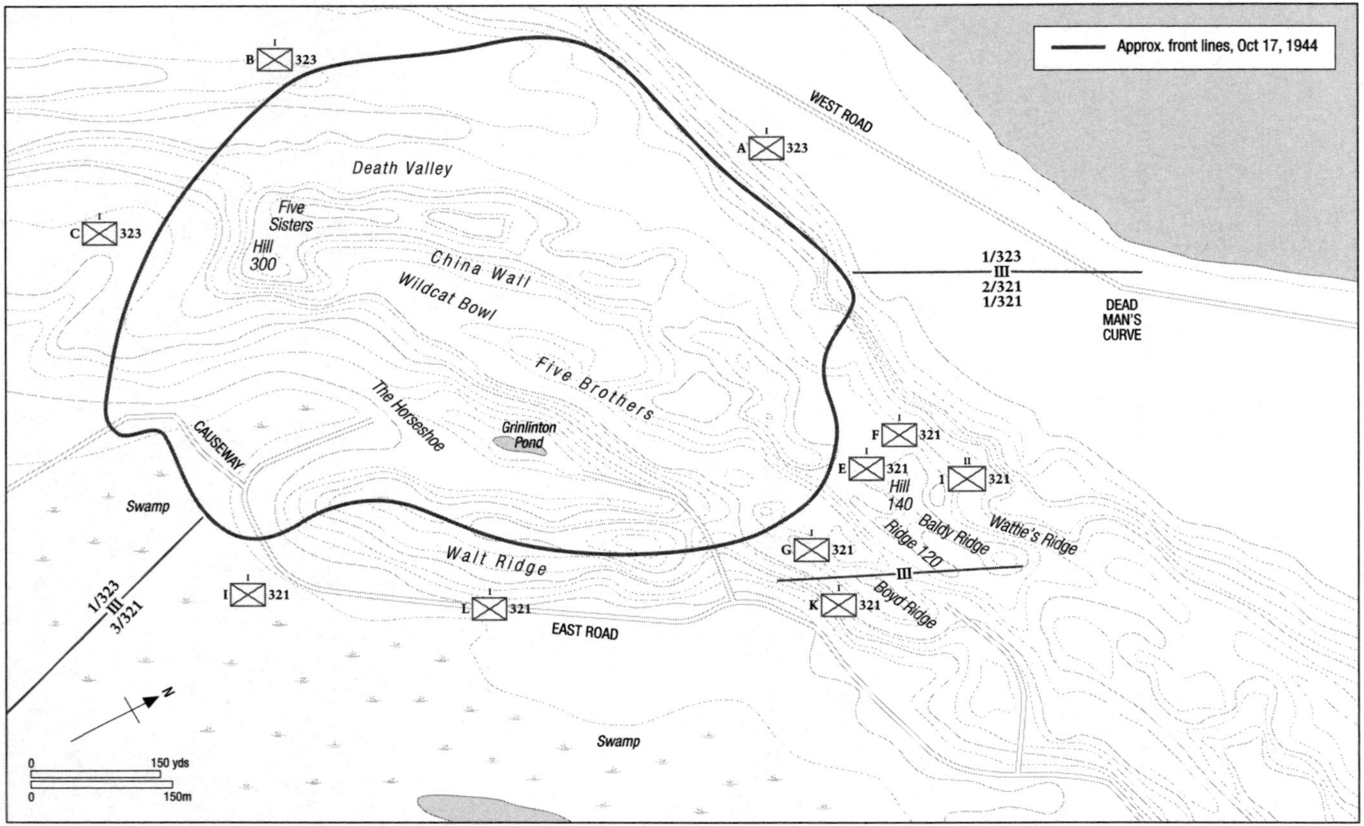

MAP 7: The Pocket

Approx. front lines, Oct 17, 1944

DEAD MAN'S CURVE

1/323
2/321
1/321

WEST ROAD

Wattie's Ridge

Baldy Ridge

Ridge 120

Hill 140

Boyd Ridge

A | 323

F | 321

E | 321

G | 321

K | 321

China Wall

Five Brothers

Death Valley

Wildcat Bowl

Grinlinton Pond

The Horseshoe

Walt Ridge

EAST ROAD

Swamp

Five Sisters

Hill 300

B | 323

CAUSEWAY

Swamp

C | 323

L | 321

I | 321

N

1/323
3/321

0   150 yds
0   150m

Chapter 10

The Fifth Marines Take Over

*The most difficult and challenging on the island ...
a complex cave and ridge fortress suitable to a fanatical
and suicidal defense.*

> Major Gordon Gayle of the Fifth
> Marines describing the
> Umurbrogol Pocket[1]

*A nether world of horror from which escape seemed less
and less likely as casualties mounted and the fighting
dragged on and on. Time had no meaning; life had no
meaning. The fierce struggle made savages of us all.*

> Pfc E.B. Sledge on the
> Umurbrogol Pocket[2]

General Rupertus had not wavered in his determination that the 1st Marine Division would eliminate the Umurbrogol Pocket – without the Army playing an important role. Dismissive of the Army's combat abilities, the proud Rupertus insisted that Marines alone would finish the job.

General Geiger had withdrawn the 321st from Angaur and sent it to Peleliu after his showdown with Rupertus on September 21. The men's heated argument had ended with Geiger ordering the relief of the decimated First Marines by the Army's 81st Division. Colonel Robert Dark's 321st Regiment had arrived on September 22, but weeks had now passed without it entering the Pocket.

To Geiger's pointed suggestions that Rupertus relieve the 1st Division's remaining active regiments – the Fifth and the Seventh, both reeling from high casualties – with the relatively fresh 321st, Rupertus replied that his Marines would "very shortly" complete the subjugation of the Pocket.[3]

With that, Rupertus then ordered the Fifth Marines into the Umurbrogol.

The Marine Corps's best-known and most highly decorated regiment, the Fifth had also been ground down by more than two weeks of fighting. While it remained combat-capable and was easily more than a match for Nakagawa's dwindling number of diehard veterans – if they ever came out for a final fight – the Fifth's hardened infantrymen were growing fatalistic.

Every night, squad leader John Murray prayed with the rosary that he kept draped around his neck. "We prayed and remembered our relentless training and hoped the two would pull us through. And as the days went by, I realized that there was a strong possibility I wouldn't get off Peleliu alive," he subsequently wrote.[*4]

A 1st Division report in early October conceded that progress had slowed against the enemy in the central ridges. "The campaign had now become a battle of attrition – a slow, slugging yard by yard struggle to blast the enemy from his last remaining stronghold in the high ground to the north of the airfield," through "rugged, almost impassable terrain requiring more time to clean out than previously had been spent in clearing all of the southern Palaus."[5]

During the Fifth Regiment's campaign in northern Peleliu and on Ngesebus, Colonel Harold "Bucky" Harris had become convinced that the Japanese were fighting an attritional battle. As a consequence, Harris more tightly embraced his philosophy of being "lavish with ammunition and stingy with … men's lives." In this respect, Harris differed sharply from Rupertus and Harris's fellow regimental commanders, Puller and Hanneken, who were older and had been molded by their experiences in World War I and the Banana Wars.

Harris intended to prosecute the Fifth's campaign against the Pocket in the same manner – and using the tactics that he had recommended to

---

*Murray survived, although he was wounded in the right knee by a sniper that was swiftly dispatched by Murray's comrades.

Puller and Rupertus after his aerial reconnaissance of the Umurbrogol in September. With his 2nd and 3rd Battalions, Harris planned to attack the enemy's fortified positions in the Umurbrogol Pocket from the north, not the south, a ridge at a time, while the 1st Battalion occupied a static position along the Pocket's eastern perimeter. Siege tactics, Harris believed, would be the most effective way to destroy the enemy's tightly integrated positions in Peleliu's highlands.

He brought in more heavy equipment and firepower: bulldozers to carve paths through the box canyons for tanks and amtrac flamethrowers; and an artillery battery to blast western-facing caves in the northern Pocket from West Road positions.[6]

Still insistent that a breakthrough was imminent, Rupertus pushed Harris to move faster, but the colonel stuck to his measured approach. "The tactical situation called for thoroughness rather than haste," the 1st Division report said. "Colonel Harris resisted all pressure to speed things up at the cost of unnecessary losses."[7]

On October 6, the Fifth's 2nd Battalion launched its first attack since relieving the Seventh Marines of the job of reducing the Pocket.

Despite all evidence that frontal assaults too often failed against Japanese fortified positions, Rupertus demanded that Harris launch a frontal assault on Baldy Ridge. "With considerable reluctance," Harris obeyed the order. "G" Company led the attack from the north, and briefly reached Baldy's summit before being forced to withdraw to its base.

While ascending Baldy, the Marines came upon the bodies of Seventh Marines killed during an earlier unsuccessful attack. They were "blackened and swollen, the flies and the birds and the maggots were working on them," said machine gunner Jim Johnston. "It was repulsive beyond imagination."[8]

Death Valley, which lay on China Wall's western side, had lived up to its forbidding nickname on October 3 when the Fifth Marines' 3rd Battalion first went into action in the Umurbrogol. The attack by the 3rd Battalion's "K" and "L" Companies that day into the western Umurbrogol was designed to divert attention from the main effort of the day: the Seventh Regiment's assault on Walt and Boyd ridges to the east.

As part of the diversion, "K" Company entered a narrow valley on the western side of the Five Sisters. The valley was a bleak place: tree limbs and rocks littered the ground; the few upright tree trunks teetered and leaned like drunken sentinels.

When a storm of accurate gunfire suddenly crashed into "K" from numerous hidden positions, the Marines discovered that enemy troops occupying caves overlooking the valley enjoyed panoramic views of the entire area. The company suffered so many casualties at one time that ammunition-bearers were called upon to carry stretchers.

The Marines withdrew. October 3 would stand as "K" Company's deadliest single day on Peleliu, with five men killed and 15 wounded.[9]

Peleliu's infernal ridges encompassed "terrain the likes of which most Americans could not even visualize, against an enemy unlike most Americans could imagine," wrote "K" Company mortarman Pfc E.B. Sledge after his company's first foray into the Umurbrogol. Often, when a volcanic eruption of gunfire forced the Marines to pull back, "not a man in the company had seen a live enemy anywhere."

Sledge described the Pocket as "a nether world of horror from which escape seemed less and less likely as casualties mounted and the fighting dragged on and on. Time had no meaning; life had no meaning. The fierce struggle made savages of us all."

Bad enough was the island's sweltering heat; worse was its putrid odor of death and excrement. Because of the island's impermeable coral-limestone surface, Japanese corpses remained unburied, and thousands of men afflicted with diarrhea were unable to practice basic field sanitation. Clouds of blowflies that had feasted on excrement and corpses hovered so densely in the air that they cast large shadows.[10]

On October 6, when the 3rd Battalion re-entered the western Umurbrogol, it was this time supported by six Army tanks. The battalion intended to push deep into the Horseshoe in order to destroy hidden 150mm mortars and rockets that were harassing the airfield. Other targets included enemy fortifications embedded in the lower slopes of Walt Ridge (formerly Hill 100) on the right and Five Brothers on the left.

During a pause at midday while the tanks were being resupplied with ammunition, two amtrac flamethrowers and a platoon of engineers specializing in demolitions and mine removal joined the offensive. When the attack resumed, the Marines, the tanks, and the amtrac flamethrowers killed many Japanese burrowed in the caves of Five Brothers and Walt Ridge.

"L" Company turned westward, climbed into a saddle separating Hill 300 and the Five Brothers, and was rewarded with a view of the valley to the west, Wildcat Bowl, still controlled by Nakagawa's men. "L" Company's sudden appearance in the saddle was met by a buzzsaw of gunfire from the eastern face of China Wall, where the Japanese had hollowed out 20 caves and linked them with tunnels and firing ports; up to 75 enemy soldiers occupied the positions, which guarded Nakagawa's nearby command post. The steel storm drove "L" from the saddle.[11]

Late in the afternoon, the tanks and amtrac flamethrowers ran out of ammunition. Without supporting arms, the situation became untenable for infantry alone, and the 3rd Battalion withdrew.[12] Ten days would pass before the Americans again attempted to advance in force into the Horseshoe.[13]

John Murray, a 3rd Battalion machine-gun squad leader, would have completely agreed with an unnamed Marine's description of the Umurbrogol Pocket as "the face of the moon defended by Jap troglodytes." When he first saw the Umurbrogol, Murray was shocked by its alien aura of "total destruction and death." Soon after Murray's battalion began fighting in its ridges, his squad had been reduced from 15 men to just five, "and most of them were sick."[14]

Colonel William Coleman of General Geiger's staff wrote, "Our language just does not contain words that can adequately describe the horrible inaccessibility of the central ridge line on Peleliu. It was a nightmare's nightmare if there ever was one." While planning *Stalemate*, "we did not fully realize the nature of the ground so it caught us pretty much by surprise when we actually came upon it. Nothing in our planning studies and subsequent development plans led us to realize how terrible it was."[15]

A sign found in a Japanese dugout concisely summarized the enemy's unbending determination: "Defense to the death. We will build a barrier across the Pacific with our bodies."[16]

Complacency could get one killed, some of the combatants discovered – too late. An artilleryman's four days of relative peace ended with his death in early October after an infiltrator climbed a seemingly unscalable 90-foot cliff in the dark and stabbed the Marine through the eye with a bayonet. A comrade of the artilleryman overpowered the infiltrator and hurled him off the cliff to his death.[17]

Inexperience could be just as fatal. Four men from the Pioneer Battalion that were sent to the Fifth Marines as replacements were all put in the same foxhole upon their arrival. During their first night on the battle line, all four of them fell asleep, leaving their position unguarded. An infiltrator crawled into their hole and hacked three of them to death. The commotion awakened the fourth man, who shot the infiltrator dead.

In the morning, when Corporal Russell Clay went to check on the replacements, he found the survivor sitting amid his dead comrades, "bug-eyed out of his skull" with shock. The pioneer was evacuated.[18]

———

Marine engineers and artillerists worked out a new piledriver-like method for advancing into the coral-and-limestone ridges. Four 105mm guns were wheeled up the West Road to Dead Man's Curve. Facing a cliffside, the gunners pulverized the coral to rubble. Then, engineers in bulldozers carved out a ramp for amtrac flamethrowers. When the ramp was completed on October 9, Lieutenant Robert Wattie's platoon from the 2nd Battalion's "G" Company hiked to the top of Baldy Ridge's western spur. Baldy had resisted capture for three days, but the spur, which became known as "Wattie's Ridge," afforded an alternative approach route. It paralleled Baldy Ridge, located to its east, and it was connected to Baldy's southern extremity.

The next day, Wattie's platoon advanced southward to explore the newly discovered access to Baldy. When the Marines began to assault Baldy from the rear, they came under concentrated fire from a large cave in a gulch between Wattie and Baldy. The platoon pulled back and let the heavy weapons – artillery and amtrac flamethrowers – plaster the cave until a landslide closed its mouth. This tactic exemplified Colonel Harris's principle of using heavy weapons to aid platoons and squads in making incremental advances.

After a shootout with small arms and grenades, Wattie's men, followed by the rest of "G" Company, overran the Japanese blocking their progress and swarmed up Baldy Ridge's southern reach, blasting every enemy obstacle in their path. By noon, the Marines had secured Baldy.

About the same time, with relative ease "E" Company seized Hill 120, the 100-yard-long razorback where the late Lieutenant James Dunn's Seventh Marines platoon had been ambushed and cut to pieces a week earlier. Capturing Baldy had eliminated the flanking fire that destroyed Dunn's platoon. Just 11 of his 48 men had gotten out alive – five of them wounded. "E" Company reported that the ground was littered with the decomposing bodies of Dunn's men.

On October 11, the 2nd Battalion lunged south toward Hill 140, which lay immediately north of the Five Brothers. Hill 140, Hill 120, and Wattie and Baldy ridges together comprised the northern boundary of the Umurbrogol, abutting the Five Brothers to the south.

Because of its height and strategic position, Hill 140 was considered one of the keystones to the Umurbrogol. The 2nd Battalion planned to seize the hill and place an artillery piece atop it to support its push into the Pocket. From Hill 140's summit, artillerists could lay cannon fire on the Five Brothers and the northern Horseshoe.

Even better, artillery on Hill 140 could deny the Japanese access to the gully between Boyd and Walt ridges, which was being used by enemy gunners to direct fire onto traffic on the East Road. With the aid of its artillery, the Marines hoped to transform the ravine into an American path into the heart of the Pocket.[19]

The 2nd Battalion's "F" Company stormed to the top of Hill 140 at a surprisingly low cost of two men killed and ten wounded, and later in the day Marines cleared the hill of bypassed enemy soldiers. "The enemy was very thick throughout our newly occupied areas, and the mopping up was a bloody procedure," the battalion report said, "with 60 of the enemy killed in a very short time."[20]

Determined to throw the Marines off the important strongpoint, that night Japanese soldiers poured out of the caves and bunkers inside Hill 140 and counterattacked with their trademark ferocity. The Marines beat them back. At least 75 enemy troops died.[21]

As planned, the Marines disassembled a 75mm howitzer, "tackle-rigged" it, and 68 Marines wrestled the components to the top of Hill 140, where it was reassembled and fired. The laborious process consumed seven hours. A second pack howitzer was muscled to Hill 140's southeastern edge, so that it could fire on China Wall and Five Sisters.

Opposite the second gun stood a Japanese observation post on the Five Sisters. Through their binoculars, the gunners spotted white-gloved Japanese officers milling around the observation post. Before the Marine gunners could open fire, however, a torrent of enemy small-arms fire from concealed positions near the observation post swept through the artillery position, killing two Marines and wounding a third. The firing position was deemed too dangerous and was abandoned for the time being.[22]

By early October, the Seventh and Fifth Marines had reduced the enemy-held area to an enclave a half-mile long and a quarter-mile wide. Major Gordon Gayle, the Fifth's 2nd Battalion commander, described the Umurbrogol Pocket as "the most difficult and challenging on the island … a complex cave and ridge fortress suitable to a fanatical and suicidal defense." Difficult indeed: its phantasmagoric features included rock spires and crevices, 200-foot cliffs, and narrow, saw-toothed ridges.[23]

Moreover, it was defended by what remained of Colonel Nakagawa's most veteran troops. But because artillery directed by Captain Wallace Slappey's spotter planes from VMO-3 had radically tamped down the Pocket's defenses, the Japanese were now able to only harass and delay.

Decomposing Japanese dead from previous battles continued to be discovered in the broiling ridges. Found near the former airport administration building were the remains of a Sergeant Ineda of the 346th Independent Battalion, in whose dispatch case was a notebook that Ineda had kept. Its entries provided a record of the demise of the 17 soldiers and eight laborers under Ineda's command. The final entry, made on September 18, reported the deaths of three of Ineda's men: one from a stomach wound, and the other two from fatal wounds to their faces. Four other men were wounded, and their injuries were described. Of course, the eighth, but unrecorded, casualty that day was Ineda himself.

A captured Japanese corporal told his interrogators that just six men from his 2nd Regiment company had survived long enough to withdraw into the ridges. The prisoner said the non-ambulatory wounded had killed themselves with grenades.[24]

Despite the enormous Japanese losses, the Horseshoe and Wildcat Bowl remained under the defenders' iron control. The two box canyons were surrounded on three sides by rock walls from which enemy troops in caves, pillboxes, and bunkers greeted intruders with machine guns, and 37mm, 75mm, and 105mm gunfire.

The Horseshoe, described as a "rock amphitheater," was 400 yards long and 100 yards wide and dead-ended in a steep hill. It was scored by a pair of long pits filled with stagnant, filthy water. Despite the water's wretched quality, at night thirsty Japanese soldiers crept to it to fill their canteens.[25]

Wildcat Bowl lay between Five Brothers' western face and China Wall's eastern side. Utterly forbidding in every respect, its surface was composed solely of exposed white coral and limestone, and was devoid of vegetation. Midway along Wildcat Bowl's 400-yard length was a perpendicular trench excavated by Japanese engineers. Ten feet wide and ten feet deep, it spanned the 80 yards separating Five Brothers and the China Wall.

Near the southern end of the bowl was a strange malformation: a 40-yard-by-100-yard depression 30 feet deep that was full of stalagmites protruding above the valley floor – like punji stakes used to impale animals. Three smaller pits lay a short distance away.

The bowl's two sides bristled with machine guns, heavy weapons, and riflemen – all ready to throw a wall of lead and steel at anyone who dared enter it. Like the Horseshoe, Wildcat Bowl was full of dangers, both visible and hidden.[26]

On October 12, the Fifth's 3rd Battalion replaced its sister 2nd Battalion, which thereafter saw no more action on Peleliu. The relief occurred under heavy sniper fire that claimed 22 Marine casualties.[27]

While the 3rd Battalion was taking tactical responsibility for the area, Colonel Nakagawa was itemizing his remaining assets in a report to headquarters in Koror. Nakagawa listed 1,150 military personnel, including naval troops; 500 rifles with 20,000 rounds of ammunition; 13 light machine guns; six heavy machine guns with 10,000 rounds; a 20mm automatic gun with 540 rounds; an antitank gun with

350 rounds; a 70mm howitzer with 120 rounds; three mortars; 1,300 hand grenades; and a dozen grenade launchers, or knee mortars, with 150 rounds.[28]

In the Home Islands, the Japanese closely followed every new development on Peleliu, esteeming the stubborn resistance of Nakagawa's men as they sought to prolong the struggle. Emperor Hirohito demonstrated his intense interest and admiration by conferring an unequaled nine "degrees of praise" on Peleliu's garrison. By contrast, most Americans were oblivious to the struggle on Peleliu.[29]

In his report accompanying the catalogue of armaments and manpower, Nakagawa wrote, "At present a fierce combat is taking place with results unknown. A unit of the enemy penetrated into Suifuzon [Boyd Ridge and the northern Pocket]. They also attacked with flamethrowers attached to tanks."[30]

Later, Colonel Tokuchi Tada, the 14th Infantry Division's chief of staff, described the situation on Peleliu as "a contest between a huge man armed with a spear and a small man armed with a short sword." The huge man's advantage of size and reach could only be counteracted by the small man's most effective weapon, infiltration and a willingness to engage in close combat, Tada said.[31]

Colonel Nakagawa, too, asserted that the Americans could be defeated "by using our close-quarter combat tactics to the utmost." That included imbedding infiltration teams in enemy-held territory to mount counterattacks and degrade the invaders' strength and morale. Tada believed that if Nakagawa's attritional strategy forced the Americans to pay a price that exceeded Peleliu's perceived value, they would withdraw.[32]

As the 3rd Battalion was occupying the 2nd Battalion's positions on October 12, "K" Company's commander, Captain Andrew "Ack" Haldane, was killed. Haldane had summoned his platoon leaders to an observation point on Hill 140 to discuss where "K" Company's heavy machine gun should be placed. When the captain raised his head to peer over the ridge, a sniper shot him in the head.[33]

Pfc E.B. Sledge and his mortar squad were moving into the ridges when they learned of Haldane's death. "The skipper is dead. 'Ack' has been killed." Sledge threw down his ammo bag, turned away from the others, sat on his helmet, and "sobbed quietly."[34]

Competent and well-liked by his men, Haldane was a 27-year-old graduate of Bowdoin College in Maine – the college where Joshua Chamberlain, the hero of Little Round Top at Gettysburg, had once taught philosophy. Bowdoin also happened to be the alma mater of 1st Division Captains Paul Douglas and Everett Pope – an oversize legacy indeed for such a small college.

Awarded the Silver Star for rallying his company to repel five bayonet charges in one hour at Cape Gloucester, Haldane believed in strict discipline but was genuinely interested in his men's welfare and gave orders quietly. "We loved him for it and did the best job we knew how," said Sledge.

Haldane's death severely depressed Sledge and his comrades; they felt forlorn and lost. "We knew he could never be replaced." Sledge wrote. "It was the worst grief I endured during the entire war." Today, Bowdoin College each year awards the Andrew Allison Haldane Cup, a gift established by officers who had served with Haldane during the Pacific War, to a graduating senior who has displayed outstanding leadership and character.[35]

The night after Haldane's death, Corpsman Joe Marquez, attached to the Fifth Marines, was wounded by shrapnel in the legs during a mortar attack in the ridges. Hearing cries for a corpsman, Marquez ignored his painful wounds and dragged himself over the rough ground to aid his comrades. "I began to crawl around to assess the damage to see who needed to be treated first," he said. "One of the corpsmen ... was the most seriously wounded and I decided to give him a unit of plasma."

Marquez could not find a vein in the dark, and he asked a lieutenant if he could request that a flare be fired over the area. It was done, and Marquez was able to start the plasma. A Marine volunteered to monitor it so that Marquez could care for the other wounded.

Other corpsmen and stretcher-bearers arrived at daybreak. Marquez refused treatment until all of his patients were evacuated. For his selfless actions, Marquez was awarded the Navy Cross.[36]

Later that day and on the next day, October 14, the Fifth Marines tightened its grip on the Pocket. From the Pocket's northwestern corner, the 3rd Battalion pushed southeastward while the Seventh Marines'

1st Battalion simultaneously attacked northward from the Pocket's southwestern perimeter.

Corsairs from VMF-114 prepared the way by dropping spare belly tanks filled with napalm with 30-second fuses attached. At times they swooped to just 50 feet above the ground. Although it was a tricky mission with the Marine lines so close to the targets, no friendly fire casualties occurred.

Captain Earl Wilson, who watched from a circling observation plane, described the aftermath. "A wall of fire boiled down near the face of the cliff, while hundreds of fiery balls rushed furiously out from the impact," he said. "At the same time, a mass of thick greasy smoke coiled up into the air and hung like a crepe ..."[37]

"It was one of the most effective weapons we were able to use," Lieutenant Colonel Lew Walt of the Fifth Marines said of napalm bombing. "It killed all who were not in caves, and last but not least, it destroyed his camouflage and stripped his fortress of any protecting vegetation." The survivors were compelled to retreat deeper into their caves to avoid the concussion and heat from the fire bombs.[38]

The Fifth Regiment's "L" Company now occupied Hill 140, where the 75mm howitzer had been carried in pieces to the summit and assembled. After dark, a Japanese squad silently scaled its sheer-sided western face, reaching a ledge 5 feet below the Marines. At a signal, the enemy soldiers hurled grenades.

A Japanese soldier pounced on Sergeant Benjamin Gailey when he jumped up, wounded by grenade fragments. Gailey struggled with his assailant, who was choking him, and tried to gouge out his eyes as they teetered on the brink of the precipice. Gailey cried out for help. A Marine with a BAR riddled the Japanese soldier, and Gailey pushed him off the cliff. Then the other enemy soldiers drew themselves up, fired pistols over the ledge, and stormed Hill 140's summit. The Marines killed them all.[39]

The Fifth's push resulted in a new line being established 200 yards deeper in the Pocket, reducing its overall size by more than 30 percent, to an area roughly 400 by 500 yards. The Marines were now abreast of the Five Brothers and 175 yards from the China Wall and Colonel Nakagawa's command post.[40]

As the Fifth Marines pushed farther into the ridges, it encountered the blackened, bloated corpses of Marines killed in combat two weeks earlier – and other revolting sights. In a rock crevice, Corporal R.V. Burgin, a forward observer with Sledge's mortar team, came upon the mutilated bodies of four scouts from an intelligence unit. "The Japs had hacked them to pieces," Burgin wrote. "They'd cut off their heads and hands... It made me dizzy and sick."

After having found dead Marines on Cape Gloucester who had been tied to trees and used by the Japanese for bayonet practice, Burgin "never had any regrets about killing a Jap in combat... I guessed I'd hate Japs as long as I lived."[41]

That day's grim discovery in the crevice was Sledge's first encounter with the enemy's retributive cruelty – and it changed him. "My emotions solidified into rage and hatred for the Japanese beyond anything I had ever experienced," he wrote. "From that moment on I never felt the least pity or compassion for them no matter what the circumstances."[42]

———

The 321st Regiment's 2nd Battalion began replacing the Fifth Marines on Hill 140 during the morning of October 15 – one month to the day after the 1st Division landed on Peleliu. The soldiers ascending the hill met the drained Marines leaving the battle line. They were "really crying, they were so happy to see us," recalled a private with the 321st – and even happier to still be alive.

The Marines descending the ridge were haggard, filthy, and unshaven, their eyes bloodshot and haunted-looking from sleepless nights and the parade of horrors that they had witnessed. The knees and elbows of their grimy dungarees, greasy with rifle oil, were torn from crawling over the abrasive coral rock, which had also ground down the heels of their boondockers.[43]

Although pleased to see them, Lieutenant Tom Stanley, Captain Haldane's successor, was dismayed by the appearance of the soldiers that relieved his men on Hill 140. "They were old men. They were 15 years older, on the average, than the men they were replacing," he said. "I felt sorry for them. Some of them [were] wearing eyeglasses. Some [of them were] 115, 118 pounds – well, hell, our own kids were no bigger than that, but they'd been in the middle of a 30-day campaign.

"But these guys that relieved us, I thought it was a crying shame," he said. "They had no more business being on that island than the man in the moon."[44]

Later that day, the 321st's 3rd Battalion occupied the positions of the Fifth Marines' 1st Battalion south of Walt Ridge and Boyd Ridge.

———

Admiral William Halsey sent a congratulatory message to the 1st Marine Division. "The sincere admiration of the entire Third Fleet is yours for the hill blasting, cave smashing extermination of 11,000 slant-eyed gophers. It has been a tough job, extremely well done."[*][45]

On the following day, October 16, the 323rd Regiment's 1st Battalion, newly arrived after capturing Ulithi, took the places of Marines in static positions west and south of the Pocket. They were initially surprised that the Marines had not dug foxholes; instead, they found "coral rocks piled up." However, the soldiers quickly grasped the impossibility of digging in solid rock.[46]

The Fifth Marines had lost 42 percent of its landing force during its 29 days on the battle line – 1,309 men of the Fifth's original force of 3,117. The Fifth now occupied the 321st's former bivouacs on northern Peleliu and Ngesebus, prior to sailing to Pavavu.[47]

Pfc Sledge's "K" Company suffered 64 percent casualties, with only 85 combat-capable men remaining of the 235 men who landed on Peleliu on September 15. Years later, he wrote that Marine veterans of Peleliu as well as other Pacific War battles believed that Peleliu was their worst experience.

Reflecting on his baptism by fire on Peleliu, Sledge described combat as "a series of changing events characterized by confusion, awesome violence, gripping fear, physical stress and fatigue, fierce hatred of the enemy, and overwhelming grief over the loss of friends." Grief made Sledge and other combat veterans reluctant to befriend replacement troops, preferring to keep them at arm's length rather than risk losing new friends.[48]

The 321st's relief of the Fifth Marines was just one of the consequences that followed the formal transfer of command from Admiral Fort, the commander of the Western Task Force, to Admiral J.H. Hoover. The strictly administrative change marked the end of *Stalemate*'s assault

---

[*]Halsey's language derogating Japanese soldiers was common during the Pacific War. Today, his words would be deemed racist and unacceptable.

phase and enabled Hoover, commander of the Forward Area Forces, to proceed with the development of Peleliu and Angaur as secured bases for future operations.

Hoover also made official the Army 81st Infantry Division's relief of the 1st Marine Division. This was little more than a formality, for most of the Marines had already left the battle front and would soon sail to Pavavu. General Paul Mueller, and not General William Rupertus, was now responsible for eliminating the Japanese holdouts in the Pocket.[49]

The conclusion of Peleliu's assault phase was based on specific objectives having been met: "the islands had been occupied and … Base Development had been initiated and could proceed without enemy interference and … the Assault Troops could be relieved by the Garrison Forces."[50]

Many of the Marines disengaging under fire from the Pocket might have disputed this, but all of the campaign's major objectives had indeed been achieved: Peleliu's airfield was operational; the Japanese defenders on Peleliu and Angaur were surrounded and were being steadily destroyed; Ngesebus and Peleliu's other outlying islands were completely under American control.

General O.P. Smith, the 1st Division's assistant commander, noted that two Pelelius now co-existed side-by-side. There was the secured southern island and the airfield, whose capture had made it impossible for Peleliu-based Japanese squadrons to interfere with General Douglas MacArthur's Philippines campaign.

Although enemy observation posts still overlooked the airfield, mortar fire on it had ceased. Japanese attempts to disrupt its operations all ended in failure, although suicide squads still sometimes attempted to infiltrate the airfield perimeter.

In the secured area that included the airfield and southern Peleliu, Seabees operated road graders and rollers, and aircraft mechanics tuned up airplane engines for the roughly 50 ground support missions flown daily. The secured area was a place of civilized amenities: four field hospitals, electricity, radios, ice machines, barracks, mess halls, outdoor movie theaters, and showers. There was a post office 300 yards south of Bloody Nose Ridge. The rear echelon troops wore laundered clothing and were clean-shaven and relaxed.[51]

Pfc Sledge had passed some of these men on his way to the second Peleliu, the unsecured Umurbrogol. The men in the safe areas studied Sledge and his thin, grimy comrades with curiosity, "as though we were wild animals in a circus parade."[52]

"Light to heavy beards itched on our faces, clotted with filth and sand fleas," wrote Pfc Sterling Mace. "We were sunburned and raw on our shoulders, in the crooks of our elbows and knees, and on our feet." They wore shredded boondockers and tattered dungarees torn at the knees, split at the bottoms, and white with dried perspiration and coral dust. "We had smoked too much and eaten too little. We were at least twenty pounds too light," Mace wrote. "The only thing clean and in good order about us were our weapons. Those we kept immaculate."[53]

Reflecting on the 17 days that he fought in the ridges, Sergeant Jim McEnery wrote, "Every one of those days was horribly the same. We were always going uphill, always under a cross fire from Japs we couldn't see in mutually supporting caves and bunkers above us. Always inching our way up some naked, rocky cliff with Japs shooting at us from distances ranging from a quarter mile to a few yards."[54]

General Smith described the situation in the ridges as "a brutally different extra-innings ball game, one where the score was kept in the number of ridges taken and how many Marines were killed or wounded in the seemingly endless process." Smith later told friends that he wondered "why we didn't simply leave the highlands to the Japanese, keep bombing and shelling them from offshore and from the parts of Peleliu we held until there were too few left to continue to fight."[55]

Before Admiral Fort's flagship, *Mount McKinley*, left the area, he sent ashore his remaining supply of beer – 500 cases, which were distributed to the front-line troops. The men were thrilled by the admiral's unexpected generosity.[56]

After the 81st Division took charge, all of the division's officers were taken on an aerial reconnaissance of the combat zone. They were imitating Colonel Harold Harris's aerial survey of the Umurbrogol in September that had convinced him that the ridges should be assaulted from the north, and not the south.[57]

Units of the Seventh Marines were the last combat troops of Rupertus's division still in action. "B" Company, driven from Death Valley three weeks earlier with heavy casualties, re-entered the rock-sided canyon on October 15, supported by "K" Company and a tank. A blizzard of mortar shells and bullets met them. "B" was able to advance just 50 yards. American tank fire, demolitions, and flamethrowers scorched enemy caves before the Marines were forced to withdraw.[58]

October 16 was a landmark in the Battle of Peleliu: the last day that the 1st Marine Division officially acted in a combat role. On that day, the Seventh Marines' 1st Battalion, led by Lieutenant Colonel John Gormley, broke off its advance through coral badlands in the so-called Southern Pocket. The next day, "B" Company of the 323rd Regiment relieved Gormley's shockingly reduced battalion – 230 men replacing, man for man, the remnants of a once 800-man Marine unit.[59] Of the division's original 27 infantry company commanders, only one remained unwounded when the Marines' combat role on Peleliu ended – Captain Preston Parish of the Seventh Marines' "A" Company.[60]

Eight Medals of Honor were awarded to Marines for conspicuous gallantry on Peleliu – five posthumously to men who threw themselves on grenades, sacrificing themselves to protect their comrades: Corporal Lewis Bausell of the Fifth Marines; Pfc Richard Kraus of the 8th Amphibious Tractor Battalion; and Pfcs John New, Wesley Phelps, and Charles Roan of the Seventh Marines. Three Medal of Honor recipients survived the battle: Pfc Arthur Jackson of the Seventh Marines, credited with destroying a dozen pillboxes and killing more than 50 enemy soldiers; Captain Everett Pope, who led the First Marines' "C" Company during its all-night ordeal on Hill 100 against ceaseless counterattacks; and Lieutenant Carlton Rough of the Fifth Marines, who fell on a grenade to spare other Marines, yet lived.[61]

The 1st Division reported 6,526 casualties on Peleliu; 1,252 of them were listed as killed or missing in action. The division said that it killed 10,695 enemy combatants.

The Marine and Army dead lay beneath nearly 1,300 white crosses arranged in neat rows in the cemetery between Orange Beach 2 and the airfield. Shattered amtracs on the nearby reef, where many of these lives had ended, served as a somber backdrop.

In their off-duty hours, volunteers graded the plots with white coral sand and planted wildflowers and shrubs. Above the cemetery gateway were inscribed these lines from an A.E. Housman poem inspired by the carnage of World War I:

> Here dead lie we because we did not choose
> To live and shame the land from which we sprung.
> Life, to be sure, is nothing much to lose,
> But young men think it is, and we were young.[62]

The 1st Marine Division spent its final two weeks on Peleliu in rest areas near Purple Beach and on Peleliu's northeastern promontories before sailing to Pavavu. By October 30, the last regiment, the Fifth, was at sea.[63]

Aboard the troop ship *Sea Runner*, 46-year-old Master Gunnery Sergeant Elmo Haney was asked what he thought of the Peleliu campaign. Haney had seen a lot of action before landing on Peleliu: he had served in World War I, in the Banana Wars, and on Guadalcanal and Cape Gloucester. Haney was known in the division for obsessively cleaning his weapons and practicing his bayonet-fighting skills.

Haney had fought with the Fifth Marines' "K" Company, but without occupying an official position. He had removed himself from the front lines in the Umurbrogol because he could no longer stand the heat or the stresses of the intensive fighting there. Replying to the question put to him, Haney said, "Boy, that was terrible. I ain't never seen nothin' like it. I'm ready to go back to the States. I've had enough after that."[64]

Chapter 11

The Army's Turn

*It became the byword of the 321st, show the bastards no
mercy, and take no prisoners. We were taught to never
trust one, [because] if you did, it would cost you your life.*
Sergeant Nolton Brown,
321st's antitank company[1]

*It was a common observance that in a long campaign,
men tend to get more careless about taking cover as the
campaign progresses, partly due to fatigue and partly,
I suppose, to fatalism.*
General O.P. Smith[2]

Until now, Rupertus, stubbornly insisting that the Marines retain the
lead role in *Stalemate*, had only assigned the 321st to support and
mop-up missions: digging out pockets of diehard Japanese on Ngesebus
after the Fifth Marines captured the islet; helping secure northern
Peleliu. The regiment had yet to carry out a primary mission against
the Umurbrogol Pocket. But now the 321st was about to become solely
responsible for destroying Colonel Nakagawa's remaining forces.

The 321st Regiment was supposed to begin replacing some of the
last Marine combat units on Peleliu on October 8, and to become
responsible for crushing the Pocket. But on October 7 Colonel Dark
was told that the 321st must first seize Garakayo Island, which lay a
little over a mile north of Kongauru Island.

The Fifth Marines had captured Kongauru when they invaded Ngesebus. Nearby Garakayo was part of a chain of islets that the Japanese had used as way stations while transporting reinforcements from the northern Palaus to Peleliu. It was believed that Garakayo's capture would disrupt and choke off access to northern Peleliu by Japanese reinforcements from Babelthuap.

The 321st's delayed deployment to the Pocket had the benefit, at least in General Rupertus's opinion, of giving the 1st Marine Division several extra days to alone complete Peleliu's conquest without the Army's assistance.

The job of capturing Garakayo fell to the 321st's 2nd Battalion. The operation on October 9 was a breeze, lasting several hours and resulting in the deaths of ten enemy soldiers without a single American casualty. "F" Company landed on Garakayo with ten amtanks, and then split into two task forces. They swept the tiny island's eastern and western beaches, meeting at the northeastern tip. Patrols pushed inland to complete the mission. The operation was over by 3 p.m.[3]

The 81st Division Operation Report said the enemy's apparent abandonment of Garakayo and the nearby northern islands clearly indicated that their defenders had departed to help defend Peleliu. Partly as a consequence, enemy resistance from the Pocket continued unabated. Garakayo was the tenth islet seized by U.S. forces in the southern Palaus since the Peleliu landings.[4]

In his announcement of Garakayo's capture, Admiral Chester Nimitz also reported that American forces had killed 12,238 Japanese in the southern Palaus – 11,088 of them on Peleliu, and 1,150 on Angaur.[5]

While the 321st was busy seizing Garakayo, Rupertus was pushing the Fifth Marines to complete the Pocket's subjugation before the Army assumed responsibility for crushing the Japanese holdouts. Already crippled by a 43 percent casualty rate, the Fifth's strength continued to ebb further as the result of the combined effects of Japanese snipers and Peleliu's oppressive heat.

The prolonged exposure to the Pocket had also caused despair to take root among the Fifth Marines; many of them now believed they would never leave Peleliu alive. Resigned to that fate, some of them stopped taking their usual precautions to elude sniper fire – with predictable results.[6]

General O.P. Smith witnessed the men's growing indifference to danger during a tank-infantry advance up a ravine. Ignoring their peril, the Marine infantrymen, waiting for the tanks to advance, sat and smoked cigarettes without bothering to first find someplace protected from enemy fire. "It was a common observance," said Smith, "that in a long campaign, men tend to get more careless about taking cover as the campaign progresses, partly due to fatigue and partly, I suppose, to fatalism."[7]

Before the 81st became responsible for reducing the Pocket, its 321st Regiment had fulfilled an important secondary role after coming ashore on Peleliu on September 23. Relegated to the fringes of the Umurbrogol, the 321st yet managed to make an impact. Exploring a rough trail that began on the West Road at Garekoru, the soldiers discovered that it ran all the way to the East Road.

The regiment assaulted and captured two Japanese strongholds guarding the road – Hill 100 and Hill B – and effectively severed the Pocket's defenders from enemy soldiers occupying northern Peleliu's hills and ridges. Rupertus had then ordered the Army regiment to clear remaining pockets of Japanese soldiers that were firing on traffic on the East Road. On September 27, Colonel Dark sent one battalion south down the road, while another battalion attacked northward.

In its drive northward, the 1st Battalion swept around both sides of Kamilianlul Mountain and its adjacent ridges, which had been largely bypassed by the Fifth Marines during its occupation of northern Peleliu. The soldiers saw many abandoned Japanese positions, but few defenders, suggesting that the 500 enemy soldiers believed to have been in this area had withdrawn.

Replacing the Fifth Marines' 3rd Battalion in northern Peleliu when the Marines assaulted Ngesebus, the 1st Battalion was raked by intensive gunfire from pillboxes and from Hill 80, which the Fifth Marines had captured two days earlier. Infiltrating enemy troops had reoccupied the hill after the Marines left.[8] This was in accord with Colonel Nakagawa's attritional strategy: reoccupy previously lost or abandoned ground, and force the Americans to fight to retake it two or three times, adding to their casualties.[9]

In a blustery downpour, the 1st Battalion assaulted the pillboxes along the East Road and in the Kamilianlul ridges. Supported by tanks and flamethrower and demolitions teams, the Wildcats destroyed the Japanese positions. They were a step closer to controlling the entire East Road – all except a loop dominated by Hill 80.

Japanese pillboxes embedded in the eastern slope of Hill 80 raked "C" Company when it attempted to edge north along the right side of the road. The enemy soldiers counterattacked, and firefights exploded up and down "C"'s advancing line throughout the morning and afternoon. By nightfall, however, "C" Company had managed to reoccupy Hill 80.[10]

Meanwhile, the 321st's 2nd Battalion was simultaneously pushing southward down the East Road, with the object of reaching the northern boundary of the Umurbrogol Pocket. As "F" Company moved down the road, fire teams ranged ahead to remove roadblocks impeding the battalion's supporting arms: the Neal Task Force's seven medium tanks, six amtracs, and an amtrac flamethrower.

"K" Company, borrowed from the 321st's 3rd Battalion, had the more dangerous job: traveling parallel to the road along a ridgeline that was defended by enemy snipers, and mortar and machine-gun positions. Intensive Japanese gunfire slowed "K"'s advance, as did the rugged terrain of plunging valleys and defiles that broke up the ridgeline.[11] "K" company got into a tight spot. Lagging behind "F" Company, "K"'s flanks became exposed and unsupported.

"Occasionally, a half dozen Japs would come out and want to give up," said radioman John Engstrom. "By this time, we pretty well knew that we were in trouble, so you couldn't take captives, you had to kill them. Maybe not right, but we never took a prisoner on Peleliu."

Captain William Murphy, "K"'s commander, was killed trying to make contact with units on his flanks, and the leaderless company stalled amid roaring enemy gunfire. Frustration and fear frayed the soldiers' nerves. "You couldn't see anything, you never saw those bastards," said Engstrom. "They were there, but you never saw them." One group piled into a room-size hole in the coral. Six of them were killed when they attempted to leave just as grenade-throwing Japanese soldiers approached. Others dashed to "M" and "I" Companies near "K"'s flanks.[12]

Reeling from heavy casualties, "K" Company was replaced by "E" Company in a composite battalion led by Major Dallas Pilliod; it consisted of "E," "F," and "I," and was supported by the Neal

Task Force. The next morning, Pilliod's battalion resumed its push south. Its mission was to destroy Japanese forces occupying the area between the 321st Infantry Trail and the northern boundary of the Umurbrogol Pocket. "I" advanced on the ridges, as "K" had done. "E" moved down the East Road, supported by tanks – the infantrymen identifying targets over the tanks' "sound power telephones." By late afternoon, the battalion reached its objective after neutralizing a chain of caves with demolitions, gasoline, and white phosphorus grenades.[13]

The 2nd Battalion was withdrawn and sent to Ngesebus to replace the Fifth Marines, and to mop up any remaining Japanese defenders who had survived the Marines' assault on the islet.[14]

The 321st Infantry Trail was now recognized as the de facto boundary between the Pocket to the south and the area north of the trail, which 1st Marine Division headquarters called the "Northern Peleliu Defense Area."

The Seventh Marines' 3rd Battalion replaced the 321st on the Pocket's northern boundary, and the Wildcats launched another assault on the Kamilianlul Mountain area, which its 1st Battalion had attacked a few days earlier. The Wildcats sealed caves and bunkers that had been missed earlier, and flushed and shot down dozens of enemy soldiers.[15]

On September 30, General Rupertus made the 321st responsible for securing northern Peleliu. The Pocket, however, remained the exclusive province of the Marines.[16]

The 321st divided northern Peleliu into two sectors, with the 1st Battalion responsible for the area north of the East Road and its junction with the West Road. The 3rd Battalion took charge of the ground between the 1st Battalion and the 321st Infantry Trail.[17]

Although the Fifth Marines reportedly captured Radar Hill during its northern Peleliu campaign, on October 1, the 321st Infantry's "B" Company learned otherwise. When a "B" platoon began ascending Radar Hill, where Marines had earlier that day sealed a massive cave, a Marine officer on the scene warned the soldiers that if the Japanese managed to dig out of that cave, it would take more than a platoon to capture the hill.

The warning portended what happened next: enemy soldiers poured out of the previously sealed cave and overran the platoon. The clash exploded into a chaotic hour-and-a-half-long firefight involving tanks, artillery, and mortars before "B" was able to take control of the situation and force the enemy soldiers back into the cave. Strong winds and rain buffeted the soldiers during their anxious night atop the subterranean enemy stronghold.[18]

In the morning, "B" Company attacked the caves and bunkers inside Radar Hill. The fortified positions teemed with Japanese troops who had survived the previous attacks by the Fifth Marines. The infantrymen forced the defenders out of holes that were roofed with coconut logs by driving a 32-ton armored bulldozer over them. When the logs crashed onto the heads of the Japanese soldiers, the enemy troops tumbled into the open and were shot. "They'd come out of there and run the gantlet," said Sergeant Lloyd Kestin of the 154th Combat Engineers. Few of them survived.

A rifle platoon and demolitions squad approached another cave on the north side of Radar Hill, and 60 enemy soldiers suddenly rushed out. They overran the attackers, who managed to kill about half of them.

Colonel Dark summoned "G" Company – it was participating with the 2nd Battalion in Ngesebus's mop-up – and on October 2, "G" and "B," supported by M10 "tank destroyers" and 155mm guns, again assaulted Radar Hill. While "B" attacked from the west and south, using ropes and makeshift scaling ladders to climb Radar Hill's sheer cliff faces, "G" supported the attack from nearby Hill 3 with covering fire. From a coconut grove east of Radar Hill, the tank destroyers laid down a barrage.

Reaching the summit in the late morning against light resistance, "B" worked its way down the northern and eastern slopes, clearing the caves with flamethrowers and explosives. At least 100 dead Japanese soldiers were counted in one cave alone.

During the attack, Sergeant William Sherry dove onto a live Japanese grenade, saving the lives of two "B" Company comrades while forfeiting his own. For this, he was posthumously awarded the Silver Star. Some of Sherry's comrades grumbled that if Sherry had been a Marine, he would have been nominated for the Congressional Medal of Honor. Indeed, Marines were awarded the nation's highest honor for doing exactly what Sherry had done. An 81st Division historian, Bobby Blair, believed that Army officers were more conservative than their Marine counterparts when recommending their men for decorations.[19]

Radar Hill was declared secured at 5 p.m. on October 2.

A Japanese soldier emerged from a cave inside the hill, waving a white rag. "B" Company's commander, Captain Wallace Moorman, told his men to hold their fire so that the man could surrender. The enemy soldier suddenly lunged at Moorman with a hari-kari knife that he had concealed in the white rag. Anticipating just such a trick, Moorman leaped aside and shot the man.

"It became the byword of the 321st, show the bastards no mercy, and take no prisoners," said Sergeant Nolton Brown. "We were taught to never trust one, [because] if you did, it would cost you your life."[20]

On Hill Row, an Army patrol came upon a Japanese medical aid station inside a well-concealed large cave that had three entrances, one of them guarded by an untended Lewis gun. Inside the cave, the Americans found 50 dead Japanese, most of them with gunshot wounds to the head, indicating that they had committed suicide. The cave had electricity and radio transmitting and receiving equipment, but few medical supplies and no bandages.[21]

As the Wildcats were methodically cleaning out the northern Peleliu caves, Imperial Marines suddenly burst from one of them. "They came out with a few hand grenades and started throwing them, then ducked back again," said James Lamson of the Antitank Company. "They only had something on their waist, and leg wrappings. They were bare from the waist up and bald-headed." A bulldozer sealed the cave with the Imperial Marines inside.[22]

Korean laborers accounted for most of the men that were captured. The soldiers may have learned from the Marines when taking prisoners how to distinguish laborers from enemy soldiers: have them raise their hands above their heads so that the captors could check for callouses. If their hands were calloused, the prisoners were presumed to be Korean laborers; if they were not, they were probably soldiers. By this method, the Marines quickly sorted prisoners into two groups and sent them to separate confinement areas.[23]

Lieutenant Colonel Peter Clainos's 2nd Battalion reached Ngesebus on amtracs during the late afternoon of September 29 to extinguish the last embers of enemy resistance. It soon became apparent that the Wildcats had work to do. Heavy sniper fire raked them from caves to the west, forcing the battalion to spend the night hunkered in water-filled shell holes on the airstrip. The next morning, Clainos's men were joined by tanks and amtrac flamethrowers and began systematically clearing the enemy-occupied caves.

Two days after coming ashore, on October 1, Clainos's men discovered several pockets of enemy fighters at Courtemanche Ridge in the northern island. Tanks were summoned and, after a pitched battle, the Japanese were wiped out. By nightfall, the battalion could claim mastery over Ngesebus and nearby Kongauru Island.[24]

Midway through October – a month after D-Day, when Rupertus had confidently predicted a campaign of just four days' duration – the 321st Regiment occupied the Marines' former positions in the ridges ringing the Pocket.

The Battle of Peleliu was not over by any means, although the Japanese soldiers who occupied the 400-by-850-yard enclave were without hope of victory, and many of them were wounded. Nonetheless, they remained determined to take to the grave with them as many of their enemies as possible.

Paradoxically, enemy deserters at the same time were turning up in greater numbers on Peleliu's beaches, hoping to escape to the Japanese-occupied northern Palaus. This development signified crumbling Japanese morale in the Pocket. Most of the deserters were killed before they could leave Peleliu.[25]

The battle had become a "siege situation," in the words of Major Gordon Gayle of the Fifth Marines. The 81st Division's commander, General Paul Mueller, intended to continue to pursue the Fifth Marines' strategy of using overwhelming firepower to achieve limited gains with the fewest possible casualties.[26]

Six weeks would pass before *Stalemate* would finally end.

The 321st joined the Umurbrogol battle after the Marines had killed more than 10,000 of Nakagawa's men. A month of bombing, shelling, and bloodletting had stripped the Umurbrogol of virtually all traces of normal terrestrial life. The alien battleground was an assault on the soldiers' senses: 110-degree sauna-like heat amid a miasma of putrefaction and tormenting insects.

The battlefield was littered with bloody field dressings, empty ammunition boxes, shell casings, smashed Japanese rifles, and "half-eaten rations rotting in the sun," recalled Marine Corporal R.V. Burgin. Empty ration cans also served as receptacles for the men's excrement; diarrhea was rampant, and its stench, commingling with that of bodies decomposing in the heat and humidity, caused men to gag. And there were the ubiquitous metallic-green blowflies, grown fat from feasting on the corpses.[27]

"The flies were terrible," said Nolton Brown of the 321st's Antitank Company. "Dead and bloated bodies were everywhere you turned. We sat down to eat a can of beans, [and] there were rotten bodies lying a few feet away. Flies as big as a half dollar [were] crawling on them and [on] you. We finally became hardened to where we paid little attention to them."[28]

Under the supervision of U.S. Department of Agriculture experts sent to Peleliu, more than 300 "sanitary squads" equipped with tanks of a DDT diesel-oil mixture began spraying unburied Japanese corpses, latrines, kitchens, messes, and standing water to arrest the spread of dengue fever. A TBM Avenger dispersed clouds of the mixture over the contested battlefields from belly tanks retrofitted with aerial sprayers. "When these planes came over trailing clouds of white dust," said Pfc Tim Nelson, "the shooting suddenly died down – even the Japs let them fly over without shooting at them."[29]

Thousands of Japanese soldiers lay dead in Peleliu's caves, gullies, and tunnels. On October 14, Colonel Nakagawa had reported that 1,150 of his original force of nearly 11,000 a month earlier now defended a 41-acre area. Nakagawa rated 80 percent of his remaining men as combat-capable, but that estimate was most likely too optimistic.

Although the Japanese bastion covered a relatively small part of the Umurbrogol, it in fact encompassed Peleliu's most rugged terrain and its densest concentration of strongpoints. It was an area crowded with cliffs; ravines clotted with jungle vegetation; deep pits; strange, other-worldly spires; and ridges riddled with caves – each of them a Japanese defensive position.[30]

The Japanese had labored hard to make mini-fortresses of Peleliu's roughly 500 natural and man-made caves. They had created blast walls of logs to buttress the caves' structural integrity. Coral-filled oil drums and reinforced concrete protected entryways from direct fire. Steel doors that could be quickly opened and closed shielded caves harboring artillery, mortars, and automatic cannons. Many caves had rear safe rooms where troops could go when the main entryway was under attack by flamethrowers and explosives.[31]

Admiral William Halsey viewed Peleliu's formidable cave and tunnel fortifications firsthand while touring the island by Jeep on October 1 – and narrowly avoided being struck by a mortar round. Days later, in a letter to his superior, Admiral Chester Nimitz, Halsey described the Japanese attritional defensive strategy and the slow, dangerous labor involved "in digging the rats out." He suggested using poison gas to kill the enemy inside their caves and tunnels, thereby minimizing U.S. casualties. Nimitz rejected Halsey's suggestion.[32]

The 321st, which had been blooded in comparatively lower-intensity combat on Angaur, was now fighting its first – and, as it would turn out, its only – major combat of the war on Peleliu. When their initial shock began to subside, the soldiers, as had the Marines before them, became inured to the brutal nature of fighting on Peleliu.

Some of the soldiers, as had some of the Marines, adopted the common practice of warriors ancient and modern. They stripped Japanese bodies of watches, money, photos, letters – and gold teeth, taken from the mouths of the corpses.

"They would bust their teeth out with a rifle butt and take the gold fillings," said Nolan Brown of the 321st's Antitank Company. "Seems that most of them had gold fillings."[33] Marine Pfc E.B. Sledge had earlier witnessed the grotesque spectacle of a Marine with a K-Bar knife attempting to pry the gold fillings from a still-living enemy soldier:

Because the Japanese was kicking his feet and thrashing about, the knife point glanced off the tooth and sank deeply into the victim's mouth. The Marine cursed him and with a slash cut his cheeks open to each ear. He put his foot on the sufferer's lower jaw and tried again. Blood poured out of the soldier's mouth. He made a gurgling noise and thrashed wildly. I shouted, "Put the man out of his misery." All I got for an answer was a cussing out. Another Marine ran up, put a bullet in the enemy soldier's brain, and ended his agony. The scavenger grumbled and continued extracting his prizes undisturbed.[34]

There were other excesses of souvenir-collecting, Sledge discovered. A comrade proudly showed Sledge his keepsake, carefully wrapped in wax paper. It was a shriveled human hand that he had severed from a corpse. He told Sledge that with a little more time to dry in the sun, it would no longer reek.

Get rid of it, Sledge told the Marine. It was not only repulsive, it was unsanitary, and if higher-ups found out about it, he would be in trouble. Others in the men's platoon unanimously condemned their mate's souvenir; bury it, or throw it away, they said. Not finding one ally among his friends, the man threw away the hand.

"The war had gotten to my friend; he had lost (briefly, I hoped) all his sensitivity," Sledge wrote. "He was a twentieth-century savage now, mild mannered though he still was."[35]

Colonel Dark's men learned to bend their definition of a foxhole to fit the peculiar circumstances. Because of the Pocket's unyielding coral-limestone bedrock, so-called foxholes often were little more than small, shallow areas enclosed by stacks of coral chunks. To cushion the discomfort of lying down on a stone bed, the soldiers covered their sleeping areas with empty "C" ration boxes – and anything else that might blunt the coral's sharp edges.

The men adapted to their uncomfortable accommodations as best they could. "I developed a favorite sleeping position: left side, left arm around neck, knees pulled up near fetal position, right hand on trench knife (later on pistol) which was next to a few hand grenades, everything ready for action," said Lieutenant George Rasula of "G" Company. "Sleep came in bits and pieces."

Their nocturnal early warning system was simple but effective; they liberally festooned their barbed wire enclosures with empty ration cans, which rattled loudly when disturbed. Many times, it was Peleliu's large land crabs that would set off the alarm – to then be obliterated by a volley of grenades.[36]

The 321st launched its first offensive on the Pocket on October 17. Attacking from the north, the regiment targeted the Five Brothers and some smaller, parallel ridges to the west. The 323rd's 1st Battalion, recently arrived from Ulithi, occupied defensive positions along the southern and western perimeters of the Pocket. Pfc James Green was one of the first 323rd soldiers to be wounded on Peleliu. "We were pinned down," he said. "We were starting to withdraw and that's when I got wounded," shot in both legs.[37]

Aerial observers helped identify targets for a pair of mortar units that set up on the Pocket's southwestern rim. A 710th Tank Battalion platoon assaulted caves north of the airstrip with its newest weapon: a flamethrower that replaced the tank's bow gun, which was usually a machine gun mounted on a tripod. Located below the turret and cannon, the flamethrower was operated by the assistant driver. It proved effective against cave openings near the ground, but its small fuel tank emptied quickly.[38]

During the 321st's first attack from the Pocket's northern rim on the 17th, its 1st and 2nd Battalions gained 125 yards, with the support of tanks that shelled caves in the Horseshoe, killing 40 enemy soldiers.

Enemy rifle and machine-gun fire cut up a "G" Company platoon in a deep ravine that ran between Hill 140 and Brother 1. In a brief span, three men were killed and a dozen were wounded, including "G" Company's commander, Lieutenant Jack Smith, who had come forward to personally lead the attack. Staff Sergeant Harry Courtemanche was killed while getting medical aid for Smith, who survived.

After their introduction to the Five Brothers, the two 321st battalions withdrew for the night.[39]

On that same day, enemy infiltrators followed labyrinthian routes through a network of caves and tunnels to an area 300 yards south of the Pocket. With knee mortars and machine guns, they surprised and drove the 4.2-inch mortar platoon and the 710th Tank Battalion's mortar platoon from their positions on the Pocket's southwestern rim.

General Rupertus recalled the Seventh Marines' 3rd Battalion from its Purple Beach rest area to eliminate the threat in the area that became known as the South Pocket. At 6:40 p.m., "I" Company attacked from positions along the West Road. Darkness prevented the Marines from recapturing the mortar positions.[40]

To demonstrate that the 321st's foray into the Pocket had not diminished their resistance, at 4:30 a.m. on October 18, the Japanese plastered the northern edge of the Pocket with mortar fire and grenades.

Hours later, Marine Captain Harry Jones, the commander of the Seventh Marines' "L" Company, was killed while directing the fire of an Army tank aiding the 3rd Battalion in clearing the South Pocket's caves. The tank struck a mine and burned, and Jones and half of the tank's crew died in the explosion and fire. Jones was the last Marine to die on Peleliu, and the third rifle company commander in his battalion to be killed.[41]

Later that morning of October 18, the 321st's 2nd Battalion renewed its attack from the north. As tanks and amtrac flamethrowers blistered caves in the Horseshoe between Walt Ridge and the Five Brothers, the soldiers reached the summits of Brothers 1, 2, and 3.

Just as the Marines had learned previously, the hilltops afforded no cover, and pre-registered enemy machine-gun and mortar fire slammed into the Wildcats from three sides. Then two Japanese platoons counterattacked from Brothers 4 and 5, forcing the 2nd Battalion to scramble off the three hills beneath an umbrella of tank fire. The battalion formed a night perimeter at the base of Brother 1.[42]

The 321st's unsuccessful forays into the Pocket and subsequent withdrawals convinced General Mueller to forsake costly infantry attacks. He instead embraced the strategy of steadily degrading the enemy's strength by siege.

Henceforth, Mueller's men would be generous in their use of tanks, artillery and mortar fire, naval gunfire, and air strikes to grind down Nakagawa's diminishing force. Mueller's approach mirrored the philosophy of Fifth Marines Colonel Harold Harris.[43]

Mueller's division also improvised. The 81st discovered that enemy troops in caves and pillboxes who somehow resisted concentrated artillery and tank fire and air strikes might sometimes succumb to a more innovative approach.

As an experiment, engineers assembled a 300-yard pipeline to a gasoline truck on the West Road, parking it as close as possible to the intended target. Then they pumped napalm through the pipeline into the enemy caves and pillboxes and ignited it with phosphorus grenades. The resulting inferno was so successful in suffocating and charring the defenders that the method was used repeatedly.

Another innovation was soldiers' use of sandbags as shields when ascending hills that lacked places to take cover from Japanese gunfire. Previously, when they reached the exposed summits of hills and found it impossible to dig holes in the tough coral-sandstone rock, they were forced to withdraw. But then they hit upon the idea of pushing sandbags ahead of them up the hills. Approaching their objective under Japanese fire, they wriggled forward on their bellies, shoving the sandbags ahead of them with poles, sticks, and rifle butts. The mobile parapets protected them from gunfire until they reached their objective, which they then fortified with the sandbags. The 321st later refined the procedure by forming a chain of soldiers, who handed the sandbags from man to man, from the bottom of the hill to its summit.[44]

The 81st Division faced a dwindling remnant of the elite Japanese veterans that for a month had flayed the Marines – and had in turn been all but wiped out by the relentless leathernecks. The ragged, besieged Japanese were hemmed in a shrinking perimeter, without hope of resupply or reinforcement.

Now that there was no longer pressure to move faster in order to meet Rupertus's illusory timetable, the Wildcats found time to send "souvenir patrols" into secured caves with lit candles. They hunted for rifles and flags to barter at the airfield with the Seabees and airfield crews, who traded fresh bread and peanut butter and jam for the keepsakes.

"There'd be dead bodies, and we would get the flags they would keep around their waists," said Roy Bergeron of "B" Company of the 321st. "When you picked up the body, you just let both ends fall out, and you take the flag."[45]

Recalled from Purple Beach on October 17 to destroy the Japanese infiltrators in the South Pocket – the ridges overlooking the West Road – the Seventh Marines resumed their attack on October 18 and annihilated enemy troops that had occupied a dozen caves.

During the morning of the 19th, the 1st Battalion of the Army's 323rd Regiment – recently arrived from Ulithi – the Army 154th Combat Engineers, and the Seventh Marines' "L" Company pressed their attack into the ridges. When "L" withdrew later in the day, Japanese artillery fire plastered the American positions, forcing the 323rd and the Engineers to pull back.

Exasperated by the failure to clear the caves, Rupertus sent the Eleventh Marines' 4th Battalion to the West Road to fire its guns point-blank into the enemy-held caves. When Marine gunners fired a 155mm high-explosive round directly into one cave and the smoke cleared, the gunners spotted Japanese soldiers throwing rocks dislodged by the blast out of the cave. The enemy troops stopped and took cover just as the Marines finished reloading the gun – having evidently calculated how long the reloading process took. The Japanese did not budge from the cave.[46]

During the 321st's third day in the Pocket, October 19, Lieutenant Colonel Clainos, the 2nd Battalion commander, requested an airdrop of napalm without the usual igniter mechanism. This was a technique that the Marines had successfully used in the Pocket, but it was the first time that the Army was employing it.

Before the mission, white panels were laid on the ground to distinguish the target area from nearby friendly forces. Fifteen seconds after taking off from Peleliu's airstrip, 16 Corsairs appeared over the Pocket. Each dropped a 30-pound napalm tank that burst on the slopes of the Five Brothers and in the northern Wildcat Bowl, sending rivulets of fuel streaming into the caves and crevices.

Then 4.2-inch mortars lit up the napalm with white phosphorus rounds. Scrambling to escape the inferno, Japanese soldiers fled their caves, pillboxes, and sniper perches in the trees, to be slain by waiting American infantrymen.[47]

The 19th was the day that the 81st Division commander, General Paul Mueller, moved his headquarters from Angaur to Purple Beach on Peleliu. A separate division "battle operations center" was established in the former Japanese headquarters building near the airstrip where Rupertus had made his 1st Division headquarters.

Marine General O.P. Smith criticized Mueller's selection of the Purple Beach area for the 81st's headquarters. It was too far from the fighting, he said. For his part, Mueller disparaged the way that the 1st Division had fought the battle, going so far as to question the Marines' combat proficiency.

Yet both the Army and the Marines had largely conducted their affairs according to their respective protocols, and the sniping only underscored their divergent war-fighting philosophies and the deep-seated resentments nursed by both services.[48]

Chapter 12

The End

I would holler out the best I could, "Come out
with your hands up." Of course, nobody ever
came out. We would pour gas in there and light it
up, and we would hear screaming, but nobody ever
came out.

Private Clifton Dantin,
321st Infantry[1]

It is easy to die but difficult to live on. We must select
the difficult course and continue to fight because of the
influence on the morale of the Japanese people.

General Sadae Inoue, rejecting a
banzai attack finish on Peleliu[2]

When General Mueller and his staff officially took responsibility for
the Peleliu campaign and the defense of the southern Palau Islands on
October 20, the 321st Regiment's mission remained unchanged: to
root out Nakagawa's diehards in the Pocket.

While serving under General Rupertus from September 23 to
October 20, the 321st reported that it had killed 1,500 Japanese soldiers
and captured 108. During this period, 98 Wildcats were killed in action
and 468 were wounded.

Before leaving Peleliu to fly to Guadalcanal with General Roy Geiger
on October 20, General Rupertus visited the Army positions near the

Five Sisters. James Fitzpatrick, a rifleman with the 321st, said, "He [Rupertus] was very disgusted with the operation. He said he was glad we had it now."[3]

The Fifth Regiment was the last Marine combat unit still on the island. It was attached as a task force to the 81st Division, and given responsibility for defending northern Peleliu and the outlying islands. General O.P. Smith remained on Peleliu as a liaison between the Marines and Mueller.[4] When Mueller openly questioned the Marines' combat efficiency, Smith responded by citing their considerable achievements in the Umurbrogol, but acknowledged that they were exhausted and depleted by their heavy casualties.

Dissatisfied with Smith's reply, Mueller asked him for a map overlay of the Marine machine-gun positions. There were no overlays, replied Smith, because the Marines were attacking every day. The Army general shook his head disapprovingly and told Smith that he would have to start a wholly new campaign – since the Marines had not finished the job. Smith silently glowered at Mueller.

Mueller also wanted to segregate the Army dead from the Marines in the Peleliu cemetery. The Army dead belonged in their own, separate area of the cemetery, insisted Mueller. When Smith objected to Mueller's plan, Mueller appealed to higher-ups. The Navy sided with Smith, and the dead soldiers remained where they had been buried.[5]

In the ridges above the West Road, the Japanese stubbornly clung to the Southern Pocket. The 323rd's "C" Company was dispatched to assist demolitions men from the 154th Combat Engineers in dislodging them. Intensive small-arms fire immediately pinned down the infantrymen. Tanks were rushed to the area and aided the infantrymen and engineers in advancing another 100 yards. Day after day, "C" assaulted the Southern Pocket with tank-infantry teams, making slow progress while methodically sealing caves so that they could not be reoccupied. "C" would stay busy ridding the Southern Pocket of its holdouts until early November.[6]

After working together for weeks, the Army tank crews and infantrymen developed a satisfying symbiotic relationship: soldiers protected the tanks while the crewmen slept, and the tanks provided a roof for the sleeping infantrymen. Before the tank crewmen bedded down, they lowered the bow machine gun through the tank's escape hatch, along with a "sound power phone." If enemy soldiers approached, the infantrymen were instructed to whistle loudly over the phone to awaken the tank crew.[7]

At 1 p.m. on the 21st, a combat patrol of volunteers from the 321st Infantry, carrying bags of grenades, assaulted Brother 1. Enemy soldiers near the summit rolled grenades downhill onto the attackers, but the patrol pushed ahead anyway, through gullies and around crags, reaching Brother 1's crest at 5 p.m. "E" Company then ascended the hill and reinforced the patrol. A human chain passed sandbags from the hill's base to the top, where a fortification sprang up.

That night, enemy infiltrators launched grenade attacks on Brother 1 and Walt Ridge. The 321st repulsed every assault, but when the counterattacks became a nightly feature, the men grew edgy. Combat fatigue cases spiked. At daybreak one day, a sergeant shot and killed a Wildcat who stood up in his foxhole; the sergeant thought he was a Japanese soldier.[8]

On October 22, the 81st Division issued Field Order No. 7. It outlined the Wildcats' first major operation since becoming solely responsible for extinguishing the Japanese resistance that still flickered in the Pocket.

Field Order No. 7 laid out a detailed plan for a four-battalion offensive preceded by napalm air strikes and a mortar barrage. The mission of the 321st's 1st Battalion was to capture China Wall all the way south to the northern slope of the Five Sisters; its 2nd Battalion's objective was the Five Brothers ridge; and the 3rd Battalion was directed to fully occupy the Horseshoe, killing enemy soldiers inside and atop Walt Ridge. Meanwhile, the 323rd's 1st Battalion would push eastward into the Pocket from the western perimeter lines to support the assault on China Wall.[9]

On the operation's first day, "I" Company of the 321st's 3rd Battalion drove southward down the length of the Horseshoe. Aided by two platoons of medium tanks, three M10 tank destroyers, and a pair of amtrac flamethrowers, the soldiers scorched enemy caves in the valley's walls. At Grinlinton Pond, the infantrymen killed 35

Japanese who fought back from holes and coral rock fissures near the water's edge.

VMF-114 dropped unfused belly tanks filled with napalm on the enemy positions in the Horseshoe, and mortar shells then ignited the napalm. To guide the pilots to their target, the soldiers placed smoke pots at the end of the Horseshoe and along its western approaches. "We were using a goodly number of belly tanks" during the air strike," the squadron's report said, "but everyone was being satisfied and Japs exterminated without commensurate loss to ourselves."[10]

By the close of October 22, the 3rd Battalion's accomplishments were impressive compared with the limited advances of its sister battalions. The 1st Battalion was stopped in the ridges before reaching China Wall, while the 2nd occupied Brothers 1 and 2, but not Brother 3; it captured Brother 3 the next day.[11]

The 323rd's 1st Battalion failed to break into the Pocket and was forced back to the West Road by swarms of Japanese soldiers flinging American grenades. Another enemy counterattack opened a dangerous gap between the 323rd and the 321st Regiments. Pfcs Ellis Smith and Lacy Pack of the 321st's "E" Company plugged the hole – and held it until morning despite both of them suffering multiple battle wounds.[12]

Pfc Hank Chamberlain described the gruesome sight of a Japanese soldier who had been flushed by a flamethrower from a cave. In the Umurbrogol Pocket, this had become a commonplace-enough spectacle, but to many of the men of the 81st Division it was new and shocking. The victim, said Chamberlain, was consumed by a "mass of fire from head to foot and his shrieks were indescribable... We put him out of his agony with enough bullets to kill a dozen men."[13]

After the 3rd Battalion's successful drive through the Horseshoe, the 321st was able to deny the encircled Japanese all access to Grinlinton Pond, their chief source of fresh water. Nonetheless, its allure for desperately thirsty men remained powerful, and it was as deadly as a flame's attraction is to moths.

The Americans planted trip flares that turned night to noon. Twenty Japanese soldiers were killed while trying to reach the pond during its first night under the 321st's control, October 23–24. When the Japanese were exposed by the flares' harsh, bright light, killing them was simplicity itself. "When they crawled along, they would trip them, we could see them, and then we would shoot them," said Bert Neil of the 321st's "I" Company.

Two nights later, a newly placed spotlight illuminated the area, and seven men in a water-carrying party blundered to their deaths. Machine-gun bullets riddled all of them. "Hardly any of them were armed," said Neil. "All they wanted was water."[14]

Most of the American soldiers did not bother trying to persuade the Japanese to surrender before sealing occupied caves, but a rare few persisted in making the attempt. Private Clifton Dantin of the 321st was one. He regularly consulted the standard English–Japanese language pocket translation issued to all Pacific Theater troops.

"I would holler out the best I could, 'Come out with your hands up.' Of course, nobody ever came out," Dantin said. "We would pour gas in there and light it up, and we would hear screaming, but nobody ever came out."[15]

By nightfall on October 24, the 321st's 2nd Battalion occupied Brothers 1, 2, 3, and 4, but not 5; its defenders would hold out for another month. Faced with the difficulty of shuttling supplies and the wounded up and down the steep ridges, the soldiers created a cable-and-pulley gondola system powered by a quarter-ton truck. Ammunition and sandbags were conveyed in wire baskets via a "high line" to the ridgetop, where the cargo was exchanged for wounded and dead men for the return trip.[16]

On the 25th, General Marcus Bell, the 81st's assistant commander, summoned to Peleliu the 323rd battalions still fighting on Angaur. They would replace most of the 321st units and assume the primary combat role on Peleliu. The 322nd remained on Angaur to mop up. Major Ushio Goto's diehards on Romauldo Hill had succumbed two days earlier to the 322nd's siege tactics.[17]

As planned, an airfield was built from scratch on Angaur, and on October 15 the first plane landed, a C-47 transport. Bombing missions were later flown from Angaur's 6,000-foot runways against targets in the Philippines.[18]

The 323rd reached Peleliu in mid-October as the 81st Division embraced the siege tactics that had ground down Goto and his men on Angaur. The strategy was ideal for an inexperienced regiment like the 323rd. Heavy weapons would soften the Pocket's defenses before troops went into action, minimizing casualties. At one point, the Army contemplated encircling the Pocket with barbed wire and observation and machine-gun posts – like a prison camp – but the proposal was not acted upon.[19]

When the 321st's 1st and 2nd Battalions withdrew from the Pocket, they were sent, respectively, to northern Peleliu and Ngesebus. The 3rd Battalion remained inside the Pocket – at Grinlinton Pond in the Horseshoe, and on Boyd and Walt ridges.

On the 25th, "I" Company captured two wounded Japanese soldiers who, when interrogated, said that 500 to 600 enemy troops were still holding out in the Pocket; half of them were sick or wounded, they said. The captives pointed to two nearby caves that they said harbored 50 to 60 of their comrades, who were armed with rifles and grenades. Their cave, they said, held 15 or 16 wounded men. Each had been issued a grenade to end his life if facing capture.[20]

By day's end on October 26, the 321st had relieved the remaining Fifth Marines' units in northern Peleliu, and the Marines were a step closer to embarking for Pavavu. However, the Marines' 8th Artillery Battalion and its 155mm guns remained on Peleliu, attached to the 81st Division artillery.

Nakagawa quickly tested the green 323rd Regiment after it took over the 321st's positions in the Pocket. The Japanese remotely detonated a mine buried beneath the spot where an "E" Company platoon was taking a rest break in the Southern Pocket. When the dust cleared, blood was splashed everywhere, one man had been decapitated, and another had lost both legs. The huge explosion on October 26 killed nine soldiers and wounded 20 others.[21]

Hours later, during the night of October 26–27, it was "B" Company's turn. A Japanese platoon attacked the entrenched soldiers three times – and each time was repulsed with the aid of heavy mortar barrages. Infiltrators slipped into the 323rd's lines and crawled beneath hammocks where soldiers slept, stabbing them through their bedding.

Steve Dombrowski's first night in a foxhole in Peleliu's west ridges was harrowing enough, and his foxhole comrade made matters worse.

In an interview with author John Peter DeCioccio, Dombrowski recalled, "On the first night in a foxhole, flares were being shot, I don't know where they came from, and the shadows of the few trees looked like the Japanese were coming after us. The fellow in the foxhole with me started shooting, thinking they were Japs. He did this for two nights, and I couldn't sleep." Dombrowski complained to his lieutenant, who replaced the man and sent him to company headquarters. Dombrowski later learned that the soldier had a nervous breakdown.[22]

Then, at 4 a.m. on October 27, fifty enemy soldiers attempted to recapture Brother 4; they failed, and 30 of them were killed.

Heavy rainfall and poor visibility through November 1 gave the 323rd a respite from combat that it used to shore up its positions and bring up ammunition, rations, and sandbags. The new arrivals also dragged more pack howitzers onto commanding high ground.

The Japanese did not let up, despite the blinding curtains of rain. A Japanese floatplane dropped two parachutes early one evening. The one recovered by American troops was attached to a wicker basket containing 60 grenades.

Even with the sketchy visibility, Japanese snipers managed to pick off American soldiers. One victim was Captain Joseph Mortimer, who led the 323rd's "K" Company in the northwestern ridges. He was shot in the back and killed. To honor the late captain, the 81st renamed the Horseshoe for him; it became known as Mortimer Valley.[23]

The night after Mortimer's death, his "K" Company repelled a strong attack on the Five Brothers after initially being driven from its forward positions. In retaking the lost ground, the soldiers killed 35 enemy troops. But the attacks on the Brothers continued through the night and the next day. All of them failed.[24]

The same night that Mortimer's men were fending off Japanese assaults on the Five Brothers, five landing barges from Babelthuap appeared in the waters 4 miles from Purple Beach. Besides carrying amphibious troops, each barge was equipped with improvised torpedo tubes; the Japanese meant to torpedo and blow up the Purple Beach anchorage and several transports that were filled with Marines who were about to sail to Pavavu.

Before the intruders could do much damage – besides riddling the tents on Purple Beach with tracer bullets – a destroyer escort and an infantry landing craft attacked and drove off the barges.

Ironically, General Mueller, criticized by Marine General O.P. Smith for locating his headquarters far from the fighting in the Pocket, came within a hair's breadth of becoming a victim of the attack. His tent was shot full of holes, and an unexploded torpedo was found on the beach near his headquarters. However, neither he nor anyone else was injured.[25]

The Americans persisted in distributing flyers that encouraged the Japanese to surrender. One said:

> Officers of the Japanese forces:
>
> As you can see if you look at the planes, the material and the ships, your best efforts are not impeding our work. American planes not only bomb you at will but they also bomb Babelthuap and the other islands north of here. Perhaps you can see the flames. Your comrades to the north have all they can do to help themselves so how could they help you?
>
> You honor and respect your men, but how can they honor and respect you if you make them die needlessly? Thousands of brave Japanese soldiers before you have realized the futility of death in such circumstances; they will live to raise families and to help build a new Japan.
>
> You still have this choice – raise a white flag and come out unarmed. We will give you water, food, shelter, and medicine for your wounded.[26]

A gaunt, dirty Japanese officer carrying a white flag surrendered the next day in Mortimer Valley. In clear English, he told his captors that he was a medical officer who had studied at Johns Hopkins University in Baltimore before the war. About 500 enemy troops remained in the Pocket, he said.[27]

The Japanese continued to attempt to parachute supplies from floatplanes to their comrades on Peleliu. On October 29, the floatplane's cargo was leaflets that were addressed to "You Reckless Yankee Doodle":

> Thanks for your advice notes of surrender. But we haven't any reason to surrender to those who are fated to be totally destroyed

in a few days later. Add to you, against the manner of your attack paying no heed to humanity, your god shall make Japanese force to add retaliative [sic] attack upon you. Saying again, against the attack paying no heed to humanity contrary to the mutual military spirits, you shall get a very stern attack. We mean cruel attack. Japan Military.[28]

A Hellcat night-fighter flown by Major Norman Mitchell from Peleliu's airfield got on the floatplane's tail and shot it down northwest of Garakayo. It was the only Japanese warplane downed by a Peleliu-based Marine pilot.[29]

On October 31, Colonel Nakagawa reported to his superiors in Koror that he had been forced to slash the ammunition ration for his 650 men by one-half. Along with 500 grenades, he said, the defenders possessed just 190 rifles, 12 machine guns, and 20 antitank bombs.[30]

While sticking to its overarching strategy of grinding down the defenders by siege, the 81st Division now identified two new objectives for attacks into the Pocket. Old Baldy – previously known as Hill 300 – and Five Sisters, it was believed, would serve as excellent observation posts for future attacks from the south into Wildcat Bowl and Death Valley, and against China Wall, the suspected location of Nakagawa's headquarters and where he was expected to make his last stand.

Intelligence officers in observation planes photographed the combat zone and studied the results of their overflights. Then, "G" Company of the 323rd attacked Old Baldy on November 2, seizing it in just one hour against feeble resistance. "G" proceeded to also scramble up Sister 4. Observation posts were established and operating ten minutes later atop both hills, and the positions were sandbagged.

An hour later, all five Sisters were secured. American soldiers could now observe all of the caves in China Wall's east face and those in Five Brothers' west face. That night, the Wildcats repulsed a Japanese counterattack, killing 38 enemy soldiers.[31]

On November 3, the 323rd's "C" Company made another stab at ridding the Southern Pocket of infiltrators. This time, after sealing a few caves, the Wildcats declared that they had been successful and withdrew to a rest area. "C" Company's two-week campaign had claimed the lives of about 100 Japanese infiltrators at a cost of 22 Wildcat and Marine deaths, and 51 Americans wounded.[32]

On the same day that the Southern Pocket was secured, "E" Company sent a 13-man armored reconnaissance patrol into Death Valley shortly after noon to learn more about the valley's defenses. Five days earlier, infantrymen supported by tanks had met little resistance when they entered the valley.

This time, the Wildcats walked into an ambush by enemy soldiers who were in a celebratory mood; it was the birth date of Emperor Meiji, whose restoration to the throne in 1867 began Japan's modern era.

The Americans were met by a buzzsaw of gunfire blazing out of caves bracketing the valley. The soldiers quickly reversed direction, leaving behind seven comrades who had been severely wounded or killed. They lay where they had fallen for more than a week before their bodies were recovered.[33]

But there were increasing signs that the Pocket's core was crumbling. During the night of November 3–4, more than a dozen Japanese soldiers tried to escape. Three were killed in a firefight, along with an American. Patrols pursued the others and rounded up eight of them on northern Peleliu, Ngabad, and Kongauru.

The prisoners said that their comrades who remained in the Pocket intended to fight to the death and had plenty of food, water, and ammunition to prolong the battle. But that was not true; the survivors were getting by on meager rations and half allowances of small-arms ammunition. Moreover, American soldiers had transformed Grinlinton Pond, their only freshwater source aside from rainwater, into a death trap.

Colonel Nakagawa was fully aware that his men's fierce defense of Peleliu was nearing its end; the day would soon come when his remaining combat-capable troops would exhaust their ammunition. "It was tentative as to whether it would last until 20 November," he wrote in a report found after the war.[34]

General Kenjior Murai, Nakagawa's co-commander, disagreed with Nakagawa's plan to continue to fight a defensive battle in the Pocket until everyone was dead. Murai wanted to end the battle with an all-out banzai attack. Although he was superior in rank to the colonel, Murai had until now been in concord with Nakagawa in his decisions, and had given him carte blanche authority to conduct Peleliu's defensive operations as he saw fit.

Unable to bring around Nakagawa to his view on this last, critical issue, Murai appealed to their superior, General Sadae Inoue, in Babelthuap. Peleliu's commanders remained in continual contact with Koror headquarters via underwater cable. Inoue, who was recovering from emergency surgery to remove a burst appendix, refused to grant Murai permission to mount a banzai attack.

"It is easy to die but difficult to live on," Inoue replied. "We must select the difficult course and continue to fight because of the influence on the morale of the Japanese people. Saipan was lost in a very short time because of vain banzai attacks, with the result that people at home suffered a drop in morale."*[35]

Another typhoon neared Peleliu on November 4. Over the next two days, the storm intensified. Rain driven by powerful winds blinded the adversaries. The Japanese took advantage of the poor conditions to slip out of the Pocket and infiltrate the Army's positions, but the battle lines did not change. The typhoon moved away on November 8.[36] The Pocket was steadily shrinking, to the point that the 81st Division stopped routinely using 4.2-inch mortars and artillery because of the risk of friendly fire casualties. Pack howitzers, however, continued to be fired directly into cave openings.

An exception was made on November 9, when the 81st Division battalions surrounding the Pocket began a three-day, around-the-clock 81mm mortar barrage on targets in the last enemy strongholds. It was a prelude to a coordinated assault scheduled for November 13 from the

---

*During questioning by his American captors, Inoue unbuttoned his shirt and showed them the scar from the surgery to remove his appendix. The surgical scar was about 6 inches long and an inch wide. "The appendix seemed to have been removed with a bayonet," one interrogator noted.

west and north against Death Valley and China Wall by the 323rd's 1st and 3rd Battalions.[37]

In anticipation of the offensive, every available noncombatant was conscripted to fill sandbags. Engineers with armored bulldozers protected by tanks built a 100-yard-long tank trail into Death Valley and removed the bodies of the Wildcats killed there nine days earlier.[38]

On November 5, a mortar detachment from the 111th Infantry Regiment had landed on Ngeregong Island without opposition. Located 9 miles northeast of Peleliu, Ngeregong was viewed by senior officers as a prospective recreation area that would double as a bulwark against attempts by the Japanese to reinforce Peleliu from Babelthuap. No enemy troops were believed to be on the islet; its seizure was expected to be easily accomplished.

It did not go altogether as planned. During the night of November 8–9, a Japanese infantry company landed on Ngeregong. Believing that they were badly outnumbered, the American mortar men hastily withdrew under an umbrella of fire from the 40mm and 20mm guns of the "Black Cat Flotilla," the four infantry landing craft that had put them ashore four days earlier.

All day long, the landing craft, along with destroyers, bombarded the tiny island. At dusk, 47 Marine Hellcats from Peleliu each dropped a 500-pound bomb on the islet. Then the Marine 8th Field Artillery Battalion shelled Ngeregong with 155mm guns from Peleliu's Akarakora Point.

General Mueller wanted to retake Ngeregong; it was vital to Peleliu's Northern Defense Sector, he said. The second invasion was scheduled for November 11.

Marine planes bombed and strafed Ngeregong the day before the landing. During the air strikes, a TBM Avenger and its three-man crew were lost when the torpedo bomber crashed on a coral reef south of the island.

When the 81st Cavalry Reconnaissance Troop landed on Ngeregong on November 11, no one was there. An hour later, the island was declared secured.[39]

———

Two thousand infantrymen from the 323rd Regiment converged on the Pocket on November 13 from three directions. Inside their collapsing

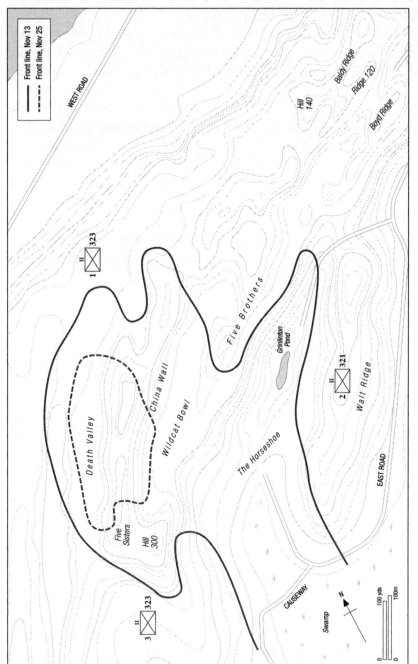

Map 8: The Last Stand

defenses, fewer than 200 Japanese soldiers continued to desperately resist from caves and fortified positions.

"B" Company attacked to the northeast through the western ridges until it was thwarted by strong opposition from five well-fortified positions. The company eliminated the enemy defenders after four hours of fighting.

An amtrac flamethrower and two tanks edged into Wildcat Bowl between the Five Brothers and Five Sisters, and blasted caves in China Wall and Five Brothers before withdrawing. At the same time, "K" and "L" Companies advanced toward China Wall and Wildcat Bowl from the north. That night, the Wildcats killed 13 enemy soldiers who attempted to infiltrate their lines.

Also during the night, "I" Company, which had attacked Brothers 2 and 5, stopped a counterattack from Brother 2 and cut down enemy troops who were walking around in the open, singing and laughing, apparently drunk on sake and indifferent to their fate. Forty-two of them died.[40]

The Wildcats proceeded over the next few days in an almost leisurely fashion, satisfied with eking out small gains each day.

"C" chalked up the elimination of an enemy strongpoint around a huge banyan tree as its accomplishment for November 16. The tree concealed a huge underground cave. Remaining true to the 81st's practice of using heavy weapons and not squandering manpower, the company drenched the position with fuel pumped through a half-inch pipeline from a petroleum truck parked 300 yards away on the West Road. Six Japanese soldiers died when the fuel was ignited with phosphorus grenades.[41]

Pfc James Ijames of the 323rd's "C" Company described the laborious process of digging out the stubborn defenders from their holes and caves: "We'd go down a ravine, any place we saw a hole that looked like a cave we'd try to shoot in it, clean them out, or dig them out anyway you could get them."[42]

Armored patrols began conducting daily sweeps through Wildcat Bowl and Death Valley on November 17, shelling and burning caves. Infantry patrols sealed caves with explosives in China Wall and Five Brothers, returning each night to their sandbagged positions.

The intensity of the fighting was falling off day by day due to the dwindling number of Japanese soldiers alive in the Pocket, but snipers still posed a deadly threat. On the 17th, Lieutenant Colonel Raymond Gates, the commander of the 323rd's 1st Battalion, was shot and killed by a treetop sniper while studying the front lines through binoculars. He was the highest-ranking 81st Division officer killed on Peleliu.[43]

That night, LCI landing craft on patrol in Schorian Harbor 2 and a half miles north of Peleliu discovered 36 flotation bladders bobbing in the water. When the seamen opened fire on the bladders, they deflated, exposing their Japanese infiltrator passengers. Most of them were shot dead.

A survivor told the Americans that 35 men, each armed with five grenades, were ordered to wreak havoc on the U.S. anchorage, and to also detonate five demolition charges besides the grenades. They then were supposed to locate places where reinforcements from Babelthuap could land.[44]

On November 21, tanks and amtrac flamethrowers roared through Death Valley and Wildcat Bowl without even attracting small-arms fire. Their Japanese defenders had evidently withdrawn from the caves along the western flanks of the Five Brothers to China Wall.

China Wall was where Nakagawa's men would fight their final battle.[45] On the 22nd, the 323rd tackled China Wall from the northern end of Death Valley. As anticipated, here lay the Pocket's last strong Japanese defensive positions, as well as Colonel Nakagawa's command post.

"The enemy in the northern part of Mt. Oyama [China Wall] are planning to capture our Defense Unit Headquarters," Nakagawa wrote to his superiors. "The enemy on the east side of Oyama Mountain penetrated our defense line and advanced towards the Defense Unit Headquarters, at the same time attacking our men, who were hidden in shelters, with flamethrowers. In this attack the casualties of our Defense Unit were heavy."[46]

China Wall's imposing height provided the Japanese with a panoramic view of the entire area, and its rugged terrain had so far protected China Wall's northern end from tracked vehicles. Moreover, the Wall's sharp perpendicular contours shielded the caves below from American gunfire coming from its summit.

At 6 a.m. on the 22nd, "F" Company, supported by tanks and an amtrac flamethrower, rolled down Wildcat Bowl along China Wall's eastern base, firing into caves. Using ropes, the Wildcats began scaling the Wall. Enemy snipers on its crest harassed the assault troops, but the Wildcats eliminated the sharpshooters, reached the top, and brought up sandbags to fortify their position.[47] While this attack was in progress, "A" Company blackened the northwestern ridges with a hose-and-nozzle flamethrower attached to a fuel truck parked on the West Road.

Although severely depleted, Japanese soldiers continued to take a steady toll of Wildcats. On November 22, Sergeant Elba Davis was killed while climbing a hill in Wildcat Bowl. When Davis briefly knelt down, the motion brought him into line with a depression at the top of the hill, from which a rifleman shot him. Later, a lieutenant from the same company was shot between the eyes while his platoon was setting up a machine gun on a hilltop. The next day, John Wick of the 306th Engineers saw an enemy sniper shoot at a soldier and hit a phosphorus grenade that was hooked to his uniform. "It exploded, setting the soldier on fire," said Wick. "The medics rushed to the soldier, but there was nothing they could do to save him."[48]

On November 23, a Japanese prisoner said that 60 to 70 enemy soldiers remained in the western ridges, and another 150 were in the vicinity of Nakagawa's command post. Many of the holdouts were ill and no longer wanted to fight, the prisoner said.[49]

Speaking to news correspondents, General Mueller lamented the fact that the Japanese had not launched large-scale banzai attacks on Peleliu as they had during other island battles. "We wish they would," he said. "We would rather shoot them in their tracks than have to go in and burn them out."[50]

Although the campaign was clearly in its last stages, the siege continued without a break. On the 24th, three bulldozers from the 306th Engineering Battalion's "A" Company began building a ramp to the 60-foot-high crest of China Wall. Its completion would permit tanks and the amtrac flamethrower to support the 323rd when it attacked Nakagawa's command post.[51]

The 323rd closed in on the Pocket's remaining strongpoints on November 25, when the ramp was completed and tanks and amtrac flamethrowers were able to reach China Wall's crest. "H" Company advanced northward along the base of China Wall, pausing to fire directly into the Japanese positions. At the same time, the 1st Battalion pushed through the western ridges toward Death Valley, killing more than 30 enemy soldiers.[52]

Japanese troops sometimes crept near the American positions and called out for a "corpsman," hoping to draw someone into the open to be killed. The enemy soldiers evidently did not know that Army troops and their medics had replaced the Marines, whose medical personnel were Navy corpsmen. The Wildcats, who knew the difference, responded to the pleas, waited for the Japanese to come closer, and then heaved grenades at them.[53]

A Japanese soldier demonstrated the survivors' desperation in slapstick fashion when he suddenly emerged from beneath a log where four Wildcats were taking a break and jumped on the back of one of them.

"Me give up, Joe! Me give up, Joe!" he cried. As the soldier struggled to rid himself of his uninvited passenger, his comrades dissolved into laughter. The new prisoner proceeded to reveal that Colonel Nakagawa and Major General Murai were dead. They had killed themselves the previous night after burning the 2nd Infantry Regiment colors and documents, and destroying their radio equipment.

Major General Murai and Colonel Nakagawa were posthumously promoted to the rank of lieutenant general.[54] Before committing ritual suicide, Nakagawa had sent a series of radio messages to his superiors at Koror on November 24. "Our sword is broken and we have run out of spears," said one message. Another said, "All is over on Peleliu." Nakagawa said that he would inform Koror of his forces' final collapse by twice repeating the code word "Sakura," the word for "cherry."

In his last report, Nakagawa said that he had appointed a Captain Nemoto to lead the 56 troops remaining in the command post area. Divided into 17 teams, they were ordered to escape from the Pocket, form raiding parties, and attack everywhere. Many of them did not even survive the night.[55]

At 4 p.m. on November 24, this message arrived in Koror: "Sakura, Sakura."[56] Yet diehards continued to resist the Americans closing in from all sides. On the 26th, tanks and an amtrac flamethrower climbed to the top of China Wall on the new ramp built by engineers. "F" Company then occupied positions atop the Wall but was pinned down by a fusillade of enemy gunfire. It was the beginning of the final act.[57]

At 10:30 a.m. on November 27, the attacking units converged on Nakagawa's command cave at China Wall. Wildcats from the 323rd cautiously entered Nakagawa's final sanctuary. It lay at the bottom of a rock formation that resembled a well; it was 40 feet in diameter, 40 feet deep, and split into two fissures just wide enough to admit a man.

At the bottom, sniper positions guarded three small caves that contained a communications center, administrative headquarters, and living quarters. The Americans walked into an abattoir, "filled with dead members of their command," the regiment's report said. One of the caves was where Nakagawa and Murai had killed themselves three days earlier.*[58] At 11 a.m. on November 27, the 323rd's commander, Colonel Arthur Watson, reported to General Paul Mueller that organized resistance had ceased on Peleliu. "The enemy had fulfilled his determination to fight to the death." It was the 74th day of *Stalemate*, a campaign that General Rupertus had predicted would last no more than four days.[59]

The 81st Division had performed the coup de grace by methodically applying siege tactics, in contrast to Rupertus's costly sledgehammer frontal assaults.

The Marine general generously acknowledged that the 321st Regiment's conduct on Peleliu, Ngesebus, and the northern outpost islands "warrants the highest praise. It was a pleasure to have this unit as part of my command during the extremely difficult operation... In the eyes of the entire 1st Marine Division, they have earned a 'Well Done.'"[60]

———

The 81st Division's "butcher's bill" reflected its more circumspect approach while on Peleliu from September 23 to November 27, as well as the enemy's waning strength – largely due to the Marines' bludgeoning assaults. The division and attached units reported 282 men killed and 1,108 wounded on Peleliu, with an additional 1,701 non-combat casualties resulting from disease, injuries, and battle fatigue. During that period, the Wildcats reported killing 3,249

*What were believed to be the remains of Nakagawa and Murai were recovered in 1993. Wagner, "The Bones of Nakagawa."

enemy soldiers and making prisoners of 180 others – the latter mostly Korean laborers. On Angaur, the Army's losses totaled 1,676 killed and wounded.[61]

Now that the fighting had ended, it was the 81st Division's turn to leave. The 322nd departed Angaur in December – the 1st and 2nd Battalions on December 6, and the 3rd Battalion three weeks later. The 323rd Regiment left Peleliu in January 1945. The 321st remained until February as the garrison fighting force under Marine General Harold Campbell. The 111th Infantry Regiment, a Pennsylvania National Guard unit, took its place.

All of the 81st Division's regiments were sent to New Caledonia. Compared with Pavavu, New Caledonia was a paradise: the rest camps set up by the Red Cross had all of the amenities, including meals served on china by waitresses.[62]

Yet Pavavu had changed during the Marines' absence. Expecting the primitive conditions that they had endured before leaving for Peleliu, the Marines were stunned by what they saw when they returned. Colorfully decorated tables lined the area near the water's edge. Behind them stood smiling Red Cross nurses handing out doughnuts and paper cups of chilled grapefruit juice.

For many men, though, the rapid transformation from struggling to survive in a slaughterhouse to kind treatment was too much to absorb at once. Shying away from the nurses and their hospitality, they sat on the beach and gazed out to sea. However, they soon enough became acclimated to the new Pavavu built by Seabees and engineers: new tents with wooden floors, electricity, mess halls serving hot food, and a well-stocked base exchange. After Peleliu, this was heaven.[63]

In the European Theater, after Allied troops liberated cities, they were feted by a grateful people before marching on to the next battle. In the Pacific War, there were no laurels, no cheering crowds – only a too-brief respite on a remote island where training swiftly began for the next campaign. At night, the men watched movies outdoors; sometimes the same film was shown and viewed so many times that the men recited the characters' lines along with the actors.

While the 1st Division was recovering on Pavavu from its ordeal on Peleliu, thousands of replacements arrived who needed training in amphibious operations. They had precious little time to prepare for the next campaign: Operation *Iceberg*, the invasion of Okinawa in April 1945. It would be the largest amphibious assault of the Pacific War – and the only U.S. offensive waged on Japanese soil. It was expected to be a bloody prelude to the looming invasion of Japan's Home Islands.[64]

Chapter 13

Aftermath

It was bones, bones, bones – left just as they had fallen
during the fierce fighting.
Hiroshi Funasaka, former Japanese sergeant,
tearfully recounting his postwar
visit to Peleliu and Angaur[1]

During a torrential downpour at 2 a.m. on January 18, 1945, seventy-five Japanese soldiers from Babelthuap disembarked from two barges and waded ashore on White and Purple beaches. The landings did not go unobserved; an alert was sent to Peleliu's garrison force, the 321st Infantry Regiment.

While the infantrymen were preparing for combat, 50 artillerymen from the 316th Field Artillery Battalion manned defensive positions near Purple Beach, where they were reinforced by 75 men from the 726th Amphibious Tractor Battalion.

The 321st then went into action at White Beach, wiping out 71 raiders and capturing two others. One of the prisoners said the attackers were sent on what was essentially a suicide mission to atone for having abandoned Peleliu amid the fighting and disgracing themselves. The assault force had been ordered to destroy planes, blow up supply dumps, and kill as many Americans as possible. The invaders' overarching mission was to disrupt U.S. bomber missions staged from the airstrip against targets in the Philippines. But the raiders failed to attain any of their objectives.

Later in the day, Private Benjamin Schiffman was shot while searching the Amber Beach area for infiltrators. He was the last Wildcat killed on Peleliu.[2]

———————

Seabees paved the Peleliu airfield's runways, built permanent hangars, and installed immense fuel tanks and other facilities. When the improvements were completed, the airfield was able to accommodate all sizes and types of aircraft, up to B-29s.

Submarine docks were constructed on Peleliu's southern shore, as were portages for battleships, cruisers, and aircraft carriers. Crews also erected large installations for tank and infantry units, and construction and maintenance units.

During the last weeks of the Peleliu battle and in the following months, the 2nd Marine Air Wing flew daily missions from the airfield against Japanese installations in the northern Palaus. Enemy antiaircraft guns claimed the lives of 18 airmen, including Major Robert "Cowboy" Stout, the decorated commander of VMF-114.

Stout died on March 4, 1945, while leading his squadron on a napalm attack against Koror's Battery Hill. As the Corsairs approached their objective from the east, with the sun behind them, the target area erupted in gunfire. Stout's wingman, Lieutenant Glenn Daniel, saw the right wing of Stout's plane tilt upward before the warplane plunged toward the waters of Molucca Harbor. The plane and Stout's remains were recovered in 1947.[3]

As the Pacific War's spotlight moved steadily northward toward Japan, the Allies' final objective, activity slowed down at the airfield. Because of the delay in securing the island, Peleliu's airstrip played a smaller role than planned in the capture of the Philippines.

Leyte was invaded in October, with carrier planes providing most of the air support. However, a photographic reconnaissance squadron that began operating from Peleliu in early October conducted missions over the Philippines and other islands until the capture of Okinawa in 1945.

From late 1944 until the end of the war, Peleliu's 600-bed base hospital was kept busy treating battle casualties from the Pacific Theater before their transfer to Pearl Harbor and Stateside hospitals.

By the end of 1944, just 24 Corsairs were flying daily missions from Peleliu's airfield. Yet it remained a way station for aircraft bound for

Western Pacific battlefields, just as Japanese pilots had previously used it for stopovers on their way to Southeast Asia. On June 11–12, 1945 alone, airfield personnel fed and housed 1,240 men who arrived on 176 aircraft and spent the night on Peleliu.[4]

The 81st Division was deactivated on January 20, 1946, in Aomori Prefecture, Japan – the first U.S. division in the Pacific to be deactivated overseas. Three months after the unit was deactivated, its commander, General Paul Mueller, became General Douglas MacArthur's chief of staff in Tokyo.[5]

___

On August 2, 1945, a Lieutenant Wilbur Gwinn took off from Peleliu in a PV-1 Lockheed Ventura on a routine patrol north of the Palaus. Around 11 a.m. he spotted what appeared to be a long oil slick. Then, he saw dozens of men in the water, struggling to stay afloat as shivers of sharks circled and attacked them.[6]

By lucky accident, Gwinn had come upon the survivors of the *USS Indianapolis*. A Japanese submarine had torpedoed the cruiser three days earlier, on July 30. The *Indianapolis* had delivered to the Mariana island of Tinian the components of the "Little Boy" atomic bomb that would be dropped on Hiroshima on August 6, and was sailing to the Philippines when it went down. The cruiser's mission and whereabouts had been kept a closely guarded secret. When the *Indianapolis* sank in just 12 minutes, damage to its radio equipment prevented a distress signal from being sent, and the cruiser's absence went unnoticed.

Gwinn radioed for help, and a PBY Catalina arrived, along with the destroyer *Cecil J. Doyle*. Other destroyers were summoned to the scene. About 300 of the *Indianapolis*'s crew of 1,195 went down with ship. Of the 890 sailors that were alive in the water on July 30, just 316 were rescued on August 2. The other 574 men died in the water.

One of the survivors was Pfc Giles McCoy, a Marine sniper who was wounded on Peleliu and who later served as a sniper on Iwo Jima. After that grueling campaign, he was assigned to "cushy" duty aboard the *Indianapolis* as a member of the 39-man Marine detachment. After the cruiser sank, McCoy managed to stay alive in the water, "kicking those damned sharks" before being rescued. He and most of the other survivors were taken to the Peleliu base hospital, where two men died.

The others sailed to Guam on the hospital ship *Tranquility* before continuing on to San Diego.[7]

After Emperor Hirohito announced Japan's capitulation on August 15, 1945, General Sadae Inoue surrendered his 14th Infantry Division and attached units in the Palaus in a ceremony aboard the destroyer escort *Amick*. Inoue's command included 18,473 Japanese soldiers; 6,404 naval personnel; 9,750 civilians; and 5,350 native Palauans. In time, most of the prisoners were repatriated to Japan.[8] After Japan's surrender, Japanese holdouts continued to hide in caves and tunnels inside Peleliu's ridges, enduring hunger and thirst, and oppressive heat and humidity. Yet, just a mile away, their former enemies enjoyed the civilized amenities of barracks life: hot, fresh food and nightly movies.

The Americans were fully aware that Japanese soldiers dwelled inside the ridges. But Peleliu's garrison force was steadily decreasing as part of America's postwar military draw down, and it became more difficult to send out patrols to hunt down the diehards, while also protecting the island's installations.

Emboldened by the American force reductions, the Japanese holdouts raided the American supply dumps with increasing impunity. Moreover, other fugitives hiding on the outlying Palau islands began to slip into Peleliu. In March 1947, a Palau native reported seeing a suspicious-looking shack standing in the middle of a swamp. He led American soldiers to it, and inside they found a cache of canned food and clothing stolen from the well-stocked American supply dumps. Also in the hideout were hundreds of rounds of .30-caliber Japanese ammunition – recently cleaned and polished.[9] Two days later, some Japanese holdouts looted a warehouse where captured Japanese weapons had been stored; two light machine guns were taken.

The raids steadily increased and escalated to brazen attacks. Two islanders were accosted while traveling to their village, and one of them managed to slash one of the attackers with a knife. A grenade was thrown at two Marines investigating a report about Japanese having been seen in a nearby cave. The Marines were not injured.[10]

Navy Captain L.O. Fox, the garrison commander, cabled Guam and Pearl Harbor for reinforcements. He also asked that a former war crimes witness be sent to make a surrender appeal to the holdouts. Fox moved the island's 35 Navy dependents from their quarters near the airfield to a more secure location – near the submarine moorage on the island's southern tip. There, they were protected by a phalanx of machine guns.

Fox's reinforcements arrived in late March 1947. One hundred twenty heavily armed Marines began conducting large-scale patrols in the Umurbrogol under the auspices of "Operation *Capitulation*." Accompanying the patrols was Admiral Hainan Sumikawa, who had testified at a war crimes trials on Guam. He brought an interpreter, George Kumi, and photographs of the Japanese surrenders at Tokyo Bay and Truk.[11]

Admiral Sumikawa drove up and down Peleliu's main roads with a Marine patrol, using a loudspeaker to urge the diehards hiding in the labyrinthine coral formations to give up; the war was over, he told them repeatedly. The patrol left behind statements signed by the admiral, along with the surrender ceremony photos.

On April 2, a Jeep patrol encountered a man standing by the side of the road. The man raised his arms above his head. At his feet lay a sawed-off carbine, three ammunition clips, a grenade, and a knife. Interrogated by Peleliu's senior officers, 24-year-old Seaman Kiyokazu Tsuchida told them that he had escaped from a cave that he had shared with about two dozen other holdouts, commanded by Lieutenant Tadamichi Yamaguchi. Seaman Tsuchida appeared to be shocked by the news of Japan's surrender.

Tsuchida said Yamaguchi shot men who tried to surrender, and he urged men who were wounded in skirmishes with Marine patrols to commit suicide. The soldier who was slashed by the islander, Tsuchida said, blew himself up with a grenade. Tsuchida warned that Yamaguchi was contemplating a banzai attack on the Marines' camp and the airfield installations. Navy Captain Fox doubled the force guarding those sites.

On April 5, Admiral Sumikawa, his interpreter, and Tsuchida returned with an armed escort to the cave from which Tsuchida had escaped, but no one was there. However, patrols soon found the holdouts' new hideout, and Tsuchida, bearing letters from the men's relatives, entered the cave and met with Lieutenant Yamaguchi. Outside, Admiral Sumikawa used his loudspeaker to promise those who surrendered speedy repatriation to Japan.

The concerted efforts were rewarded when Yamaguchi and 26 of his men surrendered on April 21. After marching past 80 Marines clad in battle dress, Yamaguchi surrendered his sword and battle flag to Captain Fox. Seven other holdouts gave up the next day.

The Japanese had survived by stealing food and supplies at night from the American warehouses. Their five-story cave hideout, lit by kerosene lamps, had running water and was stocked with American food and supplies. "They even had Kleenex," one Marine marveled.[12] Yamaguchi's men were not the last ones to emerge from their hiding places in the Umurbrogol. In 1949, a Japanese soldier surrendered to an islander, and in 1954 the last known holdout gave up – ten years after the island battle ended. He received a hero's homecoming upon his return to Japan.[13]

In 1947, the remains of the Americans killed in action on Peleliu were exhumed from the Orange Beach cemetery and sent for reburial to the men's families, or to the American military cemetery in Manila.

Over the decades, monuments began appeared on Peleliu honoring the men on both sides who had died. A stone marker at Orange Beach was dedicated to the soldiers of the 81st Infantry Division and its attached units who were killed in the battle. An obelisk of coral stones that stands atop a ridge crest in the Umurbrogol bears the inscription: "Lest We Forget Who Died: 323 Infantry, U.S. Army, 1944."

At the foot of Bloody Nose Ridge is a four-sided, 5-foot-tall Marine Corps memorial, erected in 1984. A plaque on its north side is etched with the text of the Presidential Unit Citation of the 1st Marine Division's accomplishments on Peleliu. A second plaque lists the names of the eight Marines awarded Medals of Honor for their actions on Peleliu (69 Marines were awarded Navy Crosses). Nearby is a small Shinto shrine where the descendants of Japanese soldiers killed on Peleliu occasionally hold services.[14]

On The Point is a plaque honoring Captain George P. Hunt for his dynamic leadership of "K" Company during its daring capture and defense of The Point. "Each of us who served under him at Peleliu knows, if ever a combat infantry officer deserved the Congressional Medal of Honor, it would have been George P. Hunt (Died July 6, 1991)," the plaque reads. Hunt was instead awarded the Navy Cross.[15]

Micronesia became a United Nations trust territory in 1947, the year that the Palau Islands became a U.S. Trust Territory – an arrangement that lasted 47 years. In 1981, the Republic of Palau formed a constitutional government; in 1994, it became a voting member of the United Nations. Today, Peleliu is one of Palau's 16 states, with a legislature and an island administration.[16]

Until the mid-1960s, the United States discouraged tourism on Peleliu. The ban was lifted in 1965, and one of the first Japanese to visit was Hiroshi Funasaka. The former Japanese Army sergeant was wounded and captured on Angaur, where the rest of his unit was wiped out. Funasaka burst into tears when he described his visit. "It was bones, bones, bones – left just as they had fallen during the fierce fighting," he said.[17]

After Peleliu was opened to tourists, Japanese visitors came in far greater numbers than American tourists. One reason was that the remains of the Japanese dead still lay where they had fallen; the Americans killed in action had been exhumed and reburied elsewhere. Another was Peleliu's relative proximity to Japan, 1,800 miles away, while the U.S. West Coast was 6,700 miles distant.

Until the Peleliu government stopped the practice, the Japanese visitors collected the bones of their war dead and took them to Japan for private burial. The names of the dead were added to the lists at the Yasukuni Shrine, the resting place of Japan's war dead since 1868. There, Shinto priests carried the names of the fallen in an ark to an altar, where they were sanctified as immortals.

The remains of the war dead left behind on Peleliu were cremated and their ashes placed at one of the several memorials that the Japanese erected on the island, beginning in 1967.[18] The largest, the Peleliu Peace Park Memorial, is on the southwestern coast, near where the Marines landed on September 15, 1944. It was erected in 1985 by Japan's government, in cooperation with the Republic of Palau. The stone-and-mortar cenotaph bears a plaque that in English says, "In memory of all those who sacrificed their lives in the islands and seas of the West Pacific during World War II." In April 2018, representatives of the Marine Corps and Japan's Self Defense Force gathered at the peace memorial for a wreath-laying ceremony.[19]

For the Japanese, Peleliu is a sacred place that they visit on cruise ships for the purpose of praying and mourning at the memorials.

Americans go to Peleliu to visit the battle sites and the small museum that opened in 2004 at the base of the Five Sisters. Just a handful of veterans have returned to the place where they suffered in the broiling heat and witnessed so much horror and death. Small wonder.[20]

When Peleliu natives were at last permitted to return home, they were shocked to find that their island, formerly riotously green, was now barren white rock, shimmering in the blazing sunlight. Taken aback by the dismaying transformation and the reflective glare, they instinctively covered their eyes. American soldiers helpfully distributed sunglasses to all of the returnees.

Gone was the lush, green canopy that had concealed the coral-limestone ridges and its topographical nightmares from the invading Marines. Scoured by shot, shell, and flame, the ridges and crushed white coral that lay everywhere gleamed with otherworldly brightness in the tropical sunlight.[21]

The ferocious battle had obliterated the old Palauan way of life. Besides the absence of trees and vegetation, the familiar landmarks had also disappeared, as had the island's five villages – all of them destroyed, even their cemeteries. The alien landscape, no less than an ecological disaster, was profoundly disorienting.[22]

The island slowly recovered. By 2005 there were 702 people in 196 households on Peleliu, most of them living in three villages on the northern part of the island, opposite Ngesebus. A handful enjoyed the conveniences of modern life: electricity and water, cars, and Internet service. The central island's jagged ridges regenerated their dense green covering, as Peleliu slowly returned to what it had once been: a Pacific backwater.[23]

For the returnees, the blasted landscape was demoralizing at first to their efforts to revive their economy. But they were eventually able to resume fishing and raising subsistence crops for the Koror market. The islanders were careful not to disturb the sealed caves filled with the bones of dead Japanese soldiers.[24]

Peleliu later became a popular snorkeling and scuba diving site. Its clear waters teem with colorful tropical fish, sharks, rays, anemones, and sea turtles. In recent years, diving has become an important source of revenue for the Palauans.

In the waters around the reef near the Orange and White landing beaches, the vestiges of the 1944 battle may be seen – sunken landing craft, bullets, and shells – but may not be removed because of island prohibitions.[25]

During the early 1990s, American veterans of Peleliu and the Vietnam War located Colonel Nakagawa's last command post inside a deep declivity at the northern end of China Wall. Six spent Army concussion grenades were found inside the rubble-filled living quarters. The veterans also found human remains that are believed to be those of Nakagawa and General Kenijiro Murai.[26]

In 1999, Bruce Watkins, a Marine platoon leader on Peleliu in 1944, returned to the island with other U.S. veterans. They met with a group of Japanese – none of them had fought in the battle – led by a granddaughter of General Hideki Tojo. Tojo, Japan's former prime minister and minister of war, had been hanged as a war criminal in 1948.

Watkins said the U.S. veterans were initially ill at ease mingling with the American flag-bearing Japanese. But after they warmed to them, the Americans led the Japanese visitors into the Umurbrogol. With the permission of Peleliu authorities, the Japanese recovered the bones of some Japanese soldiers from a cave. They wrapped them in colorful blankets to return them to Japan.

Afterward, the former enemies, bearing the Stars and Stripes, attended a memorial service for the American dead. It was followed by a service featuring Rising Sun flags for the Japanese soldiers who died in the 1944 battle.

There was peace at last on Peleliu.[27]

Epilogue

*I had been weighing this operation ever since it had
been broached to me ... and the more I weighed it, the
less I liked it. I felt that they [the Palaus] would have to
be bought at a prohibitive price in casualties. In short,
I feared another Tarawa – and I was right.*

Admiral William Halsey[1]

*My experience on Guadalcanal was a walk in the park
compared with Peleliu.*

Marine Sergeant James Wilson[2]

*The lessons learned were not adequately exposed to the
Marines going to hit Iwo Jima some weeks later. What
we learned was somehow not communicated to them
and they paid in blood for this mistake.*

Lieutenant Colonel Ray Davis, First Marines[3]

Operation *Stalemate* contributed little if anything to the winning of
the Pacific War. Yet despite the 74-day campaign's modest scope, it
exacted an inordinately high price in men killed and wounded. In fact,
in terms of the ratio of losses to troops committed, it was the costliest
U.S. campaign of the Pacific War.

Of the 28,000 Marines and soldiers who fought on Peleliu and Angaur,
10,786 became casualties – 2,336 of them killed in action – 38.5 percent
of those engaged, while killing 14,338 enemy soldiers on the two islands.
As they had intended, Colonel Nakagawa and Major Goto succeeded
in exacting a high cost in American blood for the victories. By way of

comparison, the overall casualty rates for the larger-scale 1945 battles of Iwo Jima and Okinawa were 23.6 percent and 27.3 percent, respectively.

Seeing that it took more than 1,500 rounds of heavy and light ammunition on average to kill each enemy soldier, overwhelming U.S. firepower clearly was the primary factor in the U.S. victory.[4] "I think those who have taken the trouble to investigate are in general agreement that the capture of Peleliu was the most difficult amphibious operation in the Pacific War... I believe that the Palaus operation has been underestimated," said Admiral George Fort.[5]

A marginal benefit might be claimed: that isolating Koror and Babelthuap in the northern Palaus kept 25,000 enemy troops out of the war. Up to 10,000 soldiers and civilians died on the islands north of Peleliu during 18 months of American bombing and blockades. The air and naval attacks also neutralized the Japanese submarine base at Koror.[6]

Victory came at such a high price because the Japanese Army had radically changed its defensive strategy after losing the Mariana Islands. Japanese military leaders who were still capable of coolly appraising their fraught situation recognized that they were losing the war.

Hoping to somehow salvage a negotiated peace, strategists in Tokyo drafted a new blueprint for combatting amphibious attacks – "Defense Guidance on Islands." Its "endurance engagement" replaced Japan's initial goal of forcing a "decisive engagement" that would win the war. Elusive during the Pacific War's early years, the decisive engagement then proved ultimately ruinous; the major air and naval battles that were fought in the Pacific during 1944 – the battles of the Philippine Sea and Leyte Gulf – hastened Japan's defeat.

Peleliu was where the new paradigm was unexpectedly thrust upon American forces. The Marine Corps was especially slow to adapt to the radically changed Japanese strategy and suffered unnecessarily high casualties. Central to the "Defense Guidance" was "fukkaku," the strategy of waging a defensive battle from an underground network of bunkers, caves, tunnels, and pillboxes.

As the Marines came ashore through a storm of artillery and mortar fire, the main Japanese force waited inland in mutually supporting, fortified positions. When they reached the main Japanese defenses, the invaders were met by intensive machine-gun, small-arms, mortar, and artillery fire. The large-scale banzai attacks that characterized the fighting on Tarawa and Saipan were conspicuously absent.

A III Amphibious Corps report concisely summarized how the enemy had profoundly altered his strategy from previous Pacific War battles. "He did not defend in strength at the water's edge, but elected to withdraw the bulk of his infantry to favorable terrain and to defend the beaches with mortar and artillery fire, and extensive beach mine fields."[7]

The fukkaku defense in depth was attritional, with the simple object of killing as many Americans as possible. The Japanese intended to continue raising the human ante for each future island battle until the losses became intolerable.

The United States, so the rationale went, would be compelled by its losses to abandon its insistence on unconditional surrender, and instead would agree to negotiations. Ideally, they would result in a peace treaty that would preserve Emperor Hirohito's prerogatives and part of Japan's crumbling Greater East Asia Co-Prosperity Sphere.

Colonel Kunio Nakagawa's transformation of Peleliu into a limestone-coral fortress became the template for later island defenses. His tactics were used effectively on both Iwo Jima and Okinawa in 1945.

David Lynch had fought on Guadalcanal, and on Peleliu was awarded the Silver Star and a Purple Heart for his deeds on Hill 100 while serving with Captain Pope's company. Lynch quickly saw that the enemy on Peleliu was behaving differently than it had on Guadalcanal. "They would fight. Then they'd back down... We'd charge in, and then they'd fall back again," he said. "So that's why we lost a lot more than we did [during earlier campaigns]."[8]

Sergeant James Wilson said that on Guadalcanal, where he was wounded, and afterward on Cape Gloucester, "we were dug in and they were hitting us. On Peleliu, we were attacking and were being shelled. They could see us. They were in the ridges over us, shooting mortars at us, artillery, and machine guns ... My experience on Guadalcanal was a walk in the park compared with Peleliu."[9]

The 1st Marine Division's special action report expressed grudging admiration for the enemy's Peleliu battle plan. "Their general scheme of defense seemed to be that of making the capture of Peleliu as costly as possible to our forces," the report observed. "This was carried out most skillfully. The planning and execution of the defense indicated that the enemy opposing us on Peleliu were first line troops, capably led, who knew their mission and carried it out in an excellent manner."

The surprisingly accurate enemy sniper fire belied the common belief that the Japanese were poor marksmen. The division postmortem of the battle concluded that the enemy troops had been thoroughly drilled in marksmanship. "Our men were frequently killed or wounded by enemy fire from positions 200 to 400 yards distant."[10]

Senior Marine officers generally underestimated the enemy and were slow to adapt to the new enemy tactics. Now, instead of Japanese soldiers perishing in futile banzai attacks, the tables were turned; Marines were being killed or wounded in frontal attacks on fortified enemy positions – just as the Japanese intended.

The First Marines' headlong assaults in the ridges, repeated daily for a week, destroyed the regiment as an effective fighting unit. General Roy Geiger's intervention stopped the regiment's self-immolation and forced General William Rupertus to utilize the Army's 321st Regiment. Yet Rupertus nearly achieved his goal of an all-Marine victory. Exercising his authority over the conduct of day-to-day operations on Peleliu, he marginalized the 321st and thrust the Marine Seventh Regiment, and then the Fifth, into the inferno of the Umurbrogol until they, too, were used up.

By then, the Marines had killed more than 10,000 of Nakagawa's men, leaving General Paul Mueller's 81st Division to extinguish the last resistance in the Pocket. Rupertus nearly completed the job with his division alone.[11]

And then there is the overriding question of whether *Stalemate* was worthwhile. Operation *Stalemate* was initially conceived to eliminate the possibility of enemy air attacks from Peleliu's airfield against General Douglas MacArthur's Sixth Army as it pushed north into the Philippines. Days before D-Day, however, that rationale evaporated with the decision to not land MacArthur's army at Mindanao, but hundreds of miles north at Leyte.

Moreover, Admiral Marc Mitscher's Operation *Desecrate* – his fast carriers' two days of air assaults on the Palaus at the end of March 1944 – had already neutralized Peleliu's airfield. The operation destroyed or damaged all of the Japanese warplanes at the airfield, and smashed most of the enemy's shipping on the island. With that raid, Peleliu's airfield had lost its potential to menace MacArthur's Philippines landings.[12]

"It would take more arguments than this writer can muster to prove [Peleliu] was worth the cost," wrote the Navy's World War II historian, Samuel Elliot Morison. "Admiral Halsey had the right idea; [the Palaus] should have been bypassed."[13] Admiral Chester Nimitz, however, rejected Halsey's recommendation; the pre-landing bombardment had already begun, and the invasion force was at sea.

Halsey later wrote that he had been dubious about the operation since May 1944, when it was first proposed during a conference with Admirals Nimitz and Ernest King. "The more I weighed it, the less I liked it." The Palaus, he concluded, "would have to be bought at a prohibitive price in casualties. In short, I feared another Tarawa – and I was right."[14]

Harold Stassen, Admiral Halsey's chief of staff and later Minnesota's governor and a perennial presidential candidate, in 1989 bluntly told historian Bill Ross: "The invasion of Peleliu was a terrible mistake, a tragedy that was needless and should not have happened."[15]

Had *Stalemate* been cancelled, the Allies' triumphal march to Japan would not have missed a step.

Ray Davis, who led the First Marines' 1st Battalion on Peleliu as a lieutenant colonel and retired from the Marine Corps as a general, said *Stalemate* will be remembered as the "most hotly contested and brutal campaign of World War II in many respects." For Davis, the destruction of the First Marines was personal. "A figure I'm not proud of is the fact that my battalion had 71 percent casualties, including me, and the whole regiment was almost as bad."[16]

The Peleliu campaign became a mere sideshow to the liberation of the Philippines, where MacArthur made good on his pledge of 1942 to return and recapture the archipelago.

Relatively unknown to the American public, Peleliu received scant press coverage as a direct result of General Rupertus's rash prediction of a quick, four-day campaign. Consequently, 30 of the 36 news correspondents accredited for *Stalemate* elected not to go ashore and scattered to battlefields promising more plentiful bylines and better story placement. They went to the Philippines and to Europe, where Operation *Market Garden* began in Holland on the same day that the 1st Division invaded Peleliu. After the initial landings on Peleliu, reports on *Stalemate* were relegated to newspapers' back pages.[17]

Peleliu and Angaur became footnotes to the Pacific War.

Stalemate derailed Rupertus's rise to Marine Corps commandant, where he was expected to succeed his friend General Vandegrift. After flying from Peleliu to Guadalcanal with General Roy Geiger, Rupertus was summoned to Marine Corps headquarters in Washington to meet with Vandegrift.

No record survives of their meeting. A Vandegrift aide said years later, however, that the commandant "had no choice but to relieve Rupertus of his command" of the 1st Marine Division because of his inept management of the Peleliu campaign.

Rupertus was reassigned to supervise the Marine Corps Schools – today known as Marine Corps University. The assignment was viewed among senior Marine officers as a "tombstone billet"; it became the epitaph of Rupertus's long career. Perhaps intending to cushion the blow, the commandant awarded Rupertus the Distinguished Service Cross.

On March 24, 1945, after attending a dinner party at the Washington Naval Yard, Rupertus collapsed and died of an apparent heart attack outside his quarters in Quantico, Virginia. He was 55 years old. During a recent routine physical at Bethesda Naval Hospital, Rupertus had been diagnosed with a heart condition. He is buried at Arlington National Cemetery.[18]

Operation *Stalemate* was flawed from its inception, beginning with the absence of Rupertus, as well as Admirals Kelly Turner and Raymond Spruance and General Holland Smith during the campaign's critical planning phase. These men had carefully organized earlier Pacific War campaigns, but their attention was absorbed by the prolonged Marianas campaign. *Stalemate* was a concatenation of plans drawn up in Pavavu and Pearl Harbor.[19]

There were myriad problems with a campaign conceived in haste amid competing operations. Too little time was allotted to train men in the use of the new amtanks and flamethrower-equipped amtracs. Amtracs were initially handcuffed to their primary role as logistical support vehicles and not seen as the tactical assault vehicles that they became. The failures extended to the drinking water that was sent ashore on D-Day in improperly cleaned oil drums, sickening hundreds of men who drank it.

For lack of shipping, the 1st Division was forced to leave behind 16 of its 46 tanks. As events demonstrated, the tanks remaining on Pavavu would have seen good use. A postmortem conducted after the battle concluded that the additional armor would have hastened the completion of *Stalemate's* early phases.

The tanks that did go ashore on Peleliu lacked adequate spare parts. Maintenance personnel suffered unnecessary casualties while salvaging parts under fire from nine tanks that were deemed complete losses.[20] Rupertus sent the serviceable Marine tanks back to Pavavu after just two weeks of combat in the belief that they would be useless fighting in the Umurbrogol's ridges. He was wrong. Thereafter, the Marines relied on the Army's 710th Tank Battalion for armored support in the ridges.[21]

Peleliu's preliminary naval bombardment was abridged because of an ammunition shortage partly due to the Marianas campaign. Guam's pre-landing bombardment alone lasted 13 days – atonement for Saipan's too-brief preparatory shelling. Ammunition was also being stockpiled for the Philippines campaign. Peleliu was allotted just two days' worth of naval gunfire. At the Marines' insistence, it was extended to three, but with the same amount of ammunition.

Yet it is doubtful that a longer, more intensive bombardment would have made much of a difference. "The bulk of the defensive positions were not capable of neutralization by the Navy," General O.P. Smith concluded.[22] Some historians disagreed. A longer bombardment would have made for a quicker campaign with fewer casualties, wrote amphibious warfare experts Jeter Isely and Philip Crowl. "The conclusion cannot be avoided that preliminary naval gunfire on Peleliu was inadequate, and that the lessons learned at Guam were overlooked... Peleliu, like Tarawa and to a lesser extent Saipan, demonstrated that the only substitute for such prolonged bombardment was costly expenditure of the lives of the assault troops."[23]

"The Peleliu fire support plan was a shocking instance of a Navy-Marine failure to learn from recent experience" during the Marianas campaigns on Saipan, Guam, and Tinian, historian Jon Hoffman wrote.[24]

Rupertus's low opinion of the Army's combat capabilities made utilizing the 81st Infantry Division's 323rd Regiment as an active reserve out of the question. He designated a Marine battalion for that role, and then hastily committed it on *Stalemate's* first day.

Few failings were worse than the tragically inaccurate maps, which were based on aerial photographs that misleadingly showed the

Umurbrogol to be a long highland covered by green tropical foliage. The jungle growth concealed a nightmarish maze of craggy hills and ravines – some connected, some standing alone. The maps also did not hint at the island's heavily fortified underground defenses – which proved nearly impervious to naval and artillery gunfire.

Rupertus was convinced that the Japanese defenses would crack, as they had everywhere previously, if brute force was applied day after day. In Rupertus's experience in the Pacific, the enemy, when enough pressure was exerted, always resorted to mass banzai attacks – and could then be destroyed. That had been the case as recently as July, when 4,000 Japanese soldiers assaulted the Marines and soldiers on Saipan, and were killed.

Rupertus's sledgehammer method lacked nuance and imagination; the punishing attacks into the Umurbrogol that destroyed the First Marines were conducted frontally, from south to north. Rupertus drove his commanders to maintain "momentum," no matter the cost. After one week, the First Marines were finished as a combat-capable fighting unit.

Alone among the 1st Division's senior officers in recognizing the futility of the frontal attacks against Japanese strongpoints was Colonel Harold "Bucky" Harris, the Fifth Marines' commander. He advocated attacking from north to south, first deploying heavy weapons and supporting arms before launching infantry attacks. For too long, his ideas were ignored, but in the campaign's later stages, Harris's approach became the norm.[25]

Exacerbating these problems were Rupertus's cold demeanor, his harsh, uninspiring personal leadership, his tendency to rebuff collaboration, and his disdain for his second-in-command, O.P. Smith, to the extent of banishing him from the division command post. Experienced, smart, and reasonable, Smith could have helped Rupertus avoid many of the mistakes that he made.[26]

Despite all of *Stalemate*'s flaws, American Marines and soldiers destroyed one of the Japanese Army's elite units – the 14th Infantry Division's 2nd Regiment – during two months of intensive combat, a notable achievement indeed.

An aspect of the battle that is rarely acknowledged, much less understood, is the intensive hatred that the Marines and Japanese bore for one another. "Marines felt it deeply, bitterly, and as certainly as danger itself," said E.B. Sledge, a mortarman with the Fifth Marines on Peleliu and Okinawa. "They were a fanatical enemy; that is to say, they believed in their cause with an intensity little understood by many postwar Americans – and possibly many Japanese as well."[27]

The Pacific War has been called a war of racial hatred. The Japanese surprise attack on Pearl Harbor planted the seed, and it germinated on Guadalcanal in August 1942, when the 1st Division first fought the Japanese in ground combat.

During the Battle of the Tenaru, wounded Japanese soldiers cried for help and killed Marines who tried to aid them. They feigned surrender and detonated grenades when approached by the Americans. The Marine commander, General Vandegrift, wrote in amazement, "I have never heard or read of this kind of fighting." The Marines adopted the practice of riddling fallen enemy soldiers to ensure that they were indeed dead.[28]

When added to Peleliu's sweltering climate and brutal combat conditions, the enemies' mutual loathing made the terrible battle even worse. Their conduct recalled bygone ages of organized primal violence. "The collective attitude, Marine and Japanese, resulted in savage, ferocious fighting with no holds barred," wrote Sledge. "This was a brutish, primitive hatred."[29]

Sadly, Peleliu's hard-earned lessons had to be relearned on Iwo Jima.

"The lessons learned were not adequately exposed to the Marines going to hit Iwo Jima some weeks later," Ray Davis lamented. "What we learned was somehow not communicated to them and they paid in blood for this mistake. They went into Iwo in a similar situation, but were not fully prepared for it."[30]

Twenty-six thousand Marines were killed or wounded on Iwo Jima while destroying 21,000 Japanese soldiers; regiments in the 4th and 5th Divisions reported casualty rates as high as 75 percent.[31]

The Japanese had not failed to pass along Peleliu's lessons to Iwo Jima's commander, General Tadamichi Kuribayashi. He was fully aware of what had transpired on Peleliu and Biak, and he modified Nakagawa's fukkaku defensive paradigm to Iwo's volcanic terrain.

The Iwo Jima campaign would have been less costly for the Marines if General Holland Smith had prepared his 3rd, 4th, and 5th Marine

Divisions for the Japanese defense in depth that the 1st Division faced on Peleliu. Undoubtedly, more of Smith's Marines would have survived the conflagration.[32]

By Easter Sunday 1945, when six American divisions invaded Okinawa, Operation *Iceberg*'s leaders were better prepared to face the Japanese attritional defense. Although this did not mitigate the extreme difficulty of digging out more than 100,000 enemy soldiers from their fortifications inside Okinawa's southern ridges, foreknowledge helped commanders cope better.

Tank-infantry teams, the widespread use of flamethrowers, explosives, and artillery, and close-air support – all developed on Peleliu – helped to sharply reduce American losses proportionate to those of the Japanese. Even so, American casualties on Okinawa totaled 49,000, more than Peleliu and Iwo Jima combined, compared with the deaths of as many as 130,000 Japanese soldiers and auxiliaries. The Japanese kamikaze onslaught on U.S. naval forces at Okinawa accounted for 4,907 lives.

Because the defeated usually do not write the history, the few Japanese soldiers that survived the Peleliu bloodletting provided few details of their experience, and their comrades are entombed inside Peleliu's ridges. It is our loss.

We know from American accounts that the raw courage displayed by Marines and soldiers in defeating Colonel Nakagawa's veteran troops on the Pacific War's worst battlefield was unmistakable and inspiring. Yet one must wonder whether the valor and sacrifice were in fact wasted.

Peleliu embodied the worst features of the Pacific War campaigns, and it is unsurprising that veterans remember it with both pride and horror.

Pfc William Finnegan fought with the Fifth Marines on Guadalcanal, Cape Gloucester, and Peleliu, where he was wounded by friendly fire and evacuated. Peleliu was Finnegan's worst wartime experience, and that includes his later participation in the 1st Division's epic 1950 breakout from the Chosin Reservoir in North Korea, where Chinese forces surrounded and besieged the division in subzero temperatures. Most historians say that the desperate fighting and suffering endured by the Marines at "Frozen Chosin" had few equals in history. To that, Finnegan said, "If I had to take a choice between Peleliu and the Chosin Reservoir, I would go back to the Reservoir."[33]

Endnotes

PRELUDE

1 Burke Davis, 215–216
2 Hunt, 22–23; Lyren, Locations 1275, 1401; Garand, 106
3 Lyren, Locations 1275, 1362; Hunt, 30–31; Hammel, *76 Hours*, 34; Ainsworth, 1; Russell Davis, 2
4 Hunt, 33–34
5 Lea, *Peleliu Landing*, 174–176; Russell Davis, 23
6 Peto, 185; Margaritis, 65; Lea, *Peleliu Landing*, 174–176; Russell Davis, 1; Sledge, *With the Old Breed*, 55
7 Donigan, "Forgotten Battle," 98
8 Lyren, Locations 1362, 1401–1426; McMillan, 264–267
9 Ross, *Peleliu*, 150
10 Hunt, 34–36
11 Wright, *Far Side*, 66; McMillan, 266–267
12 Garand, 108; Margaritis, 32, 67, 70; Lyren, Location 1426
13 Hough, *Assault*, 106; Hoffman, "Peleliu Legacy," 90–94; Wright, *Far Side*, 102; Hallas, 155
14 Ainsworth, 4–7
15 Leckie, *Strong Men*, 396
16 Hunt, 37–38
17 Peto, 189
18 Clifford West interview, Museum of the Pacific
19 Burke Davis, 215–216
20 Ainsworth, 190
21 Leckie, *Strong Men*, 398
22 Wright, *Far Side*, 69
23 Ibid., 74; Ross, *Peleliu*, 155; Hough, *Assault*, 37 fn

CHAPTER I

1 Thomason, 660–661
2 Ballendorf, 119–122, 141; Ross, *Peleliu*, 117

3 Alexander, *Storm*, 108; Murray, *Battle Over Peleliu*, 6

4 Wright, *Far Side*, 14; Murray, *Battle Over Peleliu*, 54–56, 73, 81; Hough, *Assault*, 6–7

5 Morison, 30–32; Ross, *Peleliu*, 113; Murray, *Battle Over Peleliu*, 21–25, 14; Hough, *Assault*, 7; Garand, 58

6 Alexander, "Everything About Peleliu," 28–33; Ross, *Peleliu*, 119–120; McMillan, 261; Murray, *Battle Over Peleliu*, 26–28, 31, 35, 67, 69

7 Toland, *Not in Shame*, 44

8 Wright, *Far Side*, 16

9 Murray, *Battle Over Peleliu*, 77–80

10 Garand, 70

11 Smith, 473; Sherrod, 255; Margaritis, 166; Ross, *Peleliu*, 122–124; Wright, *Far Side*, 26–32; Hough, *Assault*, 10–11; Garand, 60

12 Hoffman, "Peleliu Legacy," 90–94; Hammel, "Peleliu," 16–25

13 Garand, 63

14 Ibid., 60, 62; Hough, *Assault*, 11–13; Margaritis, 21

15 Sledge, *Old Breed*, 30

16 Camp, *Last Man Standing*, 48

17 Ibid., 50–56

18 Ibid., 104, 110

19 Ibid., 117; Moskin, 334–336

20 Moskin, 280

21 Ibid., 290–291; David Miller, 70–85

22 David Miller, 70–85

23 McMillan, 6; Moskin, 345

24 Thomason, 660–661

25 Ross, *Peleliu*, 67–69; Wright, *Far Side*, 42–43

26 Burke Davis, 202

27 Hough, *Assault*, 25–26

28 Sledge, *Old Breed*, 32

29 Ross, *Peleliu*, 62–68; Clifford West interview, Museum of the Pacific

30 McMillan, 231

31 Brehmer interview, Museum of the Pacific

32 Leckie, *Helmet*, 257

33 Ibid.; Ross, *Peleliu*, 55–58

34 Hough, *Assault*, 26

35 Alexander, *Storm*, 113

36 Ray Davis, 66–67

37 Margaritis, 47–48, 52; Iseley, 413; Moskin, 291–292; Wright, *Far Side*, 48

38 Snead, 19–20; Sledge, *Old Breed*, 34–35; Margaritis, 53–55

39 McMillan, 260, 263

40 Hammel, *76 Hours*, 60–62

41 Alexander, *Storm*, 112

42 Ross, *Peleliu*, 106–107

43 Hough, *Assault*, 30–31; Alexander, *Storm*, 113

44 Wright, *Far Side*, 49; Hough, *Assault*, 30 fn
45 Peto, 227–228 fn; Hough, *Assault*, 31 fn; Margaritis, 52
46 Margaritis, 197–198
47 Ibid., 135–136, 138
48 Manchester, *American Caesar*, 363
49 Toll, *Twilight*, 61–62; Manchester, *American Caesar*, 363–366; Margaritis, 11
50 Manchester, *American Caesar*, 366
51 Toll, *Twilight*, 88–90
52 Manchester, *American Caesar*, 370; Alexander, *Storm*, 105; Castle, 172; Wheelan, 8; Toll, *Twilight*, 88–92
53 McMillan, 268

CHAPTER 2

1 McMillan, 269–270
2 Alexander, "Everything About Peleliu," 28
3 Hughes, 338–341
4 Ibid.; Toll, *Twilight*, 120–121
5 Garand, 65
6 Duffy, 48–49; Blair, 23–24; Toll, *Twilight*, 125–126
7 Manchester, *American Caesar*, 305–306; Margaritis, 134, 129–130
8 Alexander, *Storm*, 106
9 Morison, 32, 42, 46
10 Hughes, *Halsey*, 338–341; Morison, 47; Alexander, *Storm*, 121
11 Morison, 15
12 Toll, *Twilight*, 128–129
13 Wright, *Far Side*, 40; Ross, *Peleliu*, 87–89
14 Ross, *Peleliu*, 85–87; Margaritis, 180; David Miller, 95–96
15 Margaritis, 41; Ross, *Peleliu*, 89; Garand, 63
16 Camp, *Leatherneck Legends*, 141; Alexander, *Storm*, 75
17 Garand, 80
18 Hough, *Assault*, 18–19; Margaritis, 27–28; Wright, *Far Side*, 53; Garand, 8
19 Hough, *Assault*, 34; Ross, *Peleliu*, 102–104
20 Garand, 83–84; Smith, 473
21 Ross, *Peleliu*, 102–104
22 Garand, 88
23 Ibid.; Hough, *Assault*, 100
24 Wright, *Far Side*, 49–50
25 Garand, 87
26 Ibid., 88; Marine Archives, 3rd Amphibious Corps report, 43–44; McMillan, 264; Peto, 180–181; Lyren, Locations 1183, 1063; Ross, *Peleliu*, 103, 109; Hough, *Assault*, 25, 35; Shisler, 79
27 Margaritis, 55–56
28 Hough, *Island War*, 299; Peto, 184; McMillan, 268; Lyren, Locations 1223, 1148
29 Lea, *Peleliu Landing*, 174

30 McMillan, 269–270
31 Sledge, *Old Breed*, 49
32 Fred Fox interview, Museum of the Pacific
33 Leckie, *Helmet*, 277
34 Ross, *Peleliu*, 91
35 Hough, *Assault*, 35 fn; Margaritis, 211
36 Manchester, *American Caesar*, 320; Murray, *Battle Over Peleliu*, 98
37 Morison, 34; Lyren, Location 1053
38 Lyren, Location 1275; Smith, 494–495
39 Ross, *Peleliu*, 135–137
40 Hoffman, "Peleliu Legacy"
41 Morison, 34–35; Lyren, Location 1338; Toll, *Twilight*, 511; Hough, *Assault*, 181; Alexander, *Storm*, 113; Margaritis, 157 fn
42 Margaritis, 158
43 Garand, 104
44 Ibid., 105
45 Lyman, Locations 1306–1316
46 Ibid., Location 1316
47 Wright, *Far Side*, 59–60
48 Manchester, *Goodbye*, 306–307
49 Lyren, Locations 1306–1316
50 Margaritis, 146–151
51 General Sadae Inoue interrogation, Marine Corps Archives, Carolines, Palaus, Box 1, Folder 16
52 Alexander, "Everything About Peleliu," 28

CHAPTER 3

1 Kurihara POW interrogation, Marine Archives, Carolines, Palau, Box 1, Folder 16
2 Garand, 76
3 Hough, *Assault*, 61
4 General Sadae Inoue interrogation, Marine Archives, Carolines, Palau, Box 1, Folder 16
5 Ross, *Peleliu*, 124–127
6 Hough, *Island War*, 298; McMillan, 341; Wright, *Far Side*, 21; Tokuchi Tada interrogation, Marine Archives, Carolines, Palau, Box 1, Folder 6; Garand, 69; Alexander, *Storm*, 108
7 Alexander, *Storm*, 108; Gayle, *Bloody Beaches*, 8–10
8 Hough, *Assault*, 60
9 Gailey, 40–41; Gayle, *Bloody Beaches*, 9; Alexander, *Storm*, 124; Ambrose, 358
10 Hough, *Assault*, 17–18, 106–107; Gayle, *Bloody Beaches*, 9–10; Inoue interrogation, Corporal Ko Takahashi interrogation, Marine Archives, Carolines, Palau, Box 1, Folder 16

11 General Sadae Inoue interrogation, Marine Archives, Carolines, Palau, Box 1, Folder 16; Gailey, 40–41, 46; Ross, *Peleliu*, 128–129

12 Alexander, *Storm*, 110; Toll, *Conquering Tide*, 454

13 Alexander, *Storm*, 110

14 Alexander, *Storm*, 110; Toll, *Conquering Tide*, 455–456

15 Hough, *Assault*, 16 fn

16 Daugherty, 13

17 Toll, *Conquering Tide*, 469, 487, 513–514; Toland, *Rising Sun*, 591–596

18 General Sadae Inoue interrogation, Marine Corps Archives, Carolines, Palaus, Box 1, Folder 16

19 Colonel Tokuchi Tada interrogation, Marine Corps Archives, Carolines, Palaus, Box 1, Folder 16

20 Ibid.

21 Ibid.

22 Ibid.; Alexander, *Storm*, 109; Hough, *Assault*, 180

23 Morison, 35 [from General Douglas MacArthur's Historical Report II, 297]; Isely, 412; Alexander, *Storm*, 110

24 Garand, 268

25 Garand, 72; Gailey, 39; Denby, 3

26 Daugherty, 28–29, 34

27 Daugherty, 14–28, 62; Wright, *Far Side*, 57–58

28 Leckie, *Strong Men*, 391

29 Murray, *Battle Over Peleliu*, 86; Lyren, Location 3871; Hough, *Assault*, 136; Wright, *Far Side*, 2; Hallas, 208–209

30 Gailey, 48

31 Gayle, *Bloody Beaches*, 8–9

32 Kurihara POW interrogation, Marine Archives, Carolines, Palau, Box 1, Folder 16

33 Phelan, Location 55; Hough, *Island Campaign*, 308; Manchester, *Goodbye, Darkness*, 309

34 Kurihara POW interrogation, Marine Archives, Carolines, Palau, Box 1, Folder 16

35 Phelan, Location 63

36 Gayle, *Bloody Beaches*, 8–10

37 Alexander, *Storm Landings*, 111; Phelan, Locations 39, 55, 394; Gayle, *Bloody Beaches*, 8–10; Ross, *Peleliu*, 129

38 Ray Davis, 63; Phelan, Locations 197, 227, 312

39 Phelan, Locations 31, 417, 424

40 Tada, On interrogations, Marine Archives, Carolines, Palau, Box 1, Folder 16

41 General Inoue interrogation, Marine Archives, Carolines, Palau, Box 1, Folder 16

42 Garand, 76

43 Hough, *Assault*, 17; Denby, 2

44 Wright, *Far Side*, 54

CHAPTER 4

1 Young interview, Museum of the Pacific
2 Russell Davis, 22
3 Genealogy Bank, 16 Sept 1944, *Chicago Daily Times*
4 Russell Davis, 6
5 Mace, 27–28, 49
6 Young interview, Museum of the Pacific
7 Ibid.
8 Leckie, *Helmet*, 286
9 Loren Abdulla interview, Veterans History Project, AFC2001/001/105401
10 Harrell interview, Museum of the Pacific
11 Hechler interview, Museum of the Pacific
12 Burke Davis, 217–218; Garand, 112
13 Wright, *Far Side*, 79
14 Mace, 55; Clapper interview, Museum of the Pacific
15 Hechler interview, Museum of the Pacific
16 McCoy interview, Museum of the Pacific
17 Napier interview, Museum of the Pacific
18 Hough, *Assault*, 54–55; Hoffman, *Chesty*, 274; Margaritis, 88
19 Margaritis, 64
20 West interview, Museum of the Pacific
21 Gayle, *Bloody Beaches*, 4; Ross, *Peleliu*, 129–130; Garand, 73; Alexander, *Storm*, 114
22 Russell Davis, 22
23 Hallas, 137
24 Lyren, Location 1489
25 Mace, 61–65; GenBank, 17 Dec. By USMC correspondent Walter Wood, in *Washington Evening Star*
26 Ross, *Peleliu*, 155–158; Wright, *Far Side*, 75; Clay interview, Museum of the Pacific
27 Loeschorn interview, Museum of the Pacific
28 Hall interview, Museum of the Pacific
29 Ainsworth, 8–9
30 Marine Archives, 2/1 Historical Report, Box 6, Folder 2
31 Lea, *Peleliu Landing*, 180
32 Ibid., 174–177
33 Ibid., 177
34 Margaritis, 81; Hough, *Assault*, 20
35 Hough, *Assault*, 46–47; Lyren, Location 1540; McMillan, 291–292
36 Lyren, Location 1637; Margaritis, 80–82; Ambrose, 325
37 Hough, *Assault*, 38; Lyren, Location 1619
38 Lehrack, 51–53
39 Camp, *Last Man Standing*, 180
40 Wright, *Far Side*, 88
41 Hallas, 54

42 Ross, *Peleliu*, 177–178

43 Wright, *Far Side*, 68–60

44 Ibid., 72–74

45 Peto, 190; Hough, *Assault*, 46–47; Wright, *Far Side*, 72

46 Duffy, 4; Manchester, *American Caesar*, 373

47 Morison, 19–25

48 Lyren, Location 1648

49 Berry, 72–73

50 Hough, *Assault*, 49

51 Garand, 120–121

52 Lyren, Location 1608

53 Sledge, *Old Breed*, 55–59; Sledge, "Peleliu 1944," 72–73; Alexander, *Storm Landings*, 117

54 McEnery, 209–210

55 Wright, *Far Side*, 76; Ross, *Peleliu*, 159–160

56 Hough, *Assault*, 67–68; Margaritis, 93; McMillan, 290–291

57 Douglas, 118

58 Ibid., 112–114, 118–120

59 Ibid., 119–120

60 Ross, *Peleliu*, 203–204

61 Sledge, *Old Breed*, 88–90

62 Douglas, 122–125; Paul Douglas NY Times Obit., 25 Sept 1976; mcrdpi.marines.mil

63 Hough, *Assault*, 43–44; Burgin, 130–131; Lyren, Location 2237; Garand, 118

64 Wright, *Far Side*, 60

65 Ross, *Peleliu*, 90, 102

66 Margaritis, 176–177

67 McMillan, 276–277; Hough, *Assault*, 56–57; Margaritis, 73–74

68 Ross, *Peleliu*, 172–175; Margaritis, 170

69 *Navajo Code Talkers*, 1; Chester Nez interview, Veterans History Project, AFC2001/001/54891

70 Ross, *Peleliu*, 176–177; Margaritis, 74–76

71 Margaritis, 69; Wright, *Far Side*, 83

72 Margaritis, 88

73 Ibid., 89

74 Morison, 39–40; Hough, *Assault*, 64–65; Marine Archives, 2/7 Operations Report, Box 6, Folder 8

75 Marine Archives, 1/1 Battalion Report, Box 6, Folder 1; Lyren, Location 1868

76 Lyren, Location 1859–1868; Margaritis, 70–71

CHAPTER 5

1 Hunt, 26

2 Sledge, *Old Breed*, 79–80

3 Hunt, 45–46

4 Hallas, 133; Garand, 148

5 Hough, *Assault*, 22; McMillan, 268; Ross, *Peleliu*, 187

6 Greenwood, 108–109
7 Lyren, Locations 247, 1994; Margaritis, 77; Hunt, 46–47; McMillan, 288; Garand, 112
8 Hunt, 26
9 Hough, *Assault*, 40; Lyren, Location 2054
10 Lyren, Location 1826
11 Hough, *Assault*, 41; Hunt, 26, 85; Margaritis, 79–80
12 Lyren, Location 2063; Hoffman, *Chesty*, 273; Hunt, 47
13 Murray, *Battle Over Peleliu*, 90
14 Lyren, Location 2471
15 McMillan, 286
16 Peto, 204
17 Harbaugh interview, Veterans History Project, AFC2001/001/05147
18 Marine Archives, Caroline Islands, Palaus, Box 3, Folder 13
19 Lyren, Location 2497; Hunt, 74–75
20 Sloan, 155–157
21 Hough, *Assault*, 75–76; Lyren, Location 2977
22 Camp, *Last Man Standing*, 206–207; Hunt, 91–92
23 Peto, 220–221
24 Hough, *Assault*, 75–76; Hunt, 94
25 Fox interview, Museum of Pacific
26 Camp, *Last Man Standing*, 205
27 Hunt, 91–94
28 Ross, *Peleliu*, 166
29 Hunt, 96–97
30 Peto, 221
31 Hunt, 96–97; Alexander, *Storm Beaches*, 118–119 fn
32 Clifford West interview, Museum of the Pacific
33 Lyren, Location 2157
34 Berry, 277
35 Ross, *Peleliu*, 197
36 Hough, *Assault*, 94; Margaritis, 182; Isely, 415
37 McMillan, 312–313; Hallas, 126, 155; Ray Davis interview, Marine Archives, Caroline Islands, Palaus, Box 6, Folder 1
38 McMillan, 312–313; Blair, 164; Russell Davis, 96
39 Russell Davis, 94
40 Hough, *Assault*, 9, 15
41 Mace, 68
42 Hough, *Assault*, 50
43 McMillan, 283; Wright, *Far Side*, 84; Hallas, 84; Joe Gayle interview, Veterans History Project, AFC2001/001/79326
44 Leckie, *Helmet*, 285
45 Garand, 122
46 Lyren, Location 2268; Morison, 39; Hough, *Assault*, 50
47 Garand, 122

48 Margaritis, 82–85
49 Lyren, Locations 2282, 2291; Sgt. Killeen account in Denby, 16
50 McMillan, 283–284
51 Hallas, 87
52 Ibid.; Ross, *Peleliu*, 183–184
53 McMillan, 288–289; Lyren, Location 2375
54 Donigan, 99
55 Dan Toledo account in Marine Archives, Carolines, Palau, Box 1, Folder 18; Russell Davis, 48; Lyren, Location 2358
56 Leckie, *Helmet*, 286
57 Hough, *Assault*, 51; Lyren, Location 2299; Ross, *Peleliu*, 185; Marine Archives, Caroline Islands, Palaus, 2/1 Historical Report, Box 6, Folder 2
58 Garand, 131
59 Hough, *Assault*, 54
60 Schmuck, 6; Lyren, Locations 2165, 2173; Garand, 121
61 Toll, *Twilight*, 152; Lea, *Peleliu Landing*, 186
62 Lyren, Location 2383
63 Manchester, *Goodbye, Darkness*, 310–311
64 Hough, *Assault*, 53–54; Sledge, "Recollections," 26
65 Sherrod, 256; McMillan, 287; Hough, *Assault*, 57; Donigan, 100; Margaritis, 91, 87; Schmuck, 5; Wright, *Far Side*, 91; Smith, 496
66 Wright, *Far Side*, 94
67 GenBank, 16 Sept 1944, AP story, *Chicago Daily Times*
68 Wheelan, 139; Alexander, *Storm*, 105
69 Toll, *Twilight*, 140–141; Lyren, Location 2921; Sledge, "Recollections," 26
70 Lyren, Location 2717; McEnery, 216
71 Russell Davis, 67; Lyren, Location 2777
72 Russell Davis, 67–71
73 Burgin, 133
74 Toledo account, Marine Archives, Caroline Islands, Palau, Box 1, Folder 18
75 Mace, 80
76 Sledge, *Old Breed*, 79–80
77 Leckie, *Helmet*, 287
78 Ibid., 293
79 Wright, *Far Side*, 97–98
80 Mace, 81; Shedd interview, Museum of the Pacific
81 Marine Archives, Caroline Islands, Palaus, 1/5 Journal, Box 6, Folder 4
82 Lyren, Locations 2921, 2928
83 Laurence Norris interview, Museum of the Pacific
84 Lyren, Locations 2896, 2928
85 Ross, *Peleliu*, 220; McMillan, 303; Shisler, 84; Wright, *Far Side*, 94–95
86 Toll, *Twilight*, 133
87 Ross, *Peleliu*, 221
88 Toll, *Twilight*, 143
89 GenBank, 17 Sept 1944, AP story in *Dallas Morning News*; Lyren, Location 2870

90 Ross, *Peleliu*, 222–223
91 McMillan, 303; Marine Archives, Caroline Islands, Palau, Box 6, Folder 10
92 Jack Brown interview, Museum of the Pacific
93 Denby, 37
94 Lyren, Location 2870
95 Sledge, "Recollections," 26
96 Lyren, Location 2878
97 Russell Davis, 60
98 Marine Archives, Caroline Islands, Palaus, 1st Div Special Action Report, Box 4, Folder 5; Smith, 496

CHAPTER 6

1   Russell Davis, 91
2   GenBank, 22 Dec. 1944, INS story
3   Lea, *Peleliu Landing*, 22
4   Hough, *Assault*, 63; Lyren, Location 2552
5   Hough, *Assault*, 61, 63
6   Ibid., 63–64
7   Lyren, Locations 2650, 2667
8   Hough, *Assault*, 77
9   GenBank, 22 Dec. 1944, INS story
10 Toledo account, Marine Archives, Caroline Islands, Palaus, Box 1, Folder 18
11 Clifford West interview, Museum of the Pacific
12 Margaritis, 184
13 Berry, 293; Camp, *Last Man Standing*, 213; Hough, *Assault*, 77; Ross, *Peleliu*, 244; Hallas, 156; Toledo account, Marine Archives, Caroline Islands, Palaus, Box 1, Folder 18
14 Camp, *Last Man Standing*, 227
15 Hough, *Assault*, 78; Camp, *Last Man Standing*, 227–228; Russell Davis, 91
16 Marine Archives, 2/1 Historical Report, Box 6, Folder 2
17 Ibid.
18 Leckie, *Strong Men*, 407–410; Camp, *Last Man Standing*, 230–231
19 Wright, *Far Side*, 118
20 Alexander, "Everything About Peleliu," 32
21 Camp, *Last Man Standing*, 243; Alexander, "Everything About Peleliu," 32
22 Pomroy interview, Museum of Pacific
23 Hough, *Assault*, 83–84
24 Margaritis, 93–94; Hough, *Assault*, 78; Sloan, 169–170; Hallas, 119, 209; Ross, *Peleliu*, 215–216, 315; Hallas, 209; Toll, *Twilight*, 146
25 Hallas, 116–117
26 Margaritis, 119; Lyren, Locations 3643, 3651
27 Camp, *Last Man Standing*, 231
28 Hough, *Assault*, 83; Lyren, Location 3691
29 McMillan, 457; Hallas, 131

30 Margaritis, 101; McMillan, 311
31 Hoffman, *Chesty*, 285
32 Ibid., 165–167; Wheelan, 132; Peto, 212
33 Hallas, 128
34 Berry, 277
35 Hoffman, *Chesty*, 285; Clifford West interview, Museum of the Pacific
36 Burke Davis, 206–207
37 Clifford West interview, Museum of the Pacific
38 Albert Bouley interview, Museum of the Pacific
39 Shisler, 85
40 Camp, *Last Man Standing*, 215–216; Lea, *Peleliu Landing*, 189
41 Camp, *Last Man Standing*, 218–220; Berry, 278–279
42 Camp, *Last Man Standing*, 222
43 Ibid., 222–224; Hough, *Assault*, 80–81
44 Ainsworth, 20–21
45 McMillan, 306
46 Ainsworth, 14–15
47 GenBank, 19 Sept. 1944, UP, and 22 Dec 1944, AP
48 Toledo account, Marine Archives, Caroline Islands, Palaus, Box 1, Folder 18
49 GenBank, 20 Sept. 1944, INS, in *San Antonio Light*
50 Hallas, 166
51 Lea, *Peleliu Landing*, 195
52 Gayle, *Bloody Beaches*, 46
53 Hough, *Assault*, 81
54 Napier interview, Museum of the Pacific
55 Brehmer interview, Museum of the Pacific
56 Margaritis, 96
57 Alexander, *Storm*, 123; Morison, 15
58 McMillan, 306; Hallas, 125
59 Young interview, Museum of the Pacific
60 Sloan, 155; Ross, *Peleliu*, 264
61 Hallas, 131
62 Ross, *Peleliu*, 242–243
63 Margaritis, 97
64 Lyren, Location 3668; Hallas, 131, 159
65 Camp, *Last Man Standing*, 201
66 Garand, 134
67 Camp, *Last Man Standing*, 201
68 Hallas, 196
69 Straus, 17–19, 38–39, 51
70 Straus, 44
71 Berry, 295
72 Marine Archives, Caroline Islands, Palaus, 2/1 Historical Report, Box 6, Folder 2
73 Camp, *Last Man Standing*, 247
74 Russell Davis, 98; Hallas, 129

75 Caggiano interview, Museum of the Pacific
76 Peto, 227–228
77 Marine Archives, Caroline Islands, Palaus, 2/1 Historical Report, Box 6, Folder 2
78 Hallas, 135–136; McEnery, 257
79 Fanska interview, Museum of the Pacific
80 Ross, *Peleliu*, 249–250
81 Ainsworth, 37
82 Bouley interview, Museum of the Pacific
83 Hallas, 121
84 Lyren, Location 3076; Hough, *Assault*, 63–64
85 Lyren, Location 3076; Wright, *Far Side*, 109–110
86 Lyren, Location 3076
87 Lyren, Locations 3076, 3122-3155-3202; Hough, *Assault*, 66–67; Hallas, 122–123
88 McCoy interview, Museum of the Pacific
89 Jackson interview, Veterans History Project, AFC/2001/001/89698
90 Ibid.
91 Ross, *Peleliu*, 237–238; Jackson Medal of Honor citation; Hallas, 171–172
92 Lyren, Locations 3239, 3269
93 Hough, *Assault*, 66–67; Ross, *Peleliu*, 237–241; Hallas, 123–125
94 Wright, *Far Side*, 111–112; Hallas, 126
95 Lyren, Locations 5727, 5735
96 GenBank, 19 Sept. 1944, 24 Sept. 1944, AP stories in *Dallas Morning News*
97 Lyren, Location 3292; Gayle, *Bloody Beaches*, 23

CHAPTER 7

1 Blair, 96–101
2 Sledge, *Old Breed*, 86–87
3 Blair, 4–5, 21; Hallas, 153
4 Blair, 12–13; Wright, *Far Side*, 102
5 Marine Archives, Caroline Islands, Palaus, Box 2, 81st Division Angaur folder
6 Blair, 15–16, 31
7 Wright, *Far Side*, 102
8 Blair, 19–20
9 Blair, 33–34; Hallas, 153–154
10 Alexander, *Storm*, 120; Blair, 34–38
11 Blair, 38–42; Hough, *Assault*, 107
12 Hallas, 175
13 Wright, *Far Side*, 105
14 Blair, 49–51
15 Blair, 48
16 Blair, 57, 38–45
17 Wright, *Far Side*, 105–106
18 Blair, 55; Hoffman, "Peleliu Legacy," 90–94

19 Blair, 61–64
20 Ibid., 65–67
21 Ibid., 68–73
22 Ibid., 73; Wright, *Far Side*, 106
23 Blair, 32; Morison, 47–48
24 Blair, 80
25 Blair, 78–83; Morison, 49; Toll, *Twilight*, 159
26 Blair, 83
27 Ibid., 86–90
28 Ibid., 91–95
29 Ibid., 98; Soblick interview, Veterans History Project, AFC/2001/001/33828
30 Soblick interview, Veterans History Project, AFC/2001/001/33828
31 Blair, 96–101
32 Ibid., 100
33 Ibid., 99–100
34 Ibid., 100, 104
35 Ibid., 105–106; Greenwood, 102
36 Blair, 111
37 Ibid., 111
38 Ibid., 110–118; Hallas, 254; Lyren, Location 4165
39 Sledge, *Old Breed*, 86–87
40 Valentine Ybarra interview, Museum of the Pacific
41 Mace, 89–92
42 Ybarra interview, Museum of the Pacific; Hough, *Assault*, 70–72; Lyren, Location 3310
43 Lyren, Locations 3358, 3366; Hough, *Assault*, 72–73
44 Hallas, 127
45 Sledge, *Old Breed*, 98–100
46 Thomason, 660–661
47 Sledge, *Old Breed*, 36–37, 44
48 Marine Archives, Caroline Islands, Palaus, 1st Division, Box 4, Folder 4
49 Sledge, *Old Breed*, 98–100
50 Burgin, 140–141
51 Ibid.
52 Sledge, *Old Breed*, 36–37
53 Schmuck, 7
54 Hough, *Assault*, 73–74; Hallas, 135
55 Smith, 270; Margaritis, 198
56 Margaritis, 102
57 Harrell interview, Museum of the Pacific
58 Hallas, 157
59 McCandless, 164, 166
60 Wilson, 47; Alexander, *Storm*, 121; Daniel, 74, 81–82, 89–90; Gunston, 146–149
61 Daniel, 81

62 Hallas, 158; Isely, 413, 418–422; Sherrod, 256, 258; Ross, *Peleliu*, 266, 234; McMillan, 339; Margaritis, 117; Stauffer, 17–20; Hammel, *Western Pacific*, 153; Cantrell interview, Museum of the Pacific; Daniel, 85, 87–88

63 Daniel, 87

64 Ross, *Peleliu*, 100–101; Wright, *Far Side*, 20

65 Margaritis, 114

66 Ross, *Peleliu*, 267–268; Gayle, *Bloody Beaches*, 25

67 Gayle, *Bloody Beaches*, 25–26

CHAPTER 8

1 Camp, *Last Man Standing*, 273

2 Sledge, *Old Breed*, 103–104

3 Marine Archives, Caroline Islands, Palaus, 2/1 Historical Report, Box 6, Folder 2

4 Hough, *Assault*, 182–183; Isely, 413

5 Margaritis, 100; Wright, *Far Side*, 121

6 Clifford West interview, Museum of the Pacific

7 Lyren, Location 3771; Camp, *Last Man Standing*, 253; Hallas, 163

8 Hallas, 229–230

9 Camp, *Last Man Standing*, 253; Lyren, Locations 3864, 3871

10 Camp, *Last Man Standing*, 253–254

11 Lyren, Locations 3963, 3979

12 Marine Archives, Caroline Islands, Palaus, 2/1 Historical Report, Box 6, Folder 2

13 Ibid.

14 Lyman, Locations 3963, 3979; Hough, *Assault*, 86; Garand, 157

15 Marine Archives, Caroline Islands, Palaus, 2/1 Historical Report, Box 6, Folder 2

16 Hallas, 165; Camp, *Last Man Standing*, 260

17 Lyren, Location 3794; Hoffman, *Chesty*, 283

18 Hough, *Assault*, 84–85; Ray Davis, 68–69; Ainsworth, 58–59; Hallas, 160

19 Hough, *Assault*, 85; Ray Davis, 69; Hoffman, *Chesty*, 284; Everett Pope interview, Veterans History Project, AFC2001/001/89766

20 Marine Archives, Caroline Islands, Palaus, "C" Company War Diary, Box 6, Folder 1; Ray Davis, 69–70

21 Ray Davis, 70

22 Camp, *Last Man Standing*, 267

23 Lyren, Location 4045

24 Marine Archives, Caroline Islands, Palaus, "C" Co. War DIary, Box 6, Folder 1

25 Ainsworth, 70

26 Hallas, 161–162; Pope interview, Veterans History Project

27 Pope interview, Veterans History Project

28 Lyren, Locations 4045, 4057, 4071, 4086; McMillan, 314–315; Ainsworth, 69–73; Hoffman, *Chesty*, 283–284; Marine Archives, Caroline Islands, Palaus, 2/1 Report, Box 6, Folder 2

29 Marine Archives, Caroline Islands, Palaus, "C" Co. Journal, Box 6, Folder 1; Hallas, 162–163; Ainsworth, 76–77 and fn; Hough, *Assault*, 86

30 Camp, *Last Man Standing*, 272; Lyren, Locations 4139, 4178; Hough, *Assault*, 86–88
31 Russell Davis, 107–108
32 Ibid.
33 Ibid., 99
34 McMillan, 316–317
35 Camp, *Last Man Standing*, 273
36 Russell Davis, 110
37 Ibid., Margaritis, 101; Camp, *Last Man Standing*, 273–274; Lyren, Location 4178
38 Shelby Albright interview, Veterans History Project, AFC2001/001/24553
39 Hough, *Assault*, 87, from "Tada Record, 20Sept44"
40 Hoffman, *Chesty*, 285–287; Hough, *Assault*, 86–88
41 Hough, *Assault*, 88–90; Lyren, Locations 4314, 4330
42 Hough, *Assault*, 88 fn
43 Nimitz Gray Book, Vol. 5, 2076; Cincpac Communique No. 125
44 Lyren, Location 4279; Hoffman, *Chesty*, 291; Hallas, 175
45 Lyren, Location 4200; Hough, *Assault*, 88 fn
46 Lyren, Location 4360; McMillan, 317–318
47 Ray Davis account, Marine Archives, Caroline Islands, Palaus, Box 6, Folder 1; Camp, *Last Man Standing*, 202
48 Ross, *Peleliu*, 363
49 Margaritis, 36–37
50 Ibid., 105
51 Alexander, "Everything About Peleliu," 32
52 Sledge, "Recollections," 26
53 Lyren, Locations 4097, 4108
54 Ross, *Peleliu*, 270–271; Margaritis, 180–181; Shisler, 84
55 Margaritis, 104–105
56 Camp, *Leatherneck Legends*, 146
57 Margaritis, 105; Alexander, *Storm*, 122
58 Guy Farrar interview, Veterans History Project, AFC2001/001/67778
59 Margaritis, 106
60 Margaritis, 106–107; Ray Davis, 72
61 Camp, *Last Man Standing*, 279–280, Hallas, 170; Hough, *Assault*, 106
62 Garand, 186; Ross, *Peleliu*, 274–275; Gailey, 134
63 Margaritis, 107–108; Hough, *Assault*, 88, 106
64 Hough, *Assault*, 106; Lyren, Location 4264
65 Margaritis, 179
66 Ibid., 107–109
67 Ibid., 109
68 Hough, *Assault*, 88
69 Hallas, 171
70 Nimitz Gray Book, Vol. 5, 2076
71 Camp, *Last Man Standing*, 282–283

72 Sledge, *Old Breed*, 103–104
73 Mace, 103
74 McEnery, 227
75 Clifford West interview, Museum of the Pacific
76 Sledge, *Old Breed*, 128
77 Camp, *Last Man Standing*, 283–284
78 Hoffman, *Chesty*, 287
79 Hallas, 176
80 Peto, 230
81 Lyren, Locations 4246, 4254
82 Ibid., Location 4443
83 Ross, *Peleliu*, 266
84 Bill Cantrell interview, Museum of the Pacific
85 Isely, 422; McMillan, 339
86 Lyren, Location 85
87 Hough, *Assault*, 94
88 Mace, 92
89 Lyren, Locations 5328, 5327; Wright, *Far Side*, 150; Hallas, 225–226; Stauffer, 20
90 McMillan, 337; Hough, *Assault*, 133; Ross, *Peleliu*, 289
91 Gayle, *Bloody Beaches*, 23
92 Hough, *Assault*, 90–92; Gayle, *Bloody Beaches*, 26; Hallas, 172–174
93 Hallas, 184
94 Lyren, Location 5285
95 Ibid., Location 4463
96 Margaritis, 192
97 Marine Archives, Caroline Islands, Palaus, 3/1, Box 6, Folder 3; Lyren, Locations 4472, 4480
98 Hough, *Assault*, 73; Peto, 230
99 McMillan, 319–320
100 Toledo account, Marine Archives, Caroline Islands, Palaus, Box 1, Folder 18
101 Blair, 124–125; McMillan, 318
102 Hallas, 206; Alexander, *Storm*, 123
103 Camp, *Last Man Standing*, 287–288
104 Peto, 238–239
105 Lyren, Location 6154
106 Blair, 154, 156; Hough, *Assault*, 101
107 Lyren, Locations 5369, 5378
108 Helfer, "Dog Hero," 73
109 Hallas, 215–217
110 Gailey, 124 from Benis Smith oral history interview of O.P. Smith

CHAPTER 9

1 Lyren, Locations 5531, 5539, 5285, 5294, 5310, 5508, 5516
2 Shisler, 86

3   Wright, *Far Side*, 128
4   Hallas, 179; Lyren, Location 4565
5   Blair, 129–130
6   Wright, *Far Side*, 123
7   Hough, *Assault*, 110–112; Wright, *Far Side*, 128–129; Lyren, Locations 4575, 4581; Hallas, 183; Bill Miller, "Graves Registration"; Keller interview, Veterans History Project, AFC/2001/001/19577
8   Wright, *Far Side*, 130; Blair, 127
9   Hough, *Assault*, 114
10 Wright, *Far Side*, 130; Blair, 130–133
11 Hough, *Assault*, 113–114
12 Lyren, Location 4621
13 Hallas, 185
14 Blair, 136–137
15 Ibid.
16 Lyren, Location 4636
17 Blair, 137
18 Lyren, Locations 4880, 4887; Hough, *Assault*, 115–116; Blair, 138–140
19 Lyren, Locations 4927, 4936, 4944
20 Garand, 190
21 Colonel Tada interrogation, Marine Archives, Caroline Islands, Palau, Box 1, Folder 6
22 Hough, *Assault*, 104–105; Lyren, Locations 4496, 4511, 4527, 4535, 3410; Wright, *Far Side*, 127; Ross, *Peleliu*, 280–281
23 Hallas, 217–218; Inoue interrogation, Marine Archives, Caroline Islands, Palaus, Box 1, Folder 16
24 Hough, *Assault*, 105; Ross, *Peleliu*, 282; Hallas, 186, 197
25 Garand, 207–208
26 Lyren, Location 4745; Hough, *Assault*, 117–118
27 Hallas, 189; Hough, *Assault*, 118, 120; Gayle, *Bloody Beaches*, 29; Wright, *Far Side*, 134
28 Wright, *Far Side*, 132
29 Gayle, *Bloody Beaches*, 31
30 Hough, *Assault*, 119–120; Gayle, *Bloody Beaches*, 31; Lyren, Location 4745; Hallas, 194
31 Gayle, *Bloody Beaches*, 31; Lyren, Locations 4769, 4777; Wright, *Far Side*, 139
32 Evans, "Infantillery," 50–55
33 Hough, *Assault*, 121
34 Wright, *Far Side*, 135, 139; Gayle, *Bloody Beaches*, 31
35 Hallas, 191; Gayle, *Bloody Beaches*, 31; Shisler, 86
36 Lyren, Location 4757
37 Hough, *Assault*, 120; Wright, *Far Side*, 134–135; Hallas, 192
38 Hough, *Assault*, 122
39 Lyren, Locations 4800, 4816, 4824
40 Lyren, Location 4848

41 Gayle, *Bloody Beaches*, 33; Burgin, 155

42 Lyren, Location 4979

43 Lyren, Locations 4971, 4979; Wright, *Far Side*, 136

44 Gayle, *Bloody Beaches*, 31

45 Walt, "The Closer," 37–38; Sherrod, 256–257

46 Burgin, 158; Gayle, *Bloody Beaches*, 33; Lyren, Locations 4979, 5005; Hough, *Assault*, 123–125; Hallas, 197–199

47 Burgin, 160–168

48 Lyren, Locations 5011, 5026

49 Sledge, *Old Breed*, 111–113

50 Hallas, 199

51 Ibid., 200

52 Ibid., 202

53 Sloan, 212–218; Wright, *Far Side*, 138; Ross, *Peleliu*, 300–304; Lyren, Location 5026; Gayle, *Bloody Beaches*, 31; Hough, *Assault*, 123–126; McEnery, 245

54 GenBank, 28 Sept 1944, UP in *Chicago Sun*

55 Lyren, Locations 5136, 5096

56 Wright, *Far Side*, 139; Lyren, Locations 5119, 5127; Hough, *Assault*, 128–129; Hallas, 204

57 Phelan, Location 132

58 Hallas, 203; Lyren, Location 5065; Ross, *Peleliu*, 305–307

59 Hough, *Assault*, 126–127

60 Hallas, 224, 204

61 Hough, *Island War*, 309–310

62 Ross, *Peleliu*, 307; Gayle, *Bloody Beaches*, 34

63 Smith, 551

64 Wright, *Far Side*, 133; Ross, *Peleliu*, 308

65 Evans, "Infantillery," 50–55

66 Gayle, *Bloody Beaches*, 36; Hough, *Island War*, 311–312

67 Lyren, Location 5762; Hough, *Island War*, 312

68 Shaw, 37; Hough, *Assault*, 204

69 Lyren, Location 5754

70 McMillan, 322; Lyren, Location 5209; Gayle, *Bloody Beaches*, 36; Hough, *Assault*, 144 and map

71 Walt, "The Closer," 38–39

72 Crawmer interview, Museum of the Pacific

73 Isely, 421; Lyren, Location 5209; Hallas, 256

74 Hough, *Assault*, 145

75 Lyren, Location 5224

76 Hough, *Assault*, 135; Blair, 156

77 Wright, *Far Side*, 142; Ross, *Peleliu*, 280, 313; Blair, 155–157; Hough, *Island War*, 310–311

78 Lyren, Locations 5531, 5539, 5285, 5294, 5310, 5508, 5516

79 Lyren, Locations 5531, 5539, 5547; Hallas, 225

80 Evans, "Infantillery," 50–55

81 Garand, 230–232
82 Mace, 167
83 Hallas, 215; Lyren, Location 5523
84 Lyren, Locations 5456, 5471, 5344; Gayle, *Bloody Beaches*, 40; Hough, *Assault*, 149; Hallas, 214
85 Hallas, 214–215
86 Finnegan interview, Museum of the Pacific
87 Hallas, 187–188; Sledge, *Old Breed*, 131; Wright, *Far Side*, 145; Mace, 170; Marine Archives, Caroline Islands, Palaus, 5th Marines Record of Operations, Box 6, Folder 6
88 Hough, *Assault*, 146, 148; Lyren, Locations 5402, 5418
89 McMillan, 335
90 Hallas, 214
91 Hough, *Assault*, 148–149; Lyren, Locations 55441, 5495, 5501; Ross, *Peleliu*, 314–315
92 Ross, *Peleliu*, 316; Schott interview, Museum of the Pacific
93 Lyren, Location 5523
94 Hough, *Assault*, 151–153
95 Lyren, Locations 5597, 5619, 5627
96 McMillan, 328–329
97 Ibid., 329
98 Lyren, Locations 5636, 5644, 5652, 5659
99 Gayle, *Bloody Beaches*, 36–37; Lyren, Locations 5675, 5682, 5685; McMillan, 331; Hough, *Assault*, 154; Hallas, 224; Blair, 158
100 Ross, *Peleliu*, 323–325; Hallas, 224
101 Hough, *Assault*, 150–151
102 McEnery, 248–250
103 Lyren, Locations 5479, 5487
104 Hough, *Assault*, 150–151; Blair, 155; Hough, *Island War*, 309–310
105 Hough, *Assault*, 151; Lyren, Location 5486
106 Blair, 158; Ross, *Peleliu*, 325–326; Lyren, Location 5727
107 Wright, *Far Side*, 148

CHAPTER 10

1 Gayle, *Bloody Beaches*, 34
2 Sledge, *Old Breed*, 142–143
3 Gayle, *Bloody Beaches*, 40
4 Rozell, 141–142; Hallas, 227
5 Garand, 227
6 Gayle, *Bloody Beaches*, 38
7 Lyren, Location 5823
8 Wright, *Far Side*, 151
9 Burgin, 172–173
10 Sledge, *Old Breed*, 142–144; McEnery, 247

11 Lyren, Location 5877

12 Ibid., Location 5899

13 Hough, *Assault*, 156–159

14 Rozell, 141–142; Hallas, 227

15 Garand, 219

16 Ibid., 242

17 Hallas, 227

18 Ibid., 233

19 Wright, *Far Side*, 152; Lyren, Locations 5846, 5854, 5907, 5915, 5922; Hallas, 238–239; Gayle, *Bloody Beaches*, 39; Hough, *Assault*, 160–161

20 Garand, 245

21 McMillan, 338–339; Ross, *Peleliu*, 327; Hough, *Assault*, 161–162; Wright, *Far Side*, 153; Lyren, Locations 5953, 5970

22 Garand, 248; Lyren, Location 5994; Hough, *Assault*, 164; Hallas, 241–242

23 Gayle, *Bloody Beaches*, 34

24 Hallas, 248

25 Burgin, 169–170; Ross, *Peleliu*, 311–312; Lyren, Locations 5861, 5869

26 Lyren, Location 5884

27 Garand, 11

28 Wright, *Far Side*, 153; Lyren, Location 6049

29 Alexander, *Storm*, 122

30 Hallas, 242–243

31 Ibid.

32 Ibid.; Garand, 225

33 Hough, *Assault*, 163; McEnery, 262–266

34 Sledge, *Old Breed*, 140

35 Ibid., 40

36 Sobocinski, "Hero of the Bloody Nose Ridge"

37 Hallas, 243–244

38 Walt, "The Closer, 39–40

39 GenBank, 11 Feb. 1945, Wood account, *Portland Oregonian*

40 Hough, *Assault*, 165–166 fn; Lyren, Location 6056

41 Burgin, 175; Ambrose, 352

42 Sledge, *Old Breed*, 148

43 Sledge, *Old Breed*, 134

44 Hallas, 244–245

45 Donigan, 96–103

46 Blair, 168–170; Hough, *Assault*, 166

47 Ross, *Peleliu*, 335

48 Sledge, "Recollections," 23–27

49 Gailey, 168; Ross, *Peleliu*, 335; Wright, *Far Side*, 153–154

50 Hough, *Assault*, 167

51 Hough, *Assault*, 134; Lyren, Location 5746; Ross, *Peleliu*, 295–297

52 Hallas, 218

53 Mace, 208–209

54 McEnery, 236
55 Wright, *Far Side*, 128
56 Isely, 415
57 Blair, 164–165
58 Lyren, Locations 6071, 6078, 6086
59 Gayle, *Bloody Beaches*, 41
60 Lyren, Location 6169
61 Keene, 21
62 Lyren, Location 6169; GenBank, 18 Jan. 1945, USMC correspondent Sgt John Kirby, in Roanoke Rapids, NC, *Herald*
63 Lyren, Location 6169; Hallas, 245
64 Hallas, 246

CHAPTER 11

1 Blair, 154
2 Hallas, 212
3 Blair, 158, 162–163
4 81st Division Operations Report, 61; GenBank, 7 Oct., AP in *Arkansas Gazette*
5 GenBank, 7 Oct., AP in *Arkansas Gazette*
6 Blair, 164
7 Hallas, 212
8 Blair, 143
9 81st Division Operations Report, 37; Blair, 144
10 Blair, 144
11 81st Division Operations Report, 33; Blair, 141
12 Blair, 141–142
13 Hough, *Assault*, 129–132; Blair, 144–147
14 Blair, 145–146
15 Ibid., 146–147
16 Ibid., 149–150
17 Ibid., 149
18 Ibid., 149–150
19 Ibid., 150, 153; Hallas, 204–205
20 Blair, 152–154; Lyren, Location 5176
21 Blair, 163; 81st Division Operations Report, 59
22 Blair, 157
23 Ibid., 148
24 Ibid., 146–152
25 Hough, *Assault*, 171
26 Gayle, *Bloody Beaches*, 41–42
27 Burgin, 174–175
28 Blair, 174
29 Stauffer, "Marine Aviation," 20; Toll, *Twilight*, 152–153; Wright, *Far Side*, 150
30 Blair, 171–173

31 Hough, *Assault*, 138
32 Margaritis, 135; Blair, 153
33 Blair, 147
34 Sledge, *Old Breed*, 120
35 Ibid., 152–153
36 Blair, 168
37 Ibid., 170
38 Ibid., 173
39 Lyren, Locations 6200, 6215; Hallas, 249–250
40 Blair, 178
41 Hallas, 251–252
42 Blair, 175–180; Lyren, Locations 6222, 6230, 6238
43 Hough, *Assault*, 172–174
44 Gayle, *Bloody Beaches*, 42; Blair, 195, 190; Lyren, Location 6806
45 Blair, 213
46 Ibid., 180–181
47 Ibid., 182
48 Ibid., 183

CHAPTER 12

 1 Blair, 196
 2 Hallas, 266
 3 Blair, 185
 4 Ibid., 187, 184; Ross, *Peleliu*, 336
 5 Margaritis, 192–193
 6 Blair, 184, 191
 7 Ibid., 186
 8 Lyren, Locations 6260, 6268; Blair, 191–192
 9 81st Division Operations Report, 61
10 Garand, 256
11 Blair, 192–194; 81st Division Operations Report, 73; Hough, *Assault*, 175;
    Wright, *Far Side*, 156
12 Hallas, 258
13 Wright, *Far Side*, 156
14 81st Division Operations Report, 77, 81; Blair, 202; Wright, *Far Side*, 155
15 Blair, 196
16 Ibid., 196; Gayle, *Bloody Beaches*, 42; Hallas, 258–259
17 Blair, 197
18 Hallas, 254–255; Donigan, 100; Alexander, *Storm*, 123
19 Blair, 197
20 Ibid., 198–199
21 Ibid., 200–201
22 Ibid., 173–174
23 Ibid., 206, 202–203

24 81st Division Operations Report, 81
25 Blair, 204
26 Marine Archives, Caroline Islands, Palaus, 1st Division Special Action Report, Box 5, Folder 1
27 Blair, 205
28 Nimitz Gray Book, Vol. 5, 2283, Enclosure A
29 Lyren, Locations 6336, 6344; Blair, 206, 208
30 Lyren, Locations 6329, 6336
31 Blair, 208–210
32 Ibid., 210
33 Ibid., 213; Lyren, Location 6374; Hallas, 269
34 Blair, 214
35 Blair, 213–216; Hallas, 263–264, 266; Colonel Tokuchi Tada, General Inoue interrogations, Marine Archives, Carolines, Palau, Box 1, Folder 6
36 Blair, 214
37 Ibid., 215–217
38 Ibid., 219–220; Lyren, Location 6381
39 81st Division Operations Report, 80
40 Blair, 217–222; Lyren, Location 6404
41 Blair, 223; Lyren, Location 6411
42 Blair, 228
43 Ibid., 224–226; Wright, *Far Side*, 157
44 Hallas, 269–270
45 Blair, 229; Hough, *Assault*, 176
46 Garand, 262
47 Blair, 230–231
48 Ibid., 230–232
49 Ibid., 231; Hough, *Assault*, 176–177
50 Hallas, 270
51 Blair, 234; Lyren, Location 6458
52 Blair, 234; Hough, *Assault*, 177
53 Blair, 227
54 James Ijames interview with Peter DeCioccio; Garand, 264
55 81st Division Operations Report, 9; Ross, *Peleliu*, 338; Hough, *Assault*, 177 and footnote; Blair, 235
56 Hallas, 273
57 Blair, 235
58 81st Division Operations Report, 9; Phelan, Location 582; Lyren, Location 6465
59 Hough, *Assault*, 178; Blair, 236
60 81st Division Operations Report, 7–8
61 Blair, 236
62 Ibid., 242
63 McEnery, 272
64 Ross, *Iwo Jima*, 33

CHAPTER 13

1 Murray, *Battle Over Peleliu*, 148
2 Blair, 243; Sherrod, 257 and fn; Hough, *Assault*, 168; GenBank, 21 Jan. 1945, AP in *Tulsa World*
3 Daniel, 115–118
4 Ross, *Peleliu*, 348–349; Murray, *Battle Over Peleliu*, 85, 96
5 Blair, 255–257, 251
6 Wright, *Far Side*, 162
7 Hallas, 280–281; McCoy interview, Museum of the Pacific
8 Hallas, 279; Margaritis, 206
9 Polete, 3–7
10 Ibid.
11 Ibid.
12 Ross, *Peleliu*, 292–294; Margaritis, 206–208; Polete, 3–7
13 Murray, *Battle Over Peleliu*, 129; Wright, *Far Side*, 157
14 Murray, *Battle Over Peleliu*, 129, 173–176; Ross, *Peleliu*, 354
15 Murray, *Battle Over Peleliu*, 176
16 Ibid., 136; Ross, *Peleliu*, 351–353
17 Murray, *Battle Over Peleliu*, 148
18 Wright, *Fighting Techniques*, 12
19 Cook, 447–449; Murray, *Battle Over Peleliu*, 163
20 Murray, *Battle Over Peleliu*, 173
21 Alexander, "Everything About Peleliu," 33
22 Murray, *Battle Over Peleliu*, 120–124
23 Ibid., 140; Ross, *Peleliu*, 350–351
24 Murray, *Battle Over Peleliu*, 148–151, 163
25 Ross, *Peleliu*, 351–353
26 Wagner, in *Naval History Magazine*, Vol. 17, No. 1, February 2003
27 Watkins interview, Museum of the Pacific

EPILOGUE

1 Halsey, 194–195
2 Wilson interview, Museum of the Pacific
3 Ray Davis, 71
4 Ross, *Peleliu*, 338; McMillan, 343; Blair, 255
5 Garand, 286
6 Gayle, *Bloody Beaches*, 45; Murray, *Battle Over Peleliu*, 102–103
7 Marine Archives, Caroline Islands, Palaus, Box 5, Folder 1
8 Lynch interview, Museum of the Pacific
9 Wilson interview, Museum of the Pacific
10 Marine Archives, Caroline Islands, Palaus, 1st Division SAR, 68, Box 5, Folder 1
11 Alexander, "Everything About Peleliu," 33
12 Wright, *Far Side*, 159

13 Morison, V. 12, 47
14 Halsey, 194–195
15 Ross, *Peleliu*, 143
16 Ray Davis, 68
17 Hallas, 281
18 Ross, *Peleliu*, 346–347; Garand, 285–286; Hough, *Assault*, 181
19 Wright, *Far Side*, 160
20 Garand, 273
21 Margaritis, 110
22 Alexander, "Everything About Peleliu," 31
23 Isely and Crowl, 403, Garand, 104–105
24 Hoffman, "The Legacy and Lessons," 90–94
25 Alexander, *Storm* 112–113
26 Margaritis, 172–177
27 Sledge, *Old Breed*, 305
28 Wheelan, 70
29 Sledge, *Old Breed*, 305
30 Ray Davis, 71
31 Manchester, *Goodbye, Darkness*, 343–344
32 Alexander, *Storm*, 125
33 Finnegan interview, Museum of the Pacific

Bibliography

Ainsworth, Jack R. *Among Heroes: A Marine Corps Rifle Company on Peleliu.* Quantico, VA: U.S. Marine Corps History Division, 2011.

Alexander, Joseph H. "Everything About Peleliu Left a Bad Taste," in *Leatherneck.* Quantico, VA: Marine Corps Association, Vol. 87, Issue 9, September 2004, pp 28–33.

—*Storm Landings. Epic Amphibious Battles in the Central Pacific.* Annapolis, MD: Naval Institute Press, 1997.

Ambrose, Hugh. *The Pacific.* New York: NAL Caliber, 2010.

Ballendorf, Dirk Anthony, and Merrill Lewis Bartlett. *Pete Ellis, an Amphibious Warfare Prophet, 1880–1923.* Annapolis, MD: Naval Institute Press, 1997.

Berry, Henry. *Semper Fi, Mac. Living Memories of the U.S. Marines in World War II.* New York: Arbor House, 1982.

Blair, Bobby C., and John Peter DeCioccio. *Victory at Peleliu. The 81st Infantry Division's Pacific Battle.* Norman, OK: University of Oklahoma Press, 2011.

Burgin, R.V. *Islands of the Damned. A Marine at War in the Pacific.* New York: NAL Caliber, 2010.

Camp, Dick. *Last Man Standing: The 1st Marine Regiment at Peleliu, September 15–21, 1944.* Minneapolis, MN: Zenith Press, 2008.

—*Leatherneck Legends. Conversations with the Marine Corps' Old Breed.* St. Paul, MN: Zenith Press, 2006.

Castle, Alfred L. "President Roosevelt and General MacArthur at the Honolulu Conference of 1944," in *Hawaiian Journal of History,* Vol. 30, 2004.

Cook, Haruko Taya, and Theodore S. Cook. *Japan at War: An Oral History.* New York: New Press, 1992.

Culp, Ronald K. *The First Black United States Marines. The Men of Montford Point, 1942–1946.* Jefferson, NC: McFarland & Company, Inc., 2007.

Daniel, Glenn "Bud." *Cowboy Down: A World War II Marine Fighter Pilot's Story.* Tucson, AZ: Self-published, 2014.

Daugherty, Leo. *Fighting Technique of a Japanese Infantryman, 1941–1945. Training, Techniques and Weapons.* Staplehurst, Kent, UK: Spellmount Limited, 2002.

Davis, Burke. *Marine! The Life of Lt. Gen. Lewis B. "Chesty" Puller, USMC (Ret)*. Boston, MS and Toronto: Little, Brown and Company, 1962.

Davis, Ray. *The Story of Ray Davis, General of Marines: Lessons Learned in War and Peace*. Fuquay Varina, NC: Research Triangle Publishing, 1995.

Davis, Russell. *Marine at War*. New York: Scholastic Book Services, 1966.

"The Death Ridges of Peleliu," Season 2, Episode 2 of *Against the Odds*. Amazon film, aired February 22, 2016.

Denby, D. Colt. *Peleliu Revisited: An Historical and Archaeological Survey of World War II Sites on Peleliu Island*. Saipan, MP: Micronesian Archaeological Survey Report Number 24, 1988.

Donigan, Major Henry J. "Peleliu: The Forgotten Battle," in *Marine Corps Gazette*, Quantico, VA: Marine Corps Association, Vol. 78, Issue 9, September 1994, pp 96–103.

Duffy, James P. *Return to Victory: MacArthur's Epic Liberation of the Philippines*. New York: Hachette Books, 2021.

Evans, Lieutenant Colonel R.A. "Infantillery on Peleliu," in *Marine Corps Gazette*, Quantico, VA: Marine Corps Association, Vol. 29, Issue 1, January 1945, pp 50–55.

Gailey, Harry A. *Peleliu 1944*. Annapolis, MD: The Nautical & Aviation Publishing Company of America, 1983.

Garand, George W., and Truman R. Strowbridge, eds. *Western Pacific Operations: History of U.S. Marine Corps Operations in World War II*. Vol. IV. Washington, D.C.: Historical Division, Headquarters, U.S. Marine Corps, 1971.

Gayle, Brigadier General Gordon D., USMC (Ret). *Bloody Beaches: The Marines at Peleliu*. Washington, D.C.: Marine Corps Historical Center, 1996.

Genealogy Bank, www.genealogybank.com/explore/newspapers/all

Greenwood, John T., and F. Clifton Berry, Jr. *Medics at War: Military Medicine from Colonial Times to the 21st Century*. Annapolis, MD: Naval Institute Press, 2005.

Gunston, Bill. *The Illustrated Directory of Fighting Aircraft of World War II*. London, UK: Salamander Books, 2001.

Hallas, James H. *The Devil's Anvil: The Assault on Peleliu*. Westport, CN: Praeger, 1994.

Halsey, William Frederick, and Lieutenant Commander J. Bryan III. *Admiral Halsey's Story*. New York: Whittlesey House, 1947.

Hammel, Eric, and John E. Lane. *76 Hours. The Invasion of Tarawa*. New York: Jove Books, 1985.

—*War in the Western Pacific: The U.S. Marines in the Marianas, Peleliu, Iwo Jima, and Okinawa, 1944–1945*. Minneapolis, MN: Zenith Press, 2010.

—"World War II: 50 Years Ago: Peleliu," in *Leatherneck*. Quantico, VA: Marine Corps Association, Vol. 77, Issue 9, September 1994, pp 16–25.

The Hawaiian Journal of History. Honolulu: University of Hawaii Press, 1967.

Hayashi, Saburo, and Alvin D. Coox. *Kogun: The Japanese Army in the Pacific War*. Quantico, VA: Marine Corps Association, 1950.

Heinichs, Waldo, and Marc Gallicchio. *Implacable Foes: War in the Pacific, 1944–1945*. New York: Oxford University Press, 2017.

Helfer, Sergeant Harold, "Dog Tales," in *Leatherneck*, Quantico, VA: Marine Corps Association, Vol. 28, Issue 7, July 1945, p 73.

Hoffman, Lieutenant Colonel Jon T., USMCR. *Chesty: The Story of Lieutenant General Lewis B. Puller, USMC.* New York: Random House, 2001.

—"The Legacy and Lessons of Peleliu," in *Marine Corps Gazette*. Quantico VA: Marine Corps Association. Vol. 78, Issue 9, September 1994, pp 90–94.

Hough, Major Frank, USMCR. *The Assault on Peleliu.* Washington, D.C.: Historical Division, Headquarters, U.S. Marine Corps, 1950.

—*The Island War: The United States Marine Corps in the Pacific.* Philadelphia, PA and New York: J.B. Lippincott Company, 1947.

Hughes, Thomas Alexander. *Admiral Bill Halsey: A Naval Life.* Cambridge, MA: Harvard University Press, 2016.

Hulgan, Jim. "Peleliu Parting," in *Leatherneck*. Quantico, VA: Marine Corps Association, Vol. 77, Issue 9, September 1994, pp 58–61.

Hunt, George P. *Coral Comes High. U.S. Marines and the Fight for Peleliu.* New York: Harper, 1946. Republished in 2018.

Iseley, Jeter A., and Philip A. Crowl. *The U.S. Marines and Amphibious War: Its Theory, and Its Practice in the Pacific.* Princeton, NJ: Princeton University Press, 1951.

The Journal of America's Military Past. Fort Myer, VA: Council on America's Military Past, 1998–.

Kaiser, Charles. "Former Sen. Paul H. Douglas Dies: Liberal Illinois Democrat was 84." *New York Times*, September 25, 1976.

Keene, A. "The Stout-Hearted on Peleliu," in *Leatherneck*. Quantico, VA: Marine Corps Association. Vol. 77, Issue 9, September 1994, p 21.

Lea, Tom. *Peleliu Landing.* El Paso, TX: C. Herzog, 1945.

—With Brandon M. Greeley Jr., ed. *The Two Thousand Yard Stare: Tom Lea's World War II.* College Station, TX: Texas A&M University Press, 2008.

Leatherneck magazine. Quantico, VA: Marine Corps Association, 1917–.

Leckie, Robert. *Helmet for My Pillow: From Parris Island to the Pacific.* New York: Bantam Books, 2010. First published in 1957.

—*Strong Men Armed. The United States Marines vs. Japan.* New York: Da Capo Press, 1997. First published in 1962.

Lehrack, Otto A. "A Medal of Honor, Two Navy Crosses and a Silver Star: Herman Hanneken, A Very Deadly Marine," in *Leatherneck*. Quantico, VA: Marine Corps Association, Vol. 94, Issue 11 (November 2011), pp 50–53.

Lyren, Carl. *Dogged Courage: The Struggle for Peleliu, 1944.* Self-published, 2004 (e-book edition used).

Mace, Sterling, and Nick Allen. *Battleground Pacific: A Marine Rifleman's Combat Odyssey in K/3/5.* New York: St. Martin's Press, 2012.

Manchester, William. *American Caesar: Douglas MacArthur, 1880–1964.* Boston, MA and Toronto: Little, Brown and Company, 1978.

—*Goodbye, Darkness. A Memoir of the Pacific War.* Boston, MA and Toronto: Little, Brown and Company, 1979.

Margaritis, Peter. *Landing in Hell. The Pyrrhic Victory of the First Marine Division on Peleliu, 1944*. Philadelphia: Casemate, 2018.

Marine Corps Gazette. Quantico, VA: Marine Corps Association, 1916–.

Marshall, S.L.A. *Island Victory. The Battle of Kwajalein Atoll*. Columbia, SC: Isengrim Texts, 2019. First published in 1982.

McCandless, Charles S. *A Flash of Green: Memoirs of World War II*. Ashland, OR: Hellgate Press, 1987.

McEnery, Jim, with Bill Sloan. *Hell in the Pacific: A Marine Rifleman's Journey from Guadalcanal to Peleliu*. New York: Simon & Schuster, 2012.

McMillan, George. *The Old Breed: A History of the First Marine Division in World War II*. Washington, DC: Infantry Journal Press, 1949.

Mikel, Corporal Albert. *A Salute to Lieutenant Haggerty*. Quantico, VA, in U.S. Marine Corps Historical Archives, Box 3, Folder 13, Caroline Islands, Palaus.

Miller, Staff Sergeant Bill. "Graves Registration," in *Marine Corps Gazette*, February 1945, pp 64–66.

Miller, David T., ed. *Suicide Creek and the Battle for Cape Gloucester*. Self-published, 2012.

Miller, Lieutenant Kimberley J. "The Battle of Peleliu." Washington, DC: U.S. Marine Corps World War II Committee Fact Sheet, 1994.

Morison, Samuel Eliot. *History of the United States Naval Operations in World War II. Vol. 12. Leyte, June 1944–January 1945*. Annapolis, MD: Naval Institute Press, 1953.

Moskin, J. Robert. *The U.S. Marine Corps Story*. New York and San Francisco: McGraw-Hill, 1982. First published in 1977.

Murray, J.C., Jr. *A History of the First Battalion, First Marines*. Quantico, VA, in U.S. Marine Corps Historical Archives, Box 6, Folder 1, Caroline Islands, Palaus.

Murray, Stephen C. *The Battle Over Peleliu: Islander, Japanese, and American Memories of the War*. Tuscaloosa, AL: University of Alabama Press, 2016.

Museum of the Pacific. Fredericksburg, TX. www.pacificwarmuseum.org.

Navajo Code Talkers. Navy & Marine Corps Commemorative Committee. Washington, DC: Navy Office of Information, 1995.

Naval History magazine. Annapolis, MD: U.S. Naval Institute, 1987–.

Navy Medicine magazine. Washington, DC: Bureau of Medicine and Surgery, Department of the Navy. Quarterly.

Nimitz, Admiral Chester W. *Command Summary of Fleet Admiral Chester W. Nimitz, USN. Nimitz "Graybook." 7 December 1941–31 August 1945*. Newport, RI: United States Naval War College, 2013.

Operations Report. Eighty-First Division Operations on Peleliu Island, 23 September–27 November 1944. Washington, DC: U.S. Government. Declassified 1985.

Peleliu Operation: LT3/1 Record of Events. Quantico, VA, in U.S. Marine Corps Historical Archives, Box 6, Folder 3, Caroline Islands, Palaus.

Peto, George, and Peter Margaritas. *Twenty-two on Peleliu. Four Pacific Campaigns with the Corps*. Philadelphia: Casemate Publishers, 2017.

Phelan, Lieutenant W.C., USNR. *Japanese Military Caves on Peleliu: Know Your Enemy!* Washington, DC: U.S. Marine Corps, 1945 (e-book edition used).

Polete, Sergeant Harry, and Sergeant. Edward J. Evans. "Finale at Peleliu," in *Leatherneck*, Quantico, VA: Marine Corps Association, Vol. 30, Issue 7, July 1947, p 3.

Pratt, Fletcher. *The Marines' War.* New York: W. Sloan Associated, 1948.

Ross, Bill D. *Iwo Jima, Legacy of Valor.* New York: The Vanguard Press, 1985.

—*Peleliu, Tragic Triumph: The Untold Story of the Pacific War's Forgotten Battle.* New York: Random House, 1991.

Rozell, Matthew A. *The Things Our Fathers Saw. Vol. I: Voices of the Pacific Theater.* Hartford, CN, New York: Woodchuck Hollow Press, 2015.

Sanner, Richard. *Combat Medic Memoirs: Personal World War II Writings and Pictures.* Clemson, SC: Rennas Productions, 1915.

Schmuck, Major D.M. "Battle of Peleliu," in *Marine Corps Gazette*, December 1944, pp 3–8.

Shaw, Henry I., Jr., and Ralph W. Donnelly. *Blacks in the Marine Corps.* Washington, DC: U.S. Marine Corps History and Museum Division, 1975.

Sherrod, Robert. *History of Marine Corps Aviation in World War II.* San Rafael, CA: Presidio Press, 1952.

Shisler, Gail B. *For Country and Corps. The Life of General Oliver P. Smith.* Annapolis, MD: Naval Institute Press, 2009.

Sledge, Eugene B. "Peleliu 1944: Why Did We Go There?" in *U.S. Naval Institute Proceedings*, Annapolis, MD, October 2001, pp 72–73.

—"Recollections of a Pfc," in *Leatherneck*, Quantico, VA: Marine Corps Association, Vol. 66, Issue 9, September 1983, p 22.

—*With the Old Breed at Peleliu and Okinawa.* New York: Ballantine Books, 2010. First published in 1981.

Sloan, Bill. *Brotherhood of Heroes: The Marines at Peleliu, 1944 – The Bloodiest Battle of the Pacific War.* New York: Simon & Schuster, 2005.

Smith, Robert Ross. *The Approach to the Philippines.* Washington, DC: Office of the Chief of Military History, Department of the Army, 1953.

Snead, David L. "Obscure but Important: The United States and the Russell Islands in World War II," in *The Journal of America's Military Past*, Spring/Summer 2003, pp 5–30.

Sobocinski, Andre B. "A Hero of the Bloody Nose Ridge: The Story of Pharmacist's Mate Third Class Joe Marquez and the Fight for Peleliu," in *Navy Medicine* magazine, October 2018.

Stauffer, Donald A. "Marine Aviation on Peleliu," in *Marine Corps Gazette*, Vol. 29, No. 2 (February 1945), pp 17–20.

Stephenson, Michael. *The Last Full Measure: How Soldiers Die in Battle.* New York: Crown Publishers, 2012.

Straus, Ulrich. *The Anguish of Surrender: Japanese POWs of World War II.* Seattle: University of Washington Press, 2003.

Third Amphibious Corps Report on Caroline Islands – Palau. Quantico, VA, in U.S. Marine Corps Archives, Caroline Islands, Palau, Box 3, Unclassified in 1957.

Third Battalion, Fifth Marines Record of Operations. Quantico, VA, in U.S. Marine Corps Archives. Caroline Islands, Palau, Box 6, Folder 6.

Thomason, Colonel John W., Jr. *And A Few Marines.* New York: Charles Scribner's Sons, 1943.

Toland, John. *But Not in Shame: The Six Months After Pearl Harbor.* New York: Random House, 1961.

—*The Rising Sun. The Decline and Fall of the Japanese Empire, 1936–1945.* New York: Bantam Books, 1971. First published in 1970.

Toll, Ian W. *The Conquering Tide. War in the Pacific Islands, 1942–1944.* New York: W.W. Norton, 2015.

—*Twilight of the Gods. War in the Western Pacific, 1944–1945.* New York: W.W. Norton, 2020.

United States Marine Corps Archives. *Caroline Islands, Palaus,* Boxes 1–6.

United States Navy. *Navy Department Communiques and Pertinent Press Releases, December 10, 1941 to May 24, 1945.* Washington, DC: U.S. Government Printing Office, 1946.

Wagner, Corydon, Jr. "The Bones of Nakagawa," in *Naval History Magazine,* Vol. 17, No. 1, February 2003.

Walt, Lieutenant. Colonel Lew. "The Closer the Better," in *Marine Corps Gazette,* September 1946, pp 37–40.

Wheelan, Joseph. *Midnight in the Pacific. Guadalcanal: The World War II Battle That Turned the Tide of War.* Boston: Da Capo, 2017.

Willoughby, Malcolm. *The U.S. Coast Guard in World War II.* Annapolis, MD: Naval Institute Press, 2016.

Wilson, Captain Earl. "Dressed to Kill Pilots," in *Marine Corps Gazette,* Quantico, VA: Marine Corps Association, Vol. 29, Issue 1, January 1945.

Wright, Derrick. *Pacific Victory. Tarawa to Okinawa, 1943–1945.* Thrupp, Stroud, Gloucestershire, UK: Sutton Publishing, 2005.

—*To the Far Side of Hell. The Battle for Peleliu, 1944.* Ramsbury, Marlborough, UK: The Crowood Press, 2002.

ORAL HISTORIES

Museum of the Pacific
Shelby Albright AFC2001/001/24553
Pfc Charles Allen OHO1297
Pfc Albert Bouley OHO0316trs
Navy Corpsman Oris Brehmer OHO4052trs
Sergeant Jack Brown OHO1046
Pfc Gabriel Caggiano OHO2113trs
Lieutenant Bill Cantrell, pilot OHO0253
Pfc Joe Clapper OHO2943trs
Pfc Harold Clay OHO4344trs

Pfc Martin L. Clayton OHO0981
Sergeant William Crawmer OHO2468trs
Sergeant Rudolph Fanska OHO1851trs
Pfc William Finnegan OHO0797trs
Pfc Fred Fox OHO0318
Lieutenant Otha Grisham OHO0254
Pfc Wayburn Hall OHO1014trs
Radioman Kenneth Harrell OHO1751trs
Pfc Ray Hechler OHO1553trs
Pfc Charles Loeschorn OHO3612trs
Pfc David Lynch OHO3163
Pfc Giles McCoy OHO2615trs
Navy Corpsman Burnett Napier OHO2958trs
Corporal Laurence Norris OHO3759trs
Pfc Franklin Pomroy OHO1011trs
Lieutenant John Louis Schott OHO2959trs
Corporal Robert Shedd OHO2830trs
Pfc Herman Shirley OHO3614
Lieutenant Bruce Watkins OHO0258
Lieutenant Clifford West OHO1570trs
Sergeant James E. Wilson OHO0822
Corporal James Young OHO1026trs

Veterans History Project
Pfc Loren Abdalla AFC2001/001/105401
Howard Adriance AFC2001/001/91307
Pfc Richard Benkert AFC2001/001/101814
Pfc Robert Birrer AFC2001/001/58467
Sergeant Hobart Vaughn Bodkin AFC2001/001/52954
Pfc Leslie Boland AFC2001/001/68635
Corporal John Bowling AFC2001/001/104373
Corporal Charles Boyle AFC2001/001/31955
Corporal Lester Byrum AFC2001/001/92166
Corporal Alexander Costella AFC2001/001/30258
Lieutenant Colonel Glenn Daniel AFC2001/001/60661
Lieutenant Colonel Ray Davis AFC2001/001/89653
Sergeant Arthur Dreves, C/1 AFC2001/001/80437
Sergeant Tazewell Ellett AFC2001/001/13265
Lieutenant Tom Evans AFC2001/001/91980
Sergeant Guy Farrar AFC2001/001/67778
Corporal James Cline Foster AFC2001/001/70662
Lieutenant Colonel Robert Galer AFC2001/001/16758
Major Joe Gayle Sr. 2/1 AFC2001/001/79326
Jacob Glick AFC2001/001/81308

BIBLIOGRAPHY

Sergeant Frank Gonzales AFC2001/001/51380
Corporal N.G. Gonzales AFC2001/001/77303
Major Theodore Harbaugh AFC2001/001/05147
Sergeant John Huber AFC2001/001/15568
Corporal Louis Imfeld AFC2001/001/106791
Pfc Charles Imhoff AFC2001/001/54795
Pfc Arthur Jackson AFC2001/001/89698
Corporal Marvin Jensen AFC2001/001/98637
Sergeant Gerry L. Jones AFC2001/001/84252
Corporal Norman Keller AFC2001/001/19577
Sergeant Hodge Lord AFC2001/001/13749
Sergeant Kenneth Matson AFC2001/001/111148
Pfc Otto Melsa AFC2001/001/62086
Sergeant Charles Meyer AFC2001/001/99056
Corporal Chester Nez AFC2001/001/54891
Pfc Warren Nicols AFC2001/001/88575
William Parish 2/7 AFC2001/001/105072
Corporal Victor Pichette AFC2001/001/10391
Captain Everett Pope AFC2001/001/89766
Lieutenant George Rasula AFC2001/001/14122
Pfc Herman Soblick AFC2001/001/33828
Sergeant David Sokol AFC2001/001/73402
Corporal Edward Swierk AFC2001/001/94415
Corporal Willie Vila AFC2001/001/88229
Corporal Harold Weber, AFC2001/001/99814
Sergeant Ralph Maurice Wilcox AFC2001/001/106226

Index

Figures in **bold** refer to maps.